Praise for COMMUNITY CAPITAL

Michael and Cliff are eyewitnesses, but they're also the protagonists of Community Capital, restless in their need to build institutions and compel systems to serve Black, brown, and low-income people. But their real superpowers lie in their ability to navigate and confront oppressive bureaucracy, with Cliff viewing it on a more macro level, and Michael operating on the micro.
—From the foreword by Mark Winston Griffith,
Co-Executive Director of Free Speech TV

Injustice, whether by public or private organizations, always targets the most vulnerable first. NCUA's summary closing and liquidation of Kappa Alpha Psi FCU is an essential case study of unchecked regulatory power against one of the oldest black college fraternities in America.
—Charles Filson, former CEO,
National Credit Union Share Insurance Fund

Community Capital

Community Capital

Race, Equity, and the Credit Union Movement

**CLIFFORD N. ROSENTHAL and
MICHAEL McCRAY, Esq., CPA**

Copyright © 2024, Clifford N. Rosenthal and Michael R. McCray.
All rights reserved.
Foreword copyright © 2024, Mark Winston Griffith. All rights reserved.

Memoir Disclaimer
This work depicts actual events in the life of the authors as truthfully as recollection permits and/or can be verified by research. Occasionally, dialogue consistent with the character or nature of the person speaking has been supplemented. All persons within are actual individuals; there are no composite characters. The names of some individuals have been changed to respect their privacy.

Published by
American Banner Books
P.O. Box 7412, Pine Bluff, AR 71611

ISBN (hardcover): 978-0-9846906-3-3
ISBN (paperback): 978-0-9846906-1-9
ISBN (ebook): 978-0-9846906-0-2

Book design and production by www.AuthorSuccess.com

Printed in the United States of America

Publisher's Cataloging-in-Publication Data
provided by Five Rainbows Cataloging Services

Names: Rosenthal, Clifford N, author. | McCray, Michael, author. | Griffith, Mark Winston, writer of foreword.
Title: Community capital : race, equity & the credit union movement / Clifford N. Rosenthal [and] Michael McCray ; [foreword by] Mark Winston Griffith.
Description: Little Rock, AR : American Banner Books, 2024. | Includes index.
Identifiers: LCCN 2023950893 (print) | ISBN 978-0-9846906-1-9 (paperback) | ISBN 978-0-9846906-3-3 (hardcover) | ISBN 978-0-9846906-0-2 (ebook)
Subjects: LCSH: Community development. | Credit unions. | Kappa Alpha Psi Fraternity. | African American Greek letter societies--United States--History--20th century. | Biography. | BISAC: BUSINESS & ECONOMICS / Business Ethics. | SOCIAL SCIENCE / Race & Ethnic Relations. | BIOGRAPHY & AUTOBIOGRAPHY / Memoirs.
Classification: LCC HG2035 .R67 2024 (print) | LCC HG2035 (ebook) | DDC 334/.22--dc23.

Dedication

Clifford Rosenthal

To Elayne: Together, we persisted
To Dana: Bearer of the legacy
To Carlo: Called to teach

Michael McCray

In loving memory of Julius L. Thompson, Esq.
The "Godfather" and general counsel for KAPFCU and
The Honorable John Conyers (D-MI) co-founder of the
Congressional Black Caucus and life member of Kappa Alpha Psi
fraternity; until we meet again on the golden shores of Kappa land
and pass the loving cup once more. Also The Honorable Eddie
Bernice Johnson (D-TX), Congressional Black Caucus members
who supported KAPFCU from the beginning of
our quest for financial equity.

"We've got to strengthen Black institutions. I call upon you to take your money out of the banks downtown and deposit your money in Tri-State Bank. We want a 'bank-in' movement in Memphis."

Speech by Martin Luther King, Jr., *"I've Been to the Mountaintop"*

Delivered 3 April 1968, Mason Temple (Church of God in Christ Headquarters), Memphis, Tennessee

In 2021, Tri-State Bank, a certified Community Development Financial Institution (CDFI), was acquired by Liberty Bank, another Black-owned CDFI, becoming part of the largest Black-owned bank in the U.S.

Contents

Foreword by Mark Winston Griffith ... xiii

Preface: The Historic Context by Clifford N. Rosenthal ... xix

Notes on Usage and Terminology ... xxii

Two Generations | Allied Activists by Clifford N. Rosenthal ... xxv

Black Fraternities and Economic Justice ... xxvii
by Michael R. McCray

PART ONE:
THE QUEST FOR COMMUNITY-CONTROLLED CAPITAL ... 1
by Clifford N. Rosenthal

Introduction ... 3
CHAPTER 1: Prelude ... 5
CHAPTER 2: To Serve the People ... 18
CHAPTER 3: Leader by Default ... 29
CHAPTER 4: Pursuing "People's Capital" ... 37
CHAPTER 5: Outsiders: Poverty and Race ... 52
    in the Credit Union Family
CHAPTER 6: Fighting with Friends: ... 65
    Race and the CDFI Movement
CHAPTER 7: Race and Regulation: ... 81
    Systemic Bias and Scandal
CHAPTER 8: Before DEI: Reaching the Marginalized ... 107
CHAPTER 9: The Conflicts Within: ... 123
    Increasing Success/Racial Tension
CHAPTER 10: White Boss: Didn't Know, ... 134
    Should Have Understood
CHAPTER 11: From 9/11 to the Great Recession: ... 147
    New Crises, Continuing Battles

PART TWO:
KAPPA ALPHA PSI FEDERAL CREDIT UNION: ... 161
THE FOUNDERS' STORY
by Michael R. McCray

Prologue ... **163**
CHAPTER 12: Alice In Wonderland ... 168
CHAPTER 13: Through The Looking Glass ... 193
CHAPTER 14: Rush To Judgment ... 198

| CHAPTER 15: The Mad Hatter | 204 |
| CHAPTER 16: Rainbow Pushed Out | 212 |

PART THREE: Aftermath — **231**
CHAPTER 17: From New York to Washington: — 233
  Leaving the Federation
  by Clifford N. Rosenthal
CHAPTER 18: Change Came: Signs of Hope — 243
CHAPTER 19: Coda for KAPFCU — 269
  by Michael R. McCray

PART FOUR: THE RECIEPTS: KAPFCU v. NCUA — **281**
by Michael R. McCray

APPENDIX — **283**

Appendix A — 284
NCUA Supervisory Letter to Examiners (LICUs CDCUs)

Appendix B — 292
KAPFCU Response to LUA and Request for Hearing

Appendix C — 300
Dan Moulton, CPA. Email CPA Opinion (Cash Basis)

Appendix D — 304
Balack & Williams, Legal Opinion (Total/1 Product Defect)

Appendix E — 308
NCUA Closed Door Board Transcript

Appendix F — 314
KAPFCU Response to NCUA Ex Parte Hearing

Appendix G — 318
NCUA TRO Press Release

Appendix H — 322
KAPFCU Quarterly Call Report (Financial Performance)

Appendix I — 328
NCUA "Sur Reply" to KAPFCU Complaint

Appendix J — 336
U.S. District Court Transcript & Final Court Order

Appendix K — 354
KAPFCU Motion For Reconsideration

Appendix L — 358
U.S. Treasury Department CDFI Debrief Report

| Index | 361 |
| Acknowledgments | 371 |

Foreword

By Mark Winston Griffith

I have known Cliff Rosenthal for almost thirty-five years, and Michael McCray, probably closer to thirty-five days. And within each of their writings in *Community Capital* you will find big pieces of my life.

Michael, the former official of a credit union and a few years my junior, is more my peer than Cliff. "I'm a big fan of yours," Michael said as he greeted me for the first time on the phone. "I have been following you ever since you started the 'Hip Hop Credit Union.'"

He had me at "hello."

I'm as much a sucker for compliments as the next person, especially if you praise me for the Central Brooklyn Federal Credit Union (CBFCU), which I consider one of the most important undertakings in my almost forty-year-long community-building career. But Michael's charm was not just based on an appeal to my ego; it became immediately clear to me that he understood CBFCU's place—and other credit unions like it—in the people's history of American social enterprise.

CBFCU was chartered in early 1993, the first community development credit union chartered by the first Clinton administration. At a time when neighborhood banks were notoriously abandoning Black communities, we were housed in a former bank branch, secured millions in non-member deposits, made loans to people deemed "unbankable," signed up almost 7,000 members, and grew into the largest institution of our kind—all before our third-year anniversary.

Indeed, for a moment at least, CBFCU was a big deal locally and nationally. Beginning in 1993, I and my CBFCU co-founding partner, Errol Louis, graced the pages of the *New York Times, Newsweek Magazine,* the *New Yorker,* and *Black Enterprise.* We were featured on the *PBS Newshour,* advised Congress people, and on July 15, 1993, we joined President Clinton at the White House Rose Garden ceremony announcing the Community Development Financial Institutions (CDFI) legislation.

Most importantly, we were becoming folk heroes among our neighbors and colleagues in Black Central Brooklyn for organizing and running a financial cooperative. Not some up-by-your-bootstraps shrine to neo-capitalism, but a self-governing, financially self-determining, afro-futuristic, community-based institution, grown organically among the largest urban concentration of Black people in the country. It was dubbed "the world's first hip hop credit union" by the *New York Times* after I brazenly declared in my opening day remarks that, just like rap music, we were taking beats from yesteryear and manifesting a new cultural tomorrow. And for our members, the credit union was a shiny symbol of our community's rise from generations of redlining, predatory financial services, and dependence on a hostile banking system.

Michael's name-check of CBFCU in the opening moments of our first telephone conversation impressed me because, despite its moments of fame, CBFCU has arguably become a random footnote in the annals of community economic development. CBFCU was taken over and eventually dismantled by the National Credit Union Administration (NCUA) in 1997, not unlike what happened to Michael's credit union, the Kappa Alpha Psi Federal Credit Union (KAPFCU). But by simply acknowledging admiration for the "hip hop credit union," Michael rejected the narrative of failure and shame that we reflexively project onto Black struggle and replaced it with one of achievement and transcendence.

Achievement and transcendence speak to the scale of ambition that Cliff and Michael each bring to the pages of *Community Capital.* I was a twenty-something-year-old when I first met Cliff, then the executive director of the National Federation of Community Development Credit Unions (now Inclusiv). He was perhaps the primary engineer of the conditions that made my credit union's charter possible. He was one of CBFCU's most effective champions, and a true believer in our mission.

In *Community Capital,* he recounts his professional coming-of-age and then provides the most definitive history of community development credit unions and of the community development finance movement that you are ever likely to find. Along the way, Cliff has been a mentor, an ally, a supporter of my various professional adventurers, and a cherished friend. In later years, Cliff headed up the Office of Financial Empowerment of the Consumer Financial Protection Bureau.

Cliff introduced me to Michael, a principal at KAPFCU, which occupied a specific universe within the CDFI world that Cliff describes. Michael provides a front-line, first-hand account of the National Credit Union Administration's assault on KAPFCU and his own sophisticated counter measures. I related to the trials and tribulations of KAPFCU, and its relationship to NCUA, like no other credit union story I've ever encountered. As a survivor of an epic battle with NCUA myself and as someone who saw how dispassionately the government can trample on the strivings of a Black community, I lived Michael's aspirations and pain. But unlike me, Michael actually had the boldness and technical skill to challenge NCUA in court. In that respect, Michael is a unicorn in the community development credit union world, and when he took on NCUA, he "took one for the team" fighting for social justice.

Read together, Cliff's and Michael's stories are not revising history as much as reclaiming it. Public understanding of the past typically includes headline events and recitations of what the wealthy and powerful have put into motion. We see public policy and its practice from 10,000 feet up. Rarely do we connect social advancement to the day-to-day workings of those who dedicate their lives to informing and inspiring social change, but seldom get to control it.

Michael and Cliff are eyewitnesses, but they're also the protagonists of *Community Capital*, restless in their need to build institutions and compel systems to serve Black, brown, and low-income people. But their real superpowers lie in their ability to navigate and confront oppressive bureaucracy, with Cliff viewing it on a more macro level and Michael operating on the micro. Cliff, a Russian history scholar, mastered the language of community organizing, capital formation, and public policy well enough to become a pioneer of American community development finance. Michael, a trained accountant and lawyer as well as an organizer, scholar, and whistle-blower, not only challenged the National Credit Union Administration in court, but, with hair-raising precision, deconstructed the facile arguments NCUA assembled against KAPFCU.

Michael's story is less autobiographical than Cliff's. Michael begins his section of the book by poignantly placing Black panhellenic organizations and KAPFCU in the context of Black excellence, and then juxtaposes this legacy against the faithlessness with which NCUA treats Black initiative.

But ultimately, Michael and Cliff's stories are unavoidably rooted in the personal. Michael's scenes and character descriptions are detailed and poetic, signaling just how intimate his experiences were for him—as they would be for anyone who passionately pours their dreams into a mission-driven institution and is then forced to defend themselves against hostile forces.

For his part, Cliff often meditates on the contradictions and challenges that shaped his evolution into a community development finance action figure. For instance, he considers what it means to be a white man, often in Black spaces, hustling for racial justice. He reacts to the sight of social service getting confused for social justice. He grapples with how he unwittingly falls into the role of white savior, mediator, gatekeeper, and poverty translator.

But clearly, neither of these men is pursuing personal glory. What stands out more than anything else is how they each describe the rigged system that is, well, capitalism itself. We are made present to how indifferent regulatory and government bodies can be to the fate of whole communities, while claiming to be the bulwark against injustice and exploitation in a liberal democracy. In their worst moments, these bodies are profoundly unaccountable and administratively violent towards the most vulnerable in society. And in their most insidious moments, their practices are passively racist, no matter how unintentional that racism may appear.

Michael invokes *Alice in Wonderland* to show how surreal and absurd his dealings with NCUA officials were, but they could have easily been scenes out of a Kafka novel. With one hand, federal bureaucracies come down on small financial institutions serving low-income people for not meeting financial viability standards, and with the other, they actively subvert that viability. And at one point Cliff laments:

> Implicitly or explicitly, the poor were blamed for their inability to build successful financial institutions. The GAO study illustrated the vicious cycle that made it so difficult for a low-income credit union to thrive: the members had little disposable income and thus, small savings; they required labor-intensive transactions that were "cost-ineffective;" they could only afford to borrow amounts too small to generate much surplus for the credit union. Not enough deposits meant not enough money to loan, which meant not enough income to add services to attract more depositors and generate sufficient earnings and reserves. In an aphorism that has become current common in recent years, "No margin, no mission!"

Community Capital collects receipts on just how difficult it is for people of color and poor communities to practice economic "self-help," but Cliff and Michael never draw portraits of victims, nor do they lapse into cynicism. As characters, Cliff and Michael move through their narratives with agency, as do all the credit union members and organizers who also animate their stories.

I count myself among those members and organizers. In *Community Capital* we are three-dimensional people. Often, we are even accomplices in our own undoing. But even in those moments when our best interests are thwarted, Cliff and Michael leave readers trusting that the possibilities for poor, Black, and brown people to be self-liberating are never diminished.

PREFACE

The Historic Context

Clifford N. Rosenthal

This book focuses on sectors of the financial system that do not usually make headlines: credit unions and community development financial institutions (CDFIs). Both types of institutions have missions to address financial inequity. Credit unions have a long history in the United States. They were created in the first decade of the twentieth century to serve working people who could not access loans from mainstream banks, and instead were victimized by usurers. Today, credit unions serve more than 130 million members and have total assets of more than $2 trillion. Despite their historic mission, these nonprofit cooperatives are little known or understood by most Americans, including many of their members. CDFIs emerged at the end of the twentieth century, in the 1990s, as a movement created to serve people, communities, and projects that banks deemed "unbankable." CDFIs include low-income credit unions, nonprofit loan funds, a segment of the banking industry, and special-purpose venture funds.

Credit unions and CDFIs are the "good guys," financial institutions created not to maximize shareholders' wealth, but rather to provide economic opportunity to those who have been deprived of it. However, over the last thirty years, they have not always advanced financial equity. The racial wealth gap has stubbornly persisted, reflected in and exacerbating the decline in the ranks of Black-owned financial institutions.[1] Until very recently, the credit union industry did not prioritize the preservation of Black credit unions. Neither did the CDFI Fund—an indispensable resource for community development finance—prioritize financial institutions owned by and serving communities of color.

Two linked narratives recount Michael McCray's and my respective struggles in the fight for financial equity. They are different in scope, different in style and voice, but intersecting and complementary. My story is of a decades-long campaign to rebuild a marginalized movement of low-income, predominantly non-white credit unions, which was nearly extinguished under the Reagan and Bush administrations. I led the Federation's fight for recognition, respect, and capital from the broader credit union movement; from the federal regulators, NCUA; and from the CDFI Fund, which our advocacy had helped to create.

Race is very much in the foreground of Michael's story of Kappa Alpha Psi Federal Credit Union, in which he was a key player. Although the Federation's membership included numerous community- and church-based Black credit unions, KAPFCU was unique; the creation of one of the oldest, largest Black fraternities in the country. Founded in 2004, its assets never exceeded one million dollars. Like many of the Federation's other credit unions, KAPFCU clashed with the federal regulators of NCUA. The issues were often technical, as Michael McCray lays out in meticulous detail, but they touched on the life and death of the credit union.

On August 3, 2010, without notice, NCUA seized and liquidated KAPFCU, sending out checks to close member depositors accounts. KAPFCU was effectively dead and gone.

Why was KAPFCU's case so important? For decades before and since, a steady stream of liquidations and mergers decimated the ranks

---

[1] For example, the number of Black-owned banks declined from 48 in 2001 to 17 in 2021. "Federal Deposit Insurance Corporation," FDIC, accessed January 2, 2024, https://www.fdic.gov/

of Black and other credit unions serving communities of color. Our Federation lost many small credit unions, painfully including many Black credit unions with roots in the Civil Rights movement and even earlier. But KAPFCU did what no credit union in our movement had dared to do during my 30 years at the Federation: they fought the liquidation in federal court.

KAPFCU's fate could have been—should have been—different. Had KAPFCU prevailed in court, Michael argued, *KAPFCU v. NCUA* could have been the landmark *Brown vs. Topeka Board of Education* case for the credit union movement.

Would the outcome be different today, after the changes wrought by the killing of George Floyd and the Black Lives Matter movement? "DEI"—Diversity, Equity, Inclusion—has become a watchword in government and in corporations, in philanthropy and nonprofits, and certainly in the credit union industry. Washington has invested billions of dollars in Minority Depository Institutions (MDIs) and CDFIs, much of it directed to long-neglected Black financial institutions; the private sector, philanthropy, and the broad credit union industry have joined in. To an extraordinary degree, credit union regulators have come to recognize the importance of institutions like KAPFCU; their top officials have acknowledged how NCUA's own policies and practices have perpetuated inequity and the racial wealth gap.

Although KAPFCU did not win its unequal battle with the federal government, its story should inspire others who seek justice despite formidable odds. In the words of Dr. Martin Luther King, Jr., spoken at the National Cathedral on March 31, 1968: "We shall overcome because the arc of the moral universe is long, but it bends toward justice."

Notes on Usage and Terminology

The reader will notice certain apparent inconsistencies of usage, especially but not only referring to race and ethnicity.

While "Latinx" has increasingly come into use as a nongendered term, we have not applied it retroactively or when it does not correspond to the current usage by individuals or organizations. Thus, in writing about the Federation's work in the 1990s and 2000s, Cliff Rosenthal describes its successive "Latino Credit Union Conferences" and "Latino Credit Union Network." More recently, the National Association of Latino Credit Unions and Professionals (NLCUP), which was established formally in 2020 but was active for many years previously, describes itself as "committed to our Hispanic/Latino community." Similarly, while "Indigenous" is increasingly used today, it was not commonly used in the 1970s, including by and in the organization in which Rosenthal worked in that decade.

"Minority" is a term that has frequently been discarded as implying lower status and/or minimizing the large and growing population who do not describe themselves as "white." Nonetheless, it remains an official designation used and defined in certain government and other policies and programs (e.g., "Minority Depository Institutions," or MDIs).

Finally, we have not attempted to rigorously define "low-income" or "low- and moderate-income," which are used in various contexts and by different public and private agencies. In no case should "low-income" be presumed to indicate only those people below the official poverty line, nor should it be assumed to be interchangeable with persons of color.

Key Terms

CDCUs. Community Development Credit Unions are credit unions with the specific mission of serving low-income communities.

CDFI Fund. The unit of the U.S. Treasury Department signed into law by President Bill Clinton on September 23, 1994, with the purpose of supporting financial institutions that serve majority disadvantaged communities.

CDFIs. Community Development Financial Institutions are financial institutions certified by the Treasury Department's CDFI Fund as serving predominantly disadvantaged communities. CDFIs may be nonprofit or for-profit, including credit unions, banks, loan funds, and venture funds.

CUNA. The Credit Union National Association is the largest trade and lobbying organization for credit unions.

"Divine Nine." The moniker for the National Pan-Hellenic Council consisting of the following Black Greek-letter organizations:

- Alpha Phi Alpha Fraternity founded at Cornell University (1906)
- Alpha Kappa Alpha Sorority founded at Howard University (1908)
- Kappa Alpha Psi Fraternity founded at Indiana University (1911)
- Omega Psi Phi Fraternity founded at Howard University (1911)
- Delta Sigma Theta Sorority founded at Howard University (1913)
- Phi Beta Sigma Fraternity founded at Howard University (1914)
- Zeta Phi Beta Sorority founded at Howard University (1920)
- Sigma Gamma Rho Sorority founded at Butler University (1922)
- Iota Phi Theta Fraternity founded at Morgan State University (1963)

Federation. The National Federation of Community Development Credit Unions, a nonprofit charitable organization founded in 1974 to represent and serve credit unions serving predominantly low-income persons and communities. In 2018, the organization rebranded as Inclusiv™.

Inclusiv. See Federation.

Kappa Alpha Psi. A fraternal organization founded at Indiana University in 1911 that numbers more than 170,000 members among Black college students and alumni organized in 780 chapters.

KAPFCU. Kappa Alpha Psi Federal Credit Union, started in 2003 by members of the fraternity.

MDI. Minority Depository Institution, a term used by various federal agencies.

NCUA. The National Credit Union Administration is the independent federal agency responsible for supervising federally chartered credit unions.

NCUSIF. The National Credit Union Share Insurance Fund, administered by NCUA, provides deposit insurance for all federally chartered credit unions and the great majority of state credit unions.

ABOUT THIS BOOK

Two Generations | Allied Activists
Clifford N. Rosenthal

Dual Perspectives

In this book, Cliff Rosenthal provides a 10,000-foot overview and historical context of the community development credit union (CDCU) movement while scrutinizing his journey as a white man leading a predominantly non-white organization. In his quest for community-controlled capital, he raised directly or indirectly through his advocacy $100 million in investments in low-income credit unions and pioneered the community development financial institutions (CDFI) movement. His 40-year career took Rosenthal from neighborhood co-op organizer to credit union builder, then association president, and finally federal policymaker. Rosenthal writes as a credit union practitioner shaped by his training as a Russian historian and translator. More "co-conspirator" than ally, Rosenthal is a white man battling for capital and equity in communities of color, while acknowledging and confronting his own shortcomings as a leader.

In contrast, Michael McCray gives a harrowing insider's account as a participant/eyewitness to history. McCray is a Black man fighting a federal regulator, the National Credit Union Administration (NCUA), in a white man's world. He brings "receipts"—unique access to secret transcripts, doctored financial reports, and federal court documents which undergird a compelling argument that the regulator has mistreated small credit unions, especially in minority communities. McCray takes the reader behind closed doors at an NCUA board meeting and inside the courtroom as a small credit union fights for its life against federal attorneys and the Justice Department. McCray delivers a dramatic first-person account with primary source documents and forensic insights on the landmark *KAPFCU v. NCUA* federal court case. Justifiably jaundiced, McCray's compelling writing style takes the readers on an inside-the-car, roller-coaster ride through a regulatory *Alice in Wonderland*.

Rosenthal is a historian and McCray is a whistleblower. Together, they guide the reader through a race-tinted, bifocal examination of the long and ongoing struggle to redress economic inequity. If they have succeeded, the reader will learn not only about the barriers to DEI—Diversity, Equity, and Inclusion—at the highest level of government, but gain a better understanding of the pivotal role Black organizations like the Divine Nine and Black churches play in bringing providing capital access to marginalized communities.

Black Fraternities and Economic Justice

Michael R. McCray

> **I once thought the Black Church would be the key to economic empowerment for the Black community. Now I see it may be the Divine Nine (fraternities and sororities).**
> Dr. Rick Baldwin, Ph.D. Prairie View A&M University Graduate Community Development Program

Though scarcer, fraternities and sororities are just as significant to the African American community as Black churches. These institutions have accounted for many, if not most, of all faith-based credit unions in the United States. Most are small, serving only a neighborhood or congregation. However, a network of college-educated professionals chartered the Kappa Alpha Psi Federal Credit Union with loftier ambitions.

Social and religious fraternities and sororities are part of African American high society. Thus, secret societies play a different role in the Black community than in predominantly white institutions. First, panhellenic membership is lifelong in Black sororities and fraternities. Second, the undergraduate and alumni chapters often serve a developmental role for young people in middle and high schools. This includes hosting mentorship programs and debutante balls. White institutions limit "Greek life" to college years, unlike Black institutions. For the former "I was a Pike," versus "I am an Alpha, Kappa, or Que" for the latter. Thus, the "Divine Nine" provides lifelong connections for business, social, political, and other support.

The Kappa Alpha Psi® college fraternity was born in an environment steeped in racism. Indiana became the nineteenth state of the Union in 1816. It founded Indiana University in Bloomington four years later, and Indiana became a stronghold for the Ku Klux Klan. During the school years of 1910-11, a small group of Black students attended the university. Most were working their way through school. Excluded from the "whites only" campus clubs and fraternities, they had no part in the social life of the university. They decided that a Greek-letter fraternity would do much to fill the missing link in their college existence.

Kappa Alpha Psi® became the first historically black Greek letter fraternity, chartered by the Indiana Secretary of State on May 15, 1911. The fraternity has over 170,000 members with 780 undergraduate and alumni chapters in nearly every state of the United States. It also hosts international chapters in Nigeria, South Africa, the West Indies, the United Kingdom, Germany, Korea, and Japan. One aim of the fraternity is "to promote the spiritual, social, intellectual and moral welfare of members." The fraternity promotes high Christian ideals and the purpose of achievement. The fraternity seeks to raise the sights of Black youth and encourage them to accomplish great things. Local chapters offer a range of services such as meals, scholarships, mentoring, blood drives, and public health seminars.

This book highlights Black fraternity and sorority members' involvement in social and economic justice, especially credit unions. When the National Federation of Community Development Credit Unions held its first national Faith-Based Credit Union Conference in 1992, its keynote speaker was the Congressman, Rev. Floyd Flake, a nationally-renowned advocate for economic justice and a proud member of Alpha Phi Alpha Fraternity. Rev. Flake played a major role in shaping the legislation creating the CDFI Fund—a favored initiative of President William Jefferson Clinton, who is an honorary member of Phi Beta Sigma fraternity, which also chartered a credit union. On June 15, 2021, Vice President Kamala Harris, Treasury Secretary Janet Yellen, and congressional allies announced a record 863 awards to CDFIs. Vice President Harris is in Alpha Kappa Alpha Sorority, Inc., which was recently approved for a credit union charter by NCUA. Harris became a member of the sorority when she attended Howard University.

In January 2022, a Democratic majority elected the first African American Democratic leader of the House of Representatives, Hakeem Jeffries, a Kappa member. Bill Bynum, the CEO of the most prominent Black-led CDFI in the country, is also a member of Kappa Alpha Psi. The African American Credit Union Coalition (AACUC) inducted Bynum into the AACUC Hall of Fame and honored him with their lifetime achievement award.

PART ONE
THE QUEST FOR COMMUNITY-CONTROLLED CAPITAL

Clifford N. Rosenthal

Introduction

In 1980, I joined the organization that would define my life's work, the National Federation of Community Development Credit Unions (the Federation). For someone whose political and social consciousness was shaped by the struggles of the 1960s, it was a dream job, working for a movement of cooperatives dedicated to fighting poverty and financial discrimination through collective self-help. But less than three years after I joined the Federation, our funding was gone, and with it our staff and much of our membership. I hadn't aspired to become the white leader of a predominantly non-white organization; I became one by default. For the next thirty years, I dedicated myself to raising capital and winning recognition for our community development credit unions—CDCUs—the financial institutions on the front lines of serving the people and communities shunned by mainstream banks.

In the 1980s, we struggled for the Federation's survival. Our two-person "team"—myself and Annie Vamper, an African American credit union professional from the South—fought with regulators, helped organize new credit unions, and raised investments from the new breed of "socially responsible investors." Making payroll was an uphill battle. We finally turned the corner in the 1990s, when a concept I had championed became a reality when the Clinton Administration created the Community Development Financial Institutions (CDFI) Fund, bringing tens of millions of dollars of investments to our credit unions and the Federation itself. But our decade of success was threatened by the Federation's race-tinged governance crisis, challenging my continuation as the organization's white leader. We survived that challenge, but the first decade of the twenty-first century brought a series of external crises, from the destruction of the Twin Towers a few blocks from our office on 9/11 to the Great Recession, the repercussions of which contributed to the downfall of the Kappa Alpha Psi credit union detailed in Part Two. Finally, after the economic crisis subsided, instead of retiring as I had planned, I went to Washington to launch the new Office of Financial Empowerment of the Consumer Financial Protection Bureau, where I developed policies and programs for low-income consumers.

I left behind a thriving Federation that my successor has brought to new heights. As I describe in the final chapter, Black Lives Matter and the response to the COVID-19 pandemic have brought unprecedented access to capital for the credit unions and CDFIs I served. Diversity, equity, and inclusion—the causes I long fought for—are now the banners of a growing campaign for social justice.

CHAPTER 1

Prelude

Newark Before the Riots

I was born and raised in Newark, New Jersey, on the leading edge of the post-World War II "baby boom." I was the grandchild of Jewish immigrants, driven to the United States by the pogroms of what is now Belarus. The first few months of my life were spent in the Newark ghetto above my grandparents' grocery store in the predominantly Black Central Ward that two decades later was the scene of the 1967 uprising sparked by the police beating of a Black cab driver. Later, my grandparents scraped together the money to buy a two-family house in a lower middle-class neighborhood, where our three generations lived until I was fifteen.

My father served in the Army in World War II, first in the North Africa campaign, then as a postal clerk, the only job he later held in civilian life. The Servicemen's Readjustment Act of 1944—the G.I. Bill—provided funds for college education and housing, changing the lives for millions of veterans. Our lives were not transformed. We did not join the government-funded exodus to the white suburbs; my parents remained in Newark until 1970. We were by necessity a two-income family. Postal salaries remained extremely low until an epic strike in 1970 brought collective bargaining and unionization. Thanks to my mother's work as a legal secretary, we were never poor or hungry, but were also never well-off enough to afford luxuries like summer camp or vacations at the famous Jersey shore. I would be the first in my family to attend college.

My upbringing did not prepare me for a career as the white leader of a social justice organization. I was not a "red diaper baby," a term I learned when I entered college in New York City. My family had no history of union activism or political protest. My parents were typical Depression-era FDR Democrats; they supported Adlai Stevenson against Richard Nixon, who they saw as anti-Semitic. Mine was the "cold war" generation. In school, we were taught to shelter under our desks for when the Russians would inevitably strike with a nuclear bomb. I was vaguely, anxiously aware of the trial and execution of Julius and Ethel Rosenberg as spies—mostly, I was afraid that as a "Rosenthal" I would be taken as one of them. My grandparents belonged to synagogues, but my parents did not—we were culturally Jewish, but unaffiliated with any religious institution. Overt anti-Semitism—"no Jews need apply"—had diminished from the 1930s but had not disappeared; as Phillip Roth wrote in *The Plot Against America,* there were hotbeds of Nazi sympathizers in the near Newark suburbs. Jews were still hovering on the margins of Christian white America. The messages from my parents were: don't aspire too high; don't be too visible. We were still outsiders in America.

In 1957, I joined the first entering class of the new Clinton Place Junior High School (now known as University High School). A few blocks from my house, it was a stunningly original design, with hexagonal classrooms and a spacious, attractive auditorium. It drew from my ethnically mixed neighborhood, but more widely from majority Black schools in adjoining neighborhoods. It was integrated—that is to say, white kids were in the minority, certainly in the lunchroom, gym, and locker rooms, if not in some of the advanced classes. White kids were often "asked" by Black kids for 32-cent lunch money, but notwithstanding these low-level shakedowns, there was no significant bullying, no gang wars, and no racial clashes.

In junior high school, I gained an appreciation of Black culture. In the hallways and playground, in the decades before rap, the "dozens"—we called it "hiking on" or "ranking"—were played out in witty, inventive, often hilarious verbal duels among Black students. At school dances, it was the Coasters ("Yakety Yak—Don't Talk Back") or The Silhouettes ("Get a Job" [that I could never find]), and the many Black groups of the late 1950s. The student body elected a Black president—a polished, dynamic tenth grader whose campaign speech brought down the house when his back-up group sang "Vote for George" in street-corner harmony.

Meanwhile, my neighborhood was "changing;" the euphemism for white flight. A single-family house up the street was put up for sale. I heard anxious murmurs among the adults: a Black family would buy it and somehow bring bad things to the neighborhood. Naively, ignorantly, I wondered (perhaps aloud) whether (white) people could get together and collectively buy the house to keep the neighborhood "stable." In retrospect, that racist concept of cooperative finance to preserve residential segregation embarrassingly inversely foreshadowed my later career. Fortunately, the idea went nowhere.

When I was 10, my grandparents retired and moved to Florida; a universe away from their childhoods in the *shtetls* (small towns) of the Minsk countryside. Later, as my parents were searching for a one-family house in another neighborhood, they sold the house to a Black family and we became their tenants. Our landlady lived upstairs—but she housed her brother, "Buddy," in the unfinished basement that accommodated an unused coal bin, our ping-pong table, and a train set. My father occasionally brought food down to Buddy, shaking his head in dismay that "someone had to live like that," while Buddy's family lived upstairs. There were no lectures about race or poverty or the need for compassion. There was only a simple demonstration of decency.

Twelve Years after Roth

For my first 15 years, I had lived on the "wrong side of the tracks" in Newark—not literally, but a half-mile crosstown from the more prosperous Weequahic neighborhood immortalized by the late novelist Philip Roth, who was a dozen years older than me. In 1961, halfway through my junior year, we moved closer to Weequahic High School, fulfilling my urban version of the American dream: a one-family house! With a driveway! Bedrooms upstairs and a finished basement below! Legend had it that a famous Jewish gangster had lived down the street in a house equipped with escape tunnels.

It was a culture change for me—both the neighborhood and the school. I moved from a majority Black school to one that skewed white and was still substantially Jewish. The school was not officially "tracked," although I and my friends spent most of our high school years in advanced placement classes, which were predominantly white; outside of gym class, only occasionally did we have Black classmates.[2]

One embarrassing incident has remained with me. In June 1962, I was proud to host a large graduation party in our backyard. After a while, I came back into the house and encountered my mother, who explained that several Black kids had come to the door, politely asking to join the party. She had quietly but firmly turned them away, explaining that it was a "private party." They "understood," she said.

I was anguished to realize she had turned away a Black star of the basketball team, which had thrilled us by winning the state championship. I only knew him casually, and no, I had not invited him. But he was one of our heroes, who had brought joy to 2,000 of us at our school—and my family had turned him away. I doubt that this, the latest in a young lifetime of white rejections, changed his life. Despite my acute embarrassment, the incident did not change mine. That would come later.

Crossing the River, Changing My Mind

> *I came to New York and in only hours, New York did what it does to people: awakened the possibilities. Hope breaks out. –Phillip Roth*

I finished near the top of my large high school class and won a scholarship to attend Columbia University in New York City, which we

---

[2] With several friends, I studied Swahili after school with Simon Chasen, the school's language teacher who was a renowned linguist. Our African American classmate, Wilmette Brown, later became a prominent feminist writer.

could not otherwise have afforded. I left Newark as an unsophisticated, politically-unformed centrist. I had become vaguely anti-communist as a patriotic response to the Russian launch of Sputnik in 1957. Like many of my generation, I was inspired by President John Kennedy and his call to service, but I had little awareness of the civil rights movement or racial inequality. I had not lived a sheltered life in a white suburb; rather, I had been in the white minority of an integrated junior high school, and I had lived as a tenant in a two-family house owned by a Black family. But I was not a left-wing radical nor a conscious anti-racist. I was a typical white, lower middle-class 17-year-old; the first in my family to attend college. My presumed destiny was to follow a well-trodden path to a respectable profession. The ten-mile bus ride across the Hudson was life-changing in every respect—it was an introduction to the wider world—intellectually, socially, politically.

In October 1962, a month into my college career, we were plunged into apocalyptic anxiety by the Cuban Missile Crisis; "no need to worry about exams," we joked. Meanwhile, the campus was not yet a hotbed for civil rights activism. There was a civil rights organization, the Congress of Racial Equality (CORE), but I was not drawn to it. I thought that joining demanded a purer heart than mine; an idealized conception of oppressed Black people, which contradicted my experience. I grew up in Newark, New Jersey; I questioned the authenticity of the activists who I imagined had grown up in white suburbs.

In small steps, my perspective changed. Returning to Newark for the summer after my first year, I worked in the post office during the day and volunteered at night for a college preparatory tutoring program for Black high school students, most of whom came from the ghetto not far from where I was born. I assigned them to read *The Stranger* by Albert Camus, which I chose because it was short and the language, if not the theme, seemed accessible enough for summer reading (for them and for me). It did not grab them. At the end of the summer, on August 28, 1963, hundreds of thousands of people traveled for the historic March on Washington for Jobs and

Freedom. To my lasting regret, I did not appreciate the urgency of it and did not board the bus.

"Chickens Coming Home to Roost"

My transformation rapidly accelerated. On September 15, 1963, white supremacists shockingly bombed the 16th Street Baptist Church in Birmingham, killing four young girls. Two months later, on November 22, 1963, President Kennedy was killed. For most of us, it was a radio event—there were few televisions on campus. Malcolm X, whom I had heard speak earlier in Newark, was famously quoted as describing the event as the "chickens coming home to roost," which he subsequently explained was not a statement of celebration, but a description of the inevitable result of the climate of violence and hate in the country. Eighteen months later, on February 21, 1965, I was stunned to hear a static-filled radio bulletin that Malcolm X had been killed at the Audubon Ballroom in Manhattan.

Our youthful cynicism was sparked by the dubious official narrative that a lone assassin had killed President Kennedy. Now, we were being told that members of the Nation of Islam had killed Malcolm X in retaliation for his split from the organization. Our cynicism became "left-wing paranoia," as we decided that the FBI either engineered the assassination or, at a minimum, knew about it and failed to stop it. In fact, as documents subsequently revealed, the FBI chief, J. Edgar Hoover, sought to "prevent the rise of a 'messiah' who could unify and electrify the militant Black nationalist movement. Malcolm X might have been such a 'messiah'. . . Martin Luther King, Stokely Carmichael, and [Nation of Islam leader] Elijah Muhammed [sic] all aspire to this position."[3]

Despite the epic March on Washington, despite the racist bombings

---

3 J. Edgar Hoover, "The FBI Sets Goals for COINTELPRO," *SHEC: Resources for Teachers*, accessed January 3, 2024, https://shec.ashp.cuny.edu/items/show/814. On November 18, 2021, some 56 years after Malcolm X's assassination, Manhattan District Attorney Cyrus Vance Jr. asked a judge to vacate the conviction of two Black men in the assassination. The New York City Police Department and the FBI had withheld exculpatory evidence at their 1966 trial. In October 2022, admitting the conviction was wrongful, the City of New York agreed to pay $26 million to Muhammad Aziz and the estate of Khalil Islam.

and assassinations, civil rights did not yet dominate campus activism. Rather, it was the burgeoning anti-war movement. President Lyndon Johnson had begun the escalation that would wreak massive destruction on the Vietnamese people and environment, fracture the U.S., and send millions of young Americans to war. As the U.S. escalated the war, the expanding draft personalized the war in a way it had not been for privileged white college students. Our anxiety grew. Our draft deferments would keep us safe as long as we were in college; otherwise, we would be plunged into the draft lottery, praying for a high number to reduce our chances of being called up or else finding an alternate strategy, like fleeing to Canada. Anti-war demonstrations became a way of life for those on our side of the fracture line that increasingly defined a polarized country.

The civil rights struggle and opposition to the war converged. On April 4, 1967, Martin Luther King, Jr. delivered a historic speech at New York's Riverside Church, "Beyond Vietnam," calling for a unilateral truce in Vietnam and linking the antiwar movement with racial justice. With that, we on the Left feared that Dr. King virtually sealed his fate. On April 28, 1967, Muhammad Ali became our hero by refusing induction into the U.S. Army: "Shoot [Vietnamese] for what? . . . They never lynched me, they didn't put no dogs on me, they didn't rob me of my nationality, rape and kill my mother and father. . . . Shoot them for what? How can I shoot them poor people? Just take me to jail."

He was convicted of draft evasion.[4]

In July 1967, police brutality sparked an uprising in Newark, my hometown—one of hundreds around the country. As the embers were dying down, I took my usual 107 bus from New York City to visit my parents. It dropped me on Lyons Avenue by my birthplace, the Beth Israel Hospital, a 1920s brick building high on a hill visible

---

4 Appeals kept him out of prison, but he was banned from boxing for five years at the height of his career.

from the New Jersey Turnpike. As I stepped off the bus, I found myself face to face with the armed National Guard, guarding the perimeter established to "keep our neighborhood safe." I turned away and walked the six blocks to my parents' home.

The country burst into flames in 1968. On April 4, 1968, Dr. Martin Luther King, Jr. was assassinated—the next but not the last of J. Edgar Hoover's list of potential "Black Messiahs" to die. Black communities throughout the country rose in fury. Columbia University erupted, as well. Anti-war fever, fueled by opposition to Columbia's engagement in military research, fused with outrage over racism: Columbia was attempting to seize a portion of Morningside Park, the border between the university and Harlem to the east, to build a gym that would be largely off-limits to community residents. It was imperialism right in our backyard. In protest, Columbia students and their allies seized control and occupied campus buildings. Hamilton Hall became the center for Black student and community occupiers. It became a lesson in separatism: White occupiers were asked to leave because Black students had a different perspective, centered on race; some proclaimed that they were willing to die in the struggle. After a week, Mayor John Lindsay sent in the police to end the occupation of the campus. Hundreds were arrested and scores were beaten. The Black students, notwithstanding their proclamations, negotiated a peaceful exit with a city administration fearful of sparking an outraged uprising in the broader Black community.

If the Columbia rebellion were not enough to seal my political transformation, the drumbeat of assassinations and violence through the rest of the year finished the job. On June 5, presidential candidate Robert F. Kennedy was killed in Los Angeles; in August, the Democratic National Convention in Chicago was met with bloody protests. Black Panthers were arrested, tried, imprisoned, and killed time and again. In New York, New Haven, and Berkeley, we took to the streets to protest.

What was the nature of my transformation? I did not occupy

classroom buildings in the siege of Columbia; I was among the supporters at the campus gates. I was close to finishing my master's degree and did not want to risk losing my fellowship, getting expelled, and being set adrift, exposed to the draft. I did not go to Chicago to protest the Democratic convention; I was protesting in the streets of Berkeley that summer. In 1969, when the Students for a Democratic Society (SDS) split into the Weatherman and other radical factions, I was in Europe visiting Russia for the first time, a necessary introduction to my chosen career as a Russian historian. I was a "foot soldier" in the New Left, never a leader or a "card-carrying member" of any left-wing faction in the anti-war movement, which exploded after the killing of four college students at Kent State in May 1970.

Getting (Secular) Religion

I spent a decade at Columbia, entering in 1962, completing my BA degree and continuing in graduate school, studying to become a historian of pre-revolutionary Russia. I had gained not only an academic education, but a new worldview: the secular "religion" of anti-imperialism. The wars against national liberation struggles, the lies and phony rationales of fighting against the falling dominoes of Communism, the covert undermining of democratic regimes and movements, the assassinations of Black leaders—I learned that all of it was integral to our government's effort to dominate the world. The Central Intelligence Agency (CIA) was the foreign arm, the Federal Bureau of Investigations (FBI) the domestic force against the enemies of capitalism and the U.S. government. We in the New Left played defense—solidarity demonstrations and campaigns in support of the visible Black leaders who were hunted down, sometimes killed, and often wrongly prosecuted by the government. Huey Newton, the charismatic cofounder with Bobby Seale of the Black Panther Party for Self-Defense, was jailed. Fred Hampton and Mark Clark, young leaders of the Chicago chapter of the Black Panthers, were killed in a police raid in December 1969, in an operation enabled by the FBI's

COINTELPRO operation. J. Edgar Hoover had described the Black Panthers as "the greatest threat to the internal security of the country."

In 1969, the Panther 21, accused of planning multiple attacks on police stations, were tried in the most expensive trial in New York City's history. They were acquitted on all charges.

Finding My Way

If there was to be a revolution in the United States, some of us on the Left believed that it would have to be Black led. Our role as white allies was to acknowledge Black leadership, provide legal and material support, take to the streets to raise public consciousness, and turn our attention to organizing among white America. I never believed, as some did, that revolution was imminent. I was never the first to throw a stone in the street battles of the 1960s or early 1970s. I was never arrested, nor did I seek to be. I explained—justified—to myself that although I could not be a revolutionary hero, I would commit to the struggle for the long haul.

It would not be through academia. My aspirations there crumbled on two fronts. The Columbia University student strike of 1968 shattered my illusions about the academy: most of the professors were cowed, reluctant to take a strong position, concerned with maintaining the illusory objectivity of the ivory tower. I persisted in my graduate studies for years, earned a master's degree in Russian history, but barely, through the mercy of my professors, completed my doctoral oral examinations. That was enough to convince me of my inadequacies as a future academic.

Nonetheless, I conceived a history project that, while not considered "scholarly," was for me far more compelling and socially relevant. In my research, I discovered a trove of memoirs of Russian revolutionary women of the nineteenth century. With my graduate school colleague and friend, Barbara Engel, we collected, translated, and brought to life the memoirs of these brave women; chilling narratives of armed retaliation against police brutality, life underground, and the campaign that succeeded in assassinating Tsar Alexander II in 1881. Their embrace of feminism and revolutionary populism seemed astonishingly contemporary in the feverish years of the 1960s and early 1970s.[5]

For me, the book gratified and exhausted any residual interest in becoming an academic. I regarded our book as a political act: I had produced a work of revolutionary history that inspired others on the Left and in feminist movements in the U.S. and beyond.

Organizer

I always felt that the value of a really good education is you can take more risks. –Barack Obama, Columbia College Class of 1983[6]

My half-dozen years of graduate school tedium provided me with one marketable skill: I learned enough Russian to get a freelance job translating the *Great Russian Encyclopedia*. Paid by the word, I managed to earn just enough to sustain me in my first, uncompensated career: I became a co-op organizer.

I was seeking concrete action, work that would produce tangible results and yet would enable me to link my local activity to my worldview. I focused on the Third World hunger crisis, scarcity compounded by the domination of the world food production, supply, and distribution chains by multinational corporations. I started by organizing a food co-op among the neighbors in our multiracial, lower-middle- and working-class apartment building in upper Manhattan's now-famous Washington Heights. It was one small activist

---

5 Barbara Alpern Engel, and Clifford N. Rosenthal. *Five Sisters: Women against the Tsar*. DeKalb, IL: NIU Press, 2013. Originally published New York: Alfred A. Knopf, 1975. With a foreword from a best-selling author, Alix Kates Shulman, the book attracted considerable attention, including reviews in *Newsweek* and the *New York Review of Books*. *Five Sisters* was later retranslated and published in Mexico and Turkey. In the U.S., it has been reissued multiple times and used in college courses for more than 40 years.

6 Barack Obama, *Columbia College Today* (New York: Columbia College, Office of Alumni Affairs and Development, 2005). https:// www.college.columbia.edu/cct.

step, but the food co-op was a relatively simple way to produce real benefits, and it increased the sense of community among our Black and white neighbors. In many ways, it was the most satisfying co-op experience I ever had.

In 1972, I left New York City to accompany my first wife to Hartford, Connecticut, where she had been accepted into graduate school. To engage with the community, I volunteered at a social service agency in Hartford's low-income South End, organizing a small food co-op and teaching a photography class for neighborhood youth. We lived communally for a year, but soon thereafter my marriage broke up, setting me adrift. For some weeks, I lived in a building slated for demolition. My life became more stable when I found a rented room in the city's Blue Hills area, which had spawned in a small "intentional community" of white people seeking an interracial neighborhood. For several years, I lived intermittently on the third floor of the one-family house, sharing many meals with my landlady and her two young children, one white and one (adopted) Black. It was not quite communal, but it was a warm home base providing welcome company in my otherwise unattached life.

The neighborhood proved perfect for my values and organizing impulse. I put out the call to organize a Blue Hills Food Co-op, a larger version of the co-op I had organized back in New York—multi-racial, middle- and working-class. For several years I worked without pay, lugging produce, coordinating, purchasing, and keeping the books for the co-op. I overloaded my compact car's trunk until the suspension gave out. We distributed the food weekly from the basement of a large neighboring church. I, and the co-op, had no business plan or growth goals. We saved people money, and we helped build a sense of neighborhood. That was my approach to community organizing.

Turning 30

Beyond the mechanics of food co-op organizing and operations, I began to engage with the broader cooperative movement and the food policy world. I connected with the New England Federation of Cooperatives, attended their regional gatherings, and joined the Connecticut-based Center for Farm and Food Policy. In 1975, I turned 30, marking my birthday by organizing a World Food Day event in Hartford, bringing together cooperative practitioners, nutrition advocates, and public officials.

My painful, unsuccessful efforts to complete my doctorate in Russian history were in the past and unlamented. I was divorced, unattached, and had an Ivy League master's degree with no viable career. But politically, I was satisfied with where I had come. I had published a well-received book that was educating people on the history of a struggle against tsarist tyranny. Through my food co-op and advocacy work, I was working to change people's understanding of corporate domination and imperialism. Seeking a way to translate my activism into something broader, I rented office space on the second floor above a bank in the working-class, Latinx, and multi-ethnic South End of Hartford. I envisioned my office becoming a center for political education and organizing, and I prevailed on old friends to contribute a little money. But my effort never blossomed. My grandiose vision amounted to little.

I continued to see myself as an organizer; a politically virtuous activist. I managed to get a short-lived adjunct position at the University of Hartford, teaching one subject I had never studied (ancient history), and another course that I created (America Since Vietnam). That was the summit of my academic career. I was economically marginal, earning a scant living translating the Russian encyclopedia part-time to support my unpaid avocation. But it was not a viable life plan. I found myself taking cash advances against my credit card. I needed a life change.

CHAPTER 2

To Serve the People

In debt and under-employed, I needed a full-time job. In the fall of 1975, I learned of one that seemed too good to be true. A statewide Indigenous organization in Connecticut, American Indians for Development, was searching for someone to run their anti-hunger program, and specifically to organize a food co-op. I was invited for an interview.[7]

I got the job by default. At my interview, the associate director informed me that "we were really looking for an Indian for the job, but there were no applicants, so I guess you'll have to do."[8] I wasn't offended—I was thrilled. It was my first "dream job," getting paid a full-time salary ($9,000) to work for an organization fighting for the rights of oppressed people. Along with the struggles for Black liberation, the battles of Indigenous people had broken through to the American consciousness. In 1973, the American Indian Movement (AIM) occupied Wounded Knee, the site of a massacre of the Sioux by the U.S. Calvary. Russell Means and Dennis Banks emerged as nationally prominent leaders; like Black leaders, they fell under the scrutiny of the FBI and CIA. Although everyone in my new job supported AIM and the broader movement, the organization was not

---

[7] "American Indian" was the term the organization used to describe itself.
[8] Trudie Lamb, later Trudie Lamb-Richmond, had a long, distinguished career in Indigenous advocacy and education in Connecticut. A member of the Schaghticoke tribe in Northwestern Connecticut, she became its first chairwoman. She was later director of public programs at the Mashantucket Pequot Museum and Research Center, and a representative on the Connecticut State Native American Heritage Advisory Council.

explicitly political. It functioned both as an intertribal coalition to advocate for Indigenous concerns and a social service, anti-poverty agency.

Basic Education

I needed to get educated about Indigenous people. Surprisingly, as I learned, there were more Native Americans living in Connecticut than in the state of Colorado—about 5,000. Most lived in the cities—Hartford, Bridgeport, Waterbury, and Eastern Connecticut, and many were poor. In addition to the Schaghticokes, the Indigenous tribes included the Eastern Pequots and Western Pequots, the Mohegans, and the Golden Hill Paugussetts. The Paugussetts had the dubious distinction of occupying the smallest reservation in the country: a house on a quarter acre in Trumbull, Connecticut, near Bridgeport. It was the home of Chief Big Eagle (Aurelius Piper, Sr.). It was a lesson in diversity: in addition to the five tribes native to Connecticut, the organization hosted or employed Mi'kmaq, Maliseet, Penobscot, Pasamaquoddy, Wampanoag, Mohawk, Narragansett, Hopi, Navajo, Oneida, Abenaki, Lummi, Chippewa, and others of the Indigenous diaspora. By skin color, they were as diverse as their tribal origins. Some were paler than I was, while several dark-skinned Navajos showed little evidence of mixed origins. The head of the agency was dark-skinned, and the board chair, from Eastern Connecticut, darker still. It was explained to me that intermarriage, whether with whites or African Americans, accounted for much of the differences. I learned about the cultural and spiritual importance of powwows when we cosponsored one in Connecticut. It was small, but it attracted Indigenous people from all around the Northeast. There were crafts, drumming, singing, dance competitions for men and women, and food (fry bread!); I staffed our hotdog booth. "Manuel," a young Navajo man who had found his way east to our organization, gathered much admiration for his ceremonial dress and his skill as a dancer. He was the most "traditional" of the people I met at the organization. For example, when he experienced pain in a shoulder blade, he informed us that someone had put a curse on him, directing a bone to be stuck into him.

Manuel's life ended tragically. He married the sister of one of our coworkers and began working for her father's industrial machinery company. Months after their marriage, while working on a crew, he touched a live wire and was electrocuted. The staff traveled to his wake in Chief Piper's house on the tiny Golden Hill Paugussett reservation outside Bridgeport. Manuel was laid out in traditional dress in a coffin in a small room in the chief's small house. It was the first wake I had ever attended.

Work/Life Boundaries

The organization occupied a three-story house that served both for offices and a kind of community center and waystation for young people from Maine, Colorado, Arizona, and elsewhere who passed through and sometimes occupied the bedrooms on the top floor. I did not seek to be included in the after-hours social scene, sometimes filled with personal dramas and undercurrents. But I enjoyed my working hours with my colleagues, especially the good-humored comments and jokes (occasionally with a slight edge). On one of our long food co-op delivery runs, a coworker improvised a chant, "White Man in the Indian Van."

I was hired to coordinate food projects, to set up and manage a food co-op, and to handle emergency food distribution. I was not engaged in policymaking, which seemed fine and appropriate to me as a representative of the white world. However, I delivered testimony for the organization and coordinated with the umbrella agency that oversaw our funding, a role that today might be characterized as an "equity broker." In my second year at the organization, my duties expanded to include providing energy assistance for needy families. As part of our workplan, we made a bulk purchase of blankets—ironic, if the account of Europeans providing smallpox-infected blankets to the Native population is to be believed.[9]

In one of our modest efforts to promote self-sufficiency, we used our federal grant to help the Western Pequots create a community garden on their reservation in Eastern Connecticut. I briefly met Richard "Skip" Hayward, the chief of the tribe, when he came to our office for board meetings. He left an indelible impression on me with his camouflage jacket, electric energy, and intense focus. He had begun the fight for federal recognition of his tribe, a battle that would last until their victory in 1983 (long after I left the organization). This was my introduction to the high-stakes battle for Indigenous financial sovereignty. In later years, the tribe began offering bingo and subsequently built the Foxwoods Casino and Resort, one of the world's largest, along with the Mashantucket Pequot Museum and Research Center among other enterprises. It was a universe beyond the modest, anti-poverty-funded community garden that we had helped to create.

My Idealism Challenged

Our food co-op was to serve various Native American clusters and communities around the state, bringing fresh food and baked goods. I and a few staff members drove around the state in the "Indian van" to several sites and did all the work with minimal volunteer help from our members. The organization contributed a vast amount of staff labor to the project; there was not a lot of "cooperation" among the members of the co-op. Our "business model" (not that I knew what one was) was not geared toward sustainability.

My co-op idealism was frustrated, and my commitment to "serve the people" was shaken, as I came into conflict with the executive

---

9 Memorably, I drove the company van to a wholesaler in Brooklyn, New York. As I headed back to Connecticut with a full load of blankets on July 13, 1977, a massive blackout hit New York City. Unlike earlier blackouts, it triggered extensive looting and burning—yet another blow to a city simultaneously racked by the serial killings of the "Summer of Sam" and near-bankruptcy.

director, "Kevin." My mission of promoting cooperatives had brought me to the organization, but it was at odds with his notion. For me, establishing a cooperative meant engaging volunteers with the work of the co-op, empowering them collectively, not simply delivering orders. Kevin was less interested in that. The co-op concept blurred into a social-service function. It was coupled with emergency food relief: a mobile food bank. Some families chronically did not pay for "co-op food," which was fine with Kevin, but did not align with my notion of building self-help through cooperative action.

In retrospect, it was presumptuous of me to fault Kevin for trying to provide service and build solidarity among the fragmented Indigenous population in Connecticut in any way he saw fit. But I found his alpha-male, arbitrary management style off-putting. If my objective was to "serve the people" and defer to non-white leadership, I did a poor job, as demonstrated by my disagreements with my boss. I was a white guy getting paid to do a job. The conflict revealed and reinforced my streak of rebellion against authority figures, even those who were leading the causes I embraced.

Working for an Indigenous organization was my first full-time job of any kind, and my first job as a white staff member in a social justice organization. I had taken the job with a vision of building a co-operative, but it had come to resemble direct service. There was nothing wrong with that, but I concluded that it was simply not what I wanted nor had the skills for. Moreover, I had grander ambitions than working locally. By the fall of 1977, two years into the job, I sought opportunities in Washington, DC. I was offered a job with a coalition of migrant and seasonal farmworker organizations—another opportunity to work on cooperative and food-related issues for an oppressed population.

I was grateful for my experience working in an Indigenous organization and felt warmly toward many of my colleagues despite my job dissatisfaction. After years cloistered in the university world, I appreciated working with "real" people who were not focused on academic pursuits or intellectual jousting. I had not become part of the Native American "family," as such, but I had been accepted as a useful ally. I was given parting gifts of a traditional ribbon shirt and a dreamcatcher, which I have kept for decades. In December 1977, I pulled up stakes in Connecticut.

Washington

I was hired by a national farmworker coalition not because of any expertise about the farmworker population, but because of my experience in food cooperatives and food policy. It helped that I had "field experience"—that is, working for a local minority organization rather than inhabiting the insular Beltway universe.

On my first day in Washington, my new supervisor invited me to join her and a friend for a late dinner. The friend was Leonel Castillo, who had been appointed as the first Hispanic commissioner of the U.S. Citizenship and Immigration Services. That was impressive enough—but when he asked me what *I* thought about the issues, I was pleasantly dumbstruck and could only mumble a few generalities. My introduction to the national policy scene already exceeded my expectations.

As it had been previously, my work was to advocate for groups that fell outside the predominant narrative of urban Black or Latinx poverty. Again, I needed a basic education. I learned that migrant and seasonal farmworkers endured singularly oppressive work, living, and health conditions that exacerbated poverty. They were typically immigrants of color—Mexican, Central American, Jamaican, Haitian, and others, depending on which migrant stream they traveled. Their pay was low, with few of the protections most other Americans enjoy; their hours were long and their income low, seasonal, and erratic. Their housing was way below "substandard." Children labored in the fields next to their parents as their families followed the migrant stream. Often, they moved from school to school, falling behind other students. Farmworkers' health care was often abysmal. Worst of all, they were exposed to toxic chemicals and inadequate sanitation. Crew chiefs often abused them financially and personally.

The coalition was a federation of local and regional organizations serving migrant and seasonal farmworkers. My job was to provide the member organizations with training and technical assistance on food and hunger issues, such as Food Stamps, and where possible, assist with food co-op development. Our challenge as advocates was to bring farmworkers' special situations to the attention of policymakers, who crafted program regulations that had the consequences (sometimes unintended) of excluding them. For example, farmworkers moving north with a migrant stream lacked a "fixed address" that the Food Stamp program required. The large size and extended composition of farmworker families disqualified them from certain programs. If they owned a large automobile to transport their families from harvest to harvest, the value of the car might exceed allowable asset limits.

My work managing our federal grants brought me in contact with the headquarters of the federal anti-poverty programs, the Community Services Administration (CSA), a much-reduced and far less influential successor to the Office of Economic Opportunity (OEO) that had led the War on Poverty in the 1960s. Notwithstanding the liberal-leaning politics of the Carter Administration, we were often disappointed with its failure to act aggressively on our issues, especially labor and health, where they could have made a much greater difference.

Meeting Labor Heroes

In 1979, Cesar Chavez of the United Farm Workers visited our office in Washington, D.C., to explore membership. I was thrilled to stand in the presence of the living legend. To my surprise, he did not radiate charisma, but rather a certain shyness, a physical reserve; he seemed to almost draw back from us. I met other prominent leaders of the farmworker rights movement, as well, including Baldemar Velasquez. Born to a Mexican American farmworker family, he was founder and president of the Farm Labor Organizing Committee. Velasquez was closer to our age, and much more personably accessible.[10]

In January 1979, my boss charged me with organizing and managing the biggest event in our organization's short history, a national conference in Washington. It was almost stillborn. I obtained a favorable rate at a venue that I thought would send the right political message: a Black-owned hotel adjoining Howard University. It soon came to Chavez's attention that the hotel was not unionized. That was an absolute dealbreaker for the United Farm Workers. With only weeks to go, we had to scramble to relocate, relying on the help of a local union to get an acceptable hotel.

We held sessions on the range of farmworker issues, from hunger and nutrition to health and pesticides, to immigration, education, and the census. When Chavez spoke, he did not galvanize or inspire as I had hoped. Marion Barry, mayor of D.C. and a former community organizer, gave a much more electrifying performance. I was charged by my boss with inviting senior officials of the Carter Administration for the event. They turned us down. But Senator Ted Kennedy, whose family had long been supporters of the farmworker cause, did join us. The conference ended with a true extravaganza, our Fiesta Campesina, at a theater on Columbia Road, in the heart of the Washington's Latinx and Caribbean communities. We brought in a prominent Black dance ensemble, Mexican and Chicano/a singing and dance groups, poets, Navajo dancers, and bluegrass musicians from Kentucky. It was a glorious multicultural event, and the members loved it. At the end of the long night, our board chairman, a farmworker from California, lifted me off the ground and embraced me. The next night, after the conference wound down, we had a party at my colleague's house. A young staff member from a Western farmworker organization invited me upstairs to hang out with a few colleagues. He thanked me for

---

10 While Velasquez was not then as renowned as Cesar Chavez, his organizing work over decades later won him recognition with a MacArthur Foundation "genius" grant, honorary doctorates, and many other awards.

my work and strongly urged me to continue using my talents for the farmworker cause. I was flattered but made no promises.

My First Credit Union

"Bill," the coalition's executive director, was white and male, energetic, charismatic, and undoubtedly devoted to the farmworker cause. But his "management style" was, as I saw it, improvisational, undisciplined, and fiscally questionable. Despite my misgivings about Bill's management, I was grateful when he gave me an assignment that would change my life. Bill had conceived the idea of starting a credit union to serve the staff and clients of NAFO's various member organizations. He hired a consultant to teach us the credit union philosophy and guide us through the chartering process. As a longtime cooperator, I was immediately and entirely captured by the credit union concept—a nonprofit "money cooperative" dedicated to providing savings and loan services to low-income communities.

Organizing a credit union introduced me to a huge, yet under-recognized, sector of the cooperative universe. Simply put, I fell in love with the credit unions—and specifically, community development credit unions (CDCUs), the ones that served low-income communities and communities of color. Credit unions were a proven cooperative concept with a history in the U.S. dating back to 1908; they *worked*. They were not-for-profit, organized by and for *working people* who made up their boards of directors—volunteers, not bankers. For low-income people and communities, they were a vehicle for self-help; a means of development that was not dependent on government.

After several months of training, we obtained a charter for a new credit union in July 1979. I was elected the president of the credit union—which soon became a battleground.

Solidarity

Joining NAFO introduced me to a wider and more diverse community of colleagues. The staff was multi-racial and multi-cultural, Chicano/a, African American, and Puerto Rican; my colleagues included immigrants from Central America, Cuba, and Korea, as well as white progressives of various backgrounds. It was a collection of bright, committed people who worked well together in an organization that was more chaotic than hierarchical.

In the summer of 1979, when I was serving as a mid-level supervisor, I was faced with a personnel crisis. Bill, the CEO, informed me that we had a budget crisis, and he demanded I tell him which staff members reporting to me should be laid off. I refused to name names or positions. There were extensive layoffs anyway, which we angrily blamed on Bill's poor management. I spoke with my colleagues, and we began meeting at my home to consider unionizing.

It didn't go easily. Few union locals were interested in helping; we were a small potential bargaining unit, a motley collection of nonprofit workers. Finally, a local of the United Food and Commercial Workers agreed to take us on. Bill was bitterly opposed to the unionizing effort, which he saw as a betrayal of our mission to serve farmworkers. He fought to exclude staff members from the bargaining unit on the grounds that we were allegedly "management." This opposition from an organization dedicated to workers' rights appalled me. It was a lasting lesson in the hypocrisy of the leadership in some liberal, justice-seeking organizations.

Despite management's opposition, we won our union vote. I was chosen as president of our little union shop—after having been elected as president of our new credit union. Management started spreading the false narrative that the credit union was some kind of "plot" by pro-labor union NAFO staff members. Bill's allies organized a campaign to vote me out as president of the credit union. The effort failed. Our minuscule credit union limped along; sadly, it never gained momentum among our member farmworker organizations.

Early Lessons

From my first two jobs in the 1970s, I learned lessons about nonprofits in general, social justice organizations in particular, and the vulnerabilities of credit unions and cooperatives. I learned about the kind of nonprofit leader I did *not* want to become. My first two bosses were charismatic leaders: alpha males devoted to their cause but poor managers. Our union drive taught me about the hypocrisy of management in some progressive organizations that resisted worker rights when the issue hit close to home. On the other hand, unionizing was an affirming, energizing experience of solidarity among our multi-racial, multi-ethnic staff. Finally, I learned about the dangers of a credit union becoming a political football for a sponsoring organization.

My years in Washington were among the most rewarding of my work and personal life. The capital provided me with the excitement and education I had sought. My eyes were opened to the "big picture" of Beltway policymakers and the multitude of advocacy organizations. I worked side by side with people who would become lifelong friends.

But by 1980, I had compelling personal reasons to move on. After years of our alternate weekend commutes on the D.C.-Brooklyn-D.C. circuit, Elayne and I decided it was time to marry and settle down. I gave up my apartment in Washington's Mount Pleasant neighborhood, up the hill from the national zoo, where I regularly heard the lions roaring at night (and where my apartment had been broken into multiple times despite the floor-to-near-ceiling bars on the windows and doors). I spent my last night at a friend's house up the street as the thermometer hit 90 degrees at midnight. I packed up my red Dodge Dart and headed north. I hoped to return someday. Thirty years later, I did.

CHAPTER 3

Leader by Default

I began the first day of the rest of my life in Elayne's communal house in brownstone Brooklyn, a formerly "redlined" dicey neighborhood of faded post-Victorian glory that had begun to attract middle-class "pioneers" from Manhattan and elsewhere. It was a welcome return for me to the cooperative living situation of my early years in Hartford. Moreover, with its low, shared costs, the commune greatly eased my life during my initial and later months of unemployment. I returned to New York with no job, but a plan born of serendipity. In organizing NAFO's credit union, I had learned about an organization headquartered in downtown Brooklyn, a 15-minute subway ride from my new home: the National Federation of Community Development Credit Unions (NFCDCU). One way or another, I needed to find a job at the Federation. But it would take a while.

As I commenced my new life in Brooklyn, I followed the pattern I had set years before when I moved from New York to Hartford: organize! Inspired by my experience in starting the NAFO credit union, I soon set out to organize one in Park Slope. As our bilingual brochure announced, our goal was:

> To gain local control over the economic resources of the community. Major changes are taking place in our neighborhood. Decisions which affect all of our lives are being dictated by institutions over which we have little control—large banks, insurance companies, and real estate speculators.

I gathered a small, multiracial nucleus of neighborhood activists. Together, we launched a drive to obtain the deposit pledges needed to start a new credit union, conducting outreach at street fairs and community meetings. With a famously successful food cooperative, Park Slope seemed an especially promising place for our effort. But we never achieved substantial momentum. After about a year, we abandoned the effort.[11]

Pursuing My Dream Job

The Federation had an opening that perfectly suited my interests and experience: technical assistance coordinator. However, the position would not be funded for several months. In the meantime, to enhance my chances, I volunteered at the Federation to learn about the organization and get to know my prospective boss. I waited impatiently for months. Finally, on October 1, 1980, I officially joined the staff of the organization that would define my life's work.

Jim Clark, the executive director, was refreshingly different from my previous bosses. He did not fit the mold of a charismatic leader—but that was in a good way. A devout Catholic, a noncombatant Vietnam War veteran, and a peace activist, he had an entirely different management style, one that I admired. As his laborious, months-long hiring procedure demonstrated, he was committed to treating every individual with respect and dignity. I admired his ability and his patience to deal personally with a collection of different, sometimes exasperating, staff members, which I attributed in part to his raising six daughters and sons.

The Federation was housed in an old office building in downtown Brooklyn, across from the courts and populated by "ambulance-chasing" personal injury lawyers. It had a magnificent view of the Manhattan skyline. We had the space thanks to our board chairman,

---

[11] Many years later, the Park Slope Food Co-op did affiliate with an existing credit union.

Adolfo ("Al") Alayon, whose organization, Community Action for Bedford-Stuyvesant (CABS) had an office upstairs. The Federation's staff was primarily white and young, except for the Black deputy director and one program officer. I was "middle management" in a small, free-flowing nonprofit with a national agenda. That was fine with me. I planned to focus on settling into our communal household in Brooklyn with Elayne and starting a family. Three weeks after the 1980 election, Elayne and I married in our communal living room, a wedding attended by my new Federation colleagues, many of my former colleagues who traveled up from Washington, and our families, including Elayne's 10-year-old son, Carlo. This was to inaugurate my mature, stable life.

At the Federation, I was quickly plunged into a new work "family." My first weeks on the job were a whirlwind—we convened two national conferences in six weeks. I was immersed and overwhelmed by a new scene; I knew none of the hundreds of attendees or what, exactly, they did in their community development credit unions—"CDCUs"—to whom I was supposed to be providing technical assistance. I was joining a family gathering, or, as members from the South described it, a "revival meeting." That spirit permeated the movement for years to come, but sadly faded as one Black credit union after another disappeared.

Unlike the farmworker advocacy world I had come from, the majority of the members were African American and urban. There were no Chicanos, few Latinos generally, but there was a Puerto Rican board chairman, Al. Many came from credit unions rooted in Community Action Agencies, those diminishing outposts of the War on Poverty: Dick came from Columbus, Etta from Waterbury in Connecticut, and Bob (one of the few white, rural representatives) from Iowa. Most memorably, there was Armistice Powell, the vice chairwoman of the board, a Black woman who had founded the East Oakland Credit Union in California. Her name came from her birthday: she was born on Armistice Day, November 11, 1918, when

World War I ended. Ms. Powell, typically an unsmiling presence, was a tough woman who came from a tough place. She had organized the credit union after witnessing the dignity-draining lines of people waiting in the parking lot outside a bank branch for the monthly distribution of food stamps. She believed that people deserved something better, and she founded the credit union to provide it. She was not a great fan of our predominantly white, young staff—few of whom had earned their stripes in the trenches of the antipoverty war.

I was not on the front lines of dealing with the board of directors. I listened to my boss, Jim, describing the challenges of working with a national body that was admirably grassroots and locally focused. It was not a fundraising board; it had little access to financial resources. Fortunately, the board had an exceptional chairman. Al was street-smart, politically sophisticated, and an important nonprofit entrepreneur in Brooklyn. Born in Puerto Rico, he established the first senior citizen nursing home for the Hispanic elderly in Brooklyn under the auspices of Community Action for Bedford-Stuyvesant (CABS). He had cofounded the CABS Federal Credit Union, as well. His organization was housed in the district of Representative Shirley Chisholm—the first Black woman to run for president for a major party. He informed us that when Chisholm was preparing to leave office, she suggested that Al seek her seat. He did not. Al could be frustratingly laid-back, but admirably unflustered and supremely comfortable in his own skin. On one occasion, he saved my budding career at the Federation.

My first job at the Federation was managing our technical assistance staff and preparing reports for federal funding agencies. I included a report from one staff member who mentioned—approvingly—that a particular African American credit union had "circumvented" a regulatory impediment in order to better serve its members. I did not see a problem, and I let it go. But that credit union's Black agency head, "Austin," took great offense, raging against the damned "white liberal" who was allegedly reporting to the federal government that he had violated the law. I was offended that he called me a liberal—I definitely considered myself a left-wing "radical"—but I feared losing my dream job. But Al was not overly critical or concerned; he took it in stride and smoothed over the conflict.

I drew several lessons from this incident. As a white staffer managing a federally-funded program, I was blind to the pressures and potential threats that Black people might see coming from Washington. But, thanks to Al, I learned that race-driven divisiveness would not prevail in our organization. I was grateful. We moved on.

A Change of Plans: Leader by Default

When I joined the National Federation in October 1980, I anticipated a stable career with limited responsibilities managing our technical assistance program. But in the months after Ronald Reagan's inauguration in 1981, the Federation's prospects plummeted. The funding of our dozen-person staff came almost entirely from federal grants ($500,000 out of a total of $505,000) attached to the Community Development Revolving Loan Program, which the Reagan Administration promptly set out to eliminate. Jim traveled repeatedly to Washington, waging a disheartening and ultimately futile effort to salvage the organization's funding. By the fall of 1982, all but a few tens of thousands of dollars remained to ensure an orderly close-out of our federal contracts. Jim drew a salary of a day or two a week; the rest of the staff left. We moved the Federation's computer equipment to my communal house; our Brooklyn address helped preserve the illusion of continuity. I collected unemployment and volunteered what support I could.

By the spring of 1983, there were glimmers of hope. We had raised one or two small grants from progressive foundations. More hope came that April, when I won a life-changing opportunity: I was awarded a Revson Foundation Fellowship for the Future of the City of New York at Columbia University. It came with a very livable stipend and required of me only the slightest academic commitment.

That April, Jim and I met with our board chairman, Al, at his office in Bedford-Stuyvesant. I optimistically announced a survival plan for the Federation: Jim would continue running the Federation and draw a salary, while I would help out without pay for a year. But with a house full of children, Jim could not survive on two days a week salary. He congratulated me and announced that he had to move on. Al declared that it was time to turn out the lights and close the doors of the Federation. He was proud of what the Federation had accomplished, but he did not see a path forward.

With the prospect of the fellowship to sustain me, I made the only viable offer to keep the Federation alive: I would work without a salary, with one "non-negotiable demand"—that I be given the title of executive director, a position I had never held. There were no other candidates. With nothing to lose, Al agreed. So, by default, I became the boss of a national nonprofit organization with no employees, no office, a declining membership, and a negative net worth of several thousand dollars.

Social Entrepreneur

Thus began my career as the white leader of a predominantly non-white organization that others had given up for dead. The lack of funding was a problem, but even worse was the decline in membership; the departure of credit unions that were the soul of the movement and the purpose of the Federation. Some closed their doors because the Reagan Administration was decimating the funding for antipoverty efforts, which supported the Community Action Agencies that sponsored many credit unions. Others dropped their membership because the Federation could provide little in the way of support or services.

But what mattered to me was that I was working for an organization with a proud history of fighting for economic justice. In a way, our tenuous situation was an advantage for me. I assumed leadership with the benefit of facing low expectations. Anything I achieved would be a bonus. Given the lack of alternatives, my whiteness was not a problem. The Federation was not a blank slate, but there were really no constraints on my ambition or vision. I would succeed or fail as a social entrepreneur.

Reinforcements: The "Odd Couple"

Throughout the summer of 1983, the National Federation of Community Development Credit Unions, Inc. lived in the fourth-floor study of my communal home in Park Slope, Brooklyn. The Federation's computer equipment was jammed into the room. There was no internet; our communications "system" was an answering machine—my only "colleague." Occasionally, I was pleasantly interrupted by my 18-month-old daughter, who crawled up the stairs to keep me company.

My fellowship year began in September. Returning home to my office one day, I played a phone message: "This is Annie Vamper. You may not remember me, but I've been working for the regulator, the National Credit Union Administration (NCUA). We're parting ways. I can't be helping credit unions the way I want to. Perhaps you know a credit union that could use my services."

I certainly remembered. There were few African American credit union examiners those days, and Annie had represented the agency at some of our conferences. Alabama-born, she had been one of the few Black credit union managers in the Southeast, and she had worked for NCUA on two occasions, including Operation Moneywise, the 1970s-era program that grew from the War on Poverty. I jumped at the opportunity to hire her. Our few small foundation grants would fund her part-time salary; with my fellowship, I could manage without a salary for nearly a year.

Annie was almost everything that I was not: a Black woman from the South, experienced in credit union operations and regulations, familiar with our membership, and most importantly, a believer in our mission. She was willing to work for a struggling organization with dicey prospects for survival—not necessarily what a single mother with a high-school age daughter (and two grown children) needed.

Thus began the partnership that would last the rest of the decade until her premature death in 1990.

For some months, she made a long trek from her home in Northern New Jersey to my home office. Then, we migrated to a small room in East Harlem, courtesy of our member Union Settlement Federal Credit Union. After a year, we found a "real" office in in a third-rate office building in Manhattan's decaying financial district, one block north of the Federal Reserve Bank of New York.

For several years, it was just the two of us; we were the "senior management" as well as the program staff. Annie and I divided duties to create the semblance of an organization—"smoke and mirrors," as some of our funders described it. I was the "outside" person—the advocate, fundraiser, and program developer, the "face" of the Federation, and the executive director accountable to our member-elected board of directors. Annie was the "inside" person, dealing with operations, keeping our books, and managing member relations. As a Southerner, a former credit union manager, and a former employee of the regulator, she was readily able to relate to our Black membership, but also to small credit unions generally. In addition to serving as our sole provider of technical information for our credit unions, she staffed our new Capitalization Program, which raised social investments and channeled them into local credit unions. Soon, we had the great good fortune to add a major talent on a part-time basis: Errol Louis, a Black recent graduate of Harvard.[12] Later in the decade, we added a bookkeeper, Irene, a New Yorker of Tobagan heritage with a co-op background who would serve the Federation for nearly thirty years. With this core team, we worked throughout the 1980s to rebuild the Federation.

---

12 Trained as a journalist, Errol later joined the editorial board of the New York *Daily News*. Subsequently, he became the host of the most-watched nightly television show about New York politics, *Inside City Hall*, and occasionally appears as a commentator on CNN.

CHAPTER 4

Pursuing "People's Capital"

For my 32 years at the National Federation of Community Development Credit Unions, the fight for capital was the legacy and driver for much of my work. Our credit unions needed capital to survive regulation, enough capital to make a difference in their communities. Since the 1970s, capital has repeatedly emerged as a life-or-death issue for credit unions serving poor communities. It began with a quest simply for deposits—liquidity to lend—and over time, refocused on equity, the net worth that the members collectively owned in the credit union, and that was the *sine qua non* for doing business as a financial cooperative.

The "War on Poverty"

The 1960s marked the "rediscovery of poverty," stimulated by the publication of Michael Harrington's 1962 book, *The Other America: Poverty in the United States*. In 1964, President Lyndon Johnson launched the far-reaching array of federal policies and programs known as the "War on Poverty." The Office of Economic Opportunity (OEO) was established as the federal headquarters for scores of programs implemented through a network of Community Action Agencies (CAAs) in urban and rural poverty areas. OEO adopted a credit union strategy to promote self-help among the poor, funding several hundred credit unions through the CAA network. Typically, it provided operational subsidies for staffing. Even the regulatory agency, then the Bureau of Federal Credit

Unions, joined the "war." It strove to reach poverty communities through Operation Moneywise, a financial education program, and eagerly assisted groups in chartering new credit unions (in stark contrast to later decades).

The Trouble with Poor People . . .

The well-intentioned OEO effort was under-resourced and wildly over-optimistic. It assumed that a sustainable nonprofit financial institution could be built in a poverty area in two or three years. But as a study by the Government Accounting Office[13] later concluded that one or two years of operating subsidies were insufficient. The assets of the credit unions did not grow sufficiently, primarily because of "the very limited savings that low-income families have available for deposits in the credit union."[14]

OEO's initiative provided little or no management training, support, or capital. Unsurprisingly, many of that generation of credit unions failed, giving the whole movement of low-income credit unions a bad reputation, which I was to encounter when I later joined the Federation.

Implicitly or explicitly, the poor were blamed for their inability to build successful financial institutions. The GAO study illustrated the vicious cycle that made it so difficult for a low-income credit union to thrive: the members had little disposable income and thus, small savings; they required labor-intensive transactions that were "cost-ineffective;" they could only afford to borrow amounts too small to generate much surplus for the credit union. Not enough deposits meant not enough money to loan, which meant not enough income to add services to attract more depositors and generate sufficient earnings

---

13 It is now known as the Government Accountability Office.
14 This and other studies are cited in my book, *Democratizing Finance: Origins of the Community Development Financial Institutions Movement*, Clifford N. Rosenthal with a foreword by David James Erickson, (Victoria, BC, Canada: FriesenPress, 2018).

and reserves. In an aphorism that has become current common in recent years, "No margin, no mission!"

The First Capital Crisis

With the War on Poverty quickly pronounced a policy failure, credit unions serving the poor soon ran into a capital crisis. In 1970, legislation created federal deposit insurance for credit unions for the first time, as well as an independent regulatory agency charged with administering the share (deposit) insurance fund, the National Credit Union Administration (NCUA). Many anti-poverty credit unions did not meet the new standards required for deposit insurance, and thus would have been consigned to certain institutional death. An informal coalition of "limited-income" credit unions fought successfully to include these credit unions, aided by the federal anti-poverty office, OEO. Moreover, the coalition won a special privilege. Although credit unions in general are only permitted to accept deposits from a circumscribed "field of membership," credit unions officially designated by NCUA as "low-income" were given the right to accept insured "non-member deposits" from any person or institutions outside their defined membership. In this way, Congress explicitly recognized the special challenges low-income credit unions faced in gathering sufficient deposits *within* their communities.

Following their initial success, in the spring of 1974, the informal coalition of limited-income credit unions incorporated and chose a positive, aspirational name: the National Federation of *Community Development Credit Unions*. "CDCUs" officially entered the credit union vocabulary, self-defined by the new Federation as credit unions that served predominantly low-income persons or communities.

Joining the Federation, I read about its theory of change in a 1974 document known as "The Blue Book" because of its mimeographed cover. It made the following case:

Why do poor communities remain poor? *Large amounts of cash flow through these communities but quickly flow out, as through a sieve. Income flows to absentee owners of the neighborhood businesses, not to mention banks (if there are any). There is no "multiplier effect"— the economic benefit generated when money is spent, circulated, and re-spent within a community. A community development credit union can help patch the holes, aggregate members' savings, and loan them out to locally owned businesses and residents.*

What do CDCUs need to become viable actors in community development? *Community development credit unions need capital in its various forms to stabilize and grow. But they also need access to technology, management support, and training.*

How can CDCUs jump-start their growth? *The federal government should establish at scale a fund that can provide lending capital, training, management support, data processing, and other infrastructure for the CDCU movement!*

That was the Federation's agenda for the 1970s: get Congress to provide $18 million to create a new fund to catalyze the growth of CDCUs. It was to be a fund not only *for* credit unions serving the poor, but one in which they shared ownership and control. The campaign went on for years. President Carter included elements of the Federation's vision in his urban initiative as the "Community Development Revolving Loan Fund for Credit Unions." At last, in 1979, the Federation won a partial victory. What emerged from Congress was not $18 million, but a $6 million fund, which would be run *not by the CDCU movement*, but by the much reduced, Nixon-era federal anti-poverty agency (then known as the Community Services Administration) and the regulator, the National Credit Union Administration.

The Reagan/Bush Years: Fighting for Crumbs

The CDCU Revolving Loan Fund was launched in 1980, distributing loans at 2% interest to about 30 credit unions. But soon after I joined the Federation in October 1980, we were engaged in a defensive battle to sustain it. Weeks later, Ronald Reagan crushed incumbent President Jimmy Carter, winning 44 of 50 states. Reagan conjured up an image of America as that "shining city on the hill." But his path to the shining city would be paved by getting rid of those "strapping young bucks buying T-bone steaks with Food Stamps" and "Cadillac-driving welfare queens"—racist "dog whistles." Reaganomics—also known as supply-side economics—held that a stream of wealth trickling down from the prosperous would lift up the poor. Government was the *problem,* not the solution. Straining credulity, the Reagan Administration proclaimed that they were neither racist nor enemies of the poor as they proceeded to dismantle the vestiges of the War on Poverty.

Initially, we held out some hope that the Reagan Administration would continue the CDCU Revolving Loan Program. We thought we had a strong, bipartisan argument: Our CDCU movement was dedicated to self-help and promoting the independence of the poor, a principle that ought to appeal to conservatives as well as progressives. But we soon learned otherwise. Reagan's Office of Management and Budget (OMB), under David Stockman, explicitly proposed to eliminate the miniscule CDCU Revolving Loan Fund, which did not even amount to a rounding error within a federal budget of hundreds of billions of dollars. The Fund was not even a *grant* program—it was a revolving fund designed to make *loans* at 2% interest to institutions serving poor communities. But making below-market loans flew in the face of the free-market, trickle-down philosophy of a conservative administration that publicly vowed to "starve the government." The anti-poverty office, by then only a shadow of the one-time Office of Economic Opportunity, was gutted; its remaining functions were transferred to the new Office of Community Services (OCS), headed by a dentist who had been active in the Colorado Republican campaign.

With the help of Lee Foley, a widely respected anti-poverty lobbyist who provided us *pro bono* assistance, we garnered just enough congressional support to keep the CDCU Revolving Loan Fund alive. But the Reagan Administration retaliated: if it could not abolish the fund outright, it could plant a "poison pill" that would make the fund unattractive to low-income credit unions. In a letter to the Federation's Executive Director Jim Clark on August 20, 1982, the director of the Office of Community Services, Harvey Vieth, explained the administration's philosophy:

> We discovered that a critical provision of the existing CDCU regulations contained a maximum interest rate of 2 percent on capitalization loan funds awarded under this program. I am concerned that such a rate, based on a five-year loan period, is restrictive and unreasonably low compared to the prevailing market rates [emphasis added]. During a time when interest rates are unusually high, coupled with a substantial Federal budget deficit, a regulatory-fixed 2 percent maximum interest rate on loans under the CDCU is unjustified. We are currently exploring with the Department ways in which a more reasonable interest rate can be set for new capitalization loan agreements.

To my mounting indignation, I learned that even a low-cost repayable *loan* exceeded the government's tolerance for aiding the poor. It added insult to injury: credit unions serving the poor were to help bear the cost of reducing the federal deficit. The Reagan Administration froze the fund for years. Finally, after several years, we managed to get it to release the money, but it was a Pyrrhic victory, at best. They raised the cost of the loans from 2% to 7%, a rate so high that those credit unions that won awards struggled to make the numbers work. Several of them went out of business.

I continued to pursue the CDCU Revolving Loan Fund almost obsessively throughout the 1980s. Finally, when the decade ended, we succeeded in reviving the CDCU Revolving Loan Fund on more viable terms. We failed in our original goal of bringing under control of the CDCU movement the Federation's auspices; rather, the regulatory agency, NCUA, would control the money—an unfortunate conflict of interest. But however modest and long-delayed, it was ultimately a victory; a vindication of my predecessor's campaign. The CDCU Revolving Loan Fund has gone on to become all but perpetual; Congress has renewed it each year as it has provided significant benefits to CDCUs, including not only deposits but grants to provide technology and survive various economic crises.[15]

The lengthy battle to preserve the CDCU Revolving Loan Fund taught me an early lesson in wrestling with Washington politicians for what we believed was ours. It encouraged me to pursue larger prizes—i.e., the Community Development Financial Institutions Fund—and to persist for as many years as it took.

A Fund of Our Own

If we were truly to get a source of community-controlled capital, we could not count on Washington. So, throughout the 1980s, while pursuing the federal Revolving Loan Fund, we explored other paths to build a capital fund owned by the CDCU movement itself.

In March 1981, I traveled with our members and board to Asilomar, a state-owned conference center in Pacific Grove, California. The rustic, ocean-front campus was so quiet that it unnerved some

---

15 At Inclusiv's annual conference on May 4, 2022, NCUA Chairman Todd Harper remarked that "one of our most impactful initiatives has been the Community Development Revolving Loan Fund. . . . These investments go into communities that would otherwise have unmet needs, giving credit unions additional resources to build their capacity and create more secure financial futures for their members. During 2021 alone, the NCUA awarded CDRLF grants to more than 100 low-income-designated credit unions including: 22 grants totaling more than $1 million for expanding credit union outreach to underserved communities and improving their members' financial well-being."

of our members used to urban noise; they complained to me that they couldn't sleep. There we sketched out plans for a "Capitalization Program for Community Development Credit Unions." I had learned about two sources of possible investment, both in their infancy. One was the incipient socially responsible investment (SRI) movement, which had so far mostly focused on shareholder proxy votes to urge corporations to desist in harmful practices and marketing harmful products (tobacco, alcohol, weapons, apartheid); religious organizations such as Catholic women's orders and certain national denominations were prominent in this movement. As well, there was a promising innovation in the foundation world: program-related investments (PRIs), a mechanism for philanthropies to invest in anti-poverty and social enterprises. We sketched out a business plan: borrow at below-market rates from these investors, add a mark-up of 2% for our expenses, and channel the investments to our member credit unions as insured deposits. We set a goal of raising $20 million, at which point we estimated our program would be self-sustaining.

We found early success. In November 1982, we got our first investor: the sisters of the Adrian Dominican community. We applied to them with nothing more than a vision—no collateral, no track record, no loan loss reserves. The sisters loaned us $30,000 at 8% (a below-market rate at the time). It was an act of pure faith on their part; they were risking their retirement funds. Other Catholic women's orders and communities followed. Thus, we were launched—the first community-based national financial intermediary.

Our fund grew slowly in the early 1980s—$10,000 here, $30,000 there, largely from Catholic women's orders following the example of the Adrian Dominicans. We tried without success to obtain one of those "Program-Related Investments" I had learned about. But apart from the Ford Foundation, which had pioneered the vehicle, very few foundations followed its lead. And Ford was not yet interested in us.

Unexpectedly, our fortunes changed in 1986. Sitting in the Federation's dingy office in lower Manhattan's declining financial district, I got a cold call from a man named Paul Lingenfelter, who represented the Chicago-based John D. and Catherine T. MacArthur Foundation. I did not take it very seriously; we often received inquiries that led nowhere. But to my surprise, he followed up and asked me to develop a proposal. I spent my vacation drafting a paper and submitted it to him by September. Three months later—an astonishingly short interval, as I came to appreciate—the foundation approved a $500,000 PRI in the form of a loan for our capitalization program. We closed 1986 with just short of $1 million under management.

It felt like credibility; like proof of concept. Over the next few years, we garnered additional investments from religious orders, national denominations, and then finally, in 1989, a long-term, $1 million PRI at 1% interest from the Ford Foundation. Ford's investment was the "brass ring" that we nonprofits constantly reached for. In the years that followed, the Ford Foundation made many more investments, playing an enormous role both in the Federation's growth and in promoting the entire community development finance movement. The amounts grew and the purposes expanded as we added new products like secondary capital, mortgage lending, and support to help credit unions counteract predatory lending.

By 1990, we were a full-fledged capital intermediary, a $5 million "one-stop shop" for national socially responsible investors. We developed portfolios for them, conducted due diligence on their behalf, collected interest payments, and provided impact reports. Where did we invest?

- In Marks, Mississippi, the impoverished Delta region where a credit union served the descendants of sharecroppers shunned by the local banks, which were owned by the descendants of plantation owners.
- On New York's Lower East Side, where a new credit union we had helped organize served an "unbanked" low-income neighborhood of 55,000 people.

- In San Francisco's Mission District, where our member credit union had long served immigrants from Central and South America.
- In the historically Black credit unions that proliferated in rural Eastern North Carolina.
- In credit unions formed by settlement houses (social service providers) in Chicago and East Harlem, which served single mothers and others on the margins with no hope of getting bank loans.
- In innovative "new generation" credit unions, including the aptly-named Alternatives FCU in Ithaca, New York, and the Santa Cruz Community Credit Union in California.

We were rightly proud of our financial growth and increased credibility. But even with our few million under management, we were far short of achieving *scale*. We helped our credit unions and we grew the community development finance movement, but we were not transformative.

A "Central Bank" for Community Development?

Even as we launched our Capitalization Program in the early 1980s, I was dreaming of something larger; something that not only would raise philanthropic and social investments but would build on the core principles of community development credit unions. What if we, the Federation, started our own "central bank," a "corporate" credit union in which our credit unions could place their investment funds instead of channeling money into mainstream markets and institutions? Our institution would reinvest in our members and partner in their lending. This was, at a higher level, the fundamental CDCU philosophy: recirculate the people's money and keep it within *our* system.

That was my grand vision. It had served me well in winning my fellowship at Columbia, where I enrolled in an intensive seminar in the summer of 1983 to learn the basics of banking and finance. The seminar equipped me with the vocabulary and exaggerated confidence to pitch my grand idea for "Community Development Central" to the philanthropic and credit union worlds. I raised a foundation grant to do the preliminary work, secured more than $6 million in deposit pledges from our member credit unions, and hired a rare consultant: a Black credit union professional with experience in the specialized world of corporate credit unions, who would serve as the proposed CEO of the new institution.

We unsuccessfully sought support from the mainstream credit union industry, as described in chapter 3. We submitted our business plan and application to the regulator, the National Credit Union Administration. They brushed us off with polite words, acknowledging that our proposal was well drafted, but informing us they could not justify the chartering of a new institution. It was disappointing, but unsurprising. Why would NCUA charter a national institution that might bring additional risk to the deposit insurance fund they managed?

So, my grand vision of a central bank or "Federal Reserve" for credit unions serving poor communities was not to be fulfilled. In another era—perhaps right after the urban uprisings of the late 1960s, or in the context of the Black Lives Matter movement—the result might have been different. But in the Reagan-Bush years, with America's cities relatively quiescent, there was little concern about inequities in access to capital, and no appetite to address them. I was sorry to abandon my vision, but as time passed and our Capitalization Program grew substantially, I came to realize that we were better off *without* a Community Development Central Federal Credit Union. It would have subjected us to all the rules, regulations, and constant supervision of a federal agency. And I had more than enough battles with NCUA on behalf of our members.

The New York Strategy

The Federation was a national organization. But my "Revson Foundation Fellowship for the Future of New York City" helped give us a crucial local context and platform for our work. I joined a cohort of ten high-powered New York City activists, including many of color. My classmates were passionate, experienced advocates for health care, civil rights, the arts, and more. Some later became prominent, both locally and nationally. Jill Nelson, a Black journalist who later joined the *Washington Post*, wrote the best-selling *Volunteer Slavery: My Authentic Negro Experience.* Una Tomlinson Clarke, my companion for commutes from Columbia's Morningside Heights campus back to Brooklyn, later became the first Caribbean-born woman to be elected to the New York's City Council; her daughter, Yvette Clarke, was later elected to Congress. Una introduced me to the Black political scene, specifically the Brooklyn power brokers. Under her tutelage, I held fundraisers in our house for Assemblyman Al Vann, a prominent figure in the fight over community control over schools in Ocean Hill-Brownsville, and Congressman Major Owens.[16]

My fellowship year gave me a new network, new skills, and the self-confidence to engage with the financial world. The timing was right. New York City was the money center, home to the nation's biggest banks and the site of major changes in retail banking. ATMs were beginning to proliferate in the early 1980s. Automation offered not only convenience to customers but a rationale for banks to eliminate branches—disproportionately, their less-profitable branches in low-income communities and communities of color. Without mainstream banking services, the residents and businesses in low-income communities would be consigned to costly check-cashers and predatory lenders. Community advocates and elected officials began to take notice.

---

16 Later, I would hold fundraisers for my then-former staff member, Errol Louis, and another Black colleague, Mark Winston Griffith, in their campaigns for the New York City Council.

We now had a local agenda. I put forth our credit unions as the answer to the financial abandonment of low-income neighborhoods. We approached the daunting new world of New York foundations—the bastions of old and "big" money. Our senior "team"—Annie and I—visited the New York Community Trust, a prestigious old-line charity. They agreed to support a state advocacy campaign to secure the investments and subsidy CDCUs would need to make an impact. New York State–chartered banks had just won expanded real estate investment and other powers, conditional on making "qualifying community investments" in low- and moderate-income neighborhoods. In 1985, I developed model legislation for a "New York Corporation for Community Banking," which would provide a centralized mechanism for banks to meet their CRA obligations by funding deposits in "community-oriented financial institutions, in low- and moderate-income communities"—primarily, credit unions.

We hired a lobbyist and secured 26 sponsors in the New York State Assembly for our model legislation. But it stalled in the Republican-controlled Senate and lingered in limbo for years. Despite this setback, the initiative was important in many ways. It was another valuable lesson for me in public-sector advocacy, which would later help me in developing a concept for the federal CDFI Fund. After the federal CDFI Fund was established in 1994, with its requirement for non-federal matching funds, I revived our earlier proposal for a New York State Corporation for Community Banking. Our New York State CDFI Coalition, which we had organized under the Federation's auspices, won a modest $1 million program under New York's Urban Development Corporation. It was far short of our goal, but the coalition persisted. In 2007, New York State passed into law a Community Development Financial Institutions (CDFI) Fund modeled after that of the U.S. Treasury—but without appropriations. Finally, in 2020, the first round of funding was appropriated: $5 million of a promised $25 million NYS CDFI Assistance Program. After 14 years, money began to flow to CDFIs across New York State in 2021 (although in 2023, CDFIs were still waiting for the second $5 million tranche).

Thinking Bigger: Seeds of the CDFI Fund

Throughout the 1980s, with varying success, I had pursued multiple channels and strategies to win capital for our credit unions. In the second half of the decade, I arrived at the "big idea" that ultimately would help create a new field—community development finance—and offer the hope of transforming the CDCU movement.

Expanding on my vision of the New York Corporation for Community Banking, in 1988 I began circulating a concept paper calling for the creation of a national "Neighborhood Banking Corporation." In accordance with the prevailing small-government policy environment, I proposed the most modest federal investment—a few million dollars in seed money and administrative expenses—to be supplemented by investments from banks and from the Community Development Revolving Loan Fund. I circulated the proposal, but for several years received little feedback other than objections from an advocacy organization that my idea would "let banks off the hook"—the hook being the requirement under the Community Reinvestment Act of 1977 that banks invest in low-and moderate-income areas. But over 1990-91, we gained the support of the five-year-old National Association of Community Development Loan Funds (today, OFN), which had formulated a sweeping critique of the banking system. By early 1992, we formed a loose nucleus of what we half-jokingly called the "Ad Hoc Coalition of Public Purpose Lenders," which included Community Capital Bank (the third true "community development bank" in the country); the Center for Community Self-Help (which operated both a loan fund and a credit union), the Woodstock Institute (a community reinvestment policy and action organization), and other occasional participants.

Meanwhile, candidate Bill Clinton was campaigning on a platform calling for the creation of a national network of "100 community development banks and 1,000 microenterprise organizations." After his election in November 1992, our ad hoc group formalized the Coalition of Community Development Financial Institutions, adding our efforts to the Clinton Administration's work to establish the CDFI Fund.[17]

---

17 I have described the extensive legislative and political processes leading to the establishment of the fund in my book, *Democratizing Finance*.

CHAPTER 5

Outsiders: Poverty and Race in the Credit Union Family

When I joined the Federation in 1980, I was only dimly aware of the stigma attached to low-income credit unions from the War on Poverty. Regaining respect within the credit union industry was a decade-long challenge.

From "Movement" to "Industry"

Community development credit unions (CDCUs) were—and were not—part of one of the most successful progressive populist movements of the twentieth century. Like all credit unions, CDCUs are nonprofit cooperatives, owned and democratically governed by their members, each of whom has one and only one vote. Credit unions emerged in the first decade of the twentieth century to serve the financially excluded—the working-class people who depended on usurers because they could not access loans from mainstream banks. Some of the early heroes of the credit union movement were *organizers* (which resonated with me, since I saw myself to be one), who spread the "gospel" of financial cooperatives as they "barnstormed," inspiring people in factories, offices, and in rural areas to start their own credit unions.[18] This was the narrative that made me fall in love with credit

---

18 In *Democratizing Finance*, I related the contemporary account of the ecstatic, near-religious fervor that credit union founder Edward Filene encountered in 1933 in Chicago when he addressed a meeting of more than 1,000 credit union supporters.

unions when I first learned about them and helped organize one at my workplace in 1979.

But I learned that despite its extraordinary success, this working-class movement was no exemplar of equity and inclusion. To a disturbing degree, credit unions mirrored the economic and social life of segregated America. In the South, for example, there were separate credit unions for white and Black teachers and school employees. In North Carolina, nearly 100 Black credit unions were organized in the 1930s and 1940s. On the one hand, this testified to the powerful cooperative drive of Black citizens—but on the other, it was an unfortunate reflection of America's racial divide. Up north, in Brooklyn's Bedford-Stuyvesant, an association of primarily Black Caribbean immigrants encountered thinly veiled prejudice when they sought to establish a credit union during the Depression. Despite economic desperation, a strong "common bond" (required of any aspiring credit unions), and a strong sponsor, the Paragon Association, the regulators rejected their charter application. As founder Clyde Atwell wrote, "It was the opinion of the Washington authority that the membership was not strong enough to successfully promote the program of a credit union."

It took some two and a half years for Paragon to charter its own credit union, which proudly served the community for decades.

Even when Black communities succeeded in chartering credit unions, they did not always find a warm reception among their white peers. The "building blocks" of the credit union movement were local chapters of credit unions, which in turn made up state credit union associations or "leagues." At every level, the volunteer leadership was white, and for decades, overwhelmingly male. Mrs. Rita Haynes, who began volunteering for Cleveland's Second Mount Sinai Baptist Church Credit Union in 1957 fresh out of high school, has described her decades-long effort to win respect from the local and statewide credit union officials. The feeling that she was "always the outsider," never part of the inner circle, persisted until she gained national recognition as the chairperson of the Federation, a CDFI leader, and an honoree of the National Cooperative Hall of Fame, among other awards.

The credit union movement was changed by success. As the United States began to prosper in the post-war years, credit unions paralleled the country's economic trajectory—at least, the "mainstream" of the credit union movement did. By the mid-twentieth century, the leadership of the movement was looking less at the poorest segments of the country than at the rising, increasingly prosperous, mostly white middle class. "Middle-class people need credit unions, too," they argued.

Despite internal disagreements, the Credit Union National Association (CUNA) gingerly joined in the War on Poverty, obtaining contracts from the federal government to help develop credit unions in impoverished areas. But before long, CUNA got "battle fatigue" and ceased its engagement. It deemed the federal experiment in credit union expansion a failure: "We tried that. Case closed, let's move on. Poverty is not a common bond for a credit union."

The stigma lasted. Industry leaders had a long memory, as I learned after joining the Federation. When I sought their support, sometimes they explicitly reminded me of the failures of the War on Poverty; sometimes their message was unspoken. Even in the 1990s, when I went to Congress to advocate for establishing the CDFI Fund, I met veteran Congressional staff members who brought up the failures of the 1960s.[19]

Journey to the Credit Union "Mecca"

When I joined the Federation in 1980, 99% of our budget came from contracts with the federal antipoverty agency, the Community

---

19 With the Woodstock Institute, we prepared a paper that analyzed the shortcomings of the War on Poverty initiative and argued that a well-conceived Community Development Financial Institutions Fund would avoid the errors of the War on Poverty.

Services Administration (the much-reduced successor to the Office of Economic Opportunity of the 1960s). By 1982, the Reagan Administration eliminated all of the Federation's federal funding. Struggling for our organizational life, we turned for help to CUNA. Seeking a financial lifeline, I traveled to Madison, Wisconsin—the "Mecca" of the credit union movement, where CUNA and the CUNA Mutual Group, its associated insurance companies, were located. Why had they settled in Madison, which was famously inconvenient for national air and rail connections? I heard varying explanations, the official one (there was a strong history of populism in Wisconsin) and an unofficial one (the specter of "urban issues" in Chicago).

As a long-time co-op activist, it was exciting for me to visit the home of the leading national body of the credit union movement, representing tens of millions of credit union members. But visiting CUNA and its affiliates was a cultural jolt for me. Literally and figuratively, we were CUNA's poor relations. We sat across the table from a very white, very male middle-aged group. Journalist Frank J. Diekmann later described it this way: CUNA was "up until the 1990s a largely insular, navel-gazing U.S. credit union industry/movement . . . It was a club and there were some folks with some pretty strong opinions on who was allowed in the treehouse."

Coming from multiracial, multicultural New York—arguably, my own sort of "bubble"—I felt like an alien visiting the "real" America. On one stay in Madison, I was amazed to hear a television ad for car sales in *German!*

Instead of a lifeline, a significant contribution that could help us keep our doors open, we came away with a token donation of $5,000 a year. We were outliers, not part of the family: CUNA was made up of dues-paying statewide credit union associations, made up in turn of local dues-paying credit unions. The structure was often described as the "organized credit union movement." Through it, CUNA claimed to serve *all* credit unions, ours included—hence, they argued, what need was there for our special-purpose Federation? But their picture contradicted the experience of the Federation's members. Our credit unions, especially those serving communities of color, got little respect from the local chapters or their state leagues. Many encountered thinly veiled discrimination from the "old boy" white leadership, sometimes coupled with reminders of the failures of the War on Poverty. The mainstream movement neither respected nor represented the particular needs of our community development credit unions.

Apart from our request for operating support to keep the Federation's doors open, we pitched to CUNA our vision of Community Development Central, our "central bank" for CDCUs. But this proposal, too, was rejected as redundant; there was, they argued, already a national network of wholesale credit unions to meet CDCUs' needs. We argued in vain that none of the existing corporate credit unions engaged in the kind of community investment that we envisioned for our proposed Community Development Central.[20]

Having received a token contribution from the "credit union system," we in turn played a token role throughout the 1980s. The credit union industry as a whole was doing well—*too* well according to the banking industry. Credit unions were growing in assets and membership, adding more "bank-like" services. But the banks claimed that credit union growth was fueled by their federal tax exemption, which gave credit unions an unfair competitive advantage. (They ignored the fact that credit unions had unpaid boards of directors and no stock owners demanding ever-higher quarterly profits.) For the credit union industry lobbyists, preserving the federal tax exemption was Job #1. So, rather than trumpeting to Congress the success of the larger, increasingly bank-like credit unions, they found it useful to put forth images of small credit unions like ours, serving people the banks did not serve, as the "real" face of the credit union industry.

---

20 Nearly 40 years later, on May 3, 2022, the CUNA Mutual Group Foundation announced a $1 million commitment "to build equity in credit unions led by and or serving people of color through Inclusiv's Racial Equity and Resilience Investment Fund." The investment will be used to make secondary capital investments in Inclusiv's member credit unions.

The Deal

The battle in Congress against the banks over tax exemption intensified in the 1980s. In 1990, CUNA attempted to rally the credit union industry in a united front. CUNA's leaders assumed that the Federation would fall in line with the rest of the industry. We did not.

Long-time outsiders, we were bitter that we had received only token support from CUNA for the years when we were fighting for our very survival. Various state credit union leagues, in particular, had been hoping we would disappear. But by 1990, we had survived our toughest times, raising millions of dollars of investment for CDCUs, winning major foundation funding, and gaining recognition in Washington. We had leverage; we were prepared to go our own way. When CUNA wrote to us about joining the battle against taxation, we replied that as institutions serving the poor and unbanked, we had no doubt that we would be spared taxation: banks routinely assured us that we were the "good" credit unions, doing what credit unions were supposed to be doing, and thus deserved the tax exemption. Moreover, banks were making significant philanthropic contributions and investments in the CDCU movement in order to win Community Reinvestment Act (CRA) credit—more support than we had received from the credit union industry. CUNA's CEO was furious with our response, warning us that we were making a bad mistake. But we had pried open a door to a changed relationship.

Months of contentious negotiations between the Federation and CUNA followed. We refused to simply become a division or official "affiliate" of CUNA; we insisted on retaining our own board of directors and corporate identity. Finally, on March 1, 1991, we signed a cooperative agreement with CUNA that significantly increased their support for us. We happily joined 15,000 credit union advocates one sunny day for the "Operation Grassroots" rally to preserve the tax exemption on the mall in front of Congress.

CUNA increased its financial support to the Federation substantially. Its donations enabled us to add staff, programs, and advocacy capacity. I benefited personally, as well. As part of the agreement, I became a vice president for association services at CUNA, while also remaining executive director of the Federation. I received a significant salary boost to reflect my new status. But there would be a substantial price to pay. The relationship was inherently tense. As the Federation's board chairman, "Ken," paraphrased the Bible, "The lamb will lay down with the lion—but the lamb won't get much sleep."

Recipe for Schizophrenia

Throughout our five-year alliance with CUNA, I had two sets of bosses. I was the CEO of the Federation, the employee of our board of directors, serving at the pleasure of a predominantly Black and Latinx movement headquartered in New York City. Simultaneously, I was a senior vice president of a Madison-based, overwhelmingly white trade association with a narrower industry agenda. For the first time in my life, I was part of a corporate hierarchy, participating in daily senior management conference calls.

I traveled often to CUNA's headquarters in Madison, exchanging the dangers of New York City for a Midwestern city subject to occasional tornado warnings. Through various reorganizations, I reported to officers in the CUNA hierarchy. I met only one Black senior officer, Pete Crear. He was "exceptional" demographically, but also through his qualification and experience. He had come up through the ranks, starting as the Michigan credit union league's field staff in his native Detroit; he knew first-hand the kind of small, Black church credit unions that the Federation claimed as members. Later, he successively headed two state credit union leagues. He was a dedicated spokesman for the credit union industry, although sometimes I thought I detected a slight chuckle that hinted at a healthy sense of irony in some meetings. Pete rose to become executive vice president of CUNA, but he was passed over for the presidency—continuing the still-unbroken tradition of white male leadership for the organization.[21] He was, for better or worse, a solitary trailblazer—for decades, a singular Black leader in the trade association. It was 2021 before the first state credit union league had a Latino CEO.[22] Neither CUNA, nor NAFCU, the other major national credit union trade organization, has ever had a CEO of color.[23]

The Federation's alliance with CUNA was rife with structural, cultural, and political tensions. After joining the CUNA "team," although not as a full corporate member, we were expected to sing the team song, especially on regulatory and policy matters. In 1992, the Federation's board of directors elected "Evelyne," our first African American chairwoman. A fierce advocate for racial justice, she often cited her formative experiences with the Nation of Islam. She had scant respect for CUNA, which had so little diversity besides Pete, and she had little desire to align us in lockstep with CUNA's positions. I was buffeted by near constant and conflicting pulls. I had to defend the Federation's autonomy, convey Evelyne's positions, and mediate with CUNA as best I could.

Nonetheless, for a half-dozen years, our alliance with CUNA was mutually beneficial. The Federation was finally a recognized national player in credit union politics. We were not truly part of CUNA's "family," hardly an equal, but at least we had a seat at some of the tables of power. CUNA's significant financial support enabled us to add core staff who would not be restricted to grant-funded "deliverables." I benefited personally since CUNA raised my below-market salary to a level more commensurate with my rank as a CUNA vice president. CUNA benefited from the optics of having a Black

---

21 He became the head of the World Council of Credit Unions, the first North American of color to hold that position. The African American Credit Union Coalition honored him by creating the Pete Crear Lifetime Achievement Award.
22 Juan Fernández Ceballos was hired as president and CEO of the Credit Union Association of New Mexico in June 2021.
23 Maurice Smith, CEO of Local Government FCU in North Carolina, was elected to the board of CUNA in 2010 and became the first Black elected chairman of CUNA in 2018.

woman up front amid the overwhelmingly white male leadership of the credit union industry—token diversity. Evelyne benefited from our enhanced national platform that she would probably not have achieved otherwise. She represented the Federation at high-level Washington events, such as President Clinton's signing of the CDFI legislation in 1994. Later, she was prominently pictured in the credit union industry at the signing of the Credit Union Membership Access Act of 1998. Alongside the white credit union "captains of industry," I imagine Evelyne both relished her prominence and was well aware of the token nature of her position.

Fracture Lines: CRA

Our alliance required us to hue to CUNA's line on major policy issues. The cardinal rule of political representation for CUNA (as for other industry organizations) was this: you had to speak with one voice in Washington. Dissenting opinions would enable Congress to pick and choose and weaken your arguments. It was not the paramount issue of taxation that nearly split us apart from CUNA in the mid-1990s; after all, our member credit unions had no more desire to be taxed than did other credit unions. Rather, it was the Community Reinvestment Act (CRA) of 1977, which directed banks to "meet the credit needs of the communities in which they do business, including low- and moderate-income (LMI) neighborhoods." Federal policies dating from the 1930s had officially endorsed redlining, which denied credit to people and communities of color. CRA discouraged blatant redlining, but racial discrimination in mortgage lending and other financial services persisted, as documented in an explosive investigative report, "The Color of Money," in the *Atlanta Constitution-Journal* (May 1-4, 1988).

Credit unions were never subject to CRA regulations—and the banking industry sought to change this. Our members saw first-hand the damage done by banking discrimination; they were generally strong supporters of CRA, and many participated in local CRA coalitions. But some CRA coalitions aligned with the banking lobby to demand that credit unions be placed under CRA. It was a quandary for our movement. The mainstream credit union industry argued that credit unions deserved to remain exempt because they served everyone equally, especially people of "modest means." But a portion of the Federation's membership did *not* believe that the industry-leading large credit unions served low-income populations and communities of color. Those credit unions simply weren't to be found in our communities. Neither did they provide much solidarity or support to our small, struggling credit unions; on the contrary, they often merged small credit unions or took over "our" turf. So, in fact there was significant sympathy among our membership—and certainly, on the part of our board chairwoman, Evelyne—for expanding CRA to credit unions.

When an opportunity arose to testify to Congress on the issue, Evelyne wanted to hint at opening the door for extending CRA to credit unions. That would mean a major breach of the credit union industry's solidarity, which banks would eagerly exploit. For the Federation's relationship with CUNA, supporting CRA would be a deal-breaker, pure and simple. Our board was officially opposed to the expansion of CRA to credit unions. I was ambivalent, at best, about our position. Despite my mixed feelings, I was alarmed at Evelyne's intended testimony; I wrote an urgent memo to the board reiterating our official position and stating that no one was authorized to express any contrary position. I'm sure that my intervention infuriated Evelyne, but she backed off, and we managed to avoid a crisis—for the time being.

The tenson over community reinvestment continued when the chairman of the regulator, NCUA, proposed a "CRA-lite" regulation for credit unions. I dutifully opposed it, increasing tensions with Evelyne, who had a close relationship with NCUA's chairman. I was trying both to follow our board's adopted policies and to keep our relationship with CUNA intact. It was uncomfortable. I felt more like a cynical politician than a movement champion.

At its peak, CUNA provided us with annual support of about $250,000. It was extremely helpful, but as the Federation grew, it was no longer an indispensable lifeline. In the mid-1990s, CUNA went through its own crisis, as two business lines—mortgages and credit card processing—failed, taking down CUNA's CEO in the process. Understandably, CUNA concentrated on getting its own house in order and tightening its belt. It greatly reduced its financial support that had cemented our alliance. The formal alliance did not rupture but it became less of a focus for both parties.

From the 1990s, despite the tensions between us and the credit union "mainstream," the Federation achieved growing acceptance in the industry. It was reflected symbolically in the annual Herb Wegner memorial awards presented in Washington by CUNA's affiliated charity, the National Credit Union Foundation. That was the best kind of recognition for us—the opportunity to tell our story to an audience of nearly 1,000 prominent credit union leaders and dedicated volunteers. The Federation received the foundation's award in 1992, a year after our alliance with CUNA was formalized.[24]

Black Faces in a Sea of White

Despite the welcome recognition that the Federation and the CDCU movement achieved, the credit union industry remained predominantly white. Each year, when I attended CUNA's Governmental Affairs Conference, the largest event in the credit union industry, I saw thousands of white faces with only scattered Black and brown representatives. The attendees were not rich bankers and lobbyists; for the most part, they were senior staff and volunteer board members of credit unions. Anyone from a member credit union of CUNA could attend—if they or their credit union had the budget for airfare, three

---

[24] Evelyne's youth credit union project was honored shortly after our alliance with CUNA was formalized. In 1999, our board member, Earnest Johnson, a legendary credit union organizer of Black credit unions in the South, was honored. A series of CDCU leaders were honored after 2000, including myself.

or four nights in a Washington hotel, and the substantial registration fee. Unsurprisingly, small and resource-poor credit unions, including many serving communities of color, were under-represented. There was no mistaking the overall demographic. If you came from an already marginalized group, you were all but invisible.

I got an important lesson about the long road toward racial representation from "Paul," a widely respected figure among Black credit unions, the industry generally, and the Federation in particular, which benefited from his volunteer efforts. When I interviewed him in 2016, he described the lonely, stressful path he traveled for years in the credit union movement: "I was the only one, or one of few, in every meeting I went to, everything I was involved with, so I had to pretty much be the standard bearer everywhere I went. Being an African American male back in the seventies, you had to be bold, but you had to be careful how threatening you were, [lest others would] look at us as, 'Oh, well, are you going to war with me over this [negotiation].'"

He went on: "They were stereotyping, insulting, condescending, underestimating . . . . In the early part of my credit union career . . . . the so-called credit unions leaders were very condescending from my vantage point, and I never accepted that. It took courage to be bold, to bet on yourself."

For decades, as Paul described to me, there was no systematic bonding among Black leaders. At meetings like CUNA's Governmental Affairs Conference, "They tended to go to restaurants and just talk among themselves."

Like other credit union people, they griped among themselves about the usual regulatory and other issues (but probably as well the difficulties that some had in advancing in the profession). By the 1990s, Paul was the CEO of a large "mainstream" credit union. He met with a handful of his peers at CUNA's GAC, and along with several others, pushed the group to formally organize the African American Credit Union Coalition (AACUC). "I said, 'No more going to a restaurant and bitching and complaining. We're going to be out on the street where everyone can see us.'"

They secured an exhibit table, where a dozen or so of them gathered, and soon started attracting attention. "People started looking around because they weren't used to seeing that many African Americans together.... I wanted my [colleagues] to know that being together and drawing attention has value, because people become curious. If they become curious, they ask questions. If they ask questions, they get a good understanding. If you have understanding, you have a movement. If you have more movement, you can have more progress."

In ways large and small, the credit union industry needed to change. Even through the 1990s, it was not hard to find evidence of racial bias and "microaggression." At CUNA's Governmental Affairs Conference in Washington, the exhibition hall is a popular event; lunch is free, and at a hundred booths, vendors entice credit union attendees by offering product giveaways and drawings for prizes. Lest outsiders take advantage of this opportunity, there are always security guards outside the doors. For years, when the Federation's board held our own meeting in Washington at the time of the GAC, our board members could not afford CUNA's lofty registration fees, and so they did not have the credentials to enter the exhibit hall. "George," one of my white board members, told me the story of walking into the exhibit hall unquestioned, despite the lack of a conference badge. When he suggested to one of our Black board members that she do the same, she tried—only to be turned away by the guards. To avoid future embarrassment, we prevailed on CUNA to waive registration fees for Federation board members so they could get the credentials needed to attend the exhibit hall and the conference sessions.

Change came slowly to the credit union industry, but it has come, as described in chapter 17.

CHAPTER 6

Fighting with Friends: Race and the CDFI Movement

Origins: Where Did the CDFI Movement Come From?

When people talk about the origins of the CDFI Fund, they often (respectfully) attribute the origins of the founding generation, of which I was a part, to civil rights activism. That is not quite accurate. There is no question that we all were committed supporters of civil rights, but few of those on the leading edge of building the CDFI movement came from civil rights or antiracist organizations, with the exception of Shorebank founders described below. Nearly all of the original CDFI leadership cohort were white. We were involved in economic justice work, movements against nuclear power, neighborhood and housing advocacy, reinvestment, philanthropy, and other progressive activities (and even banking).

The inspiration for Bill Clinton's vision came from Shorebank (originally, South Shore Bank on the South Side of Chicago), the nation's first community development bank, and the Grameen Bank in Bangladesh. Shorebank had a unique leadership team: two were white, Ron Grzywinski and Mary Houghton, and two were Black, James Fletcher and Milton Davis.[25] Fletcher had been Midwest director of

---

25 I met Jim Fletcher when we served on the Federal Reserve Board's Consumer Advisory Council in 1989. Earlier in the decade, when I was formulating the concept of a "central bank" for CDCUs, I met with Ron Grzywinski.

the Office of Economic Opportunity (OEO), the antipoverty agency, and Davis had been a leader of the Chicago chapter of the Congress of Racial Equality (CORE). Some researchers and advocates have mistakenly described Shorebank as a Black bank, which it never was, notwithstanding the civil rights engagement of its founders. And decades after its founding, Shorebank encountered community resistance when it bought one of the few remaining Black banks in Chicago.[26]

This is not to diminish the enormous importance of Shorebank, nor to diminish the commitment of its founders to racial and economic justice. Shorebank provided a vision and a model of a new kind of banking, and without it, there might never have been what became the community development banking movement. Shorebank prominently testified to Congress and favorably impressed members of key committees (especially because it was a for-profit institution). But Shorebank was not, and did not see itself, as a movement builder—they were bankers. Only later did it join our CDFI Coalition, as did the First Nations Development Institute and new associations for microenterprise lenders and venture capital. Until Southern Development Bank sent a Black representative, the initial leadership group of the CDFI Coalition was entirely white.

CDFIs and the Community Development Universe

Over 1991-92, our ad hoc coalition of credit unions, loan funds, a bank, and a community investment advocacy group adopted and attempted to define the term, "community development financial institution."

---

26 In 1995, Shorebank moved to merge with the largest Black-owned bank company in the U.S., Indecorp in Chicago. While Shorebank won regulatory approval and had the support of many Black community and political leaders, it encountered opposition from the local Black Leadership Development Institute, the Metropolitan Area Black Churches, and others. *The Wall Street Journal* described the controversy as "an emotional, nationally significant debate about race and economic empowerment." See John R. Wilke, "Power Struggle: Plan to Sell Black Bank to a White One Stirs Protests in Chicago," Wall Street Journal (November 13, 1995).

We were attempting to establish our niche in the complex landscape of community-based and community development related organizations, entities, and financial institutions. There were Community Action Agencies (CAAs, many of which were established as the outposts of the War on Poverty of the 1960s); Community Development Corporations (CDCs, which in the 1980s predominantly concentrated on housing); and Community Housing Development Organizations (CHDO, organizations certified by HUD, the U.S. Department of Housing and Urban Development). Among financial institutions, there were credit unions and banks (both government-regulated) and revolving loan funds (mostly nonprofit charitable organizations). In the credit union sector, there were the "ordinary" credit unions, and the small subsector (Community Development Credit Unions, or CDCUs) that concentrated on serving low-income people and communities; among banks, there were Minority Depository Institutions (MDIs), which were predominantly Black.

On the government side, there were numerous federal agencies involved with community development programs, including HUD, the U.S. Department of Health and Human Services (HHS), the U.S. Department of Agriculture (USDA), the U.S. Small Business Administration (SBA), the U.S. Department of Commerce (EDA), and the U.S. Department of Treasury (CDFI).

What did "community development" mean? For decades, among philanthropies and government, it generally focused on physical development. It encompassed real estate development—bricks, mortar, land, and buildings—but it is more complex and expansive, because it involves human needs and interactions. For example, building a new corner store is a real estate development project. In contrast, clearing the homeless population and training urban growers so that property can be acquired to build a grocery store in an inner-city food desert is a community development project.

But the movement I represented had deliberately adopted the name of "*community development* credit unions" in 1974, when the

Federation incorporated. For us, community development was "people-centric" rather than solely "place-centric." Yes, our credit unions provided financing to small, local businesses, or for housing renovation or home purchase. But to us, financially empowering people was as important as revitalizing the neighborhoods in which they lived. I fought that battle for years, with uneven success. Even today, when philanthropies, investors, and government think of and invest in community development, they think in terms of housing units or commercial square footage created.

So, when we advocated for the creation of the CDFI Fund, we had to convince the Clinton Administration that the CDFI tent must be a big one, encompassing not only the institutions that created or renovated the physical environment, but institutions that provided credit and financial services to individuals who had been excluded or neglected by the mainstream banking system. Thus, the emerging CDFI world included a range of institutions, including revolving loan funds, microenterprise lenders, venture capital firms, banks, and credit unions, all of which needed to demonstrate that their predominant activity was providing finance or investment to low-income and/or non-white and other "target" communities or populations.

Black Financial Institutions and the CDFI Fund

As early as the 1980s, Congress acknowledged a crisis for minority financial institutions. In 1989, responding to the failure of hundreds of savings and loan institutions, Congress passed the Financial Institutions Reform, Recovery, and Enforcement Act (FIRREA). Section 308 of FIRREA instructed regulators "to preserve the number of minority depository institutions; [and] Preserve the minority character in cases of merger or acquisition . . . . [and] Promote and encourage creation of new minority depository institutions." These included, but were not limited to, Black financial institutions. When the new CDFI Fund was making its way through Congress over 1993-94, the National Bankers Association (NBA), which represented Black banks, called for the CDFI Fund to automatically certify Black banks as CDFIs. It was unsuccessful; Black banks had to meet the same certification criteria as any other applicant to the Fund. The NBA did not join the CDFI Coalition or play a major role in CDFI advocacy. Meanwhile, little progress was made toward the goal of preserving and promoting Black financial institutions. By 2001, there were only 48 Black banks in the country; by 2021, only 22 remained. Finally, in December 2020, thirty years after FIRREA, Congress finally took aggressive action to preserve and protect minority depositories through the COVID-19 appropriations legislation.

The disappearance of minority financial institutions went beyond banks. Black-owned credit unions have a long history in the United States, dating back to at least the 1930s. The Federation had many Black member credit unions that were founded by civil rights activists in the South. In the North, financial apartheid was not as sharply defined as in the South, but access to housing finance and other credit was also widely denied to African Americans. Hundreds of credit unions were founded in Black churches; unfortunately, the trajectory of Black credit unions paralleled that of Black banks over the last four decades. Their ranks have been steadily reduced.

One tragic example chronicled in this book is the story of KAPFCU. It was organized by Kappa Alpha Psi, the premier African American Greek Letter Fraternity founded on January 5, 1911, at Indiana University. The fraternity designed KAPFCU to be a vehicle for African American engagement in banking, finance, and economic development. In the official language of its charter, credit union membership was open to Kappa Alpha Psi Fraternity, Inc. members, spouses, children, relatives, employees, and affiliated organizations. It was (like all credit unions) a stand-alone financial institution, owned and governed by its members. But unlike the majority of predominantly Black credit unions, which typically serve a church or neighborhood, KAPFCU was the first "virtual" credit union authorized by NCUA, with eligible members throughout the nation.

Purpose of KAPFCU

- To engage in charitable activities and extend financial aid through grants, gifts, contributions, or aid or assistance to qualified individuals.

- To acquire or receive from individuals, firms, associations, corporations, trusts, foundations, or any governmental subdivision unit or agency by deed, gifts, purchase, bequest, or otherwise cash securities, and other property, tangible or intangible, real or personal, and to hold for the purpose of which the Richardson/Plano Guide Right Foundation (Corporation) is organized.

- To acquire, construct, maintain, and operate rehabilitation projects or redevelopment projects in accordance with the provisions of the State where such activities may occur (i.e., Richardson, Plano, Addison, Carrollton, Garland, Mesquite, or Dallas).

- To encourage, promote, and participate in the education, rehabilitation, and management of youths and related facilities and services for the benefit of residents of the metroplex where such activities may occur (i.e., Richardson, Plano, Addison, Carrollton, Garland, Mesquite, or Dallas), in such a way as may appear feasible and appropriate. To transact such other business and do any other things incidental to and connected with said purposes.

- To do whatever is deemed necessary, useful, advisable, or conductive, directly or indirectly, to carry out any of the purposes of the Richardson/Plano Guide Right Foundation (Corporation), including the exercise of all other power, rights, privileges, and authority conferred on and enjoyed by corporations, generally, by virtue of the provisions of the Texas General Not for Profit Corporation Act.

- To accept and hold all assets accepted and received under the terms and conditions hereof exclusively for charitable purposes, and unless otherwise requested by the donor and authorized by the board of directors, all assets shall be held as unrestricted funds, and net income there be applied for charitable purposes or the assistance of qualified individuals or charitable organizations and public charities (which are supported by private donations or public taxation), contributions for which are deductible under the Internal Revenue Code 1954 including, but not limited to the promotion of education; social and scientific research; the care of the sick, the aged, infirm, and handicapped; the care of children; the improvement of living, working, recreational, and environmental conditions or facilities; and such other charitable education and social purposes that will assist the betterment of the mental, moral, social, and physical conditions of the inhabitants of America, regardless of race, religion, sex, place of national origin, or political persuasion according to the discretion of the board of directors.

I drafted my early call for a CDFI Fund and co-organized the CDFI Coalition with the explicit hope that a federal CDFI Fund would stem the hemorrhaging of Black, Latinx, and other low-income credit unions. But the CDFI Fund was not a regulator and thus was not covered by the 1989 legislation. It did not have an affirmative mandate to favor "minority" institutions. Consequently, an important opportunity to address financial inequity was, if not irrevocably lost, long deferred. For more than two decades, the overwhelming majority of the CDFI Fund's grants and investments went to predominantly white-run community development loan funds. The loan funds did supply capital to Black and other communities of color—but they were neither owned nor governed by people and communities of color, nor did they provide retail banking services like small loans and savings accounts.

Disparate Impact

How did it happen that (predominantly white-run) loan funds became the foremost beneficiaries of the CDFI Fund? It was not personal bias of the Fund's leadership; many of the presidentially-appointed directors of the Fund were people of color. Rather, bias was systemic and unintentional, with roots in the legislation itself.

Early in the legislative process, Congress had contemplated prioritizing depository institutions—government-regulated banks and credit unions—over other types of community lenders. However, there was a political problem. President Clinton's program envisioned "100 community development banks." In fact, only three such banks existed in the country, and creating new ones from scratch—"de novo"—would have been lengthy, not to mention capital-intensive. On the other hand, there were several hundred community loan funds and credit unions. The bill drafters decided, and we in the CDFI Coalition agreed, that all types of community lenders could be considered "community development banks," equally eligible for funding. Since our CDFI Coalition consisted both of depositories and loan funds, equal treatment for both was an inevitable compromise for us; the Coalition would have splintered and fallen apart otherwise. However, the Federation's credit unions lost an important advantage. Had I foreseen the outcome, I might have decided to fight harder for the depository preference, even at the risk of alienating allies. Instead, I "took one for the team."

Ultimately, Congress settled on weak language directing the Fund to "consider" in its investment decisions applicants that were, or planned to become depository institutions. The CDFI Fund never implemented such considerations.[27] The ostensibly level playing field between depositories and unregulated loan funds produced one-sided results. Over the Fund's first two decades, banks and credit unions combined received less than 20% of the major "financial assistance (FA)" funding, while loan funds obtained 80% of those grants and investments and dominated other CDFI Fund programs, like the New Markets Tax Credit program.

Fighting the Devils in the Details

The CDFI legislation was signed into law on September 23, 1994. The law set the broad parameters, but the new Fund had to write

---

27 To my knowledge, no loan funds transformed into credit unions, and only two loan funds gave birth to credit unions, one coming only in 2021.

the rules and regulations that would determine where and how the money would flow. Consequently, over 1994-1996, the Federation engaged in the obscure, technical advocacy struggles that were critical to achieving equity—the effort to ensure that the Fund's rules and policies not only *appeared* to be neutral and equal-handed but would actually produce equitable outcomes and would not unintentionally disadvantage minority institutions. One problem was that the Fund's rule writers had limited knowledge of credit unions. My job was to educate them in the realities of small, struggling credit unions who every day, all day, confronted the financial inequities plaguing Black and other poor communities.

One big problem was the *matching funds* requirement. Bill Clinton's political philosophy dictated that the CDFI Fund should not be just another "big government" initiative, but one that would leverage investment from the private sector. All grants and investments from the CDFI Fund were to be matched, dollar for dollar, by nonfederal investments of like kind (i.e., grants for grants, loans for loans). Preferably, these funds would come from the private sector; in practice, this meant that the match would come primarily from banks and foundations.

How would this affect low-income credit unions, whose capital came from their members? They typically did not solicit or obtain foundation or corporate donations and grants. In contrast, grant-seeking was a core business for nonprofit loan funds, which were generally structured as 501[c](3) charities. Many had established relationships with foundations and with the major banks, who provided them with grants that counted toward banks' Community Reinvestment Act (CRA) requirements. (In contrast, those banks tended to view credit unions and community development banks as competitors rather than as potential allies.)

Without access to matching funds, few low-income credit unions would have won investments from the Fund. The smallest and poorest credit unions—especially those that were Black, Latinx, and/or rural, far from the headquarters of banks and foundations—would likely have been shut out altogether, another blow against equity. My task was to convince the Fund that it would be unfair and perverse for the CDFI Fund to reward those institutions that could access matching funds from corporations and foundations, while disregarding the community-generated net worth that credit unions amassed from their members by retaining a portion of the earnings generated from their operations. Fortunately for the Federation's credit unions, we prevailed on this crucial issue. The CDFI Fund permitted credit unions to use their retained earnings or net worth to match Fund grants.

I was less successful in another critical area. The very structure of the Fund's application process implied "disparate impact." The huge, complex process was essentially a grant competition, which inevitably favored those institutions with the capacity and experience to compete. Credit unions did not typically employ grant-writers; they were in the business of gathering deposits and making loans in poor communities. The Fund's application asked questions, demanded data, and sought impact indicators that were more readily generated by loan funds than by credit unions. It's not that credit unions lack data: They generate extensive, standardized reports for federal examiners. They serve hundreds of thousands of low-income member-customers, especially those of color, but they don't routinely track the kind of impact data most valued in Washington, like housing units or jobs created—the main lenses through which government and philanthropy tend to view "community development."

The First Awards: Shock and Disappointment

The establishment of the CDFI Fund was the "holy grail" of my decades-long quest for capital for our credit unions. I had drafted the first paper calling for such a fund and had catalyzed the Coalition of CDFIs to advocate for it. CDCUs had long struggled as the only banking institutions with the explicit mission of serving low-income communities. I saw the CDFI Fund as a crucial source of donated equity that low-income credit unions could leverage to obtain additional deposits, initiating a virtuous cycle of growth and reversing their decline in communities of color. If there was one issue that I felt I "owned," it was the CDFI Fund. Our members were content to have me campaign for it, but it was not the focus of their hopes and plans. Some were skeptical that it would become a reality; others were cynical that they would benefit, since the federal government had so often dashed their hopes. But after the CDFI Fund became law in 1994, their interest grew, and the stakes rose.

In the summer of 1996, the CDFI Fund made its breathlessly awaited first round of awards. Unfortunately, our members' skepticism proved largely justified. Dozens of CDCUs struggled through the exhaustive federal application process, yet only a scant half-dozen received awards—less than one-tenth of our membership. Our few winners were worthy institutions that served poverty communities from the South Bronx to the East Side of Cleveland to the Navajo reservation. But I had envisioned and hoped for something more expansive, a full-blown commitment to nurture existing credit unions and incubate new ones in communities of color. My biggest disappointment came when the Fund rejected one particular credit union, the recently chartered Central Brooklyn FCU organized by two brilliant young Black men (one of whom was my former staff member) and was known nationally as the "hip hop" credit union. I had invested my hopes in it as the harbinger of a new generation of credit unions.

Why so few? Our credit unions, I was certain, *deserved* to get a major share. We were the largest grouping of minority-owned, minority-run financial institutions in the country. Our credit unions were found in all the financial gaps, the unprofitable markets and "banking deserts" that banks ignored: the Deep South, Indian Country, the neighborhoods that were home to Black churches from Harlem to Chicago's South Side, to South Central Los Angeles. Surely, I thought, the CDFI Fund would recognize and prioritize support for our credit unions.

But nonprofit loan funds dominated. Most of them were only a few years old, whereas our credit unions had spent decades serving the poorest communities—Black, Latinx, Asian, and Native American. Our institutions had the greatest needs; we served the "bad credit risks," even while suffering from regulatory pressure to meet "industry standards" and raise capital. No one claimed that the loan funds were unworthy. But, we asked, could not the Fund have found a way to make more, smaller awards rather than the relatively large investments they made in a handful of institutions?

I personally had a lot riding on the outcome—perhaps too much. Perhaps my response reflected white privilege: I did not expect to lose. Sadly, many of our members may have been less surprised at the outcome. They had felt the sting of disappointment at the hands of the government far longer and more acutely than I had. But my reaction literally paled in comparison to that of my African American board chairwoman, "Evelyne."

Confrontation: Fighting with Friends

Shortly after the awards were announced, I led a briefing session for our members and others in Washington. I tried to temper our members' disillusionment; the competition for government money is always intense, and there are always more losers than winners. A big mistake! Evelyne angrily confronted me, which surprised and upset me. But more than that: she confronted the head of the CDFI Fund, an Asian American woman who was a highly respected longtime supporter of community investment. Evelyne denounced her and the Fund as racist. She likely voiced the feelings of a number of our members, although few of them would have engaged a federal official the way she did. I'm sure the director was stunned.

I was stunned, as well, embarrassed but also plunged into self-doubt: was I playing the classic role acting as a white mediator, defending a racist system, and attempting to "cool out" the righteous rage of our members?

Afterward, I tried to argue our case with the director that the Fund had ignored the neediest communities in the country. She pointedly questioned whether I was arguing that "need" should take precedence over "performance." I haltingly replied that, of course, both had to be considered, but that "performance" should not be evidenced solely by a professionally done application, elaborate business plans, and a track record of raising bank and foundation money. Some of our smallest credit unions had demonstrated "performance" through decades of experience serving and surviving in the hardest-to-serve low-income markets.

I did not win. As I learned, the Fund leadership favored those that they perceived as providing the greatest impact in order to justify the Fund's existence as a Clinton Administration start-up in a hostile legislative environment.

Throughout the 1990s, I continued my battle with the CDFI Fund. It was not a fight against enemies: the Clinton Administration and its appointees were vigorously supportive of the CDFI Fund; they shared our core values.[28] But the playing field was never level. The Fund's applications, its procedures, its metrics, its desired impacts all were rooted in a framework that comfortably fit the largely white-led nonprofit sector, to the disadvantage of small credit unions with limited staff resources but a record of serving Black, Latinx, and other low-income communities. Year over year, the Fund's resources went overwhelmingly to the loan funds—consistently, around 80%.[29]

To this day, I regret the race-charged confrontation of my board chairwoman with the Fund's director. I was not proud of the uncomfortable mediating role I played. But I regret even more the disparate

---

28 Later, the George W. Bush administration's appointees in the early 2000s were not ideologically hostile to the Fund and indeed were supportive of some of its programs. Nonetheless, as presidential appointees, they were obliged to support President George W. Bush's efforts to cut back the CDFI Fund or, in 2005, consign it to a likely death by "consolidating" it with other federal programs.
29 A detailed analysis appears in *Democratizing Finance*.

impact that the Fund's allocations produced. For decades, we had witnessed the relentless erosion of financial institutions run by and for communities of color. The CDFI Fund was by no means a disaster; in so many ways, it has been the best federal vehicle to promote community economic development. But early on, it chose "impact" over "equity."

White Gatekeeper?

How, then, to deal with our, and my, bitter disappointment with the first actions of the long-sought CDFI Fund?

Evelyne threatened to take her anger to Congress, to denounce the CDFI Fund. The anti-Clinton forces, led by Rep. Newt Gingrich, would have been delighted to use her criticism to wipe out the Fund altogether. I was alarmed. But how to turn things around to ensure that our credit unions could benefit from the Fund?

I consulted with Martin Eakes of Self-Help, a white CDFI leader and longtime colleague who had fought on behalf of Black credit unions in North Carolina for decades. He was extremely influential within community development circles and had been key in getting the CDFI Fund legislation passed. He quietly advised the CDFI Fund that it was essential—for purposes of politics as well as equity—to find a way to reach the Black and poor institutions that had largely lost out.

The Fund recognized this and introduced a significant policy change. The Fund decided to begin providing capital to national intermediaries, which in turn would "downstream" funding to small institutions that otherwise stood little chance in competing with larger, more sophisticated applicants. This gave the Federation a major opportunity. In the second funding round, we won a grant of $3.25 million, which we used to make equity-like loans and grants to our smaller member credit unions. The Fund's grant helped transform us: it greatly expanded our assets and net worth and enabled us to offer our members capital of a type and volume that we had never before been able to provide. In subsequent rounds, we repeatedly won large CDFI Fund grants, enabling us to build significant net worth and leverage tens of millions of dollars of loans and deposits.

The Fund's policy change was a win for the Federation and for the CDCU movement. It was a win for the CDFI Fund, which "pacified" some of its most vocal critics. But it raised a difficult question for me: Was I, through the Federation, playing the role of *white gatekeeper,* providing the "respectable" institution that could speak the government's language and play by its rules? The Federation was an intermediary between the sources of capital and the communities that needed to benefit from it. It may have been a step *toward* equity—but that was not enough.

Earlier, when Congress was still working through the details of the CDFI Fund, I had pressed for language that would set aside a portion or window of the CDFI Fund for small, "non-competitive" institutions, credit unions, and others. My CDFI Coalition colleagues informally referred to it as the "Rosenthal amendment." It did not become law. So, throughout the 1990s, I worked to establish such a program through the Fund's administrative policies. Finally, in 2000, the Fund established the Small and Emerging CDFI (SECA) program. Our credit unions and other small CDFIs were at last able to compete directly for funding on more equal grounds, if only for smaller amounts of capital.

Persisting Inequality

Even this policy change did not ensure equitable outcomes of the CDFI Fund. On April 20, 2021, Bill Bynum, the CEO of the Hope Enterprise Corporation and its affiliated credit union, perhaps the most prominent Black-led CDFI in the country, testified to Congress that a capital shortage still affected institutions like his: "Even though minority-led CDFIs have performed better in reaching minority communities, which often have the greatest need for financial services, these CDFIs have historically had the least amount of resources to do this work. Over the last 15 years, white-led CDFIs have had a median asset size twice that of minority-led CDFIs. In some years, it has been three times as high."[30]

Systemic bias persisted not only in the CDFI Fund's Financial Assistance grant programs, but in the multi-billion-dollar New Markets Tax Credit (NMTC) program, the largest program administered by the CDFI Fund. Annie Donovan had an insider's view of the CDFI Fund from her four years as director. Subsequently, as chief operating officer of the Local Initiative Support Corporation (LISC), one of the largest CDFIs, she decried the low share of awards to minority-owned applicants.[31] She argued that the "disproportionate results reflect the same deeply-seated structural barriers that prevent minority-owned enterprises from accessing credit in other parts of the economy." She attributed it to the competitive process, which resulted in organizations "with smaller balance and smaller staffs" tending to be judged as having lower capacity, especially if their track record showed that they had made corresponding smaller investments. She urged a set aside for "small or emerging minority- and Native-owned applicants." She noted that similar "on-ramps" had been created for Native CDFIs and Small and Emerging CDFIs.[32] Her arguments echoed mine of decades earlier.

The correlation between race and small institutional size is not purely coincidental; rather, it is a feature of a systemically racist capitalist society. It becomes a self-fulfilling, self-replicating dynamic—those who have more can get more.

---

[30] His remarks to the U.S. Senate Committee on Banking, Housing and Urban Affairs were entitled *"An Economy that Works for Everyone: Investing in Rural Communities."*
[31] Annie Donovan, "Dismantling Structural Racism in Community Development Finance," Local Initiatives Support Corporation, August 11, 2020, https://www.lisc.org/our-stories/story/dismantling-structural-racism-community-development-finance/.
[32] See the discussion of the CDFI Fund's Small and Emerging CDFI program above in this chapter.

CHAPTER 7

Race and Regulation: Systemic Bias and Scandal

Deposit Insurance Changes the Credit Union Movement

In the early decades of the twentieth century, credit unions operated as "pure" cooperatives—that is, they were groups of people united by a "common bond" (of employment, geography, or association) engaged in what we would now describe as character-based "peer lending." Simply put, members pooled their savings, established their loan policies, made loan decisions, and shared any losses. Governance was (as it is today) one person, one vote, regardless of the amount of a member's savings or credit. Regulation was relatively light, solely on a state-by-state basis until 1934, when the Federal Credit Union Act was passed. Organizing new credit unions was a simple process—gather at least seven people to pledge deposits of $5 (in whole or over time) and assemble volunteers to serve as the elected board of directors, the credit committee, and the supervisory committee.

Legislation in 1970 brought major changes. A new, independent agency, the National Credit Union Administration (NCUA), replaced the former Bureau of Federal Credit Unions, and with it, for the first time, federal deposit insurance was provided to eligible credit unions by the National Credit Union Share Insurance Fund (NCUSIF), which is parallel and comparable to the FDIC that insures bank deposits. But not all credit unions were eligible. To qualify for deposit insurance, a credit union had to demonstrate it had sufficient capital (i.e., equity or net worth). Many credit unions serving low-income communities did not, which would have meant an early death: an uninsured institution would have no chance to survive if all its peers were insured. Credit unions that served low-income communities, including many communities of color, banded together to advocate for inclusion in the new deposit insurance program. With help from the federal anti-poverty agency, most survived. Moreover, recognizing that credit unions serving poverty communities faced chronic challenges in raising capital, Congress granted credit unions designated as "limited income" by NCUA the exclusive power to raise "non-member deposits," in contrast to other credit unions, which could only raise deposits from their circumscribed "field of membership."

Capital, limited-income designation, deposit insurance—these were the interrelated issues that repeatedly engaged the Federation in our battles with the federal regulators, NCUA.

Different

There is much to be said for a regulated financial industry. Credit unions (like banks) have standardized accounting and financial reporting that provide a high degree of transparency.[33] They report dozens of different statistics and ratios for lending, assets, liabilities, and more, not to mention maintaining compliance with a host of consumer regulations. To evaluate the "safety and soundness" of credit unions, NCUA has a rating system (from "1", the highest, to "5" the lowest, for credit unions on the verge of termination). "Peer statistics" are one of NCUA's major tools—ratios compiled by aggregating the reports for the thousands of credit unions. Examiners use these statistics to guide their analysis as they supervise and rate credit unions.

---

33 I came to appreciate the advantages of standardization when I visited Russia in the early 2000s, after the dissolution of the former Soviet Union. Hundreds of "credit unions" sprang up subject to various provincial rules and without standardized accounting, which made it difficult to grow a mature, stable industry nation-wide.

I spent my career arguing with regulators that our credit unions were *different* from most of those thousands of other credit unions reflected in peer statistics. Our differences were important and valuable. We served populations that few other financial institutions were interested in serving. We were in neighborhoods where other financial institutions—including "mainstream" credit unions—generally were not found. We served Black, Latinx, Asian, Indigenous, immigrant, and white communities of all ethnicities (including a few nonconforming "outliers" in progressive university communities like Santa Cruz and Ithaca). It was no accident that our credit unions' financials did not match up to their more prosperous mainstream cousins: if your business was serving low-income and credit-challenged people, your losses, earnings, net worth, and other characteristics would look different from industry norms. Typically, members have smaller average deposits and take out smaller loans than industry averages; often they are more labor-intensive and thus less profitable or "efficient." In a low-income community, many members have lower and/or fluctuating incomes, reflected in irregular repayment histories; rather than "A" borrowers, they may be classified "C" or even "D." Consequently, a community development or low-income credit union may have higher than average rates of loan delinquency—a flashing red light for regulators, which became one of the deciding factors in the case of KAPFCU.

The CDCU differences were magnified in the case of KAPFCU. It differed from industry "peers" not only because it served a Black membership, but because of its particular business model. Not only was it a low-income designated credit union (LICU) and CDFI-certified institution, but it was also the first "virtual" credit union authorized by the NCUA. It was not neighborhood- or community-based; it operated on a national footprint, with no brick-and-mortar office. it had to maintain a presence at all sanctioned Kappa Alpha Psi caucuses and conferences. Because it was required to attend regional (12 provinces) and national meetings, its travel expenses differed widely from most other credit unions, far "out of line" of peer expense ratios. Another difference grabbed NCUA's attention. Even low-income credit unions make larger loans to more prosperous members to cross-subsidize their administratively expensive portfolios of small loans. KAPFCU was known to Black student athletes and alumni, some of whom went on to become professional basketball or football players. Making larger auto and other loans to these members looked quite different from the operations of a neighborhood credit union.

> ### CDCU Loan Portfolios
>
> For example, KAPFCU has the benefit of being sponsored by Kappa Alpha Psi Fraternity and an internationally known and well-respected brand. College students all across the country are familiar with Kappa Alpha Psi, including student-athletes. Some of them went on to become professional athletes. Consequently, KAPFCU provided auto financing for NFL and NBA players. They viewed auto financing at KAPFCU just like General Motors and GMAC. These are not your typical low-to-moderate income borrowers that are the typical members of LICUs or CDCUs. However, the survival of community development credit unions requires them to balance their loan portfolio with lending to middle-income and high-net-worth individuals for several reasons.
>
> ### 1. Administrative Costs
> Credit Unions must ultimately disburse their deposits as loans. KAPFCUs model was to provide substantial loans ($5,000) that could serve as "emergency funds" for their hard-to-serve membership population. NCUA examiners tried to limit KAPFCU to $500 loan limits for hard-to-serve borrowers as a "safety and soundness" concern. KAPFCU had a $475,000 loan portfolio. That would be 1,000 individual (troubled) borrowers, 1,000 credit reports to review, and 2,000 loan files to maintain,

etc. In contrast, KAPFCU can administer 100 loans (at $5,000) with their volunteer staff. Micro-loans create administrative burdens for small credit unions to administer.

2. Portfolio Risk

You want to offer loans to a mix of credit-worthy borrowers, while it is "God's work" to lend to low-income individuals and individuals with lower credit scores. However, to maintain a viable loan portfolio, you also have to have middle-income and credit-worthy borrowers to balance your loan portfolio. You can't maintain a loan portfolio with all sub-prime paper. You have to have some "A" and "B" borrowers to allow you to offer services and loan products to "C" and "D" borrowers.

3. Loan Size

Auto financing to professional athletes and other high-net-worth individuals is the most efficient tool to deploy capital that KAPFCU possesses. Including $25,000 to $50,000 auto loans is a much more efficient method to deploy a $475,000 loan portfolio versus $500 individual loans.

Tragically, NCUA's regional examiners "weaponized" these and other differences against KAPFCU.

Where the System Meets the Road

A credit union's face-to-face encounter with the credit union regulatory system comes when an examiner periodically visits to assess the credit union's operations and finances. Until recent years, the examiner—most commonly a "he," and more often than not, a white "he"—arrives at the credit union's doors as an authority figure, armed with industry-wide peer statistics and the credit union's historical performance. His job is to identify shortcomings and require the board and staff of credit unions to rectify these. Few credit unions are perfect; each credit union receives a list of conditions to be rectified in a timely manner. It can be an intimidating process, especially for the volunteer boards of credit unions and for their managers, whose jobs may depend on the examination results.

It is a near miracle that CDCUs do as well as many of them do given their divergence from industry norms, which are compiled from thousands of credit unions, many of which serve more middle-class members. The crucial outcome of an examination is reflected in the components of its CAMEL score (the quaint acronym summarizing a credit union's financial condition in terms of its capital, asset quality, management, earnings, and liquidity). These are the inputs for the numerical top score of "1" to the bottom-most "5," a message to pack your bags because you will soon be closed.

It all sounds very objective. But even NCUA acknowledges that there is a subjective element: "examiners use their professional judgement and consider both qualitative and quantitative factors when analyzing a credit union's performance."

How to assess the differences when the numbers of our credit unions looked different? The low credit scores, the small emergency loans without collateral, the loans for old used cars with minimal book value, the loans to small businesses with seasonal fluctuations of income and late loan payments—were these evidence of poor performance? Did they indicate a manager's or board's incompetence? Or were they inherent to a credit union's business model of serving an economically stressed low-income community?

Given their acknowledged power to make subjective interpretations and assessments, examiners can find, highlight, and criticize shortcomings in almost every credit union; mistakes and oversights happen. But it is crucial to identify whether a deficiency is material and consequential, truly a threat to "safety and soundness" and thus to the solvency of the deposit insurance fund that NCUA administers.

In my years as CEO of the Federation, I frequently received from our members complaints about difficult encounters with their examiners. When these came from credit unions of color, was this evidence of racism? Occasionally, I heard a blatantly racist story. I was shocked, but perhaps should not have been surprised when a credit union from Texas reported that an examiner had told their board, "Black people don't know how to run a credit union."

More commonly, racism was subtler, expressed through disrespect, condescension, or excessively harsh subjective judgments. An examiner might question a credit union's business model (and implicitly, the community they served): "Why do you even have a credit union, you're not offering enough services, you're just a savings club?"

Or: "Why are you making loans to *those* people, who have obvious problems on their credit files?"

Frequently, examiners encouraged boards to abandon the credit union and merge with a larger, "more efficient" institution. Or worse, they may refuse to allow a credit union to merge and prematurely rushes it into liquidation—KAPFCU's fate.

In Part Two, Michael McCray, trained as a CPA and lawyer, explains the "death spiral" that wrongly resulted in the closure of that credit union. In brief, the problem started with:

> . . . the forced change to GAAP full accrual accounting, which tracks and recognizes expenses over time rather than recording them only when paid.[34] Daily monitoring (tracking) caused KAPFCU's record-keeping deficiencies; the record-keeping deficiencies caused the decline in KAPFCU management ratings; the decline in management ratings caused the drop in KAPFCU's overall CAMEL

---

34 NCUA Rules and Regulation allow small credit unions with less than $10 million in assets to report on a "cash basis" or "modified cash" basis. See 12 U.S.C. § 1782(6)(C)(iii), which states that small credit unions are exempted from the mandatory GAAP treatment that the examiner imposed on KAPFCU under the "de minimus exception" to the standard accounting principles. Regrettably, Region IV officials forced KAPFCU to report on a full accrual basis from 2007 to 2009.

rating; the drop in the overall CAMEL rating made KAPFCU ineligible for federal funding assistance; the resulting ineligibility for federal funding assistance and NCUA corporate stabilization caused the deterioration of KAPFCU's capital position. Together the record-keeping deficiencies and subsequent deterioration of KAPFCU's capital base necessitated the [punitive NCUA] Letter of Understanding and Agreement (LUA). But for NCUA's actions the forced change to GAAP full accrual accounting KAPFCU would never have been in a financial or management condition that subjected it to an LUA at all.

Proving racism or other unfair treatment was difficult. To defend our credit unions, I elevated their questions and concerns up the supervisory ladder of NCUA. But despite their complaints, most credit unions were ultimately unwilling or unable to document incidents of examiners' disrespect or unduly harsh judgments—which is what made KAPFCU's challenge to the regulators so extraordinary. They feared they could not win: given the mountains of rules, regulations, and procedures governing credit unions, an examiner can readily produce "the facts," instances of a credit union's shortcomings that would justify his actions. Our credit unions also feared retaliation. Win or lose, examiners can make life difficult for a credit union; they can criticize its financial performance, aggressively downgrade loan quality, and press for merger or even liquidation. Running a credit union with the specific mission of serving a low-income community is a tough job. A nonprofit charity may have a bad year and show a net loss without incurring mortal danger. For a credit union, an unprofitable year or decreasing net worth is a bright red flag. And the danger mounts with every new economic crisis.

In the decades before deposit insurance, relations between the regulatory agency and credit unions were generally less adversarial. However, after the creation of the National Credit Union Share Insurance Fund, which is backed by the "full faith and credit" of the United States, NCUA acquired a compelling interest in protecting the insurance fund, which is backed by the "full faith and credit" of the United States.[35] That interest in preserving NCUSIF's assets increasingly overrode NCUA's historical relationship of supporting credit unions. At one meeting with NCUA, I was surprised—although perhaps should not have been—when one senior official declared bluntly that all he cared about was protecting the insurance fund. In practice, for examiners and NCUA, the prevailing approach seemed to be: if in doubt, liquidate or merge a credit union. There was little incentive for an examiner to err on the side of lenience. To my knowledge, no examiner was ever penalized for pressing to merge a "troubled" credit union, even if it had hopes of recovery.

Virtually all of our credit unions were too small to inflict serious losses on the National Credit Union Share Insurance Fund if they failed. Moreover, the costs of liquidation or merger were sometimes greater than the costs of letting a small credit union work out its problems and return to health. Nonetheless, over the decades and through various administrations, NCUA policymakers effectively concluded that our small credit unions were thorns in their side. It was "inefficient" for NCUA to spend their examiners' time on these small institutions when they could be spending it on larger, more sophisticated credit unions; better that there be fewer, but larger, credit unions in the United States.

Credit unions lived or died by the numbers. But there was no number, no calculus of what the loss of a credit union would mean for a low-income community or community of color. Consider, for example, what is lost with the closure of a Black church credit union

---

35 "Full faith and credit" means that the federal government will "bail out" or reimburse depositors for their accounts (up to specified limits) if an institution fails. Ordinary people learned what full faith and credit meant in the 1980s, when years of rampant banking deregulation led to widespread speculation, fraud, and the failure of hundreds upon hundreds of Savings and Loans (S&Ls). Their depositors were made whole up to the insured limit through the federal government's guarantee.

that was formed during the eras of overt racism and bank redlining—a credit union that has survived for decades through the volunteer labor of its parishioners, often as a kind of "economic mission" of the church. Credit unions like that were part of the shared history of the credit union movement, a living legacy and reminder that credit unions existed to serve the underserved and marginalized.

The Big Picture

The hard reality is this: small institutions are mostly on the wrong side of financial evolution. From the time I joined the credit union movement in 1980, there has been an unrelenting trajectory of consolidation both among credit unions and banks. In the credit union industry, the number of institutions has shrunk dramatically (from about 20,000 in the 1970s to 5,200 today), even as total assets have climbed above $2 trillion, and membership has increased to more than 130 million people. Increasingly, the largest credit unions account for the lion's share of assets, members, and political influence. (As for banks, the concentration of assets, customers, and political power in the four or five biggest institutions is even more pronounced.) Small institutions are disadvantaged because they lack the efficiencies and economies of operation that come with scale. Increasing regulation compounds the dilemma: much regulation is one size fits all, tailored to the large institutions. All credit unions (and all banks) complain about regulation—but the regulatory burden is especially hard on small institutions.

When NCUA publicly announces the "voluntary" merger of two credit unions, one of which may be a small CDCU, it often uses the boilerplate phrase that the merger was undertaken to "provide better service for members." Certainly, this is sometimes true. But for decades, we saw repeatedly that when a small CDCU was merged into a larger "mainstream" one, the latter soon shuttered the CDCU's office. Moreover, the loan policies of the larger, predominantly white credit union were ill-adapted for a low-income membership, especially one of color. Whereas in a small, tight-knit credit union, personal knowledge might mitigate a low credit score for a member seeking a loan, in a merged institution, she would likely face more rigid, standardized underwriting and possibly outright rejection or a higher rate for a loan because of "risk-based" pricing. So, embedded in the narrative of industry "rationalization," there was real loss.

It was a painful for me to watching the thinning ranks of Black and Latinx credit unions over three decades. Some *chose* to give up their charters because the mounting burdens of regulation and operational complexity proved too much for volunteer boards and understaffed management. Others tried to resist when NCUA forced a merger, and they asked desperately for the Federation's help—usually at the eleventh hour, when their fate was all but sealed. We argued with the regulators, we complained, we pleaded—but we had no legal staff, and as our chief advocate, I rarely was able to save an institution that NCUA was determined to close.

"Casework"—intervention for individual institutions—had its limits. To effect change, we had to fight for top-level regulatory policies and procedures that would recognize the valuable role our credit unions played in serving low-income communities, people of color, and immigrants who would otherwise go without affordable financial services.

Was it Racism?

Over my career, I took personally the steady stream of mergers and liquidations of credit unions serving Black, Latinx, and Indigenous communities. Some I had helped organize; others I knew from my visits to South Central Los Angeles, Minneapolis, and North Carolina.

My colleagues who formerly worked for NCUA argue that it was *not* racism or discrimination that led to the decline of Black and other credit unions of color. Charles "Chip" Filson, formerly a high-ranking official of NCUA, argued that:

NCUA does not respect members' rights. Be they Black, brown, or white; young, old, or in between; male or female. When member-owned institutions, created through volunteer labor, are summarily closed or merged, the systemic failure that allows this will either be changed or there will be no more cooperative movement. Injustice, whether by public or private organizations, always targets the vulnerable first. Be they the economically fragile, or the uninformed and unempowered. When violation of rights is left unchallenged, the inequities will extend across the entire population.[36]

Even if, as Filson argues, NCUA is even-handed and race-blind in its lack of regard for small credit unions, that does not refute the disproportionate racist impact of its policies. The "vulnerable" among credit unions are disproportionately of color. The credit unions' own vulnerabilities reflect those of their membership: disproportionately, their members are among the last hired and the first fired, lack steady full-time work, or are employed in the service economy or other low-paid jobs. They often have limited or no emergency savings to carry themselves through periods of unemployment. Consequently, credit unions serving low-income communities and communities of color are often at risk for higher loan delinquency, greater loan losses, and decreased net worth—all red flags for regulators.

It is not a coincidence that institutions serving non-white communities are disproportionately small; it is a consequence of capitalism and racial inequality. They often suffer a vicious cycle of smallness: lacking resources and capacity, they cannot expand their services and membership, which means that they cannot generate income to add more services and attract more members. Finally, the loss of a credit union serving a community of color often has a disproportionately harsh effect, since the community may be unlikely to find other

---

36 Chip Filson, "The End of Kappa Alpha Psi FCU's Journey to the 'Promised Land' (Part II of II)," Just a Member, February 26, 2021, https://chipfilson.com/2021/02/.

satisfactory financial sources. Thus, the loss of a Black-owned financial institution both results from and perpetuates systemic inequality.

Historically, in the eyes of the regulator, "small" has not been beautiful, sustainable, or a priority—a view that some within the credit union industry shared. All kinds of small credit unions were indeed being lost; arguably, my own perspective was skewed because the Federation's membership consisted predominantly of small credit unions that served communities of color. Perhaps my perspective was skewed—but I do not believe it was wrong to call out a threat to financial equity.

Bias: Explicit and Implicit

In the 1930s, federal agencies unabashedly promulgated explicitly racist policies and regulations that devastated and disadvantaged Black and poor communities for decades. The Federal Housing Administration created and sanctioned redlining by denying insurance to neighborhoods with Black populations. Other federal housing policies discriminated by providing or withholding subsidies; they favored white homeowners and excluded Black homeowners, and they permitted restrictive covenants that prevented Blacks from buying homes. There is a long list of policies that the federal government either knew, or should have known, would perpetuate discrimination and deprive Blacks and other people of color of opportunities to build wealth, especially through housing.

In the last few decades, no federal regulatory agency would consciously promulgate regulations or policies that would *explicitly* disenfranchise and discriminate against Black Americans and communities of color. The National Credit Union Administration certainly did not, could not, and would not issue rules that explicitly targeted Black, Latinx, Asian, or Indigenous communities. Rather, some of the biggest battles I fought with the agency were against implicit bias and *disparate impact*—rules and policies that on their face were neutral but would bring outsized harm to credit unions serving communities of color. One instance highlighted the damage.

The Credit Union Scandal of the Century

Race, sex, politics, embezzlement—the Franklin Community Federal Credit Union scandal of 1988 had it all. It broke on the eve of the election in 1988 that would make George H. W. Bush president. It arrived suddenly and shockingly in Omaha, Nebraska. Credit unions are routinely the most boring institutions in the financial world; generally, the industry is quite content to fly under the political radar. Suddenly, the industry was embroiled in a scandal of corruption and vice exposed by an article in a fabled investigative weekly, New York's *Village Voice*.

The Franklin Community Federal Credit Union was a small, predominantly Black, low-income institution, headed by Lawrence King, Jr., a one-time Democrat who switched allegiances when Ronald Reagan was elected in 1980. King became a high-profile actor in the Republican Party, chairing the National Black Republican Council. He sang the national anthem at the 1984 Republican convention, and at the 1988 convention, and entertained 1,000 people, including former President Gerald Ford, in a rented warehouse used to stage the Mardi Gras parade in New Orleans. He lived lavishly, renting an expensive townhouse in Washington that he claimed was made possible by his wife's wealth; King himself only drew a $16,000 yearly salary from the credit union. King employed an interesting model, a credit union operating in tandem with a nonprofit organization. Seeking to expand his influence nationally, he pitched his model to the only Black member of Reagan's cabinet, HUD Secretary Samuel Pierce (who later was investigated for political favoritism and influence-peddling).

An anonymous source communicated to NCUA that King was converting credit union deposits to his personal use. On November 4, 1988, the FBI, IRS, Treasury Department, and Omaha police raided and shut down the credit union. They soon announced that King had embezzled $34 million of "non-member deposits." The investigation by the *Village Voice* exposed tawdry details that went far beyond financial misconduct: among these were allegations that King was involved in the sexual abuse of children, allegedly transporting teenagers from foster care to parties around the country for the sexual edification of King's guests.

At every level, the King scandal was a disaster. King was a highly visible, respected figure in Omaha. His credit union and nonprofit affiliate were highly valued by the local Black community. King's downfall brought disappointment, a sense of loss, disbelief, and suspicion of the government's "persecution" of this honored community leader.[37]

Disparate Impact: Choking Access to Capital

The Franklin Community Credit Union disaster damaged the Federation and the entire CDCU movement. Lawrence King was ostensibly in the same "business" as ours: raising deposits from socially responsible investors, often religious institutions. King's staff went as far as to forge my signature on the Federation's letterhead to solicit investments from organizations like a Catholic women's order in South Dakota, which had unwittingly invested $2 million in what proved to be a Ponzi scheme. These were not insured deposits, of course—they were only entries on King's fraudulent second set of books. (The sisters went to court to eventually retrieve their funds.)

The biggest blow for our movement came from the regulators. Weeks after the Franklin scandal became public, the three-member NCUA Board, then under former Republican Senator Roger Jepsen, took an unprecedented action: it issued an "emergency" regulation that restricted the ability of credit unions to raise more than 20% of their deposits from nonmember sources (chiefly, philanthropy and faith-based organizations). This scarcely mattered to mainstream credit

---

37 Disregarding (if possible) King's corruption, his organization undoubtedly served needs in the Black community—so much so that the Federation was permitted to help organize a successor credit union in Omaha after Franklin's demise. King was convicted of embezzlement charges and served 10 years in prison.

unions, who were restricted to raising deposits from their defined fields of membership. The "20% rule" only affected low-income-designated credit unions, the majority of which were Black. The regulation limited their access to capital that they needed to thrive.

To us, it was a clear case of *disparate impact*, discrimination by effect rather than by stated intent. Low-income credit unions, which were mostly Black and Latinx, were the *only* federal credit unions empowered to accept non-member deposits, according to law dating to 1970. Thus, NCUA's new restriction *only* affected these institutions—essentially, our Federation's membership, even though the regulations did not name them.

We were outraged. Since the 1960s, the lack of access to capital was acknowledged as a primary cause for the failure to thrive of low-income credit unions. Now the regulators were restricting that access. They saw the problem as King's low-income credit union having access to *too much money*; we saw the problem as a case of massive fraud and embezzlement, undetected by the regulatory agency charged with examining and supervising the credit union. Embezzlement, of course, was never the sole province of Black credit unions—but when it occurred on a large scale at mainstream, predominantly white credit unions, there was no rush to promulgate regulations restricting their deposit-gathering.

I reached out to the Lawyers' Committee for Civil Rights Under Law to explore a suit against NCUA. We learned that the courts pay substantial deference to federal agencies, being reluctant to second-guess their judgment. We faced a high barrier: we would need to prove that NCUA's actions were "arbitrary and capricious." Could we, should we, have pressed a case we were so unlikely to win? Perhaps it would have been more courageous to fight. But I counseled our board not to pursue the case against all odds; we could barely sustain our staff of three or four people.

For years, I was on a personal crusade against NCUA's "20% rule," which made low-income credit unions apply for permission any time they wished to obtain philanthropic or other non-member deposits exceeding that portion of their assets. The comparison I invoked was this: imagine a town in which Black people were restricted to a 9:00 p.m. curfew—unless they begged for a waiver or special permission. Eventually, grudgingly, NCUA made technical changes that made it somewhat easier for a credit union to obtain waivers—a modest victory that brought no justice and little joy.

Guilt by Association

After the Franklin scandal, our Black credit unions felt the weight of guilt by association, especially if they happened to have a nonprofit affiliate that "looked like" King's model. Our members reported to me that their examiners arrived with a suspicious attitude; NCUA was determined that there would be no more Franklin Community FCU scandals on their watch. Over the next several years, under the Bush administration, NCUA thinned the ranks of designated low-income credit unions—the only ones empowered to raise philanthropic capital from non-member deposits. The list of officially designated low-income credit unions shrank from 325 to 195. Our movement was further marginalized.

Was NCUA's action racist? Did it consciously seek to starve low-income communities of capital? There was not a conscious plan, but the agency felt the need to protect its reputation, damaged by the scandal, not to mention the deposit insurance fund. Promoting financial equity—allowing philanthropic capital to flow into capital-deprived communities—was not a priority. Low-income credit unions, including credit unions of color, were acceptable "collateral damage." Their special challenges merited no special government privileges or considerations.

Government-Starving Republicans and "Compassionate Conservatives"

The Reaganism of the early 1980s was unapologetically antigovernment to the core, asserting that government was the *problem* for the United States, not a solution. Reagan's Director of the Office of Management and Budget, David Stockman, had literally singled out the paltry $6 million CDCU Revolving Loan Fund my predecessors had fought for as a waste of government money. Their policies were harsher than the "benign neglect" that had previously marked right-of-center administrations.

But there was another strain in Republicanism, achieving meme-like status in President George H. W. Bush's call for a "kinder, gentler nation" in his presidential campaign of 1988. Bush lauded the "thousand points of light" (and created a foundation bearing that name), individuals who had served their communities in various capacities—*not* as representatives of an intrusive government, but as volunteers. Within the Reagan and Bush Administrations, we occasionally found officials sympathetic to our work. The three-person National Credit Union Administration board included Mrs. Elizabeth Flores Burkhart; the first Latina appointed to the board. She had been deputy treasurer of Reagan's 1980 campaign. The oldest of 13 children from a tiny, rural Texas town, she was gracious and within the limits of her position, helpful to us. (I recall a ceremony with then-Vice President George H.W. Bush at the Old Executive Office Building when she maneuvered me to the front of the room to have my picture taken with him.) But there were limits; Mrs. Burkhart enjoyed little influence within the NCUA board.

Our Road to the White House

Within the Reagan administration, we also encountered a gentleman who seemed to embody "compassionate conservatism." A courtly, concerned gentleman from the administration's Low-Income Opportunity Board, Morgan Doughton, learned about our credit unions' work in advancing self-help among low-income people—which coincided with the White House's interest in strategies to reduce welfare. Doughton encouraged us to prepare a report for the White House on our movement and our policy interests. He had no money to offer us, though. That was not in the Reagan Administration's playbook.

We had no budget for this research effort, but anything that attracted the interest of the White House was bound to attract the attention of the two national credit union organizations, CUNA and NAFCU, which maintained lobbying offices in Washington. Grudgingly, they came up with a few thousand dollars to help our project. They would come to regret it.

We developed a research protocol, prepared questionnaires, and obtained computer assistance from a New York City nonprofit to analyze masses of regulatory data. On December 17, 1986, we presented our report, *An Analysis of the Role of Credit Unions in Capital Formation and Investment in Low- and Moderate-Income Communities*, to the Executive Office of the President. The following April, we brought our national conference to Washington, where we met with Reagan Administration officials in the Indian Treaty Room (ironic!) of the White House's Old Executive Office Building.

In our report, we presented a series of policy recommendations, including a call for the establishment of our "central bank"—our Community Development Central Credit Union—along with the revival of the Community Development Revolving Loan Fund that my predecessors had fought for throughout the 1970s. The two mainstream credit union organizations were not pleased. CUNA opposed our proposal for Community Development Central; the National Association of Federal Credit Unions (NAFCU) opposed special regulatory treatment for CDCUs. They dissociated themselves from our recommendations.

We had succeeded in raising the visibility of our CDCU movement, a major step in our campaign for recognition from regulators, policymakers, funders, and especially, the credit union industry. On the other hand, the project reinforced our status as troublesome credit union outsiders. The mainstream credit union organizations placed a high premium on "speaking with one voice" in Washington; our voice was out of tune.

Although we did not win friends within the credit union industry, there was another, crucial audience for our work. We had spent years trying in vain to make a breakthrough with the Ford Foundation. We made the short trip uptown from our offices at the edge of New York's Wall Street for years of pleasant lunches in their dining room in the famed "ivory tower" of the foundation world, on 42nd Street a block from the United Nations. The Ford Foundation had focused its giving on place-based approaches, especially community development corporations; our approach, targeted to the people who lived in impoverished communities, was not on their radar at the time, nor was our work on credit and banking. But now, with our report, we had acquired some of the "currency" of the foundation world: we had a *study;* we had *data.* We could now speak Ford's language. Ford initially funded our pilot project, aimed at documenting clusters of low-income credit unions in North Carolina, Chicago, Philadelphia, and New York City. Thus began a decades-long history of major investment and grant support from the Ford Foundation that not only strengthened the CDCU movement but helped incubate the CDFI movement.

An "Endangered Species"

Our struggles continued throughout the waning years of the George H. W. Bush Administration. Mergers and liquidations of our credit unions continued; NCUA restricted access to philanthropic capital by terminating the low-income designation of hundreds of credit unions. Arguing that credit unions like ours were an "endangered species," we took our story to Congress. On February 27, 1991, we secured a room in the Rayburn House Office Building for a briefing session on "Preserving Financial Services in Low-Income Communities." It was moderated by our Associate Director, Errol Louis, and included a presentation by our board member, Robert Jackson, CEO of Quitman Country FCU, who explained "how 'non-member deposit restrictions' halt the flow of capital into low-income communities" like his own in the impoverished Mississippi Delta.[38] Some 10 congressional offices were represented, including staff of the chair of the Congressional Black Caucus.

Banks vs. Credit Unions: Credit Union Expansion and "Prompt Corrective Action"

The tide turned in 1993, when Bill Clinton was inaugurated as president. The regulatory pressures on our movement eased, as Clinton installed a liberal Democrat as chairman of the National Credit Union Administration. But the perpetual political battle between credit unions and banks heated up. Banks won a major victory in their attempt to limit the expansive "fields of membership" in which credit unions were permitted to operate.[39] The Supreme Court agreed with the banks that a federal credit union's field of membership could not encompass multiple diverse occupations or other associations. This ruling could have crippled the credit union industry by restricting growth. The credit union industry mobilized to obtain legislation that would circumvent the problem and permit credit union expansion. The campaign was successful, and H.R. 1151—the Credit Union Membership Access Act—was signed into law in August 1998.

It was celebrated as a huge, crucial victory by much of the credit union industry. We in the CDCU movement had mixed feelings about credit union expansion; too often, we had seen large, predominantly white credit unions move onto "our turf" and "cherry-pick" profitable middle-class members within our institutions. But opposing the legislation was not viable; none of us wanted to have banks dictate the future of our cooperative system. However, there were other aspects of the legislation that represented a real threat to our movement.

---

38 Robert Jackson became the first Black state senator since Reconstruction for his district.
39 Federal credit unions are not open to the entire public. Their charters specify groups with "common bonds" or "fields of membership" within which they are authorized to enroll members.

It's About Capital. Always.

The critical issue for our movement was, as always, capital. A credit union's ratio of net worth (equity) to total assets could spell the difference between survival and liquidation.

NCUA summarized the provisions of the new law this way:

> A new net worth standard of 7% of assets will be established for insured credit unions . . . .For credit unions not meeting these standards, progressively more stringent "prompt corrective action" [will be applied]. . . . The lower the credit union's net worth the more stringent the actions become . . . . Administrative actions will apply to credit unions below 4% net worth.

This was a major change. For many decades, credit unions had managed to survive, for better or worse, without rigid capital standards. Those days would be over, effective in 2000. NCUA gained a much stronger, more threatening hand with which to regulate credit unions.

It was no consolation for us that NCUA officials themselves had not necessarily sought the new regime, "Prompt Corrective Action" or PCA. The "villain" was higher up: Congress, which had passed the law. And higher still: it was the assembly of guardians of the global financial system in Basel, Switzerland, that ultimately stood behind the sterner requirements for capital. It was yet another nasty "trickle-down": the smallest financial institutions around the world, like credit unions, inevitably suffered under a system designed primarily with an eye toward constraining powerful large institutions.

NCUA implemented a system that went a long way toward making credit union regulation parallel that of banks. It was easy to foresee the consequences for our low-income credit unions. In vain, I pleaded our case to Congress and the national credit union organizations to exempt low-income credit unions from PCA. I did win some concessions.

Prompted by bank complaints, the legislation limited the percentage of "member business loans" a credit union could carry on its books. Because CDCUs were important providers of loans to local small businesses, especially but not only in communities of color, this was important to their business model. We won "exceptions [to the limits for] credit unions that have a limited income designation or participate in the Community Development Financial Institutions program."

The other technical concession proved crucial—we hoped. As NCUA stated it, "A separate system of prompt corrective action must be developed for 'new credit unions'. . . defined as credit unions that have been in operation for 10 years or less and have less than $10 million in assets."

This was helpful because without greater leniency, there would essentially never be a new credit union created to serve a low-income community. (Even so, very few credit unions of any kind were chartered after 2000.) NCUA's regulation provided relief from the provision that "all federally insured credit unions *with assets of $10 million or more* [emphasis added] must follow generally accepted accounting principles [GAAP]." Generally, this meant that credit unions larger than $10 million required a CPA audit, which could be much costlier than a less extensive review by an accountant.[40]

Thus, the $10 million asset threshold was helpful to our very smallest institutions, disproportionately likely to serve non-white low-income communities, like Black church-based credit unions. It usually did not become contentious—with a major exception that constitutes the case of KAPFCU. By ignoring or overriding the

---

40 As summarized by Michael McCray, "the difference between full accrual accounting (GAAP) and accounting on a cash basis is significant. Cash-basis accounting is simple and straightforward. An institution simply documents how much was spent or received at the time the transaction occurred. Full accrual accounting requires estimates and more extensive record keeping. Accrual accounting attempts to track revenues and expenses when they originate or "accrue" rather than when they are paid (as in a cash basis; see Part Two, Chapter 12).

statutory exemption for small new credit unions, over the express objections of KAPFCU starting in 2007, KAPFCU argued that NCUA exceeded its authority and usurped the prerogatives of the credit union, with devastating consequences to the credit union.

Prompt Corrective Action (PCA) did not come into effect until 2000. In practice, it would ensure that regardless of the administration in charge of NCUA, Democrat or Republican, the tensions between the regulator and the regulated could only increase.

Small Victories: Regulatory Policy

Unable to exempt our credit unions from the rigors of PCA, we turned our attention to those areas of regulatory action that we *could* influence; in particular, the interaction between examiner and credit union. NCUA provides "supervisory letters" and guidance to its examiners. We sought to shape these documents by providing NCUA with data and analysis detailing the economic context of our credit unions and their communities. For example, we demonstrated that although loan delinquency was indeed higher for our credit unions than for the typical "mainstream" credit unions, it did not translate into loan losses at a correspondingly high rate. Our advocacy bore fruit. In February 2005, when NCUA issued a guidance, "Supervising Community Development Credit Unions," that included a white paper "designed to facilitate examiners' understanding and ability to supervise the unique challenges faced by LICUs [low-income credit unions] and CDCUs."

We were pleased; in many ways, we could have written the document ourselves. NCUA enumerated accurately and extensively many of the distinct and difficult conditions affecting our credit unions' members conditions that we had repeatedly emphasized to the agency.

- Unsteady employment (often temporary jobs with long hours)
- Part-time employment with multiple jobs or side businesses
- Unstable residency (often rent or live in public or subsidized housing)

- No health insurance
- Lack of affordable childcare
- Dependence on supplemental security income (SSI) or social security disability (SSDI) benefits
- Prevalence of English as a second language
- Low share account balances
- Need for small dollar loans
- Limited financial resources
- Limited, negative, or no credit history
- A need for labor-intensive services (e.g., money orders, financial education and/or counseling, check cashing).

In our world, that counted as a major victory. But what mattered most was how this guidance was implemented on the ground. In January 2010, NCUA issued to all examiners another official letter, entitled, "Supervising Low Income Credit Unions and Community Development Credit Unions," intended to "provide examiners guidance on issues they might face when supervising low-income credit unions (LICUs) and self-designated community development credit unions (CDCUs)."[41]

The guidance discussed the characteristics, benefits, and unique challenges of our types of credit unions and included an appendix describing available resources. Examiners were also directed to remember that "all federal credit unions have a continuing obligation to meet the financial service needs of people of modest means."

However, our advocacy victories mattered only to the extent that NCUA's supervisory letters actually guided its field examiners. In practice, these official guidances did not always supersede or override

---

41 "Community development credit union" was the term the Federation had adopted for credit unions serving predominantly low-income memberships. Only NCUA's "low-income designation" had official status in making credit unions eligible for non-member deposits and later, secondary capital.

examiners' recommendations to sanction, liquidate, or merge what they saw as "troubled" credit unions. Ultimately, "safety and soundness" trumped communities' financial needs. One credit union reported to me that an examiner walked into a credit union board meeting and expressed his disdain for the "guidance" by flinging it across the table.

The bottom line was this: the ranks of small credit unions, and low-income credit unions in particular, continued to decline. As a colleague from CUNA wrote, "NCUA was dead set to kill off small credit unions. I think we failed every time we tried to get NCUA to spare a small credit union."

Rarely were new credit unions formed to replace them—the regulatory and financial barriers to chartering new credit unions of any type were steep and growing. Credit unions, once a movement, now constituted an industry, which was inexorably consolidating. Today, there are fewer separate credit unions than at any time in almost one hundred years. On average, they are larger and serve more members; more and more provide bank-like services. They are still nonprofit, still cooperatives, still democratically governed. Yet few operate in communities of color.

CHAPTER 8

Before DEI: Reaching the Marginalized

What's In a Name?

For 32 years, I worked for an organization with the unwieldy name of the National Federation of Community Development Credit Unions. There was no snappy acronym—NFCDCU? NatFed? As CEO, I tried to have people recognize us as "The Federation"—but there were others in our arena, especially the Federation of Southern Cooperatives, so that didn't work.

Awkward as it was, I valued the name and what it represented. "Federation": we were an association of autonomous local credit unions, voluntarily joined together to amplify their power at the national level. "Community development"—this distinguished us from all the other types of credit unions and conveyed a positive, aspirational image. Originally, the organization had been known as the federation of "limited Income" credit unions, which communicated constraint and limitation; my predecessors changed it to "community development" in 1974. We changed the logo several times, but we did not manage to settle on a compelling brand.

When I joined the Federation in 1980, we had about 100 member credit unions out of a universe of nearly 20,000 institutions—about 0.5%. After we lost our federal funding in 1982, and with it much of our ability to provide services, our membership dropped by half. How were we to increase our impact and reach more communities of color and low-income people? Over my 30 years as the Federation's leader, we pursued multiple strategies:

- Organizing new credit unions
- Connecting with unaffiliated peers
- Building bridges within the credit union industry

Organizing New Credit Unions: Spreading the Credit Union Gospel

By the time I joined the Federation, the organizing fervor that characterized the early credit union movement had long since ebbed. For decades, the ranks of credit unions had grown dramatically, spurred by organizers with a near-religious zeal who barnstormed the country, organizing new credit unions wherever they found a handful of like-minded people of "modest means" in need of access to credit they could not obtain from banks. The momentum was interrupted but not ended by World War II. By 1955, there were more than 16,000 credit unions; by 1969, there were more than 23,000.[42]

But from the 1980s, more credit unions merged or were dissolved than the number of new credit unions that were formed each year—a trend that has continued to this day. A debate emerged: were credit unions a "movement" or an "industry?" There were fewer, but larger credit unions; their collective assets and membership increased dramatically.[43] But the overall growth of the credit union movement did not solve the problem of those who were left behind. Many small credit unions serving low-income communities and people of color disappeared; the larger surviving credit unions rarely filled the gap. The national and state credit union organizations, which for decades had vigorously supported the organizing of new credit unions, largely

---

[42] During the 1960s, there were 9,992 new credit unions formed; in the first decade of the 2000s, 73 new credit unions; by the 2010s, 22 formed. See, Luis G. Dopico and Taylor C. Nelms, "What Is Old – and New – about Credit Union Mergers?," *Credit Union Times*, November 22, 2019, https://www.cutimes.com/2019/11/22/what-is-old-and-new-about-credit-union-mergers/?slreturn=20231130155310.

[43] As of December 31, 2022, there were 4,760 federally insured credit unions with 135.3 million members. https://ncua.gov/newsroom/press-release/2023/ncua-releases-2022-annual-report. Privately insured credit unions are not included.

retreated from fostering new institutions. Thanks to liberalized federal rules in the 1980s, it became easier for people to join established credit unions than to start new ones, a laborious process that often was abandoned by community groups daunted by the burdensome chartering process.

Why was an organization and a mission like ours necessary?

In fact, the need in low-income communities for credit unions was growing in the early 1980s. Blatant "redlining" was less prevalent, although it had not disappeared. But fueled by sky-high prime interest rates—up to 21%—banks were upscaling their fees and "pruning" their branch networks to eliminate less profitable outlets, especially in low-income neighborhoods. Communities protested, and politicians began to take notice. The convergence of these trends created a need and an opportunity for the Federation.

In January 1984, midway through my fellowship year studying banking and finance at Columbia University, I was invited to address a conference of 200 bankers, regulators, community advocates, and foundations hosted by the New York Federal Reserve Bank. I asserted that mainstream banks were leaving low-income neighborhoods for good, and that community development credit unions—CDCUs—could and should fill the gap. If the government was not inclined to *force* banks to serve low-balance, small-loan customers, it should subsidize the nonprofit credit unions that *would* serve them. It was a logical argument, but with little experiential grounding. We needed proof of concept.

Four months later, I received a call that would change the trajectory of our movement. Manufacturers Hanover Trust, the last bank standing in a neighborhood of 55,000 people, had announced plans to close its Lower East Side branch at Avenue B and East Third Street—the heart of "Alphabet City," a famed neighborhood that was home to thousands of low-income people, including many immigrants as well as struggling artists and musicians. Community organizations protested, claiming the bank was abandoning the neighborhood just as it was beginning to make progress against the rampant drug trade. They wanted to find another bank to take MHT's place, but none were interested. Someone, somehow learned about credit unions, and a local housing activist contacted us.

I knew little about the mechanics of credit unions. But I knew something about organizing: for a decade, I had helped organize multiple food cooperatives and even a credit union. I saw myself in the historic tradition of the earlier credit union organizers like the legendary Dora Maxwell.[44] I became the Federation's evangelist-in-chief, explaining the concept to community groups eager to achieve a measure of economic empowerment by starting a credit union. What I lacked in operational expertise, I made up for with passion for the effort. Crucially, in the fall of 1983, I had hired Annie Vamper, an experienced credit union manager and former examiner who became the advisor-in-chief, teaching groups what it took to run a credit union.

Over 1984-86, we worked intensively with neighborhood organizers on New York City's Lower East Side, preparing business plans, providing board training, and assisting with negotiations with the $80 billion MHT bank that, under the pressure of the Community Reinvestment Act (CRA), agreed to provide start-up capital for the aspiring Lower East Side People's Federal Credit Union. The newborn credit union opened the boarded-up doors of the abandoned bank building on May 1, 1986, with a ribbon-cutting by Borough President and future New York City Mayor David Dinkins.

The Lower East Side People's FCU would become our "flagship," the living demonstration that a community development credit union could succeed and replace a bank.[45] After the victory on the Lower

---

44 Dora Maxwell (1897-1985) was credited with organizing hundreds of credit unions. The credit union movement honors her with a social action award named after her.
45 In 2021, 35 years later, the credit union had 8,700 members, $82 million in assets, and branches in East Harlem and Staten Island, as well as its headquarters on Avenue B and East 3rd Street.

East Side, other neighborhood groups contacted us for organizing assistance. The message of economic empowerment was compelling: a CDCU was a vehicle to win community control over the cash that flowed through poor neighborhoods, only to be "exported" to absentee owners and big corporations. We helped charter credit unions in the Bronx and for a citywide housing organization on the West Side of Chicago and for a Native American community on the North Side, as well as in Texas, Nebraska, and Vermont. All were predominantly low-income; all except Vermont were in communities of color.

But perhaps the most dramatic organizing initiative, and the one with the sharpest racial implications, was played out in South Central Los Angeles. It began as a comedy of errors. In 1988, Annie and I were separately contacted by competing groups interested in starting an expansive, community-wide credit union. We discovered the potential conflict only after arriving in Los Angeles. Which of these two Black community groups would we work with? Visiting one neighborhood group, we spoke to "Bill," an easy-going, welcoming man, who casually informed us that there would be no problem, as he opened his desk drawer to show us a handgun.

We began to sweat. Fortunately, we were able to divide up and speak with both groups, with the help of a long-time ally from the National Economic Development and Law Center, who had also been called to help. To our great relief, the competing groups decided to join forces. That night, as Annie and I drove to our hotel near the USC campus, we heard a series of loud sounds. "Was that what I think it was?" I asked her.

"Yes, gunshots," she answered.

We worked for two years to help prepare a charter application. It was rejected by the National Credit Union Administration on the grounds that the expansive proposed "field of membership" of South Central was too large, that it did not constitute a "common bond." Then, on April 29, 1992, South Central erupted in days of violence, outrage prompted by the acquittal of officers charged with brutalizing

Rodney King, which was captured on video and circulated worldwide.

NCUA reconsidered its rejection. Within months, it approved a charter for the South Central People's Federal Credit Union with boundaries corresponding almost exactly to the curfew lines that had been drawn around the neighborhood at the time of the uprising. That fall, I jammed in a car with a few of the credit union organizers for a two-hour drive from Los Angeles to San Diego, where the head of NCUA ceremonially presented a charter to the group.

The South Central People's FCU survived only a few years. But in 1994, another credit union we helped organize in Los Angeles with the help of Episcopal Relief and Development was chartered: the diocese-wide Episcopal Community Federal Credit Union, which continues to serve a predominantly Latinx and Black membership with nearly $7 million in assets.

Connecting: Credit Unions and the Black Church

Although we helped organize a mini-wave of new credit unions in the 1980s, we were swimming against a strong current. We could never add credit unions faster than they were being lost to the movement. The War on Poverty of the 1960s was gone and was not coming back. Many credit unions tied to the network of anti-poverty Community Action Agencies were gone. The loss of anti-poverty credit unions in Black neighborhoods was particularly painful because their membership was generally community-wide. But churches, the time-tested pillars of the Black community, remained and became a focus of the Federation's outreach in the 1990s.

Many Black churches served as economic as well as spiritual anchor institutions for their communities. During the decades of de jure and de facto segregation, hundreds of Black churches organized credit unions to provide loans that parishioners could not get from white-owned banks. Credit unions were economic self-help, and they often were recognized as "ministries" of their churches. Some ministers became "evangelists" for credit unions, encouraging the formation of credit unions as their careers took them from one congregation to another.

In 1990, we initiated our decades-long outreach to Black faith-based credit unions with a pilot project funded by Trinity Church, our neighbor on Wall Street in New York City. Trinity's focus was on church credit unions in New York City. The Ford Foundation became interested in this work, and in 1991, they gave us a grant to expand our program nationally and beyond Black churches to other faith-based institutions.

I can't claim to have developed a strategic plan to engage church-based credit unions, nor did I fully anticipate the energy and enthusiasm our outreach would generate. One cold, rainy morning in March 1992, we traveled to a midtown Manhattan church that had agreed to host our First National Church Credit Union Conference. I expected a handful of local credit unions to participate, along with a few national invitees. But as I reached the church, I was greeted by a representative of a credit union who had traveled from Baltimore, as well as others who had traveled from across the country to participate—150 people in all. Our keynote speaker was a nationally renowned African American leader in community economic development: Rev. Floyd Flake, congressman from Queens, New York, and the pastor of a mega-church, The Greater Allen A.M.E. Cathedral of New York in Jamaica, Queens. Over six feet tall, with piercing hazelnut eyes, intense, powerful, and no-nonsense in his demeanor, he was at the same time warm and extremely accessible to our members. He elevated our event, exciting our members and reinforcing the message that we might have the capacity to make an impact in Washington. An elder statesman and ecumenical leader, he was adept in dealing both with Democrats and Republicans in order to wield the levers of government to benefit low-income communities and community-based organizations.

Black, and to a lesser extent Latinx, faith-based credit unions played a growing role in the Federation over the course of the decade.

We established a national advisory committee that included some of our church credit union leaders as well as leaders and scholars of national Black denominational groups. We held national faith-based conferences in Cleveland in 1994 and in Nashville, headquarters of the National Baptist Convention, in 1996. We published a newsletter called *Church Connections* and compiled a database of faith-based credit unions. In 1995, we published a guide, *Faithful Stewardship*, which explored some of the issues specific to Black church/credit union relations. In particular, we discussed the delicate balance inherent in these partnerships. Although the credit union was often embraced as a component of, or embodiment of, the church's economic ministry, it was a distinct legal entity. Some pastors took a hands-off approach instead of promoting it among the parishioners, and their credit unions languished. On the other hand, problems sometimes arose when a pastor was *too* close to the credit union—for example, by influencing it to make loans outside its guidelines. Some church credit unions failed to thrive because members of the congregation feared the loss of privacy if others learned about their personal finances.

The predominantly Black credit unions of the War on Poverty were typically neighborhood-wide. But structural, social, and demographic characteristics limited the reach and impact of many Black church-based credit unions. Their charters were typically limited to members of the congregation, employees, and others closely associated with the church. It was possible to seek a charter expansion, but to serve the broader community, a church credit union would have to satisfy regulators that it had the necessary capacity. However, many were trapped in a vicious circle of smallness, with limited services. In addition, some lacked motivation; they were content with being insular, tight-knit cooperatives. That may appear anomalous today, but it very much resembled how most early credit unions operated in the United States and elsewhere.

For our movement, with its commitment to community

development, it was frustrating: the *need* for church credit unions, along with the *potential,* was huge. In New York, the stunted growth of some church credit unions was especially frustrating. We saw historic, politically influential African American churches with tiny credit unions sustained by a handful of dedicated volunteers. A prime example of squandered potential was the credit union associated with Congressman Floyd Flake's church. The church was huge, and the scope of the projects it launched—housing, small business, a school—was impressive. But the credit union remained small, and eventually went out of existence.

There were important, if too few, exceptions to this scenario. One shining example was the Faith Community United Credit Union in Cleveland, which originated with a single church, Cleveland's Second Mount Sinai Baptist Church in 1952. By 1990, it had become a community-wide institution on the East Side of Cleveland, acquiring a bank branch building as a result of Community Reinvestment Act negotiations. More recently, I was inspired by the example in Chicago of a network of predominantly Black church credit unions that recently celebrated its tenth anniversary. By the conventional wisdom, these tiny credit unions with assets of a few hundred thousand dollars each should have disappeared by now. But they formed a thriving coalition of credit unions of various denominations to share ideas and resources.

As significant as the expansion of the Federation's membership, our outreach to Black churches led to the emergence of a generation of leaders for the Federation. From 2000 through my departure from the Federation in 2012, except for two years, all our chairpersons were African American women, and two of the three came specifically from credit unions that had originated in Black churches. Mrs. Rita Haynes came from Faith Community United Credit Union in Cleveland, and Mrs. Eunice J. Rogers came from the NRS Community Development FCU in Birmingham, Alabama; Mrs. Lynda Milton came from Houston Teamsters FCU. They helped us heal after our internal conflicts of the 1990s and later, to navigate the external challenges of the new millennium, from Y2K, to 9/11, to the Great Recession.

Today, in the wake of Black Lives Matter, there is evidence of new energy among some Black church credit unions, helped in part by the awakened interest in "banking Black." The efforts of my successors at Inclusiv have energized and brought new resources to Black church credit unions.

Building the Latino Credit Union Connection

Our faith-based initiative was not exclusively targeted to Black credit unions; we had member Latinx church-affiliated credit unions in Southern California, South Texas, and the Northeast, especially. But the enthusiastic response among Black credit unions prompted us to initiate a broader effort targeting Latinx communities.

In 1995, we initiated a preliminary effort to organize a Latino CDCU Network. We already had one important human resource on board. I had hired Ignacio Esteban to be the Federation's representative at CUNA's offices in Madison, Wisconsin. He came to us from our member credit union in Apopka, Florida, that predominantly served migrant and seasonal farmworkers. Fully bilingual and with frontline experience working in a credit union, he was a valuable addition to our team.

At our annual meeting in 1996, we held our Foro Latino, the first Spanish-language credit union event at any national credit union gathering in the United States. Three years later, during our twenty-fifth anniversary year of 1999, we held the First Latino Credit Union Conference on U.S. soil, a high-profile event in Texas, coordinated by our Program Officer Deyanira Del Rio. We attracted several prominent credit union officials, but the industry as a whole still was paying scant attention to the Latinx population, even though it was growing steadily through immigration from Mexico, Central America, and South America. We advocated with CUNA Mutual to develop loan forms in Spanish, which would have greatly assisted credit union members who were not comfortable with legalistic English-language loan documents. However, it was not yet ready to undertake the expense and labor required to get state-by-state approval for Spanish-language legal documents.

The 2000 census changed attitudes in the credit union industry. It documented the rise in the Latinx population, including in Southern states like North Carolina and Georgia. It became increasingly obvious that there was an underserved market with a pressing need and pent-up demand. In North Carolina, for example, immigrant workers were largely unbanked. As a result, many carried cash or kept it (sometimes quite literally) "under the mattress."

The birth of a new credit union in Durham, North Carolina, in 2000 was a landmark event. The Latino Community Credit Union (Cooperativa Latino) was organized "as a grassroots response to a wave of robberies and muggings of Latino immigrants in Durham, North Carolina." Formed with the assistance of Self-Help Credit Union, El Centro Hispano, and the North Carolina State Employees' Credit Union, the Latino Community Credit Union signified the growing prominence of immigrant and Latinx populations in places where they had previously been invisible. It grew faster than any new CDCU in our history, adding a dozen branches around North Carolina and tens of thousands of members (not only Latinx immigrants).[46] That credit union changed the paradigm: it became nationally—and even internationally—renowned as the standard for a financial institution serving immigrants, many of whom had no or bad experience with banks in their home countries. Its CEO, Luis Pastor, born in Spain, was an increasingly sought-after voice nationally for the issues and needs of immigrant communities.

Our membership had always included credit unions serving predominantly Latinx communities, especially in the Northeast and Southwest. But our outreach efforts from the late 1990s increased

---

46 As of 2021, its assets approached $700 million, and its membership topped 100,000.

their numbers and visibility within our membership. Some of our new members, especially in the West, served broad communities and were considerably larger than our historically Black-run credit unions. There were few overt manifestations of tension between the Black and Latinx credit unions. But as I later learned from board members, there was indeed an uneasy undercurrent of resentment as the Latinx population in the U.S. and Latinx credit unions rose in prominence.

At each annual meeting we provided breakout sessions and forums for credit unions serving Latinx populations. In 2004, the Federation celebrated our thirtieth anniversary by bringing our annual conference to San Juan, Puerto Rico. Several members grumbled that it was some kind of vacation "junket," but it was far from that: it was a recognition of the growing importance of Latinx credit unions in our membership, as well as a deliberate effort to engage the large number of credit unions and *cooperativas* on the island.[47] In 2006, we added a staff member who would spearhead the Federation's outreach to Latinx credit unions. Pablo DeFilippi, a Chilean immigrant, had come through a Federation training program and later became the CEO of our "flagship" Lower East Side People's Federal Credit Union in New York. We hired him as our representative in Madison, Wisconsin, where he had worked for the World Council of Credit Unions. With his leadership, we worked to address services and issues for our credit unions serving immigrants, including international money remittances and acceptance of Individual Tax Information Numbers (ITIN) to meet federal customer identification requirements.

Disability Outreach

It was not only racial and ethnic groups who were excluded from the mainstream banking system. In the first years of the new millennium,

---

47 It would take the disaster of Hurricane Maria in 2017 to greatly expand the collaboration between Inclusiv (as the National Federation was then known) and the credit union movement of Puerto Rico.

we met the dedicated leadership of the National Disability Institute (NDI), including Michael Morris and Johnette Hartnett, who educated us about one of the most financially marginalized sectors of American society: persons with disabilities. We learned about the numerous, often counter-productive financial and social constraints on the disability population. The poverty rate of persons with disabilities is sky high; many people with physical, cognitive, psychological, or other disabilities are unable to find employment at a living wage. Those who do may face regulations and rules that restrict them from earning income or building savings. To exceed government limits could be a matter of life and death, since it could entail the loss of critical Medicaid or other medical benefits. The proportion of people with disabilities who are unbanked is even higher than among the general population. Unsurprisingly, people of color are disproportionately affected. Early in the new century, we began a formal collaboration with the National Disability Institute, seeking to break through the issue-specific silos in which many advocacy organizations work. Working with NDI, we attempted to educate policymakers about the poverty/disability/financial exclusion nexus. Disability issues were poverty issues; banking issues were disability issues. Government asset and income limitations were (and are) major issues: restricting people to the most minimal savings and employment income intensifies the cycle of poverty, often confining them to part-time, lowly paid, or no work at all and elevating the daunting barriers to economic self-sufficiency. "Logical" regulations with the ostensible aim of targeting government assistance to the neediest sometimes has perverse, counterproductive consequences.

Reinforcing our connection, at our gala thirtieth anniversary conference in Puerto Rico, our keynote speaker was Kathy Martinez, who was born blind and whom I met in her role as Assistant Secretary for Disability Employment Policy at the Department of Labor. For several years, I served on the advisory board of NDI, succeeded by our staff member, Pam Owens. With NDI, we developed and obtained funding for a pilot project to connect persons with disabilities to positions in New Jersey credit unions. After my retirement from the Consumer Financial Protection Bureau, I consulted with my long-time colleagues at the National Disability Institute to develop initiatives for CDFIs to expand their services to persons with disabilities.

Early in the 2000s, we forged another connection with disability advocates. One day, Charlie Hammerman visited the Federation's office to learn about CDFIs and the CDFI Fund. I informed him that the Fund was a potential source of equity capital for financial institutions that served "other targeted populations"—that is, segments that were poor but were not defined by racial, ethnic, or geographic characteristics. It was clear to me that he could make a compelling case for a CDFI that served this "other targeted population." Charlie, who had a financial background, managed an incipient fund, and had a personal connection to disability issues, pursued the case and ultimately succeeded. In recent years, a portion of the CDFI appropriation has been designated for institutions serving persons with disabilities.

Over my long career, I never met advocates more passionate and dedicated than those who served the disability community. It is gratifying to see that CDFIs serving the disability community have now formed their own formal coalition.

Credit Unions and Youth

In our effort to expand the boundaries of our movement, we targeted one more population segment for special outreach: youth. Spurred initially by one of our credit unions with a successful youth program, we raised foundation funding to promote pilot credit union programs throughout our membership. We down-streamed grants to credit unions from Brooklyn to Mississippi to Seattle, mostly serving Black and Latinx young people. We convened special youth tracks at our annual conferences. It was eye-opening and inspiring for us to see young people, predominantly those of color, showcasing their learning.

One credit union youth group from San Francisco's predominantly Latinx Mission District made a particularly strong impression, demonstrating to us how children as young as 10 (sometimes even younger) not only learned about personal finance, but also equaled their elders in their understanding of credit union philosophy and operations. This youth project subsequently went on to establish an independent organization that has grown far beyond its original credit union sponsor. Led by Margaret Libby, who began as an AmeriCorps*VISTA volunteer for the Federation, MyPath has become a nationally-renowned nonprofit promoting financial education and economic mobility for low-income working youth.[48]

Changing the Brand—Keeping the Essence

In 2018, years after I departed the organization, my successor, Cathie Mahon, led the rebranding of the National Federation of Community Development Credit Unions as Inclusiv (no "e"). I was wistful—something of our, and my, history was lost. But undeniably, the name was easier to communicate, and most importantly, it conveyed the unchanged essence of what we had always been about: inclusion of people and communities who had been abandoned or ill-served by the mainstream banking system. Inclusiv is no longer the association of small, marginalized credit unions that I had joined decades before. It now boasts more than 400 member credit unions, with nearly 17

---

[48] While we at the Federation were unaware of it at the time, KAPFCU and its parent organization were particularly engaged with serving young people. Most of the fraternity's members joined as college-age students. The fraternity's Kappa League also provided significant youth outreach and development activities for high school students. Kappa Alpha Psi and KAPFCU created their CARE Program (Credit Abuse Resistance Education) to help young people become responsible with credit as well as their GLAD Program (Greeks Learning to Avoid Debt), a financial literacy training targeted toward college students. Kappa Alpha Psi Fraternity gave free memberships in KAPFCU for all new fraternity initiates. As a result, the median age for KAPFCU membership was less than 25 years of age—in contrast to the median age of 47 for all credit unions nationwide (10 years older than the U.S. median), a source of concern for an industry that worries about an aging membership.

million members and total assets of nearly $250 billion. Nearly 100 of its members each have more than $500 million in assets. Whereas the National Federation's membership represented a scant 1% or 2% of all credit unions during my time, Inclusiv's membership today accounts for about 8% of the entire credit union industry, which has consolidated to about 5,000 institutions, down 75% from its historic peak of more than 20,000 institutions. More than 400 credit unions, the majority of them Inclusiv members, are now certified as mission-focused Community Development Financial Institutions, following the path that the National Federation of CDCUs opened in 1994.

For many years, the National Federation of CDCUs was the lone organizational torchbearer for diversity, equity, and inclusion within the credit union movement. Inclusiv has gained allies in the African American Credit Union Coalition (AACUC), the National Association of Latino Credit Unions and Professionals (NLCUP), the National Disability Finance Coalition, and the African American Alliance of CDFI CEOs.

CHAPTER 9

The Conflicts Within: Increasing Success/Racial Tension

Throughout the 1980s, when the Federation was a struggling, marginal organization, the elected board of directors, which always had a majority of people of color, was basically content for me to develop ideas, start programs, and do what was required to keep the lights on. But from 1990, the stakes got bigger as we raised millions of dollars in investments and raised our profile in the credit union world. The decade would present the gravest test of my role as the white leader of a predominantly non-white organization.

Moving on Up

Purely by chance, I learned of a unique real estate project that would bring us the trappings of respectability. The Wall Street crash of Black Monday in 1987 accentuated the decline of the one-time hub of finance. Building occupancy plunged. One developer took advantage to assemble a tax-enhanced deal to transform a Depression-era building on Wall Street into the Association Center for national and international nonprofits. We got a spectacular deal: one year rent-free, with a major allowance for remodeling the space and a 15-year, below-market lease. In 1992, we moved from a cramped, dilapidated space—suitable for a "movement-type" organization—into a suite of offices with East River views for everyone. Now, literally as well as figuratively, we were on the margins of Wall Street—the last building before the highway and the East River. Six months after we moved in, a December northeaster sent flood waters from the river up the street and into our lobby, marooning us until the tide went out—our first experience of climate change. The relations between the elected board of directors and staff would change, as well.

A Warrior's Rise to Power

Toward the end of the Reagan years, we held our annual conference in Washington. Ironically for us, we held our plenary session at the National Republican Club on Capitol Hill. Modest as it was—100 participants—it was our biggest turnout since 1981. The National Credit Union Administration (NCUA) sent an administrator to meet with us. One of our members—"Evelyne," whom I knew only slightly—rose to make a speech sharply critical of the agency. She was smart, charismatic, and fearless in confronting power, and she created an approving stir among our members.

Evelyne came from a small credit union that had formed decades earlier in a Black Baptist church and expanded into the community. Years before, she told us, she had been part of a "women's auxiliary" of Elijah Muhammad's Nation of Islam. She explained that she left because she didn't accept the lesser roles assigned to women in the movement. Nonetheless, she explained, she had learned valuable lessons from the experience, becoming acutely attuned to power dynamics and "reading the room."

Our membership was still quite small, and Evelyne was elected from our sparse New England region. She rose in a few years to be elected vice chairwoman of the Federation's board. She, and we, expected that she would soon rise to the chair. But the next step proved bitter and divisive.

Our white chairman, "Ken," had served since 1985, the years when our very survival was in doubt. After years of struggle, he took particular pride in leading us through the negotiation of our landmark alliance in 1991 with the Credit Union National Association (CUNA), as described in chapter 5. There was an unwritten understanding that Ken would step down in 1992, after the alliance was in place, making way for Evelyne to assume the chair as the first Black and first woman to occupy that position. But before the board election, Ken decided that he wanted to remain for one more year to enjoy the fruits of his accomplishment—our enhanced status and "respectability" in the credit union industry. This forced a contested election, putting him in opposition to Evelyne. His action was tone-deaf, and it brought tensions out into the open. To Evelyne and others, his action seemed to shout, "double cross."

The board held its election for chairman in a small hotel room at our annual conference. Ken appointed a non-Board member—a white male college professor—to collect and count the secret ballots. He did so, promptly announced that Ken had won, and then, stunningly, walked out of the room carrying the paper ballots in his pocket. Evelyne felt multiply betrayed, first by Ken's decision to stand for election, then by the manner in which the election was conducted. I could hardly blame her. The following year, she did assume the chair, serving until tensions with the board, with the membership, and with staff reached an unsustainable level in 1999, threatening to tear apart the organization.

The Brewing Conflict

Some change in the board/staff relationship was inevitable. For the decade when we were fighting for our survival, I had operated under chairmen—one Puerto Rican, one white—who were content to let me run our marginal organization. Now, with greater industry recognition, with millions in social investment under management, and with a shared victory in the creation of the CDFI Fund, the Federation was worth fighting for, and about. I was a (white) executive director serving under a (Black) chairwoman, who made her presence and demands felt in policy, program operations, member relations, and crucially, in finance. Certainly, there was a racial component to the friction between us. But some of the problem was systemic—underdeveloped governance (not unusual in a small, relatively new organization), reflected in a board/staff role confusion and inadequate or easily transgressed boundaries. In the end, a series of conflicts of interest nearly destroyed us. Some were about money; others were not.

In 1982, we established our Capitalization Program as a vehicle to raise funds to reinvest in our member credit unions. The Federation was not only a membership organization, but a publicly supported 501(c)(3) charity, which was essential to raising grants and investments. Our status required us to insulate the organization from self-dealing or favoritism. So, when we established our Capitalization Program, we placed decision-making under an "arm's length" committee, primarily composed of outside advisors who had no financial or other conflicting interest in our members.

After Evelyne became board chair, she claimed an ex officio, non-voting role on our Capitalization Committee. That was within her rights. But when her own credit union applied to the committee for loans and grants, she needed to recuse herself from the committee's deliberations. She left the room for the vote, but nonetheless, influenced the committee to award her credit union tens of thousands of dollars in grants and a high-risk, long-term secondary capital loan of $250,000. At a minimum, the optics were uncomfortable; years later, the consequences would prove to be far worse.

Other issues threatened the Federation even more gravely. Evelyne stepped into a regulatory conflict, embroiling our members in North Carolina, home to the largest, oldest concentration of Black community credit unions in the country. They were a crucial portion of our membership, and they had a state network of their own, the North Carolina Minority Support Center, which the Federation had helped incubate. In January 1999, the National Credit Union Administration liquidated one of the Center's members and ours, the allegedly insolvent 63-year-old Bricks Community Federal Credit Union.

It was my job, not a board member's, to lead our regulatory advocacy. It was typically a frustrating and futile job. We could sometimes delay or mitigate NCUA's actions, but we won few outright victories; the regulator had access to information that we did not, and generally the courts made any challenge all but unwinnable.

Evelyne took it upon herself to lead the response to NCUA,

specifically charging the regulatory agency with racism (notwithstanding the fact that the liquidation was initiated by the only Black regional director of NCUA). It was true that NCUA often acted harshly or with little concern for the communities affected, especially Black and other minority communities. But the North Carolina Minority Support Center was furious with Evelyne's intervention, including specifically her attack on NCUA and the (Black) Regional Director for racism. As the Center's chairman wrote to us, "This position was uncalled for and far from the most productive way to help a troubled institution . . . . [especially] given that the additional 14 [Black credit unions] are the ones which must deal with the residue of this tactic."

The Center reproached her for "scapegoating" it, implying that the Center was somehow "complicit" in setting the credit union up for failure. It demanded to know whether Evelyne's intervention was within the bounds of her role as Federation chairwoman; whether she was authorized by our board; whether we supported her actions, including financially; and what "corrective action" we were prepared to take.

We faced the disastrous possibility that the largest single grouping of Black credit unions in our membership would leave us unless our board took action. Other members, as well, complained that they would leave the Federation unless something was done to contain Evelyne. It is not an exaggeration to say that the future of our organization, and our movement, was at stake.

Meanwhile, yet another conflict was bringing us to a showdown. Evelyne's credit union had an exemplary youth program. It inspired us, we promoted it, and we obtained a major grant to replicate it nationally. We employed a staff member to manage the program and divided the grant money to nearly a dozen credit unions from Bedford-Stuyvesant to Seattle. We allotted a portion of the grant to Evelyne's own credit union, providing that they assisted with certain training and development tasks for the youth project. But after a while, they began to demand a larger share of the grant (even though they had not performed as our arrangement required). Sadly, this program to empower young people in low-income, minority communities became so contentious for the Federation that we took the unprecedented step of *turning down* a major foundation grant because we feared reputational risk.

In 1999, the conflict escalated. Evelyne's credit union threatened to take legal action against the Federation, asserting ownership of their "unique" youth credit union concept (even though youth credit union programs date back to the early twentieth century). We assembled our national board for a crisis meeting in Saint Louis. It is hard to imagine a more bitter, divisive scene. To our disbelief, Evelyne asserted that she—as the manager of the credit union *and* as the chair of the Federation—had no conflict of interest. She continued to take her credit union's side, berating our board. There were heated, virulent exchanges; at one point, the board sent both Evelyne and me into the hallway.

Given Evelyne's refusal to acknowledge her multiplying conflicts of interest, the board decided to vote on her removal as chairwoman (not as a board member, which would have required a vote of the membership). The decision would be made at a follow-up meeting at our headquarters in New York City—scant weeks before our upcoming twenty-fifth anniversary conference, the largest in our history.

I flew home from a board meeting in Saint Louis drained physically and emotionally. Arriving late at night in Brooklyn, I walked into a glass door in my house and lacerated my thigh. Bleeding profusely, I did not have the energy to go down the block to the hospital for treatment.

Showdown

The board of directors traveled to New York for the decisive meeting at our offices on May 6-7, 1999. I was not a board member and was not in the room for the crucial vote; the Federation had always maintained separation to ensure that governance was the sole province of the member-elected board of directors. I could not and did not lobby directly for her removal. On the other hand, I could scarcely claim neutrality when various directors and members brought their complaints to me. Evelyne had no doubt what side I was on. At one point, I was asked to retrieve a corporate document that Evelyne had demanded. As I was looking through a drawer in the file room, I turned around to find her literally in my face. She had narrowly lost the vote. She bitterly charged me with orchestrating her removal as chairwoman. I stammered that it was a board action, not mine. That was literally true, but I had not discouraged the board members from taking action and I was not displeased by the outcome. The board included 10 African Americans, four whites, two Latinx members, and one Asian member; of the 17, nine were women and eight were men. I never learned the exact breakdown of the votes, but clearly, they did not break strictly along racial lines; at least one white member told me he could not bring himself to vote to remove a Black woman, regardless of her actions. I subsequently learned that Evelyne blamed the vote to impeach her on the Black men on the board who she thought lacked the courage to stand with her.

Evelyne went public, taking her complaints to a credit union publication. An investigative reporter eagerly pursued her charges: Evelyne's erroneous assertions about the funding of our youth credit union project, her misleading claims of a lack of financial accountability, and her claims that she was being removed because she was "outspoken" on behalf of credit unions. Amid preparing for the largest event in our history, we had to engage in damage control. The board refuted the assertions about youth program funding, pointing to Evelyne's conflict of interest, and flatly denied that Evelyne was "removed for being outspoken on behalf of our credit unions." The reporter demanded access to our funders (which we were not obliged to provide) and hounded them for incriminating information (of which there was none).[49]

---

49 Years later, after Evelyne was convicted of federal charges, the reporter sheepishly apologized.

A few short weeks remained before our gala Twenty-Fifth Anniversary Conference, June 17-20, 1999, at the rebuilt World Trade Center's Vista Hotel, which terrorists had bombed in 1993. It was the highest profile event in our history. We had conducted a year-long fundraising campaign and secured "A-list" speakers, including Ralph Nader, Rev. Jesse Jackson, Sr., a representative from the Ford Foundation, the head of the National Credit Union Administration, and others. We had record registration of 500 members, supporters, and funders. Evelyne spread rumors that she would attend the business meeting of the membership with a crew of her former colleagues from the Nation of Islam. We took her threats seriously and hired security. She let it be known that she was going to introduce a docket of charges that would result in the membership rising up to fire me on the spot.

I felt unbearable tension. If the board and membership endorsed Evelyne's made-up charges against me—or even if they only demanded that she return as chairwoman—it was clear to me that it would be untenable for me to remain in the organization that had been central to my life for nearly 20 years.

High Noon

The three-day anniversary conference began inauspiciously with a convocation at historic Trinity Church at the corner of Broadway and Wall Street. Thereafter, we moved to the Vista Hotel at the World Trade Center for two days of keynote speakers, panels, and workshops. The conference was scheduled to conclude on Saturday night with the official business meeting of the Federation's membership. It was there that Evelyne would bring her docket of charges—still unknown to us—that would cause the members to remove me.

A small but telling drama played out before the membership meeting. Reverend Jesse Jackson Sr. made a belated and brief appearance. We gathered a few dozen members in the hallway for an impromptu dialogue. As we stood in a semicircle, Rev. Jackson walked around the front row, greeting people. He walked straight past Evelyne, who was smiling in expectation of recognition that never came. Reading between the lines, we concluded that Jackson, a savvy politician, had learned of Evelyne's fall from grace.

Late Saturday afternoon, the annual membership meeting began. The rumored contingent of Evelyne's former colleagues did not appear; instead, there were a half-dozen of her friends, family, and supporters, who were orderly and dignified. As I was preparing to walk into the meeting room, two Black board members of the Federation assured me that they "had my back"—precious reassurance at a precarious time for me.

Sadly, the spectacle was embarrassing more than anything else. Evelyne had chosen "Phillip," a board member who was a legendary Black credit union organizer from the South, to present her case. He began to read her assertions from an impressive-looking binder—but the charges were so confusing and groundless that our board officers responded that they simply didn't know what Phillip was talking about. In the end, the presentation just faded out. The day was getting late, and attendees were eager to head to the pier on the East River for our two-hour cruise around lower Manhattan. One member, an outspoken white woman who headed a West Coast credit union, stood up and declared that the members had "had enough"—it was time to move on. Only a few hands were raised in support of Evelyne. Her action to remove me failed utterly—case closed.

After the meeting was adjourned, I hurried from the Vista Hotel to the South Street Seaport, where the boat awaited us for a celebratory cruise around lower Manhattan. I was joined by my wife and my 81-year-old mother. As the boat was about to depart, my daughter Dana ran across the pier to join us, still in her high school prom dress. We sailed off into the Manhattan evening. I was liberated from the crushing burden of anxiety, dread, and anger that I had borne for months.

Aftermath

We tried to shield staff from the bitter internal conflict that primarily enveloped the board and me, but they certainly would have seen the scenes that unfolded at our membership meeting. Some knew much of what was going on, others less. Some later told me that they saw Evelyne as a powerful, talented person who went astray and did not use her powers for the greater good. They were not asked to take sides, and they did not. I expect that their primary emotion was relief that they were free to do the mission-driven work that had brought them to the Federation. No one left. We moved on.

As for the board of directors, they carried on anxiously for the year after our anniversary meeting, lest Evelyne tried to run for the board again in 2000 and try to reclaim power. She did not, but she did proceed to wreak vengeance on us. She violated the terms of our $250,000 loan to her credit union and refused to provide the required financial disclosure, a federal violation. I issued a complaint to the National Credit Union Administration, which in 2003 seized the credit union and conducted an audit. They discovered major embezzlements. Our loan was lost, as were the investments of others. We would never recover a cent.[50]

Coming to Terms

There was no joy in Evelyne's downfall and our "vindication." She was a charismatic, resourceful leader, capable of kindness and generosity. She sought power and recognition for our Black credit unions and the Federation itself. But that drive was accompanied by, sometimes inextricably linked with, and ultimately overshadowed by her drive

---

50 In March 2008, Evelyne was convicted of 44 federal charges, including embezzlement, concealing records, bank fraud, and filing false tax returns. That September, she was sentenced to 54 months in a federal prison—reduced by more than half from the sentencing guidelines in consideration of her record of service to the community. She was ordered to provide $1.4 million in restitution.

for personal power, which was manifested in her disregard for organizational discipline, for ethics, and for the law—and simply for the common good of our movement of financial cooperatives. Our members, led by our board of directors, took the difficult, painful step of removing a leader—Black and female—who was putting our entire movement at risk. It was an affirmation that the CDCU *movement* was larger and more important than any individual.

The board drew a crucial lesson about the need to address governance, both in their relationship with the CEO and also regarding the development and succession of the elected leadership. In 2001, during the weekend leading up to 9/11, they met at a retreat center in rural New York and adopted changes including board duties, term limits, and officer tenure. As well, they delineated the executive director's sphere of action and developed a more formal assessment process.

Over the next decade, the board was chaired by a succession of African American women except for one two-year period. Despite repeated external crises during the first decade of the new century, the Federation stabilized and normalized. The board adopted systematic annual appraisals of the executive director. It offered criticisms of my style of management, which sometimes suffered from my instinct to improvise and to go off in too many directions. I gave them too much information, not enough information, not the right kind of information. But all these were part of a healthy accountability process, delivered without rancor or controversy. We moved on, and we moved ahead.

CHAPTER 10

White Boss: Didn't Know, Should Have Understood

I never wanted to be a boss, much less the white boss of a predominantly non-white organization. I took over the National Federation of Community Development Credit Unions in 1983 by default, after the organization lost virtually all of its funding and all its staff. I was devoted to the mission, had a vision, and was willing to work without a salary for a year to try to make a go of it. The board chair and cofounder, Al, rightly perceived that the organization had nothing to lose, and so granted me my only request, that I be given the title of executive director for the first time in my career. It was a position without staff, without resources—a blank slate, except for our legacy—and thus a perfect arena to test my drive to become a social entrepreneur. It was a drive to *create,* to build something—yes, something that was "*mine,*" but a way to build value for the CDCU *movement,* for the cooperative common good. These drives were not mutually contradictory; at best, they were aligned and mutually reinforcing. But there was an underlying tension between my sense of personal ownership, and the primacy of the *movement,* embodied by the Federation, which truly owned what we created. The internal conflict that wracked the organization in the 1990s would magnify that tension.

A few months after I assumed leadership of the Federation in 1983, I had the good fortune to gain a Black colleague, Annie Vamper, a former credit union manager and later federal examiner from the

South. For a decade, until her premature death in 1990, we were essentially a partnership, dividing the organization's external and internal duties between us. Over the next two decades, I hired a series of African American women for the deputy or associate director position. "Deputy director" is often a thankless job, and indeed, I delegated to my second-in-command many of the administrative and personnel tasks that I had no taste for. Although Annie was a credit union "lifer," none of her successors, while supportive of our mission, aspired to spend their careers in the credit union industry. After five or so years, most moved on to other fields.

Throughout the 1980s, Annie and I constituted the "senior management," the fiscal office, and the program staff. We were barely an "organization" at all. When we managed to win grants and contracts, we hired staff for projects that typically lasted a year or two. Only in the 1990s did we have the resources to build out the organization, reaching a peak of about 20 employees late in the decade. We were able to build a multiracial, multiethnic staff. New York City had large populations of first- and second-generation immigrants, especially from the Caribbean, and many of our staff members claimed these origins; others had roots in the Philippines, Turkey, Africa, Puerto Rico, Chile, Ukraine, Mali, and Korea. There were, of course, African Americans and white people at various levels. By most standards, we were a diverse group.

When we had money, we held facilitated staff-building exercises, once at the Akwaaba Mansion in Brooklyn's Bedford-Stuyvesant, another at a well-equipped rural Connecticut conference center, courtesy of funders. As a small, evolving organization, we had plenty to do in order to formulate and agree upon a mission statement, a vision statement, and a work plan. I cannot say that we plunged deeply into issues of race and gender; we spent considerable time learning about each other's personalities and work styles, using exercises like the Myers-Briggs personality inventory. Although many of us were initially uncomfortable with Myers-Briggs, we learned about each other's preferred ways of interacting—for example, why one person worked right up to deadline, irritating his boss (me) and other staff; when to share information; and when a closed door meant a closed door. We gained a greater appreciation for our colleagues when each told their life story. It was enlightening to learn that one very reserved Black man had not joined us simply for a job, but as a way of continuing the legacy of community service of his father.

This is not to idealize our multiracial, multigenerational staff. But we were a mission-driven nonprofit organization, and I recruited staff who broadly shared our values. From what I perceived, internal frictions were driven more by personality differences than by group identity, but it is certainly possible that I missed what was going on below the surface. In today's environment, our dialogue would likely be more urgent, deeper, and harder, exposing both underlying racial and gender issues.

Since Black Lives Matter, activists of color have questioned whether white people should have any role in leading social justice organizations. The argument has prompted me to look back at my career. I know that neither my left-wing/progressive background, nor the 30 years I spent working alongside and for communities of color spared me from missteps, misconceptions, and implicit bias in my career. I made some mistakes out of naivete or ignorance, some simply because my assumptions as a white male were inherently different from those of people of color, whose experience led them to see the world differently. Perhaps the lessons I drew over decades gone by are obvious and/or obsolete. If the white leaders of today have freed themselves from old patterns, all the better; if not, they still have substantial work to do.

Radical Blindness and White Northern Ignorance

I described in chapter 3 an incident that nearly ended my career at the Federation soon after it had begun. I infuriated a Black CEO of a member credit union when I sent a quarterly report to a federal funder that he saw as implying that his credit union had done something illegal. I neither intended nor perceived that. But he saw Washington as a potential enemy; despite my decades as an avowed radical opponent of the government, I somehow assumed that Washington was fair and objective in this "nonpolitical" grant management matter (this despite the aggressive dismantling of the anti-poverty infrastructure by the first Reagan Administration). Nothing came of it; no inquiries or investigations. But the incident was a cautionary one for me, a basic lesson that white people and people of color often view the world quite differently.

Soon after I became leader of the Federation in 1983, Mr. James Gilliam invited me to visit the Saint Luke Credit Union that he had cofounded in the 1940s. I flew into Raleigh-Durham airport, rented a car, and headed east to rural Bertie County. I passed a building with a faded sign for Gilliam's farm implements business. "Oh," I exclaimed on meeting Mr. Gilliam, "was that your family's business?"

As a white Northerner, my ignorance about the about the legacy of slavery and persistence of racism in the South was embarrassing. "Not exactly," he tactfully replied.

I stayed at Mr. Gilliam's home, and the next day he drove me around the county. Only years later, when the Federation presented him with a lifetime achievement award, did I learn what that trip had meant. No white man had ever stayed in his house. Driving around with me sitting next to him in the front seat was a rare and potentially dangerous act, even in the early 1980s.

Role Models

Largely because of my ambivalence about being a "boss," I often failed to see the impression my comments made on the staff, and specifically staff members of color. Trying to be transparent and to empower staff, I routinely shared accounts of my meetings with public officials and funders. After one such meeting, I ranted about the unprofessionalism of a state official who kept me waiting while she checked her horoscope. The official was a Black woman. So was my staff member, who was obviously distressed and confronted me, informing me that my outburst was inappropriate and a bad example for staff.

From my perspective, this was not a race matter. A state official was acting disrespectfully to the public that paid her salary; I would have acted no differently had it been a white man. But my staff member was right that I was not modeling admirable behavior. And probably especially hurtful for her, I was criticizing another Black woman professional—who could easily have been her.

Fortunately, our staff found other role models to inspire them. We had senior staff of color at the Federation, including the Black women who served as deputy director and as board chairpersons. But as I later learned, some staff members were particularly inspired by our volunteer Capitalization Committee, which included several prominent Black credit union leaders who had succeeded despite the obstacles in an overwhelmingly white-dominated movement and who were now "giving back" by donating many demanding, unpaid hours to the Federation's work, analyzing and making determinations on our members' investment and grant applications.

White Manager

I never wanted to be a boss, but I *especially* never wanted to be a manager. I was not good at it. And I was especially not good at it when race entered the picture. Some of my shortcomings were associated with liberal overcompensation. I made every effort to hire non-white staff, and indeed we had a diverse office, including many talented people of color. But in several instances, I was guilty of the "soft bigotry of low expectations." I tolerated substandard performance or retained employees of color that I should have terminated. I didn't always demand excellence, and as CEO, I did not always deliver it for the organization.

I don't think my failure served those employees or the organization well. We were fortunate in finding talented people who were willing to work below their market value (often, for many years). But for years, we did not pay the competitive wages needed to consistently attract top financial, legal, and technical talent as our balance sheet grew and our business became more complex. Yes, our budget was limited, but I suffered from a lingering anti-poverty view that sacrifice was necessary if one is to work for "the cause." I was underpaid; therefore, it was fine for others to be underpaid.

Firing non-white employees was especially difficult. As CEO, hiring and firing were both ultimately my responsibility. But there were instances in which I delegated the dismissal of a staff member to their supervisor. It was not exactly inappropriate, given the job descriptions and reporting lines, but it was not, I felt, a "stand-up" action on my part. There was one particularly delicate instance in which I informed the board that I planned to dismiss an African American staff member for inadequate performance. I was worried that it could become racially divisive. The board agreed with my action, and they delegated a Black board member to provide backup for me. We managed to negotiate the situation without lasting damage; the organization was spared racial turmoil. I was grateful; it avoided a painful conflict for the organization. But I was left with a sense of my own shortcoming as a manager, and specifically, as a white manager. I should have handled the matter myself and dealt with any consequences. I never would have sought board support in terminating a white person—and I did not feel good about relying on them in this situation.

Confronting the Savior Complex

The most difficult, painful part of my job was dealing with dead and dying member credit unions. With few exceptions, troubled institutions were insular and protective of their problems until the eleventh hour, when liquidation or merger was imminent. Often, they accompanied their pleas for help with complaints that their examiners were prejudiced; that they had exaggerated the credit union's operational and financial deficiencies. I heard their pleas and was quick to take their side against the regulators. But it was hard for me to prove that the regulators' actions were illegitimate because they were "arbitrary and capricious" or overtly discriminatory; we often lacked the full, factual story. Occasionally, we won a temporary reprieve or got an examiner replaced; in a few instances, we were able to inject capital to buy time for the credit union. But it was virtually impossible for the Federation to save them from their eventual demise. I could not be the savior they needed and wanted.

The savior syndrome is probably all too common among all workers in the "helping" professions. In my career at the Federation, my membership included the smallest, most fragile institutions in the financial system. Against the odds, these credit unions served the low-income communities and communities of color that banks avoided as unprofitable. The failure rate of small businesses, in general, is high; as for resource-poor, thinly capitalized, collectively owned businesses—credit unions—it sometimes struck me as little short of a miracle that as many survived as did.

But there were frequent failures, and when we lost member institutions, I had little emotional distance to insulate myself. Each loss hurt. At some level, I experienced their failure as *my* failure, a repudiation of my reputation, my competence, and of the narrative I wove for our funders about our noble, successful institutions. What could we do? Wherever possible, the Federation provided capital, technical assistance, or advocacy in Washington. But ultimately, only the credit unions could save themselves—not the Federation, not me personally. Their successes were *their* successes; their failures were *their* failures. To deny that simple truth was a denial of their agency; a misplaced sense of ownership. It was the unfortunate flip side of my passion for these institutions, my wholehearted desire for them to succeed.

Not all "saviors" are white. But it seems to me that my version of the savior syndrome suggests a strain of white entitlement: people like me somehow believe we *deserve* success and are offended when we do not achieve it. If that is a luxury, it is one not given to most Black and other communities of color. As for me, with each failure of a member credit union, I questioned the value of my work—sometimes colored by resentment at the credit union that didn't validate my self-image. I hope and believe the next generation of leaders, white and other, will function more effectively, unencumbered by the savior syndrome.

Crimes Against the Commons

The most painful questions arose when a credit union failed not because of difficult finances, but because of embezzlement or betrayal of trust.

Sometimes it was the inappropriate but "well-meaning" action by a manager, covering up a cash discrepancy of a teller, even by filling the gap with her (the manager's) own money. Sometimes it involved changing the loan payment due date for a hard-pressed member, which distorted delinquency statistics. Those things were wrong, and they might unfortunately, sadly, result in the loss of the credit union. But they were not evidence of high criminality.

On the other hand, there were grievous, indefensible criminal actions, including theft on a grand scale. In the 1980s, as I described in chapter 7, we were confronted with the huge scandal of Franklin Community Federal Credit Union in Omaha, whose Black CEO, Lawrence King, stole tens of millions of dollars from social investors. In the 1990s, I was heartbroken by the liquidation of a credit union in the South whose treasurer, a veteran Civil Rights marcher, misused $1 million of credit union funds to buy land. In one of the poorest regions of the South, a credit union was destroyed by the long-running, million-dollar embezzlement by an employee who lost money gambling at the casino that was supposed to "revitalize" the local economy. Unfortunately, there were numerous other cases, some ending tragically in suicide.

What to make of these incidents? Were people of color more prone to dishonesty, less capable of running credit unions—as some people in the credit union industry believed? Surely not. As Ibram X. Kendi reminds us, it is inherently racist to ascribe race-wide characteristics to the actions of an individual—to make "individuals responsible for the perceived behavior of racial groups and [to make] racial groups responsible for the behavior of individuals."[51] Black credit union officials steal; Latinx credit union officials steal; Asian and Pacific Islander credit union officials steal; and certainly, white officials steal. Was it a problem only for small credit unions, which lacked the resources for internal controls? To the contrary, there are recent examples of (white) trusted officials of billion-dollar credit unions who have embezzled or engaged in destructive lending practices.[52] My "universe" was predominantly antipoverty credit unions in communities of color; unsurprisingly, the scandals I saw tended to originate there. I happened to be working with a skewed sample.

Willie Sutton, famous bank robber in the 1930s, explained why he robbed banks: "That's where the money is." There is money in credit unions, too, including credit unions in communities of color. Robbing a credit union, like robbing a bank, was a crime—but to my mind, stealing from a credit union was worse; it was a crime against *the community*, against the members of *the cooperative*. These crimes violated my brittle shell of idealism, my earnest belief that credit unions were inherently honest, admirable institutions that embodied the best of human cooperation, free of the greed and corruption that characterized the capitalist economy. What's more, white liberal that I was, I fallaciously believed that Black people, more than white people, were supposed to honor those principles. While I nursed my injured pride, the communities directly affected did what they had always done. After all, communities of color had faced defeat after defeat and responded with resilience. As Maya Angelou wrote: "And still I rise."

---

51 Ibram X. Kendi, essay in *How to Be an Antiracist* (New York, NY: One World, 2019), p. 92.
52 In one nationally notorious case, a white second-generation CEO of a large New York City credit union was convicted of bribery that contributed to the impoverishment of immigrant taxicab owners and devastated the industry, leading to suicides by at least a half-dozen drivers.

The lessons I learned were not only for white people, but for idealists of every color and gender. No financial institution is immune to betrayal of trust, not even the most progressive, dedicated, community-controlled cooperative. Control structures, oversight, and supervision are indispensable in a community enterprise. These are inglorious, thankless, essential tasks. There is a useful aphorism translated from a Russian proverb (and cited by President Ronald Reagan): "Trust but verify."

Victimology and Black Achievement

Another trap related to the "white savior" syndrome was viewing all African Americans and people of color through the lens of their victimhood. Unquestionably, credit union leaders of color faced a harder path; their communities were systemically disadvantaged and oppressed. The credit union industry was not an early leader in opening paths for advancement for people of color—or for that matter, women. The leadership—nationally, statewide, and locally—of credit union associations was overwhelmingly white and male; so were the largest credit unions, the billion-dollar giants.

But to view the people of color in the credit union movement solely as victims deflects from and minimizes their agency, their accomplishments, and their resilience. The Federation sought out and connected with many accomplished Black credit union leaders who made their way in the credit union industry despite the obstacles. We recruited them for our Capitalization Committee, and from 2000, we had a series of distinguished Black board chairwomen (followed shortly after my departure from the Federation by the first Latina chairwoman).

Over the past decade, it has been gratifying to see a critical mass of Black credit union leaders becoming a visible force in the broader industry. Attending the Washington gatherings of the African-American Credit Union Coalition each year, I have seen the attendance increase from dozens to a few hundred, including not only Black and Latinx credit union officials, but officials from the "mainstream" industry and regulators who have come to pay their respects. I have met scores of accomplished, self-assured Black professionals, some from my generation, but increasingly from younger generations.

It has been a long time coming, and the work is not yet done. But the voices for financial justice are more numerous and louder than ever in the credit union world.

Gatekeeper

If you become an intermediary, do not expect to be well-loved—especially if yours is a *membership* association, as we were—a nonprofit federation of dues-paying organizations each of which had a claim on our resources. In 1982, we established the first community-based national financial intermediary in the country, our Capitalization Program. We raised funds from national sources in the name of and for the benefit of our credit union movement. To insulate us from internal politics, we established an arm's length committee of non-members to allocate investments to members. The structure has worked well to this day—except for an episode in the late 1990s.

Another effort at intermediation proved disastrous. We obtained a major grant from a foundation for a youth project, distributing subgrants to about ten credit unions and keeping a portion to fund one staff position along with various administrative costs. It fueled an acrimonious conflict, replete with threats of legal action when one member credit union demanded a greater share. The conflict was so divisive that we abandoned the project, turning down the prospect of a major grant.

Credit unions in general, and small credit unions in particular, fared poorly in the opening round of the CDFI Fund in 1996. I took it personally. For years, I had argued unsuccessfully for a separate funding window for small institutions. Only after the Fund assessed the outcome of its first awards round did we win a partial victory. The Fund opened its application to intermediaries that could in turn channel investments to small, "uncompetitive" institutions. The Federation took advantage of the opportunity. We applied for and won millions of grant dollars that we provided to our members as grants and/or high-risk loans.

We provided a useful function. We distributed capital that many small credit unions could not have obtained on their own. But we, the Federation, benefited from the process financially as well; the grants from the CDFI Fund and foundations helped build the Federation's net worth. This wealth did not enrich management, but rather was owned by our members collectively. We clearly added value. But were we playing the role of the "credible" (white-led) intermediary, comfortably accommodating the accountability and performance requirements of (white) funders and investors? Would equity be better served if the moneyed institutions dealt directly with those "on the ground," accommodating *their* needs and building *their* capacity?

A Final Bias: Ageism Meets Racism

I spent my career fighting the bias against small, non-white, and poverty-fighting financial institutions. For years, credit union industry officials lamented aging boards, which were seen as resistant to change, unable or unwilling to attract the younger generation; these credit unions were anomalies, doomed to extinction in the dynamic marketplace. Examiners often pushed these institutions—some of which were based in Black churches—to liquidate or merge. Defending them was my job; we developed programs to help them, and it was easy for me to react righteously, when I heard members complain of examiner bias or condescension. But was I free of bias myself?

Only recently, in writing an article for my former organization, did I fully come to terms with the ageism and, yes, racism that pervaded *my* view no less than the mainstream industry's. I interviewed a number of very small, Black, faith-based credit unions. One, in particular, impressed me. Like others I had known, the board consisted largely of people past the usual retirement age. Some had spent as much as 30 years volunteering for their credit unions. However small, these credit unions were well-managed institutions, and their board volunteers took pride in them. They conscientiously attended the many trainings volunteers needed to keep current with the voluminous credit union rules, regulations, and procedures. They were exploring ways to add new services. In their personal lives, many of them were retired or current professionals—in health, social services, or the public sector. They were, in short, accomplished, dedicated individuals of a generation who had to make their way and earn respect from a grudging white world. Many were either themselves, or the children of, the generation that had come north in the words of Richard Wright and captured by Isabel Wilkerson, seeking the "warmth of other suns."

I was embarrassed to realize the degree to which I had privately shared the industry's view of these volunteers as relics, irrelevant to the future of credit unions. I was doubly embarrassed to realize that I, in my seventies, was the same age as some of the people I interviewed. Only now, as an elder myself, have I come to fully appreciate the contributions and importance of these pillars of the Black community.

CHAPTER 11

From 9/11 to the Great Recession: New Crises, Continuing Battles

For the Federation, after a decade marked both by growth and internal conflict, the first decade of the twenty-first century was a time of internal stability. The crises were externally driven by political terrorism, climate catastrophe, and economic disaster. Late in the decade, the election of Barack Obama seemed to offer a new era of racial equality. But our struggles for economic equity and regulatory fairness continued.

9/11

The century began with a crisis that never happened. In the final years of the old century, there was growing alarm that a coding shortcut (using two digits instead of four to designate years—e.g., "99" instead of "1999") would cause computer systems to fail when the calendar rolled over to a new century. It is estimated that billions of dollars were spent to reprogram the systems that industry, government, and all the other sectors of the economy relied upon. Nothing much happened.

But the next year, our sense of normalcy was shattered irrevocably. In the first week of September 2001, the Federation's board held a retreat in a camp in upstate New York to address our governance issues, a pressing concern after the collective trauma we had undergone in the 1990s. The weekend concluded, and the board headed back to their homes around the country. On Tuesday morning, the terrorist attack on the World Trade Center struck a few short blocks west of our office.

Our building was immersed in the cloud of debris from the successive explosions of the twin towers. I sat in my tenth-floor office overlooking the East River, watching the papers that an hour ago sat on people's desks float by toward Brooklyn, and watching the apocalyptic exodus of thousands of New Yorkers walking up the FDR Drive and fleeing on boats. One of our staff members was caught in a stalled train coming from New Jersey; another, heading to our office for his first day of work, had to turn back; others emerged from the subway to the chaotic scene. Flights were cancelled, and several board members had to scramble to rent a car to drive home across the country. Thankfully, we lost no one.

At 5:00 p.m., I finally left the office and walked through the deserted streets, past the abandoned food carts, to make my way across the Brooklyn Bridge, when I heard yet another building explode: 7 World Trade Center. Reaching Brooklyn, I saw signs asking for blood donations. Tragically, none was needed; the dead far outnumbered the wounded.

Lower Manhattan was cordoned off for a week or more. When I finally returned, passing through security, I walked past the ghostly remains of the food carts with molding food inside. No New Yorker will forget the poignant homemade signs posted everywhere begging for information about missing loved ones. The air was acrid, as it would be for months; a bitter reminder any time we emerged from the subway. We had no mail deliveries for two weeks. Telephone service was out and then spotty for days.

The decade of disasters, natural and human, continued. The climate crisis had not yet become as unavoidably obvious, but in 2005, Hurricane Katrina devastated the Gulf Region, killing nearly 2,000 people, disproportionately Black and poor, in New Orleans. To help our damaged credit unions in the Gulf region recover, I started a Katrina relief fund. Beginning with contributions from individuals, we raised nearly one million dollars, thanks to major contributions from the John D. and Catherine T. MacArthur Foundation and the Jewish Funds for Justice. We distributed grants to help our credit unions in Louisiana and Mississippi recover.[53]

A Changing Membership

Over the decades, the profile of the Federation's membership has changed. Moreover, I pressed for a strategy with the potential to change us.

When I joined the Federation in 1980, our membership included many surviving credit unions, primarily African American, from the War on Poverty period, and our board reflected it. These institutions tended to be small, but open to the entire Black community. As the Reagan Administration dismantled and starved the anti-poverty network, many of these credit unions faded away. Over the course of the 1990s, through our faith-based outreach, we added a substantial number of Black church credit unions, and in the 2000s, they were prominently represented on our board, including as chairwomen. But with notable exceptions, these institutions were narrower and more insular than the community-wide predominantly Black credit unions of the War on Poverty age. They were often the most precarious and vulnerable among our members, given their limited resources and often, their aging volunteer leadership. Their ranks were steadily eroded through mergers and liquidations. Most found it difficult to obtain resources from the CDFI Fund that I had so long fought for.

The Federation's thirtieth anniversary year, 2004-05, would prove to be the worst period ever in terms of the merger and liquidations of CDCUs. The entire credit union industry was shrinking by hundreds of institutions each year—on average, 3% of the total. The

---

53 The ASI FCU in New Orleans used the contributions to establish a community center in the Upper Ninth Ward. It named the center after me to recognize my efforts in initiating the relief campaign.

erosion was worse for small credit unions: 8.4% for credit unions under $10 million in assets—and worse yet for our membership. Over 2004-05, we lost 11% of our membership through mergers and liquidations—from Little Haiti in Miami to the Latinx South End of Boston; from a long-established credit union in East Harlem, to a fledgling, Black-led credit union in Denver. North Carolina, home of the largest concentration of Black credit unions, lost institutions with histories of 40 years or more.

Although the Federation itself was relatively stable with some 200 members, we were still marginal players in the credit union industry. We were not on a road to achieve broader impact—to "scale up." Observing the erosion year by year, I explored a new paradigm: what if we could combine the mission-driven focus of our "traditional" low-income credit unions with the scale and capacity of select larger "mainstream" credit unions? Would this both expand the CDCU movement's outreach to underserved communities and enhance the Federation's own capacity? This approach made strategic sense economically for the Federation (through dues contributions) and politically (through our alliance with prominent, "mainstream" institutions). But our smaller credit unions were uneasy and concerned about losing their voice in the one association specifically for credit unions like theirs. I understood their concerns. An abundance of large, bank-like (primarily white) credit unions—even well-intentioned ones—could overshadow the grassroots, poverty-fighting credit unions that long were the essence of the Federation.

Nonetheless, in May of 2003, the Federation's membership committee adopted a proposal to create a new, associate membership category for "Community Development Partners"—those credit unions that "have an interest in and provide services of underserved communities." Our goal was to reach more low-income communities, strengthen our "traditional" smaller members through partnerships with larger institutions, and strengthen our voice within the credit unions industry, elevating the attention on the needs of low-income communities and credit union members. We reached out to large credit unions that did not serve *predominantly* low-income communities but whose work intersected ours or member credit unions. Our "value proposition" for them was somewhat thin: we offered Community Development Partners an opportunity to join a good cause with an advisory voice, but no voting rights.

However, thanks to the Ford Foundation, which was interested in seeing us move to scale, we were able to provide some material incentives. Ford provided grant funds that we redirected to induce large, non-CDCUs to partner with CDCUs and expand their services in low-income communities. Some opened new branches and others developed joint programs with or provided technical support to our CDCUs. Over several years, we recruited nearly 50 Community Development Partners, including a number of the 10 largest credit unions in the country. But over time, some Community Development Partners drifted away because they were dissatisfied with associate membership in an organization that did not grant them full voting rights.

Our image within the credit union industry benefited from our new initiative as we emphasized our commitment to a core principle of the cooperative movement—"cooperation among cooperatives." We moved further beyond our previous "outsider" (some thought "rogue") posture. I was confident that I had initiated the right *business strategy* for the Federation as an association. But I harbored doubts: was it right for the *CDCU movement?* Had I, in fact, put us on the path that diverged from our historic mission? The Federation existed for the *movement,* for low-income communities, and if the movement was in trouble, what was becoming of our mission? At credit union industry gatherings, we were told we were the "heart and soul" of the credit union movement. We wanted to be and do much more than that. We wanted to make a difference, to make a tangible impact on communities of color and low-income people. My hope was that allying with the mainstream "giants" of the credit union industry would help us achieve that.

The CDFI Fund: Continuing Inequity

Throughout the 2000s, I continued our advocacy with the federal CDFI Fund. Although we had won the establishment of a designated funding window for small CDFIs in 2000, the share of CDFI grants going to credit unions remained small throughout the decade: annually, an average of 80% of the fund's "Financial Assistance" award dollars went to the predominantly white-led community development loan funds, while less than 20% went to credit unions and banks *combined*.[54] Contrary to the Fund's initial guidelines, it never gave consideration to CDFIs that either were, or planned to become, depositories. The fund's application materials remained more suitable for loan funds than depositories or venture funds. In response to our arguments, the Fund argued that the majority of certified CDFIs were loan funds, and that the awards to that sector tracked their numerical preponderance. Confidentially, one senior official of the fund told us that credit union applications simply "weren't as good" as the loan funds.

Meanwhile, the largest pool of CDFI Fund money was out of reach for almost all credit unions. Few had the capacity to participate in the complex New Markets Tax Credit Program, which channeled billions of dollars through banks, special purpose entities, and CDFI loan funds for projects in designated low-income areas. Neither could our credit unions take advantage of the CDFI Bond Guarantee program, which required applications for $100 million or more. Of course, one problem was that the CDFI Fund "pie" was quite limited under the administration of President George W. Bush. In fact, the administration had tried to eliminate the fund in 2005 by consolidating it with other community development programs. That effort failed, but appropriations remained at a historically low level.

On the morning of November 5, 2008, I gathered our staff in our conference room on John Street in lower Manhattan. Barack Obama

---

54 A detailed analysis of the CDFI Fund's award history appears in *Democratizing Finance*.

had won a historic victory. For millions of us, it was an emotional time. I choked up as I recounted to my staff how in the 1960s, my cohort had dreamed—fantasized—of a revolution. Obama's victory, I said, was the closest the country would come in my lifetime.

But Obama inherited an economy on the brink of disaster, as one major financial institution after another failed. The Great Recession was reaching full force, wreaking financial havoc on the communities our credit unions served. There were massive losses of low-wage and service-sector jobs, home foreclosures, and other rippling economic losses that disproportionately hurt people of color. In turn, our credit unions—some of which were as precarious as the members they served—were severely challenged. The good news for our field was that Obama was a strong supporter of CDFIs. Working with Congress, his administration provided a special appropriation in 2009 and a large increase to the CDFI Fund's annual funding.

Our Paths Meet

The Federation's first meeting with the founders of KAPFCU came at our annual conference in June 2008, in Dallas, Texas; KAPFCU's home base. We had typically assisted the chartering of most new credit unions, but not so for KAPFCU. They had been established in 2004 without our assistance by financially sophisticated people, including Michael McCray and Victor Russell. Although we could not claim the Federation's usual "midwife" role in birthing their institution, their type of start-up credit union was precisely the kind of institution that I had always envisioned the CDFI Fund supporting.

Tragically, it did not work out that way. Through the circumstances described by Michael McCray in Part Two, KAPFCU was denied a CDFI grant of $100,000—retracted, remarkably, after it had been presumptively approved. As well, KAPFCU was denied a $26,000 secondary capital investment from the Obama Administration's Community Development Capital Initiative (CDCI, described below), the equity-like Treasury Department investment program that the Federation had fought for. Between the two programs, federal investment totaling far less than $200,000 would have likely ensured the survival of a promising, innovative, Black-led community development financial institution.

Doubling the Pain: Cooperative Collapse

Adding to the devastation of the country's overall economy in the Great Recession, the credit union industry suffered another harsh blow, attributable in part to the subprime mortgage disaster.

Throughout my career, I was frequently critical of the credit union industry and what I saw as its drift from its working-class, purely cooperative roots. Still, I admired and was proud of the financial structure that credit unions had created in the 1970s. Seeking to reduce their dependence on the banking system, credit unions had banded together and created a multi-tiered structure to circulate money within the movement. Most states had a wholesale or "corporate" credit union in which local credit unions invested their excess cash; one level higher, investments were channeled into a national "bankers' bank," U.S. Central Credit Union.

In the first weeks of 2009, U.S. Central crashed. Pursuing competitive returns for credit unions, it had incurred unsustainable paper losses on its investments in subprime mortgages—the very mortgages that disproportionately victimized communities of color and low-income people. A number of the state corporate credit unions crashed and were liquidated. The costs of these failures were passed down the chain to the local credit unions through increased fees that they paid to the union deposit insurance fund. True, the losses were allocated proportionately based on asset size, but many of our credit unions were especially vulnerable, having suffered disproportionately from the Great Recession. Every lost dollar hurt.

The failure of U.S. Central and the other corporate unions was not only an economic shock to the credit union movement, but for some of us, a harsh blow to our morale and any idealistic belief that we could somehow escape the capitalist-dominated banking system. We saw the bare truth: markets are everywhere; money is fungible, flowing throughout the system; absolute purity is hard to achieve. Market-rate yields are sometimes achieved through investments in the misery and disproportionate victimization of communities of color. Had the Federation ever succeeded in chartering our Community Development Central Credit Union—our own "central bank" for CDCUs—we might have been able to invest in affordable housing and other uses that *benefited* our communities, rather than subprime mortgages and derivatives.

Fighting for Capital in the Great Recession: The CDCI Program

Washington sought to stabilize the banking system by providing hundreds of billions of dollars to major banks through TARP, the huge, controversial Troubled Asset Relief Program. As usual, small institutions—those that were not "too big to fail"—were given short shrift. And in particular, the institutions that served low-income and minority communities were all but ignored.

I and other CDFI leaders began to meet informally to press for access to TARP. We partially succeeded. After deliberation, the Treasury Department decided to create a program that would invest in certified CDFIs. Only depositories—that is, banks and credit unions—would be eligible; the unregulated nonprofit loan funds were excluded. In any case, the formal announcement of the Community Development Capital Initiative (CDCI) brought limited joy. In October 2009, with only a day or two notice, I joined my CDFI colleagues, mainstream bankers, and financial industry lobbyists at a White House briefing to announce the program.

Disappointingly, this was not held in the White House Rose Garden, unlike the original CDFI Fund announcement in 1993, but rather in a suburban Maryland records-storage warehouse that had received a Small Business Administration (SBA) loan. I traveled to a remote DC Metro stop, walked uncertainly through a semi-forested area, and arrived at a bleak industrial warehouse. We waited in rows of folding chairs, without access to water or bathrooms, until finally President Obama and senior administration officials arrived. When they announced the outlines of the TARP-offshoot Community Development Capital Initiative (CDCI), we were disappointed. There was no talk of equity capital, only loans at a below-market rate and in amounts too small to make much impact.

With our allies, we continued our advocacy, aided especially by the support of Treasury's CDFI Advisory Committee, headed by Bill Bynum, CEO of Hope Credit Union, the largest Black credit union and CDFI in the Southeast. Over the next few months, the Treasury Department elaborated and improved the terms. On February 3, 2010, I joined colleagues at a small briefing at the Treasury Department, where Secretary Timothy Geithner announced a revised and improved CDCI program. Frustratingly, final details were not yet complete and would not be for 60 days. This was a major problem, because the funds needed to be obligated by the end of the fiscal year, September 30, 2010.

A Bittersweet Victory

In total, the program had a projected cap of $1 billion. Individual investments were proportionate to the size of the recipient credit union or bank. We won an important victory for our credit unions: the investment was to be in the form of *secondary capital*, equity-like loans that could boost the net worth of low-income credit unions and help them survive the damage from the Great Recession. I was pleased that this validated the Federation's pioneering role in inventing secondary capital in 1996. (A comparable structure was offered to banks.)

So, yes, we had won a hard-fought victory for the small institutions that served "Main Street" rather than Wall Street. But inequities persisted. Our credit unions (as well as banks) had to get approval from their regulators. For credit unions, this meant getting NCUA to consent. No "troubled" or struggling institutions would pass muster, even those—especially those—in some of the hardest-hit communities.

What was worse were the inordinate regulations and restrictions in areas like executive compensation. These regulations were intended to prevent TARP's big-bank recipients from providing "golden parachutes" to their executives. But the same rules applied even to the tiniest institutions like our credit unions: to get the CDCI funding, even low-paid credit union staff had to foreswear bonuses and some raises. It was preposterous and unjust. Our smallest credit unions often paid their staff little more than the minimum wage. But if they didn't sign and agree to the terms, the credit unions could not receive CDCI funding. Moreover, there were extensive monitoring and other legal and technical restrictions. For example, applicants had to provide "opinion of counsel" from a lawyer affirming that they were legally able to do everything required by the investment agreement. But most of our credit unions had no access to lawyers who could render this crucial opinion. I enlisted the aid of the Lawyers Alliance of New York, which provided enormous *pro bono* aid directly to some credit unions and helped secure legal resources for others around the country.

There was another major obstacle to overcome. Credit union regulations were at odds with the particular terms and requirements of the federal government's CDCI investment. We needed to get the NCUA to quickly alter its secondary capital regulations. For once, we did not have to go to battle with NCUA. In record time—a few short weeks—NCUA issued rulings that made it possible for our credit unions to participate in this crucial federal CDCI program. It was probably the high point of my 30-year adversarial relationship with NCUA.

Disparate Impact: The Same (Damn) Rules for Everyone

The CDCI program was a painful example of disparate impact that disadvantaged our credit unions. The Treasury Department's TARP rules were indeed "the same for everyone"—but they were designed with the largest banks in mind, lest the American public view TARP as a bailout that would reward banks and their senior management. The rules were intolerably onerous and inappropriate for the smallest community-centered financial institutions. Consequently, many of our credit unions declined to participate, even though they needed the capital. Some found the loan terms economically unfeasible; it especially pained me that our credit union in New Orleans that had suffered greatly from Hurricane Katrina decided it could not make the numbers work, and so they declined to participate. Other credit unions feared that accepting government money would bring bad publicity, making them targets for the bank lobby and right-wing critics. Finally, others failed the financial "viability" test the program required regulators to apply. (Sadly, South Shore Bank, the country's first community development bank, was denied CDCI funding and was liquidated in 2010.)

By the deadline, September 30, 2010, 48 credit unions received $69.9 million in equity-like secondary capital investments. The level of participation disappointed me—there could have been so much more. But despite the frustrating federal process, despite the missed opportunities, I was proud of what we achieved. Even a few of our smallest credit unions were able to participate, including five faith-based African American credit unions. My entire career had been dedicated to bringing capital to our credit unions. By the numbers, this was the largest achievement of my career in bringing capital to our movement.

Meanwhile, the Obama Administration proclaimed CDCI a victory for equity. "It's a common misconception that TARP funds only went to large Wall Street firms, but the CDCI program is yet another example of how TARP is providing critical assistance to Main Street financial institutions," said Herbert Allison, Treasury Assistant Secretary for Financial Stability.

Right-Wing Backlash

The CDCI program was a pittance compared to the hundreds of billions provided to bail out banks: CDFI credit unions and banks collectively received less than $600 million. Nonetheless, it drew baseless partisan fire. Soon after the investments closed on September 30, an assistant professor from Louisiana rushed out a study, "Political Influence and TARP Investments in Credit Unions." He alleged that credit unions located in the districts of members of the Democratic-led House Financial Services Committee were three times more likely to receive TARP CDCI investments than other eligible credit unions, and that political influence could have accounted for the skewing of Treasury investment. But virtually every piece of "evidence" he cited was factually wrong, down to the number of applicants, the approval rate, and where the money went.

I was furious. I drafted point-by-point rebuttals to the spurious research; our consultant, Terry Ratigan, diplomatically suggested modifying my language. But it is easier to make a spurious assertion than to erase the initial impressions made by unsubstantiated, misleading charges. The main lesson I drew was the unremitting enmity of conservative forces even to extremely modest public-sector support for institutions serving communities of color and the poor. As the author of the disingenuous study himself noted, "Credit unions received $69.911 million dollars from the TARP or less than one 10,000-th of the monies authorized." I took this as a continuation of the ideologically motivated resistance I had encountered from my earliest days at the Federation, when we fought for years to preserve a miniscule federal loan program for CDCUs.

PART TWO
KAPPA ALPHA PSI FEDERAL CREDIT UNION: THE FOUNDERS' STORY

Michael R. McCray

Prologue

> "Why, sometimes I've believed as many as six impossible things before breakfast."
> –*Alice's Adventures in Wonderland* by Lewis Carroll

Black Achievement: AACUC Hall of Fame Induction

My heart pounded and I beamed with pride as I introduced KAPFCU's founder and my Kappa brother, Victor Russell, at his induction into the African American Credit Union Coalition (AACUC) Hall of Fame in 2017. Victor is a towering man of average height, with salt and pepper hair, bushy eyebrows, and a pronounced mustache. He is fair-skinned with freckles and hazel eyes, with a slender build as a former student-athlete who pitched (baseball) his way through college. A reformed investment banker, Vic wore tailored suits with silk ties and Italian leather shoes. He spoke of founding the Richardson Plano Guide Right Foundation and the Kappa Alpha Psi Federal Credit Union.

> When I arrived in Dallas-Fort Worth in 1994, I saw many social and economic opportunities to improve African American lives. The Southwest business community was trying to recover after the Savings and Loan collapse. I recalled several creative ideas that I could develop through the Kappa Alpha Psi fraternity.
>
> As I drove from Chicago, I reflected on several philanthropic missions that my fraternity had instilled in me over my 21 years

as a member and life member. These experiences opened my mind about engaging in and building upon my fraternity's proven community events and social fundraising strategies. As of the spring of 1997, the hunt was on to create a viable entity through my Kappa Alumni Chapter, Richardson Plano Alumni of Kappa Alpha Psi Fraternity. The first thing on my agenda was to create a 501(c)(3) private foundation specializing in multiple areas.

The State of Texas's initial approvals in 1998 enabled the Richardson Plano Guide Right Foundation's (RPGRF) first-ever Black and White Ball in 1999 to proceed. This exceptional Black and White Ball covered a weekend of events and receptions in the second week of June 1999. Community dignitaries, business partners, and political leaders gathered at the Intercontinental Hotel in Addison, Texas.

As I launched the RPGRF and chaired the initial 1999 Gala with a team of dedicated Kappa Alpha Psi Fraternity members, all roads opened up. We evaluated other enterprising opportunities after establishing this footprint in the community. After a second and third Black and White Ball, I headed into August 2002. I researched financial strength in the African American community through Kappa Alpha Psi and eight other Black fraternities and sororities in 2002-2003.

We tested initial focus groups for a successful financial institution at the Southwestern Province (SWP) meeting in Arlington, Texas, in March 2003. The test was at the SWP Board meeting with about 450 to 600 in attendance that weekend to seek the board's support to purchase a "bank." However, understanding the challenges and the unlikeliness of raising the capital requirements to launch a bank, I re-stated our case and stipulated to the board in their second round of meetings that I would lead a team. We formed Kappa Alpha Psi Federal Credit Union.

My background from Bear Stearns Investment Bank allowed me to arrange meetings with the Texas League of Credit Unions through February 2004. I sought the guidance and blessing of one of the nation's largest and most proficient credit union trade associations. Based in North Dallas, I could set various meetings to learn and get help from the executives—the same hour or same day. This access improved my relationships and allowed me to lead the team and file for our charter in Region IV of the Southwest. This Region IV office [of the National Credit Union Administration] was based in Austin, Texas.

After the initial submission of two or three revised applications into July 2004, the [NCUA] administrator said, 'Kappa Alpha Psi, the ones in red, I remember you guys. Y'all would get drunk and party all the time.' So, I had to make a trip to Region IV. I met with the NCUA to discuss and arbitrate our point of view.

I vividly explained to the NCUA Administrator that the Kappa Alpha Psi fraternity consists of professionals and college-educated men. Kappa is not like the typical college fraternity that ends after graduation, such as white fraternities. He acknowledged his college fraternity but said it had no post-college support.

We successfully chartered the Kappa Alpha Psi Federal Credit Union as a national federal institution in 2004. Our rights to operate and take in deposits included Puerto Rico, Guam, and the Philippines. I attended 12 Kappa Provincial meetings by Spring 2005 to inform the fraternity and encourage KAPFCU membership.

Throughout 2004 and into August 2010, we operated the first "virtual" NCUA charted internet-based credit union platform. Rep. Eddie Bernice Johnson (D-TX) celebrated KAPFCU as the first federal African American financial institution in Texas.

We grew from zero dollars to $1 million in deposits. KAPFCU received significant NCUA designations that benefit high school and undergraduate college students (young adults). In addition, we secured CDFI certification, CCR certification with the federal government's GSA division, and applied for CDFI Grants. KAPFCU received approval for $100,000 from the CDFI Department of Treasury as one recipient of millions of dollars allocated to grow credit unions. The CDFI Fund would have awarded our allocation on August 19, 2010.

Bill Bynum and Victor were both honored in the AACUC's Hall of Fame, with Bynum receiving the Pete Crear Lifetime Achievement Award. A Black man from North Carolina, Bynum had to navigate the Deep South, Mississippi Delta culture to make his mark and garner national recognition. Bynum grew a tiny community development corporation (CDC) from the closet of a small Methodist church to a billion-dollar regional financial powerhouse, using with a $3 million Empowerment Zone/Enterprise Community (EZ/EC) grant.

He is the founder and CEO of Hope Community Federal Credit Union, the most prominent Black-led CDFI in the country. Various philanthropies recognize and honor his outstanding work, and he has served on the advisory board of the CDFI Fund. I was the desk officer assigned to support Hope Enterprise Corporation when I worked for the U.S. Department of Agriculture (USDA). I was a technology and community development specialist for the Clinton White House's Federal Empowerment Zones and Enterprise Communities Program.

My Journey

I met Victor Russell, my Kappa fraternity brother, when he thunderously threw a pair of NCUA examiners out of the law office in the middle of a federal examination.

As a lawyer and CPA, I advocated for civil and human rights, including free speech and whistleblower protections. I was knowledgeable about USDA and regulatory sciences. I also had experience pushing back against government overreach and abuse, first at the USDA and then within a prominent social/charitable organization. I had exposed wrongdoing in the venerable community action organization, ACORN.

I had prior experience fighting the federal government or powerful special interests. In 2007, I received the "No FEAR Award" in Washington, D.C., from the No FEAR Institute, founded by civil rights icon Reverend Walter Fauntroy. The Notification and Federal Employee

Anti-discrimination and Retaliation Act of 2002 ("No FEAR") was the first civil rights legislation passed in the twenty-first century.

Volunteering for KAPFCU called upon all the education and advocacy experiences of my long career. KAPFCU was an excellent fit for its fraternal parent organization. The credit union knew its members and provided second-chance credit and/or emergency funds to an at-risk and hard-to-serve population. Thus, KAPFCU routinely encouraged members to pre-pay their loans to mitigate any associated risk.

I offered my expertise to Victor and KAPFCU. I started working on the Advisory Board for KAPFCU to oversee compliance and lead community development initiatives. With my support, KAPFCU became the first and only African American fraternal credit union to be certified by the federal CDFI Fund. We became the first "virtual" credit union operating on a national footprint. We became part of the CDCU movement through the National Federation of CDCUs, as well as a member of the African American Credit Union Coalition.

CHAPTER 12

Alice In Wonderland

> "It's no use going back to yesterday, because I was a different person."
>
> —Alice to the caterpillar in *Alice's Adventures in Wonderland* by Lewis Carroll

Capital: A Matter of Life and Death for Credit Unions

On August 3, 2010, the National Credit Union Administration (NCUA) served a surprise liquidation order on Kappa Alpha Psi Federal Credit Union (KAPFCU). In response, the tiny African American credit union sought constitutional due process from the NCUA. The core of the conflict was capital, or net worth—the amount of equity a credit union has over and above what it owes to depositors or creditors.

Credit unions are subject to punitive "Prompt Corrective Action" (PCA) if they cannot maintain an adequate ratio of net worth to their total assets. For most credit unions, this means a Net Worth Ratio (NWR) of 7% or higher. KAPFCU claimed NCUA was liquidating the credit union based on the false impression in the media that KAPFCU's crucial NWR had dropped to 1.95% and "had no reasonable chance for recovery."

KAPFCU was a new credit union, starting from scratch with a zero net worth ratio (0%). The credit union had built its NWR up to

1.95%, or "minimally capitalized," as of March 31, 2010—and even higher to 3.67%, or "moderately capitalized," by June 30, 2010, after which date NCUA elected to close or "liquidate" the credit union.

The NCUA chose the unusual and extreme measure of liquidation without consideration of conservatorship or a merger. KAPFCU had suffered only one loan loss (for less than $4,500) in its six-year operating history. By NCUA's own rules and regulations, new credit unions have ten years to become "adequately capitalized" and achieve a net worth ratio of 7%.

Thus, the NCUA decision to liquidate KAPFCU on August 3, 2010, was ill-advised, improper, and legally actionable. NCUA rushed to liquidate KAPFCU not because it was failing, but because KAPFCU was becoming too successful—that is, recovering too quickly. The steep decline in KAPFCU's NWR to 0.58% on December 31, 2009, resulted from NCUA's levy of $6,700 on KAPFCU. The assessment was imposed on federal credit unions because of massive losses caused by exposure to real estate risk or mortgage-backed securities incurred by the large "corporate" (wholesale) credit unions—losses that had nothing to do with KAPFCU's actions, since it had no exposure to the real estate risk or mortgage-backed securities.

CORPORATE STABILIZATION

Corporate Stabilization was a monetary assessment charged against all credit unions following the mortgage crisis to save corporate credit unions. As a result, the NCUA eased credit union capital requirements across the board, resulting in restated "hurdle" rates, including a "hockey stick," which lowers capital requirements during the stabilization period.

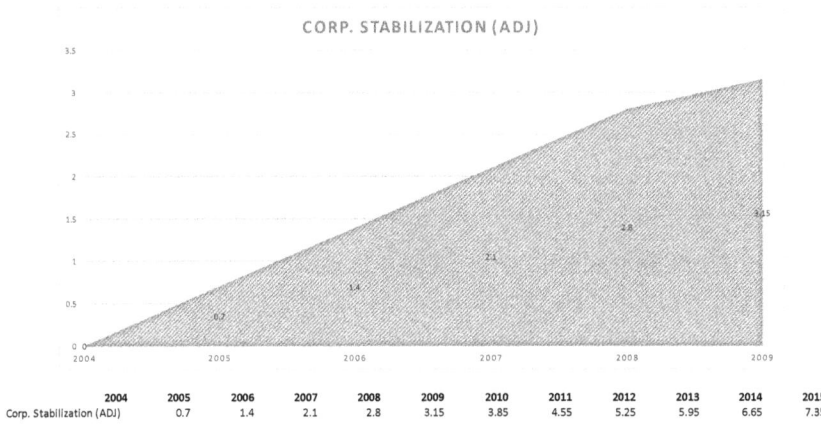

CORP. STABILIZATION (ADJ)

	2004	2005	2006	2007	2008	2009	2010	2011	2012	2013	2014	2015
Corp. Stabilization (ADJ)		0.7	1.4	2.1	2.8	3.15	3.85	4.55	5.25	5.95	6.65	7.35

KAPFCU, like all federally insured credit unions, was required to replenish the federal deposit insurance fund to make good the hundreds of millions of dollars of losses of those larger corporate credit unions. NCUA's own supervisory guidance stated that credit unions should not be adversely judged for losses because of corporate stabilization. Thus, by June 30, 2010, KAPFCU's NWR, adjusted for the corporate stabilization assessment and computed on a cash basis, was 4.93%, which meant that KAPFCU had complied with a Revised Business Plan (RBP) approved by NCUA.

There is a strong public policy need for NCUA to offer special benefits to credit unions, like KAPFCU, that are designated "low income." These include NCUA Technical Assistance Grants (TAG) and other support services to aid credit unions, which provide desperately needed development and financial services to traditionally underserved and hard-to-serve populations. Regrettably, NCUA evaluated KAPFCU as if it were a mature credit union, defined as being ten years old with $10 million or more in assets. The accounting rules and regulations are entirely different for these small, new credit unions—but KAPFCU was improperly evaluated based on the much higher standard by NCUA examiners.

Ignoring the improvement in KAPFCU's NWR to 3.67% by June 30, 2010, NCUA opted to move forward with liquidating the credit union. KAPFCU challenged NCUA's action, bringing the case to the federal district court in Washington, D.C.

Ironically, KAPFCU's court case may be the most significant challenge to the NCUA's authority in recent memory. This tiny African American credit union was contesting the constitutionality of the Federal Credit Union Act and NCUA's rules and regulations themselves. KAPFCU's chief complaint was that it had not been afforded the full flexibility allowed under NCUA rules, regulations, and supervisory authority for credit unions of similar size and character.

Confrontation

> An angry sun glared off the tinted glass of a small law office in Richardson, Texas. I waited for my cousin, the proprietor, to return. Tall in stature but slight in height, Julius Thompson is a brilliant attorney who is the general counsel for KAPFCU. He provides legal expertise and guidance to the fraternity enterprise. He also offers his offices, file cabinets, and conference room to support the KAPFCU effort.
>
> Friends and family call him the "Godfather;" Julius Thompson, the bald barrister with a caramel coffee complexion. Julius has a knack for networking and connecting people. He also recruited

me to assist KAPFCU with government relations and community development expertise to help grow the fledgling credit union.

While waiting for Julius to arrive, I observed the circle of life outside the ground floor windowpane of the Julius Thompson Law Office. A few army ants overwhelmed an injured yellow jacket. The insect pismire soldiers banded together to hoist away their winged trophy. However, a giant black spider thwarted their progress. Licorice-colored insects battled over the wounded carcass of the decaying onyx and gold prize. The black widow grabbed the hornet, pulling it away from the ants. The spider was larger and more robust than any individual ant and had much longer legs, which made it faster. But instead of racing the insect militia, the spider spun some web and slowly thrusted the wasp onward.

Her gossamer threads ensnared the wasp and cleaved it from the ants. It was not quick and decisive but a delicate, iterative process. She spun another layer of webbing and then trawled the wasp some more. Each layer entombed the wasp in thicker webbing, weighing it down and protecting it from the onslaught of the angry ants. Each tug pulled the prize further from their reach.

Turning their attention from the hornet, the ants swarmed the spider. As she elevated the yellowjacket above the reach of the ants, she exposed her long legs to the swarm. First, she moved quickly, confident in her prowess. Then, she slowed as the ants attacked her joints. An insignificant few at first, now a platoon of ant reinforcements extended across the windowsill, windowpane, and exterior wall into the courtyard. While meaningless individually, together, the ant column could overrun the stronger predator if given enough time to organize.

At 6:02 p.m., an alabaster male with stern, square cheekbones and thin lips walked into the conference room at Julius Thompson PLLC to conduct the quarterly examination of KAPFCU, the only federally chartered Black-owned financial institution in the state. He wore a dark conservative suit, a busy patterned tie, and polished leather shoes. He was clean-shaven with amber hair and piercing cobalt eyes. NCUA Supervisory Analyst Tony Rausch personified the Texan view towards minority-owned financial institutions. Privileged, aggressive, and assertive, his demeanor was best described as "typical Texan," exuding his white male privilege. Empowered as a federal official, he was assertive regardless of whether he was right or wrong. Ultimately, being a "Fed" means that you never have to say you're sorry.

Total Disaster

A loud commotion erupted inside the conference room of the small legal office and real estate title plant. Tony Rausch, a "good 'ol boy" from Texas, versus Victor Russell, a fast-talking hustler from Chicago. They congealed like oil and water. However, Victor had transformed from Chicagoan to Texan, donning ten-gallon hats and ornate belt-buckles with Italian suits—even Black people do rodeo in Texas.

During the regular quarterly examination, Victor Russell described the current operations of KAPFCU and his plans to increase revenues by origination fees for residential or commercial mortgage transactions. Tony's eyebrows rose. "Slow down, Victor, before you try to jump into high finance. You guys are just sitting on your deposits. If you want more money, make more loans to your members."

Victor sat upright, interlocking his fingers. "We are trying to mitigate our risk. In banking, we say, 'know your customer.' We know our members and make loans to individuals we know will pay us back."

"Very good, because that's the only way you can legitimately make money to generate revenues," said Tony.

Victor argued that KAPFCU was not issuing or holding mortgages on the credit union's balance sheet. Instead, KAPFCU would only make referral fee income by finding qualified borrowers for other financial institutions. Rausch balked at this and declared that KAPFCU could not generate mortgage fee income because of real estate risk. "I will not let you do that, Victor."

"What do you mean, you won't let us do this? You don't run our credit union—we do!" Victor bellowed.

"That's not how small credit unions operate." Tony replied, "You must grow your loan portfolio. Make your money from member loans."

Victor rose to his feet. "That's one way we can make money, but that's not the only way," he replied, wagging his finger for emphasis, "If we want to have car washes or bake sales, there shouldn't be any limit on how many extra services we provide as long as we don't have any loan exposure."

Tony matched his glare. "I don't know who you think you are, Victor. You could be J.P. Morgan, Jr. I won't allow KAPFCU to get involved in mortgages or residential brokering even if it is off-balance sheet activity."

Victor's nostrils flared in outrage.

"And another thing," Tony glared, "no more unrecorded expenses. You need to set up a reserve account to book debits for your data processor."

"Say what?"

Tony said, "I'm looking through your call report and you're not paying or consistently paying for your data processor."

"That's because Total/1 is not just a vendor but a potential partner. We're working with them to expand their services to all minority credit unions," Victor answered. "They aren't charging us because we are negotiating a business relationship with them to go after other minority credit unions."

Victor gloated, "Total/1 has not started collection activities because KAPFCU is negotiating a partnership with Total/1 to recruit AACUC members."

Tony stared blankly.

"Look, Tony. We are the first virtual credit union allowed by the NCUA. The entire credit union industry, especially Black ones, is going to look to KAPFCU to see how we did it. We are the tip of the spear for online credit unions," Victor said. "We are the perfect partner to expand Total/1 services to the African American credit union movement and we can earn a 25% commission for promoting the platform."

He leaned back in the conference chair and formed a steeple with his fingers.

"You're not as smart as you think, Victor. You guys are showing 20% returns from your loan portfolio, but you don't have any loan products over 15% interest."

Surprised, Victor's eyes widened.

"How did you do that, Victor?

Victor's nostrils flared again.

Tony waved his hands, mimicking a magician. ". . . abracadabra?"

Victor's eyes darted down and right.

"F*ck you!" Victor Russell pushed the conference room chair back. "No harm, no foul!"

"F*ck you!" Tony Rausch leapt to his feet as well.

The KAPFCU board members broke up the two hot-headed finance gurus and rushed the NCUA examiners out of the law offices of Julius L. Thompson, who summarized the meeting.

"That went well, Victor!"

The conference room erupted in laughter.

The relationship between credit unions—especially LICUs—and NCUA examiners is often fraught with tension and animosity. NCUA examiners are federal agents who sometimes act like patrolmen policing dangerous neighborhoods. The famed Los Angeles mystery writer Walter Mosley would have described the relationship as "just another game of cops and n*ggers." Sometimes tensions boil over, just like the Watts Riots in 1965 that Mosley writes about.

Debating Safety and Soundness

Loan pre-payment became an issue when Tony Rausch confronted Victor Russell during an NCUA examination, charging the credit union with overstating or overcharging interest. Victor did not know it yet, but Total/1 had a software defect that miscalculated loan pre-payments as additional interest payments, which inflated interest income. After being notified about this product and informed of their software malfunction, Total/1 ceased all collection efforts from KAPFCU. However, KAPFCU maintained extra reserves (arrears) in case Total/1 requested payment. Region IV NCUA examiners accelerated punitive prompt corrective action, writing up KAPFCU under "safety and soundness" concerns.

To address PCA and respond to the NCUA letter of understanding and agreement (LUA), which prescribed required remediation steps, Region IV officials referred KAPFCU to the Office of Small Credit Union Initiatives for assistance. As a result, the NCUA assigned one of its economic development specialists to assist KAPFCU in preparing revised business plans and net worth restoration plans while implementing NCUA-approved policies and methodologies.

Carl Banks, a seasoned financial analyst, was an imposing figure with a stocky build. Hazel-skinned with curly chocolate hair, he dressed like a typical Fed, wearing quality suits and polished leather shoes. Carl possessed decades of financial expertise, institutional knowledge of the NCUA system, and an affinity for small grassroots credit unions across the country. Cerebral and imaginative, Carl Banks was an expert in NCUA financial modeling.

With over 20 years' experience at NCUA, Carl had a heart for underserved people—and knew all the "tricks of the trade" in the NCUA system. He explained the incentives for NCUA examiners to find things to write up, whether they were violations or not. If a small credit union implodes and an examiner misses the red flags, then they can lose their jobs. Many examiners write up low-income credit unions and CDCUs not because they are mismanaged, but because they serve an underserved or hard-to-serve market.

KAPFCU submitted a secondary capital plan to raise up to $100,000 in equity-like debt; a power that was at the time reserved for low-income credit unions. Region IV officials acknowledged that KAPFCU's plan satisfied the relevant NCUA rules and regulations but denied the secondary capital plan. The denial was intentional and malicious, because the rationale provided by the credit union conflicted with the relevant NCUA rules and regulations and was unrelated to any so-called "safety or soundness" concerns, which we believed were pretext for intentional and malicious treatment of the credit union; an excuse for NCUA's arbitrary and capricious refusal to adhere to the relevant rules, regulations, and supervisory authority.

NCUA Region IV officials denied and refused to approve KAPFCU business plans, restoration plans, and asset/liability management programs. In particular, the denial of the Secondary Capital Plan was a malicious attempt to liquidate KAPFCU, even though the plan was prepared by an NCUA economic development specialist and complied with all NCUA requirements. The officials became hostile towards KAPFCU after our minority credit union insisted that the examiners follow NCUA rules, regulations, and supervisory authority regarding new, small, low-income, and community development credit unions.

Missing The GAAP

Rausch didn't answer the bell for round two of the subsequent KAPFCU examination. Instead, a stout, salmon-skinned woman in a leopard print blouse entered the room. Carolyn Penaluna replaced Rauch as the supervisory analyst for KAPFCU. With short-cropped rosy hair with burgundy roots, she looked like an analyst because of her non-athletic build and functional rather than designer eyeglass frames. She looked like someone who made their living reviewing spreadsheets tethered to a desk rather than toiling with her back or hands in the gym. She was disarmingly mundane.

Hardworking and smart, Penaluna possessed a non-confrontational demeanor. She was a stickler for the rules; at least some of them. Penaluna was pleasant and unassuming—unlike the bellicose Rausch. She was an NCUA worker bee who believed "you can catch more bees with honey instead of vinegar." This change in personnel deescalated tensions between KAPFCU and NCUA Region IV. She quietly implemented the previous NCUA policy recommendations and switched KAPFCU to reporting on full accrual accounting to capture data processing costs.

A CPA for a Fortune 500 company, Bill Whitehead served as the treasurer for KAPFCU. Whitehead had cocoa skin, sepia eyes, and midnight relaxed hair. Baby-faced with a medium build, He wore designer suits and shoes. He was a Black man working in a white world, and a naturally affable guy. Whitehead climbed the corporate ladder. He knew how to go along and play the game: don't create powerful enemies, and never piss off white people. In contrast, Vic was a hustler from Chicago who graduated to finance and real estate. Michael (Mac) was a solo practitioner turned politico and served as a freelance consultant. There was no corporate ladder to success for them. They relied on free markets and the law of the jungle—you eat what you kill—so they could identify the opportunity and seize the moment to advance.

Whitehead was deferential to authority. Thus, he was reluctant to challenge Penaluna because she insisted on keeping KAPFCU on full accrual. I argued KAPFCU was not required to stay on full accrual accounting according to NCUA rules and regulations. Penaluna started PCAs against KAPFCU after the examination. Region IV issued an LUA to protect the "safety and soundness" of the share insurance fund.

Because of NCUA's actions, KAPFCU suffered a steep decline in net worth and concomitant GAAP record-keeping discrepancies. This lowered KAPFUC's capital position and overall management (record-keeping) ratings under CAMEL, which constricted KAPFCU's access to NCUA grant funding and secondary capital.

Cash (Basis) is King

NCUA rules and regulations allowed small credit unions with less than $10 million in assets to report on a "cash basis" or "modified cash" basis. Federal regulation 12 U.S. Code § 1782(6)(C)(iii) states that small credit unions are exempted from the mandatory GAAP treatment that Penaluna imposed on KAPFCU, under the *de minimus* exception to the standard accounting principles. This became the central dispute that precipitated the downward spiral in KAPFCU's management, record-keeping, capital position, and overall CAMEL ratings. It ultimately resulted in NCUA's LUA and PCA.

KAPFCU sought a legal opinion about the contract dispute with the Total/1 services vendor. The credit union's board of directors released the reserves or arrears into net worth after the statute of limitations on the contract dispute expired. KAPFCU also sought professional legal and accounting consultation regarding proper accounting treatment.[55]

Region IV officials claimed that KAPFCU's change in accounting methods was a disingenuous attempt to "cook the books" by not recording a data processing contract with a third-party vendor. However, the board of directors had deemed the data processing contract uncollectible. Thus, KAPFCU disputed the unenforceable contract, which was barred by the applicable statute of limitations. That being the case, the change in accounting methods did not affect how we reported the data processing contract. An unenforceable contract was not a liability under either full accrual or modified cash accounting. Thus, the change in accounting was *not* about KAPFCU trying to "cook the books."

---

55 "Credit unions for which adoption of the accrual basis of accounting is not required or practicable should use the modified cash basis of accounting." Dan Mouton, CPA. See Appendix C: CPA Opinion (Cash Basis).

Contrary to NCUAs false assertions, KAPFCU sought to change back to a modified cash basis for four legitimate business reasons:

1. To Comply with NCUA Supervisory Authority. An NCUA supervisory letter recognizes the strong public policy considerations supporting low-income credit unions and community development credit unions. It mandates that NCUA examiners compare low-income and community development credit unions to other low-income and community development credit unions when performing supervisory evaluations and contacts, and therefore, not discriminate against minority/community credit unions simply because they operate on low-income business models.

After receiving the supervisory letter, KAPFCU contacted the trade association for small, low-income, minority, and community development credit unions. The Federation polled their membership and reported that no LICUs or CDCUs under $10 million in assets use full accrual accounting. We notified Region IV officials of this and requested a list of the low-income credit union peers that KAPFCU was being compared to. KAPFCU needed to go back to modified cash accounting to be fairly compared to other low-income and community development credit unions, as required by NCUA supervisory authority. But Region IV officials ignored this request.

2. To Improve Record-Keeping. KAPFCU had no full-time staff. It operated through an all-volunteer board. We developed a streamlined and straightforward operational model that could be implemented with limited or non-existent staff. KAPFCU projected it could hire a full-time manager once it built its loan portfolio to $875,000 and achieved a 75% asset deployment ratio.

Full accrual required KAPFCU to maintain 35 to 40 sub-ledger accounts every month. Any error, no matter how small or immaterial, would be negatively evaluated by NCUA examiners and recorded as "persistent record-keeping" errors. For example, the record-keeping errors pegged on KAPFCU amounted to eight transactions out of thousands, totaling less than $1,400; a non-material amount under standard accounting practices, since KAPFCU had over $800,000 in total assets. KAPFCU needed a full-time branch manager to employ full accrual accounting, which we did not have.

Modified cash accounting only required that KAPFCU maintain four or five sub-ledger accounts. Our volunteer staff was able to maintain this level of record-keeping. In fact, when we were on modified cash accounting in 2005 and 2006, we had no record-keeping problems. It was only when we were forced to use full accrual accounting from 2007 through 2009 that KAPFCU experienced any persistent record-keeping problems or difficulties. KAPFCU's record-keeping improved when it went back to modified cash.

3. To Control Expenses. Modified cash basis accounting gave KAPFCU management more control over the operational performance of the credit union. It allowed KAPFCU management to better match revenues to expenses. KAPFCU had "seasonal spikes" in membership that corresponded to back-to-school-related activities. Our membership fee income fluctuated accordingly. From an operational management perspective, it was helpful to hold off on certain larger expenses and pay them during periods when we had increased income. This is perfectly legitimate and allowable under modified cash accounting. And, contrary to Region IV officials' contentions, there was nothing nefarious or improper about doing so.

4. To Improve its CAMEL Rating. The CAMEL rating is a composite rating of the overall health of a credit union, ranging from 1 (best) to 5 (worst). It comprises five individual components, some objective while others are subjective: Capital Adequacy ("C"), Asset Quality ("A"), Management ("M") Earnings ("E"), and Asset/Liability Management ("L"). NCUA adopted the CAMEL rating system in

October 1987. Its purpose is to provide an accurate and consistent assessment of a credit union's financial condition and operations in the five areas. It is not a "report card," but is instead an internal tool to measure risk and allocate resources for supervision.

NCUA distorted KAPFCU's CAMEL rating due to applying the wrong accounting method in 2005 and 2006. Only when forced to use full accrual accounting did our rating drop to CAMEL 4 (unacceptable/failing) from 2007 through 2009. The deterioration was because of persistent record-keeping problems that lowered KAPFCU's overall Management ("M") rating, understated KAPFCU's capital position, and lowered our Capital Adequacy ("C") rating—because of NCUA-imposed uncontrolled, runaway expenses.

Our record-keeping improved when KAPFCU went back to a modified cash basis in 2010, which should have improved our management ("M") rating and improved our net worth position to "moderately capitalized" (3.67%), reflected in an improved capital adequacy ("C") rating. Thus, KAPFCUs overall CAMEL should have improved back to CAMEL 3, at least.

Thus, contrary to NCUA assertions, the data processing contract was not why KAPFCU sought to use cash basis accounting. Instead, the refusal to follow NCUA rules and regulations convinced us that NCUA's Region IV was intentionally trying to liquidate KAPFCU.

The CDFI Fund Awards

KAPFCU received its designation as a certified Community Development Financial Institution (CDFI) by the U.S. Department of Treasury on August 26, 2006, a "red-letter" day. Created by the Riegle Community Development and Regulatory Improvement Act of 1994, it was the same year I joined the U.S. Department of Agriculture.[56]

The CDFI Fund's mission is to expand the capacity of financial institutions to provide credit, capital, and financial services to underserved populations and communities in the U.S.. The CDFI Fund announces a fresh round of technical and financial assistance award every year. On August 19, 2010, Donna Gambrell, Director of the U.S. Treasury Department's CDFI Fund, prepared to announce new awards at the Lower East Side People's FCU in New York City, a $26 million credit union that the Federation had helped organized in 1986.[57] The Federation expected the fund to distribute the largest amount of money in its history because of the $247 million allocated in 2009. The Federation also asked credit unions that received money through the Community Development Capital Initiative program of the Treasury Department to let it know. "Since the Treasury is not making individual approvals public, we need your assistance to track that progress. Therefore, it is imperative that you let us know when you receive your 'preliminary approval letter,'" wrote Brian Gately, the Federation's Senior Consultant for Small and Emerging Credit Unions, who had been an examiner for the NCUA. Brian became instant "BFFs" with me and Vic and was the central point of contact between the Federation and KAPFCU.

Come to Jesus

The relationship between KAPFCU and Region IV continued to deteriorate as NCUA implemented its PCA: the examiners would find, or make up, any excuse to write up the credit union or claim KAPFCU had violated the LUA. For instance, the regional administrators wrote up KAPFCU for being "too dependent" on grant income.

---

56 In 1995, I blew the whistle on $40 million in waste, fraud, and abuse in the Clinton White House Empowerment Zone Initiative.
57 In 2008, KAPFCU hosted Donna Gambrell as a featured guest during a reception honoring African American leaders in the credit union industry.

However, an NCUA white paper[58] recognized that low-income and community development credit unions use grant income and operate on a different business model. KAPFCU was a federally certified CDFI and Community Development Entity (CDE). These designations provided us with significant opportunities in terms of both capitalization and technical assistance. We were eligible to apply for financial assistance (FA) and technical assistance (TA) grants from the CDFI Fund to defray the costs of launching new services and lending platforms (i.e., credit card, ATM, and mortgage brokering services).

KAPFCU kept very detailed minutes of board and advisory board meetings. Kenny Burnett was a young, dark-skinned fraternity brother who worked in technology and kept copious notes. In fact, he was *too* proficient at keeping minutes. NCUA examiners often used board deliberations, as opposed to board actions, as an excuse to write up KAPFCU in quarterly examinations. KAPFCU should have received a kind of credit union "Miranda" warning—"everything you say can and will be used against you." However, in response to purported record-keeping deficiencies, KAPFCU hired the Texas Credit Union League to provide back office services.

KAPFCU minimized its office expenses by utilizing a shared office service in Addison, Texas. A small office for storing files and records and access to the shared conference room and coffee dispenser was all KAPFCU really needed. This arrangement was perfect for conducting meetings with clients and regulators. Julius L. Thompson PLLC. previously housed KAPFCU in the back-office of the law firm.

The next shoe to drop was an emergency meeting requested by Richard Lynn, NCUA's Region IV Director, a dark-haired man with a receding hairline that was greying around his temples. He wore a sharkskin suit with a crisp white shirt and colorful tie. With piercing eyes and an interrogator's gaze, Director Lynn conducted the

---

58 NCUA Supervisory Letter to Credit Unions 10-CU-01.

closed-door meeting with the board of directors at the offices of KAPFCU. He demanded we meet without Victor.

The purpose was a "come to Jesus" meeting about KAPFCU's progress in addressing the required corrections in the LUA and to assess operating prospects for KAPFCU. The real reason for the meeting, we understood, was to convince the board of directors to replace the president/chairman.

> Director Lynn began, "What are we going to do about Victor? KAPFCU is being mismanaged, including profligate spending by the CEO. How else do you explain spending over $1,000 in credit union funds for the NBA All-Star game?"
>
> All eyes turned towards Kenny, a bald man with mocha skin and glasses. Kenny Henderson was an IRS supervisor and the chairman of the supervisory committee for KAPFCU. Tall and authoritative, the brown-skinned "Kojak-like" figure said, "We already investigated this claim when the examiners flagged it before. We paid no expenses for the NBA all-star game. However, we found $94 in questionable bar charges that weekend. Victor bought a round of drinks for some of our VIPs, which he promptly repaid."
>
> All eyes turn back towards Director Lynn.
>
> Richard Lynn is stunned by that revelation. "KAPFCU is in trouble, and I'm here to save it. The question is, which one of you men will step up and replace Victor?"
>
> Silence.
>
> "What about you, Steve?" Director Lynn said. "You're next in line. Are you willing to take the helm to save the credit union?"
>
> Steve Ellis, Vice Chairman of KAPFCU, has cocoa skin with wavy hair. Smooth as Tennessee whiskey, Steve has an easy Creole cadence from Southern Louisiana. "Excuse me, sir, Vic paid not some—but all—of the bills and the organizing costs for establishing KAPFCU. We will not turn our back on him now."

The central tenets of Kappa Alpha Psi include manliness,

brotherhood, and fidelity. Thus, the KAPFCU board refused NCUA's offer to condemn or desert its founder. Instead, the KAPFCU board of directors stood by Victor and refused to offer any replacement, which vexed the Region IV director.

The Credit Union Tsunami: NCUA "Stabilizes" Corporate Credit Unions

The Dow Jones dropped 504 points in a single day in September 2008, when the mortgage bubble burst, precipitating the foreclosure crises. Many financial institutions, including banks and credit unions, were negatively impacted. Early in 2009, NCUA assessed costs on all credit unions to recapitalize the deposit insurance fund for the expenses of the large, failed "corporate" credit unions following severe real estate-related losses resulting from the sub-prime mortgage bubble.[59] KAPFCU sustained a $6,700 loss because of the NCUA corporate stabilization assessments.

Although all federally insured credit unions were required to contribute to the Share Insurance Fund (administered by the NCUA, the Share Insurance Fund insures individual accounts up to $250,000, and a member's interest in all joint accounts combined is insured up to $250,000), NCUA supervisory guidance stated that credit unions should not be punished or prejudiced for losses because of corporate stabilization. Thus, on a cash basis, KAPFCU's net worth ratio (NWR) after the corporate stabilization assessment was 4.93% (as of 6/30/2010), which meant that KAPFCU operations complied with its Revised Business Plan (RBP) previously approved by NCUA.

---

59 Corporate credit unions were like "bankers' banks," wholesale institutions which invested idle funds for local credit unions and provided other services.

ADJUSTED MODIFIED CASH BASIS

This chart illustrates KAPFCU's interim performance adjusted to "modified cash basis." Large and mature credit unions are required to operate on GAAP full accrual accounting. In contrast, small and emerging credit unions can operate on a modified cash basis.

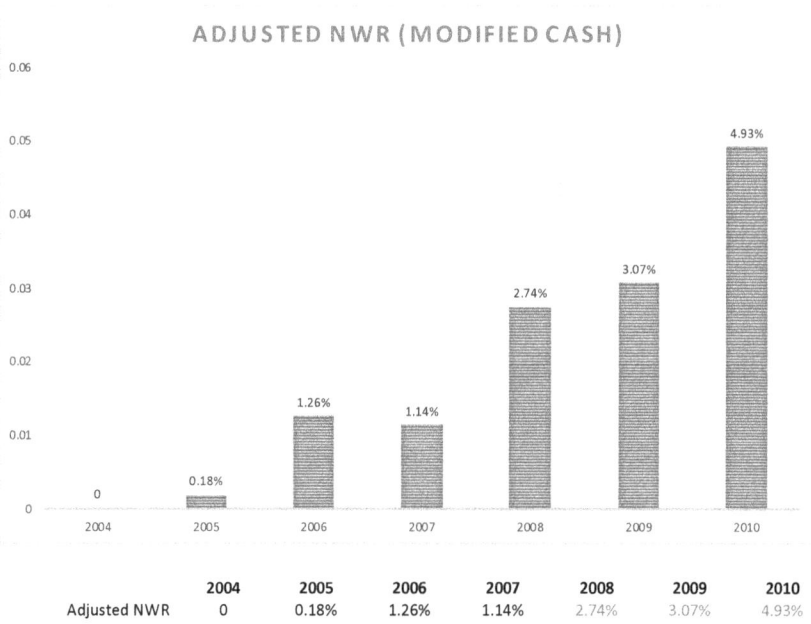

	2004	2005	2006	2007	2008	2009	2010
Adjusted NWR	0	0.18%	1.26%	1.14%	2.74%	3.07%	4.93%

NCUA chastised KAPFCU for failing to comply with the approved RBP. However, NCUA failed to acknowledge that they approved this RBP prior to the corporate stabilization assessments. Thus, money was taken from KAPFCU (as it was from other credit unions) because of the failure of the large corporate credit unions, but these loss assessments were entirely unrelated to KAPFCU operations. KAPFCU had no exposure to real estate or mortgage-backed securities.

The NCUA assessment treated all credit unions "the same." However, that does not mean they treated all credit unions "fairly" or "equally," which is the difference between equality (equally) and equity (fairness). For example, consider a hypothetical traditional family of four; father (adult male), mother (adult female), son (adolescent male), and newborn daughter (baby girl). The father gets injured in a motorcycle accident and needs six pints of blood to survive. An "equal" solution: take two pints of blood from everyone equally. You will save the father, but you will kill the newborn baby girl. An "equitable" solution: take four pints from the mother, two from the son, and none from the baby. This would save the father and preserve the family.

The NCUA sacrificed innocent low-income credit unions to save large corporate credit unions that engaged in risky lending practices. NCUA stated they would exempt any credit union with no previous "write-ups" from stabilization. However, there are no "unblemished" low-income credit unions or CDCUs because they serve financially disadvantaged and hard-to-serve markets. NCUA showed a steep decline in KAPFCU's net worth ratio down to 0.58% on December 31, 2009, because of the corporate stabilization assessment of $6,700 imposed on KAPFCU, which had no exposure of its own to real estate risk or mortgage-backed securities.

Size Matters: NCUA and Small Credit Unions

There is no shortage of otherwise level-headed leaders within credit unions who swear NCUA's secret goal, sworn to in some sort of covert ceremony held in the parking garage beneath its Alexandria, Virginia, headquarters, involved the sacrifice of young examiners in order to put small and medium-size credit unions out of business. I found it "interesting" that NCUA's "real feelings" towards small credit unions—seemingly at odds with what Chairman Matz proclaimed all the time—were voiced by a high-level NCUA official at a public forum for credit unions.

In a message to Cliff Rosenthal in August 2010, Dan Morrisey, the long-time volunteer Treasurer/CEO for the Queen of Peace Arlington FCU, described the apparent contradiction between the NCUA's "official" support for small credit unions and what actually guided senior agency officials. As Morrisey reported, a credit union representative at a public meeting questioned whether NCUA was, in fact, giving larger institutions more time to work out problems than it does smaller and midsize CUs. "The size and the sophistication of the credit union is a factor," said John Kutchey, Deputy Director of NCUA's Office of Examination and Insurance. "We have about 800 exam staff, and we have a pipeline to manage that process. If it is in imminent danger, we will take it over, as we did with WesCorp and U.S. Central. But the larger the financial institution, generally, the more sophisticated its management team and the more confidence we have in their ability to manage their way back to profitability. Speaking frankly, size does come into play. Our charge is minimizing the loss to the insurance fund. But if we need to take it over, we take it."

Kutchey said that it's not very difficult to find a merger partner for an ailing credit union that's in the $300 million in asset range or smaller. "But when it gets to the billion-dollar level, now you have about 140 credit unions that could take it over. In the $3 billion to $5 billion range, I can count on two hands the number that can take them."

As Cliff Rosenthal pointed out in chapter 5, it is not a coincidence that Black-led and other non-white credit unions are disproportionately small, reflecting the cavernous wealth gap in the country.

Know Your Customer

Secretary Karey Barnett took the roll call of a telephonic board meeting for KAPFCU. Victor Russell, Steve Ellis, Bill Whitehead, Kenny Henderson, Michael McCray, and Kevin Burnett announced their attendance.

Kevin Burnett is tall and barrel-chested with salt-and-pepper hair styled in a goatee. The deep baritone has a passion for helping youth, and he is the advisor for the local Kappa League for high school students interested in college. Depending on whom you ask, Kevin is either the conscience of the credit union or a majestic pain in the ass.

Midway through the financial report, Kevin asked, "Am I the only one concerned that we've been operating for nearly five years, and we've never made a loan to an undergraduate?"

There was an uncomfortable silence as the question seemed to come out of the blue. The board members fidgeted nervously.

Victor spoke first. "We help the undergrads through our GLAD and CARE programs. We teach financial literacy and provide debt counseling to our undergraduate chapters."

Kevin cut him off. "That's just the stuff we tell the media and the government."

Victor's freckled face turned red. "Brother, please! That's not just PR, it's for real. Once they graduate and get a job, they will already have access to KAPFCU to borrow money."

"There you go again." Kevin's voice boomed louder. "Is KAPFCU really about helping develop our youth, or is it just about making money?"

Several voices chattered amongst themselves before Henderson, the supervisory committee chairman, weighed in. "That's not fair, Kevin. We are about helping all of our fraternity brothers, but this is a federally regulated financial institution. They have to pay the money back."

Kevin was undeterred. "We receive grants and benefits from the NCUA because we serve a majority young adult population. That's how we got our low-income credit union designation."

Simple and plain, that comment silenced the chatter.

"This young man needs $5,000 to pay for tuition to stay in school. So, are we a brotherhood or a bank?'"

All eyes fell to the floor.

Victor spoke first. "I hear you, but we aren't giving away free money. It's not a grant or a scholarship—it's a federally insured loan. It has to get paid back."

"We make $5,000 loans to brothers with less than perfect credit all the time."

"Yeah, but we know them," Victor replied. "We know how much they care about the frat/bond. We know how much they volunteer and are active with the fraternity. We know how they make money, and how they handle their finances."

"So, it is just about the money!"

"No!" Mac replied, "In underwriting, this is called 'Knowing Your Customer.'"

Kerry agreed with Kevin. "Victor, we've got almost $10,000 in loss reserves, and we've never had a bad loan. We can afford to take a chance on this young man if we are really about making a difference and not just making money."

The impassioned plea won the day and persuaded the KAPFCU to approve a $5,000 emergency loan to our first undergraduate borrower.

While any Kappa or family member can join, the strength of the KAPFCU board was their ability to underwrite outside or beyond a credit score or profile by providing loans to active fraternity members who volunteered their time and were well-known and respected by the brotherhood.

Thus, the "security" for our uncollateralized loans included a form of "social" insurance. No active member wanted to be the brother who damages the fraternity. This is how KAPFCU maintained a zero-default rate for five years. Lending to undergraduates presents a different proposition because they have yet to develop any meaningful status within the fraternity.

KAPFCU Firsts and Achievements

- First/Only African American Fraternal Credit Union With The Federal CDFI Certification
- Access to $3.9 Billion In New Markets Tax Credits for Business/Real Estate Development Financing
- Access to $1.1 Million in Financial and Technical Assistance Grants from the Department of Treasury
- KAPFCU Applied for $100,000 Grant from the U.S. Department of Treasury CDFI Fund
- First/Only Low Income/Community Development Credit Union to Operate on a National Footprint
- KAPFCU Became a Member of the National Federation of Community Development Credit Unions (Credit Unions United to Serve the Underserved)
- KAPFCU Developed a Mission to Service a Traditional Hard-to-Serve Market and Was a Member of the African American Credit Union Coalition (AACUC)

CHAPTER 13

Through The Looking Glass

> "We're all mad here."
>
> The Cheshire Cat from *Alice's Adventures in Wonderland* by Lewis Carroll

Arbitrary and Capricious

Debbie Matz, Chairman of the NCUA, has sandy hair with blond highlights; a petite woman with a big job, Matz issued a letter to credit unions about "Supervising Low-Income Credit Unions and Community Development Credit Unions." The letter provided guidance on the characteristics, benefits, and unique challenges of low-income credit unions and community development credit unions.[60]

The supervisory directive was provided to examination staff and shared with the boards of directors of all federally insured credit unions. Matz was a woman making it in a man's world of politics and finance. Her policy instincts were sound, but the NCUA rank and file seemed to circumvent her best intentions.

The NCUA board voted to liquidate KAPFCU in a closed-door meeting on August 3, 2010. Region IV officials made several false or misleading statements which influenced the NCUA board to

---

60 See chapter 7.

wrongfully liquidate the credit union. The ultimate decision to liquidate was based on a determination that "KAPFCU was minimally capitalized with no reasonable chance to reach adequate capitalization within ten years."

Keith Morton, Cory Phariss, Carolyn Penaluna, and Ron Blouch knew KAPFCU had an NCUA-accepted and approved revised business plan and net worth restoration plan. In a personal vendetta against Victor Russell, they claimed he spent over $1,000 of equity treating people to the NBA All-Star game weekend. This was the final straw, and the NCUA board approved their recommendation to liquidate KAPFCU.[61]

Mission accomplished.

Phariss knew that the credit union's supervisory committee examined the allegations of improper debit card transactions. They found no NBA All-Star game-related charges. The charges were travel-related expenses for board meetings and regional conferences for the fraternity. The supervisory committee identified only $94 in questionable charges, which Victor promptly repaid.

Tragically, the NCUA summarily liquidated KAPFCU a "moderately capitalized" credit union that had experienced a 600% increase in its net worth ratio to 3.67% and which was operating under an NCUA-approved revised business plan and net worth restoration plan without due process, based on lies, supposition, and innuendo or a personal vendetta against Victor Russell and KAPFCU management.

Victor Russell was spending the day working in one of his commercial real estate client's offices in Dallas, Texas. The receptionist informed him there was an important phone call for him. Victor picked up the receiver and his eyes narrowed in rage. "What do you mean, you're at our office? Why the f*ck would you be at our office?" Victor added, "Without us?"

---

61 See Appendix F. NCUA Closed Board Transcript.

A gleeful voice answered over the receiver, "We're liquidating you, Victor. And I need all the keys, computers, and client files for KAPFCU," Phariss said.

The director for NCUA Region IV, Cory Phariss, is an olive-skinned white man with spiked black hair. He has droopy eyes with a double chin and a collar slightly too tight for his neck. Like most federal employees, Cory is a career climber. He's a go-along-to-get-along type of guy and not one to rock the boat, especially for small or minority credit unions.

"Just wait a minute. I'm on my way." Instead, Victor clicked on the three-way line and dialed me.

"What do you mean, they liquidated us?" I asked. "We just had our best quarter—ever!"

"Look Mac, they are at the mutha_f*cking office right now!" Victor said, "What can we do?"

"This can't be right," I said. "We've only had one bad loan!"

Victor interjects, "And I want to kick his ass. I was trying to keep a God damn college kid in school. I knew we shouldn't have bailed his ass out!"

"You mean NOT helped him stay in school?"

"Whatever, Mac. I mean, whoever vouched for him should have paid this loan off." Victor said. "He was a first-payment default."

"Just calm down and read the paperwork to me, Vic," I said. "We have to have some rights to appeal. This is bullsh*t."

Liquidating a Black Credit Union: Tragic and Unwarranted

The surprise NCUA liquidation was improper because KAPFCU was "moderately capitalized" and well on its way to "adequate capitalization" when examined under the NCUA rules, regulations, and supervisory authority applicable to new (less than 10 years old), small (under $10 million in assets), low income

(LICU) and community development credit unions (CDCUs).

False Representation: KAPFCU was "minimally capitalized" with a real net worth under 2%.

In Fact: KAPFCU was "moderately capitalized" with a net worth (cash basis) of over 3.6%.

False Representation: The published LUA had no positive effect on KAPFCU.

In Fact: KAPFCU had substantially complied with the published LUA, which had resulted in a 600% increase in NWR, an NCUA-approved revised business plan, an NCUA-approved net worth restoration plan, and a LUA regulatory plan of action.

False Representation: Liquidation was the only available option because KAPFCU management was not willing to cooperate or merge with any other credit union.

In Fact: KAPFCU had passed a formal board resolution authorizing collaborations with other credit unions up to and including a voluntary merger. KAPFCU and Hope Credit Union were already in merger discussions, which were documented in KAPFCU board minutes.

False Representation: Victor Russell mismanaged KAPFCU and treated guests to over $1,000 in travel and expenses for the NBA All-Star game.

In fact: No expenses were made for the NBA All-Star game. The KAPFCU supervisory committee investigated these allegations and found only $94 in questionable (restaurant/bar) charges that Victor Russell promptly repaid.

False Representation: KAPFCU was mismanaged because Victor Russell advanced a car loan to his wife without entering it into the computer system.

Distortion Of Truth: The oversight was accidental. The initial entry did not properly post to the data processing system. The loan was repaid in full, with interest, within 60 days, and KAPFCU enacted new policies to prohibit management officials from entering transactions on their own or family member accounts.

False Representation: KAPFCU's business plans were all unacceptable because of their over-reliance on grant income rather than income from operations.

True Statement: KAPFCU was eligible for significant grant funding as a low-income credit union and certified community development financial institution and was positively evaluated by the CDFI fund. The NCUA issued a supervisory letter concerning examining LICUs and CDCUs that acknowledged significant grant resources and admonished examiners NOT to negatively evaluate credit unions for having low-income and/or community development business plans.

False Representation: KAPFCU was not concerned with safety and soundness considerations.

In Fact: KAPFCU agreed to comply with all the NCUA rules and regulations applicable to small, low-income, and community development credit unions.

False Representation: Liquidation was warranted because KAPFCU had no reasonable chance of recovering.

True Statement: KAPFCU was "moderately capitalized; made a 600% increase in its net worth ratio; was operating under an NCUA-approved revised business plan (RBP) and an NCUA-approved net worth restoration plan (NWR); was eligible for $100,000 in secondary capital; and NCUA knew KAPFCU would have been awarded a $100,000 technical assistance grant from the CDFI fund on August 19, 2010.

CHAPTER 14

Rush To Judgment

"Curiouser and curiouser!"
Alice from *Alice's Adventures in Wonderland* by Lewis Carroll

A Rush to Judgment

I called Victor Russell after reading the transcript from the closed-door NCUA board meeting, "It's messed up what they did to us, man."

"I know, right?" Victor replied. "But what do you see?"

"The NCUA board members refused to dissolve KAPFCU at first," I said. "They recognized that cash basis vs. accrual accounting increased expenses and created our net worth ratio problems."

"That's good."

I explained, "Region IV officials convinced the NCUA board to liquidate KAPFCU based on a series of lies and false representations in an ex-parte proceeding."

"Which is total bullshit." Victor said, "We need to demand a personal meeting with Debbie Matz or get a hearing before the entire NCUA board."

"They ain't gonna listen to us, Vic," I said. "They're trying to screw us."

"Well, if they won't listen to us, then we need to get [Representative] Eddie Bernice Johnson," Victor said, "and the whole freaking Congressional Black Caucus to reach out to NCUA on our behalf."

"If that doesn't work, Vic, we need to take them to court ASAP."

Victor nods. "Who do we know in Washington, D.C.?"

Representative Eddie Bernice Johnson (D-TX) wrote a letter to Debbie Matz requesting a meeting or emergency hearing for KAPFCU. NCUA officials ignored the emphatic request from a distinguished Congressional Black Caucus member. They also ignored KAPFCU's frantic meeting request in a last-ditch effort to stop the surprise liquidation.

> I issued a press release announcing KAPFCU's decision to sue NCUA. If successful, KAPFCU v. NCUA could be the Brown v. Topeka Board of Education[62] case of the credit union movement. It was one thing to announce a lawsuit and issue a press release—but another thing to secure competent legal counsel for federal litigation.
>
> Victor called on his fraternity brothers in Alexandria. A small law firm near the nation's capital answered the call for help. Vic and I debriefed Ken Bynum, partner in the boutique law office of Bynum and Jenkins, along with another fraternity brother, Robert Cooper, about the case.
>
> Ken Bynum is a Black man navigating the marble halls of power and influence in Washington, D.C. Mocha-skinned with a bushy mustache with a tight Afro, Ken wears bow ties and designer suits with Italian loafers. In addition, he is active in the Democratic Party, his local church, and is a proud member of Kappa Alpha Psi Fraternity.
>
> "We need your help, Ken," Victor said. "In a personal vendetta against me, Region IV officials decided it was easier to liquidate KAPFCU under false pretenses rather than follow NCUA rules and regulations to remove management."

---

62 *Brown v. Board of Education of Topeka, 347 U.S. 483 (1954)*, which held the Equal Protection Clause of the Fourteenth Amendment to the United States Constitution prohibits states from segregating public school students on the basis of race. This marked a reversal of the "separate but equal" doctrine from Plessy v. Ferguson that had permitted separate schools for white and colored children provided that the facilities were equal.

"NCUA has been granted broad authority by Congress and can use a 'subjective standard' to address performance under letters of understanding and agreement. However, KAPFCU contends that any such subjectivity must be objectively reasonable and cannot be exercised arbitrarily or capriciously."

"We believe the NCUA's actions were intentional and malicious because they were based on a defective record of lies, supposition, and innuendo presented in a closed-door board meeting," I said. "There had been long and contentious deliberations concerning KAPFCU's compliance with the LUA. However, KAPFCU had turned the corner in its management and operations. This action surprised KAPFCU."

Substantial Compliance with LUA: A Record of Compliance and Operational Improvement

- KAPFCU had completed a regulatory action plan to ensure LUA compliance
- KAPFCU was operating under an NCUA-approved and accepted revised business plan
- KAPFCU was operating under an NCUA-approved and accepted net worth restoration plan
- KAPFCU had experienced a 600% increase in net worth since December 31, 2009
- KAPFCU was "moderately capitalized" (3.67%) by NCUA standards
- KAPFCU was in negotiation with a well-capitalized credit union mentor (Hope Credit Union)
- KAPFCU had a $100,000 CDFI Fund technical assistance grant application pending
- KAPFCU had resolved record-keeping deficiencies through an expanded backroom contract
- KAPFCU had implemented an NCUA-approved Allowance for Loan and Lease Losses (ALLL) program for adequate loan loss reserves

I continued: "NCUA exceeded its authority and usurped the prerogatives of the KAPFCU board of directors by changing KAPFCU financial statements to reflect full GAAP accrual contrary to NCUA rules and regulations regarding credit unions under $10 million in assets, and over the express objections of KAPFCU since 2007. This central dispute precipitated the downward spiral in KAPFCU's management and capital position, record-keeping, and CAMEL ratings. This caused the LUA and prompt corrective action."

Vic said, "NCUA allowed Region IV officials to pick a number 'out of thin air' and declare that their number was our net worth ratio. Then NCUA liquidated KAPFCU based on Region IV's false assertions and lies rather than KAPFCU's actual financial performance. KAPFCU could never defend its financial statements before liquidation."

Ken asked, "Why would they do that, Victor?"

"That's easy. The NCUA rushed the liquidation because it knew about the [pending] technical assistance award. The NCUA has been in contact with the U.S. Department of Treasury's CDFI Fund regarding the KAPFCU funding application since April 2010. Thus, NCUA 'rushed to liquidate' the credit union because it knew that KAPFCU was going to receive a $100,000 technical assistance award from the CDFI Fund."

Robert Cooper of Cooper and Crickman said, "The record shows that the liquidation was part of a personal vendetta against KAPFCU management. It was a malicious effort to remove Victor Russell. Region IV officials engaged in concerted actions and liquidated the credit union rather than using other less extreme corrective measures, e.g., a cease-and-desist order, conservatorship, voluntary merger, etc. Under NCUA rules and regulations, there are 14 steps before liquidation. KAPFCU was only on step nine."

The Capital Question

NCUA liquidated KAPFCU in a rush to judgment. KAPFCU was well on its way to achieving adequate capitalization and correcting the deficiencies in question. Under the applicable NCUA rules and regulations, new credit unions like KAPFCU are allowed ten years to reach "adequate capitalization," a ratio of 7% net worth to total assets. Thus, on a straight-line basis, this equates to 0.7% per year.

NETWORTH RATIO BENCHMARK CHART

New credit unions have ten years to reach a 7% capitalization rate. The Net Worth Ratio Benchmark Chart illustrates the average "hurdle" rates credit unions should maintain to achieve the NCUA capital requirements.

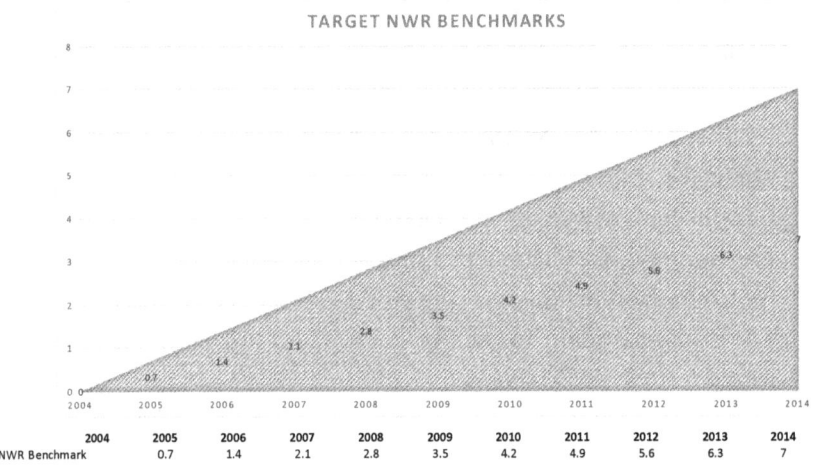

	2004	2005	2006	2007	2008	2009	2010	2011	2012	2013	2014
NWR Benchmark		0.7	1.4	2.1	2.8	3.5	4.2	4.9	5.6	6.3	7

Five years into its operation, KAPFCU was a "new" credit union, well within the ten-year benchmark. As the difficulties with NCUA examiners continued to mount, KAPFCU had returned to modified cash accounting and focused on expanding its traditional nonprofit activities until it restored the credit union operations. Because of this strategy, KAPFCU experienced a 600%[63] increase in net worth from December 31, 2009, through June 30, 2010.

---

63 *The Financial Times* confirmed that KAPFCU experienced the highest-ever quarter increase in the history of financial institutions, quarter over quarter.

FULL ACCRUAL PERFORMANCE

This chart illustrates KAPFCU's interim performance on "GAAP Full Accrual Basis." Large and mature credit unions are required to operate on GAAP full accrual accounting. In contrast, small and emerging credit unions can operate on a modified cash basis.

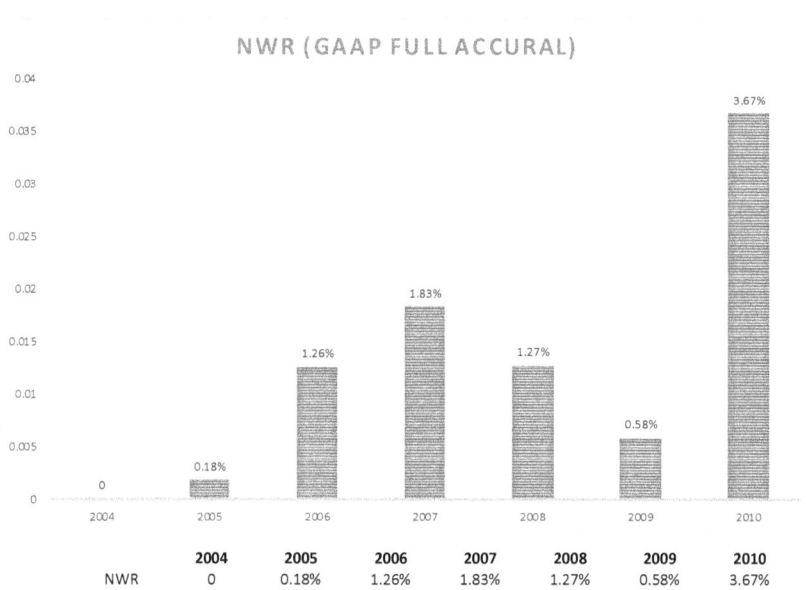

	2004	2005	2006	2007	2008	2009	2010
NWR	0	0.18%	1.26%	1.83%	1.27%	0.58%	3.67%

In its fifth year of operation, we would expect a new credit union to have a 3.0% to 3.5% net worth capital ratio. KAPFCU achieved a 3.67% NWR by June 30, 2010, which is moderately capitalized. KAPFCU was on track and on its way to attaining adequate capitalization by its tenth year of operations. Unfortunately, Region IV officials lied about the true financial condition and other significant deficiencies in NCUA's malicious attempt to liquidate the KAPFCU. Had it received a fair opportunity to be heard, KAPFCU would not have been liquidated. However, if some form of administrative action was required, it should have been a cease-and-desist order, conservatorship, or voluntary merger.

CHAPTER 15

The Mad Hatter

"Off with their heads!"
The Red Queen from the film adaption of *Alice in Wonderland*

KAPFCU v. NCUA: Our Day In Court

Sunlight, dust mites, and anticipation filled the federal courtroom in Washington, D.C., along with an overflow audience. Dozens of dapper African Americans aged 20 to 65, in hues from a box of Godiva chocolates, adorned in crimson and cream business attire, along with a gaggle of reporters attended the initial hearing for KAPFCU v. NCUA.

"All rise!" bellowed the courtroom bailiff.

The Honorable Emmet Sullivan, an African American, took the bench and acknowledged the members of the venerable organization, Kappa Alpha Psi, present in the courtroom.

Government attorneys Fred Haynes and Damon Frank flanked Cory Phariss and took their place at the defendant's table. They seemed genuinely surprised by the turnout for the hearing. At the plaintiff's table, directly across from them, sat Ken Bynum, Victor Russell, and me; the KAPFCU team.

The deputy clerk announced the case: "Civil Action 10-1321, Kappa Alpha Psi Federal Credit Union versus National Credit Union Administration. Counsel, identify yourselves for the record."

Ken stood. "May it please the Court, Ken Bynum of Bynum and Jenkins on behalf of Kappa Alpha Psi Federal Credit Union, along with Ken Crickman from Cooper and Crickman. Good morning."

Judge Sullivan responded, "Good morning, counsel."

Fred rose. "Your Honor, Fred Haynes for the government. With me at the counsel table is Damon Frank, a trial attorney with the Credit Union Administration. We have the regional director, Keith Morton. He's from Region IV, which supervises this credit union, and we have the supervisory examiner, Cory Phariss, who supervised it."

Ken addressed the court and stated that the NCUA started the liquidation in error. The agency took KAPFCU's charter mistakenly because the credit union's financial condition was not that dire. KAPFCU asked for NCUA to reinstate the charter or issue a temporary stay to allow KAPFCU to merge with another community development credit union.

Judge Sullivan nodded. "This is not an unreasonable request." He was dismayed when the government's attorney, Haynes, said they weren't authorized to negotiate or agree to these terms. And neither could any of the NCUA officials present in court.

Judge Sullivan became indignant. "The NCUA was properly served with the complaint and was notified of this hearing. Yet they didn't bother to come to court with anyone empowered to negotiate? I'm going to set another hearing date. You make sure that you or your client have authorized NCUA officials present on that day."

"Yes, your honor!" both government attorneys sheepishly nodded to his request.

Phariss, NCUA Region IV Director of Supervision, said, "We brought a witness, your honor. A vendor who wants payment from KAPFCU."

Victor and I quickly conferred with Ken. "Total/1 sold us a defective product that miscalculated our interest income," I said. "We complained about this after our poor examination. As a result, they started no collection activities or efforts. But we maintained a special reserve account to pay them if necessary. We got a legal opinion and then released the special reserves into our general reserves after the statute of limitations ran out on the contract dispute. These f*ckers just went into our bank account and took $30,000 and gave it to a vendor after the statute of limitations had expired."[64]

Victor said, "We shouldn't be here at all. We got liquidated after our first bad loan. We have $475,000 in loans on the streets and had one bad loan for less than $4,500 to a college student, but we have $10,000 in loan loss reserves."

KAPFCU argued that NCUA's Region IV officials had exceeded their authority and usurped the prerogatives of the KAPFCU board of directors by improperly contacting the third-party vendor in a tortuous and malicious attempt to reaffirm the debt and liquidate the credit union.[65]

U.S. District Court Judge Emmet Sullivan said that he likely lacked the authority to stop the liquidation. However, he ordered the agency to argue why the court should not stop it by Friday, August 13. The order also gave the credit union until August 16 to explain why the court could stop the liquidation.

Ken nodded but told Judge Sullivan he had evidence that NCUA accessed KAPFCU's computer records and changed KAPFCU's financial statements ("call report") after KAPFCU sued in court. Government attorneys defended NCUA officials not by denying KAPFCUs explosive allegations—NCUA examiners misappropriated their money—but by arguing that NCUA's unilateral action did not result in any misrepresentation of KAPPFCU's financial position.[66]

---

[64] Region IV improperly usurped the credit union's board role in an attempt to liquidate KAPFCU by forcing them to book/record an unenforceable debt. KAPFCU had a contract dispute with a data processing vendor. KAPFCU elicited a legal and a CPA opinion about the disputed matter. After the four-year Texas Statute of Limitations expired, KAPFCU passed a formal Board resolution deeming the debt uncollectible and released the special reserve into retained earnings.

[65] See Appendix D: Balack & Williams, Legal Opinion (Total/1 Product Defect).

[66] See Appendix I: the NCUA "Sur Reply" brief.

Judge Sullivan said, "I understand your concerns and will take it under advisement. However, my order still stands." The NCUA had until noon on August 13 to explain the liquidation to the U.S. District Court for the District of Columbia. KAPFCU also had until August 16 to argue why the court should stop the liquidation.

Chip Filson: NCUA And A Black-Founded Credit Union (Part I of II)[67]

In 2010, NCUA's regulatory activity reigned unchecked. Even though the economy was on the mend, its penchant for shutting down credit unions was unabated. It would ultimately lead to liquidating five corporate credit unions in September—the most catastrophic decision in credit union history.

On August 3rd, 2010, six years after founding, Kappa Alpha Psi FCU ($750K, Dallas, TX) fell under NCUA's knee, having been served a surprise order of liquidation and charter revocation.

In the regulatory environment, one might assume this was just another small credit union falling prey to economic circumstances. But then something happened that no other credit union had dared in this situation. The credit union appealed NCUA's action, filing a complaint, contesting the order on both factual and constitutional grounds.

KAPFCU requested a temporary restraining order against NCUA: "Petitioner fears that before a show cause can be held, the Respondent will complete what has already been threatened, and that is to liquidate assets, spend money, enter or break contracts, and disrupt the ongoing operations of the credit union."

In response, a federal judge in D.C. granted a temporary injunction and scheduled a hearing on the issue in the time provided for an appeal.

---

[67] Quoted with permission. Chip Filson, "NCUA and a Black-Founded Credit Union (Part I of II)," CUInsight, February 26, 2021, https://www.cuinsight.com/ncua-and-a-black-founded-credit-union-part-i-of-ii/.

The Credit Union's Brief History

Kappa Alpha Psi FCU, chartered in 2004, was in its sixth full year of operation when NCUA struck. Classified as a "new" credit union, that is, in operation for less than 10 years and its total assets did not exceed $10 million. NCUA Regulations provide that 'new credit unions' must be 'adequately capitalized' or (7%) NWR within 10 years.

NCUA based its liquidation order on the credit union's net worth ratio, asserting that because the financial institution was minimally capitalized at the end of the first quarter of 2010 with no reasonable prospect for becoming capitalized, prompt corrective action was warranted.

The credit union notes its first-quarter net worth ratio was 1.95%; by June 30, 2010, the second-quarter, however, the credit union is moderately capitalized with a net worth ratio of 3.67%—a 600% increase since its December 31, 2009, rating.

These numbers, for reasons never explained, were not reflected in the credit union's second quarter 2010 Call Report posted by NCUA.[68] Who altered Kappa Alpha Psi FCU's second quarter Call Report to make it appear insolvent? What was the basis for the change? Why was the credit union not contacted?

"Cooking Our Books"

In 2017, following the AACUC Hall of Fame induction and Pete Crear award ceremony for Victor Russell and Bill Bynum, respectively, Victor and I met Helen Godfrey Smith from the African

---

[68] The NCUA changed KAPFCU's financial statements and Financial Performance Report/FPR report post-filing after the NCUA assured the court that the government would not take any adverse actions. By illegally and improperly changing KAPFU's financial statements, NCUA exceeded its authority and usurped the prerogatives of the KAPFCU board of directors. In addition, acts of concealment are admissible evidence of culpability.

American Credit Union Coalition (AACUC) for dinner at the Capital Grille.

Helen is the matriarch of the African American Credit Union Coalition and President of Shreveport Federal Credit Union. A diminutive woman with a roux complexion, she's a Creole cook from Southern Louisiana. The tawny Southern belle had a knack for getting her way by making the regulators feel like they bested her.

A wealth of information and industry knowledge and relationships, Helen is a proud member of Alpha Kappa Alpha sorority, and she nominated Victor Russell for induction in the AACUC hall of fame. I ordered double-cut lamb rib chops with parmesan truffle fries and drinks for the table while Victor regaled Helen about KAPFCU's run in with the NCUA.

"I am so sorry that this happened to you all, Victor."

"They just took our money and gave it to our data processor, Helen, **after** the statute of limitations had expired. They weren't even trying to collect."

Helen shook her head. "That's messed up, Victor. We've complained about the examiners doing this to other AACUC members."

"You have?"

Helen said, "They just went in your cash drawer and took your money, and then used it to pay whoever they saw fit. They usurped the management prerogative of the board. That's not an act of oversight."

"Exactly!" Victor said. "Even if we wanted to pay them, we could have negotiated the bill down to pennies on the dollar. They had a defective product that got us into trouble with the examiners."

"You're not the only one," Helen said. "But the NCUA agreed to stop allowing the examiners to do this. It's paternalistic, and the examiners treat minority credit unions like children. They wouldn't do this to any other credit unions."

"Exactly!" Victor sighed. "Lynda Milton (CEO of Houston Teamsters FCU) told us they set us up from the very beginning." AACUC members knew Carolyn Penaluna intimately. She was reputed to be a 'Black Widow' within the African American credit union community. Region IV assigned her whenever they wanted to close a minority credit union. But unlike Tony Rausch, she killed them softly rather than with bluster.

Helen said, "I'm glad you guys joined AACUC. We've been watching Kappa since you launched. And we thought you were doing great! We had no idea that KAPFCU was having so much trouble until after the NCUA published the LUA."

HOPE Emerges For Nation's First Virtual Credit Union To Avert Liquidation[69]

A federal judge yesterday gave troubled Kappa Alpha Psi FCU 24 hours to work out an emergency merger with HOPE Community FCU to avoid a wholesale liquidation by NCUA. But a Justice Department lawyer representing NCUA told Judge Emmet Sullivan even if a merger deal could be reached it would be too late to avert the liquidation, which the NCUA Board put into motion for the nation's first internet-only credit union on August 3. "The bell has been rung when we placed it into liquidation. There's no way to stop it from ringing," said Fred Haynes.

In an Orwellian situation reminiscent of an ongoing lawsuit over WesCorp FCU, Haynes told the judge the Federal CU Act allows a credit union's board to challenge a liquidation order by requesting a court-directed show cause order, but even if the court finds no cause for the liquidation there is no mechanism to reverse the liquidation order. "The bell has been rung, your Honor," said Haynes, during a court hearing yesterday.

In WesCorp, a federal court has allowed NCUA to assume the roles of both the defendants, the WesCorp management and directors, and the plaintiffs, seven credit unions suing the management and board, according to provisions of the Federal Credit Union Act.

---

69 Melinda Haehnel, "HOPE Emerges For Nation's First Virtual CU To Avert Liquidation," *Credit Union Journal Daily Briefing*, August 11, 2010.

Judge Sullivan was not swayed by NCUA's position on Kappa Alpha Psi, a six-year-old credit union chartered by the nationwide African American college fraternity that counts only $750,000 of assets and depleted all of its net worth paying assessments for NCUA's corporate credit union bailout. The judge, asserting that the merger proposal by HOPE Community would allow the fraternity to avoid the stigma of a liquidation and discourage the credit union's 1,341 members from withdrawing their deposits, urged the two sides to negotiate on a merger.

But Haynes insisted that no one, outside of the NCUA board, is authorized to overturn a liquidation order. That has never been done before. Haynes also informed the judge that none of the three NCUA board members is available to represent the board, having all scattered for the board's annual August recess.

Judge Sullivan ordered NCUA to make one of the board members available for an additional session this afternoon. Even if it required getting NCUA Chairman Debbie Matz hooked in by teleconference from her vacation in Jackson Hole, Wyoming. "Someone has to be able to speak on behalf of that board," a clearly frustrated Judge Sullivan glared.

Under a proposal by HOPE Community, a well-known Mississippi community development credit union, it would assume all the member deposits and loans—just 41 loans for $400,000. But the CDCU will need some time to analyze the loans, lawyers for Kappa Alpha Psi told the judge, perhaps as long as a week.

Ken Bynum, a lawyer representing Kappa Alpha Psi, asked the judge for an order giving it until next Wednesday to negotiate a final deal with the HOPE Community. "If they take it into liquidation, a hostile environment will ensue. There will be a run on deposits," he said.

CHAPTER 16

Rainbow Pushed Out

> "No, no!" said the Queen.
> "Sentence first — verdict afterward."
> The Red Queen from the film adaption of *Alice in Wonderland*

NCUA Preempts the Court

On Friday, August 13, 2010, NCUA filed a brief in the D.C. Federal Court of Judge Emmet Sullivan responding to the complaint by Kappa Alpha Psi FCU challenging NCUA's liquidation order of August 3. Several hours later, NCUA began liquidation, mailing checks to the credit union's savers and assigning loans to the agency's asset management unit.

The credit union had until noon, Monday, August 16, 2010, to file its reply to NCUA's brief. NCUA's liquidation nullified further court review.

Why liquidate the credit union before the court's expedited legal process had even run its course? The credit union was serving the mission of the largest Black professional fraternity using a virtual business model. No checking accounts, no ATMs, and no debit card withdrawals—just regular savings to fund loans to students and Black professionals to support "achievement"—a fraternity goal.

The risk of any NCUSIF loss was de minimus. The credit union's lawyers were *pro bono*. Their goal was to merge the credit union if the NCUA wanted to cancel the charter. They sought an impartial hearing for this request. Their motive was to preserve the pride and dignity of their fraternal colleagues who began the effort and to continue a credit union offering for members.

> Victor and I hurried through a scurry of squirrels on the cobblestone streets of Alexandria to meet in the law office of Bynum and Jenkins. Robert Cooper greeted us as co-counsel from Cooper and Crickman. We joined counsel Ken Bynum and Robert Cooper in the French door-lined conference room to discuss legal strategy.
> Smart and aggressive, Rob is an excellent legal researcher. To his credit, Rob is more "gung-ho" than his more reserved lead partner. Ken shifted in his seat while maintaining a serious poker face, like a card shark playing with rounders in Las Vegas.
> Judge Sullivan told KAPFCU to provide legal authority to enjoin NCUA from liquidating KAPFCU. I suggested malice, racial discrimination, and constitutional violations against KAPFCU, while Rob briefed due process arguments for Bynum and Jenkins.

The Due Process Arguments: Credit Unions and Banks, Individual and Corporate Constitutional Rights

Due process requires that legal proceedings must be carried out fairly and under established rules and principles. In the banking industry, courts have held that due process was satisfied by a post-deprivation hearing. However, the question here was, "Does being heard *after* the liquidation has already taken place satisfy Fifth Amendment due process requirements for a natural person credit union?" Are the due process protection considerations the same for corporations as distinct from individuals in membership cooperatives? Thus, this was a "case of first impression"—that is, a legally significant case that could establish a legal precedent because it was the first time this factual scenario would be considered by a federal court.

There are two fundamental differences between banks and natural person credit unions—individual association versus corporate form, and initial capitalization levels. Banks and credit unions differ greatly. First, banks are for-profit commercial enterprises, while credit unions are not-for-profit associations. Second, banks are *corporations*. Natural-person credit unions are unincorporated associations of individuals. Third, the courts have long held that constitutional protections differ between corporations and individuals. The courts have only held that corporations are entitled to First Amendment protections. Hence, post deprivation hearings (i.e., after an action has resulted in loss of life, liberty, or property) do not violate banks' due process rights since courts have not held that corporations are entitled to Fifth Amendment due process protections at all.

However, natural-person credit unions, as cooperative associations of individual members, are different. They have full constitutional rights and are entitled to individual due process protections. Thus, a post-deprivation hearing did not satisfy individual Fifth Amendment due process protections. Therefore, KAPFCU believed that the NCUA liquidation and dissolution order was unconstitutional because it was based on a closed-door meeting, and because a post-deprivation hearing could not satisfy individual Fifth Amendment due process concerns as a natural-person credit union. KAPFCU believed its due-process rights were doubly violated.

- "Substantive Due Process" requires laws and regulations to be related to legitimate government interests and not contain provisions that result in unfair or arbitrary treatment of an individual. Here, KAPFCU believed that this statutory scheme, which allowed post-deprivation hearings without the opportunity to enjoin or stay the liquidation as applied to natural-person credit unions, resulted in unfair and arbitrary deprivation of liberty and property.

- "Procedural Due Process" requires adequate notice before the government can deprive one of life, liberty, or property, and the opportunity to be heard and defend one's rights. KAPFCU did not receive adequate notice, was not given an opportunity to be heard, and could not defend its rights.

Robert nodded. "It's not a question of whether NCUA was right or wrong regarding the liquidation. The question is whether KAPFCU had a fair opportunity to be heard prior to the deprivation and loss of their property or liberty. The NCUA contends courts have held that due process considerations were satisfied by a post-deprivation hearing in the banking industry."[70]

I nodded with Rob. "We don't need to argue that this was just an unfortunate mistake, Ken. We need to say that it was a discriminatory and malicious liquidation."

Ken's gaze fell toward the floor. "Those are strong words, which we will have to prove in court."

"The credit union world is watching our case because they think NCUA mistreats small credit unions," I said. "Especially minority-serving credit unions. We have reached out to the Credit Union National Association, and they're on board. As well as the National Federation of Community Development Credit Unions and the African American Credit Union Coalition. "This case is bigger than just us. KAPFCU is the tip of the spear for fairness and reform for NCUA," Victor said. "We even contacted Jesse Jackson and got Rainbow Push interested because this is a case of racial discrimination in banking and finance, except we're a credit union."[71]

(The Reverend Jesse Louis Jackson, Sr., founder and president of the Rainbow PUSH Coalition, is one of America's foremost civil rights, religious, and political figures. Over the past forty years, he has played a pivotal role in virtually every movement

---

70 However, courts have also held that aggrieved banks are entitled to have their charters reinstated in the case of unlawful or wrongful liquidation. See, Stocksdale S&L Complaint (Illinois) filed against the FDIC or OTC during the S&L Crisis. Federal courts overturned the regulator's overly aggressive and unnecessary action and restored the S&L to its key shareholders.

71 The Rainbow PUSH Coalition was the product of a social justice movement that grew out of the Southern Christian Leadership Conference's (SCLC) Operation Breadbasket. Founded by Rev. Dr. Martin Luther King, Jr., Operation Breadbasket sought to combine theology and social justice and to effect progressive economic, educational, and social policy in America. In 1966, Dr. King appointed Jesse L. Jackson, Sr. to serve as the first director of Operation Breadbasket in Chicago.

for empowerment, peace, civil rights, gender equality, and economic and social justice. On August 9, 2000, President Bill Clinton awarded Reverend Jackson the Presidential Medal of Freedom, the nation's highest civilian honor.)

Ken had finally heard enough.

"Listen, Vic, I know Jesse Jackson. I volunteered for his presidential campaign in 1988." Ken paused, "And I won't have anything to do with him or Rainbow Push anymore."

Flustered, Victor and I leaned back and sulked in our respective conference chairs.

"We pulled a superb judge, Emmet Sullivan, who seemed receptive to our arguments." Ken said, "I know him from Christmas and cocktail parties. All we have to do—is try not to piss him off."

"Listen Ken, nobody cares about an individual small credit union, but we have the chance to make this a landmark civil right case, complete with media, publicity, and industry support," I pleaded.

"I have a small practice working in the DMV [D.C., Maryland, and Virginia]. I'm not trying to take on, or piss off, the federal government or the Justice Department," Ken said. "The math is the math. KAPFCU was 'moderately capitalized' when it was liquidated. I want to argue that case respectfully before Judge Sullivan and against the Justice Department." Ken glared, "Therefore, we will not go to the media. We're not giving interviews. We will not issue any more press releases. And we will not make this a media spectacle or enrage the federal government."

Exasperated, Victor and I sighed together and looked at each other in dismay.

"At least I'm not. If you want to get another lawyer, that's fine," Ken said. "But I'm not trying to be Jesse Jackson, if that is what you want. I'm only willing to argue that the NCUA made a mistake and accidentally liquidated KAPFCU improperly."

Loquacious and loud, perhaps the best word to describe Vic is "maverick," which is great for a businessman but cause for concern for a witness in a federal court proceeding. Knowing what to say, and more importantly, what not to say, is paramount in this arena. Ken made the call and refused to put KAPFCU officials on the stand. Chagrined, all we could do was argue that NCUA made a mistake, which tied KAPFCU's hands. In the end, Ken argued the NCUA made an innocent mistake and threw KAPFCU on the mercy of court, specifically Judge Emmet Sullivan.

NCUA Jumps the Gun, Liquidates First Virtual CU[72]

NCUA said it won't wait for tomorrow's court hearing on liquidating the tiny Kappa Alpha Psi FCU and has gone ahead and liquidated the $750,000 credit union serving the national African American fraternity. The NCUA announcement comes as lawyers and directors for the credit union were scheduled to meet tomorrow morning with NCUA lawyers to argue why the credit union regulator should hold off liquidating the six-year-old institution—even after the presiding judge questioned whether he has the legal authority to hold off NCUA. "NCUA has a statutory obligation to pay members their shares and give them access to their funds as soon as possible." John McKechnie, chief spokesman for the agency, said. "Kappa, the first all internet-only credit union, was liquidated Friday, and mailing checks to members began that day." The NCUA move comes as the Kappa lawyers were trying to stave off a full liquidation and the stigma it would bring the fraternity. They want to engineer a merger instead, into HOPE Community FCU of Jackson, Miss. But NCUA told the court there was no hope of resuscitating the tiny credit union and it was in the best interests of Kappa's 1,341 members and the National CU Share Insurance Fund to liquidate the institution. Lawyers for Kappa were unavailable for comment.

---

72 *Credit Union Journal Daily Briefing,* Tuesday, August 17, 2010.

Victor slammed down the phone. "What the f*ck, Mac! Every time they write a story about KAPFCU without talking to us, the brothers go nuts and start blowing up IHQ [International Headquarters]. If we lose their support, we're really screwed."

"I know, Vic. It's nuts. Here's what gets me. It was clear as glass that Judge Sullivan blasted NCUA for not sending any authorized officials to the hearing. Everyone in the courtroom could see that."

"That's right."

"But the Credit Union Times writes it up like Judge Sullivan chastised KAPFCU for not being prepared to negotiate, and we had our CEO and board chairman sitting at the plaintiff's table."

Victor nods.

"They were pissed off because we refused to talk to them and give our side of the story."

Victor said. "But they should not have lied about what really happened, right?"

"But this is America."

"Staying strong and silent is going to get our asses kicked, Vic."

"We might win some brownie points with Judge Sullivan in federal district court, but we're losing in the court of public opinion. And if we lose the Nupes [Kappa members], then we lose the war."

KAPFCU v. NCUA: The Final Judgement

A murder of crows circled the stone-faced federal courthouse in Washington, D.C. NCUA had until Friday, August 13, at 12:00 p.m. to explain to the U.S. District Court for the District of Columbia why the court should not have prevented it from liquidating the Kappa Alpha Psi Federal Credit Union. The agency announced it would liquidate the credit union on August 3, but the credit union went to court to stay and reverse the liquidation.

The agency said the credit union's liquidation was warranted because it was "minimally capitalized" based on its March 31 financial statements. But in its legal briefs, the credit union claims that as of June 30 it had raised its capital ratio to 3.67% and that NCUA's examiner had validated those financial reports.

The credit union is working toward a merger with the $129 million Hope Community Credit Union, but the details have not been finalized. In its court documents, the credit union contends that publishing the liquidation order is "defamatory, casts KAPFCU in a false light, and has caused erosion of public confidence."

However, instead of waiting for the judicial proceedings to conclude, NCUA Officials rushed to dissolve KAPFCU. NCUA "jumped the gun" and sent out the liquidation checks while the case was still pending in court **before** the next scheduled hearing.

The hearing was over before it began. Judge Sullivan's courtroom demeanor and attitude toward KAPFCU had drastically changed by the second hearing.

> We listen as Judge Sullivan rules from the bench:[73]
>
> - First, current regulations allow NCUA the authority to conduct a surprise liquidation in this manner. Second, KAPFCU had no business giving large auto loans to professional athletes. They should lend to everyday college students and graduates *instead*.
>
> - Even if NCUA made an initial mistake regarding the financial statements, they could have liquidated KAPFCU for other reasons. The rise in delinquency rates and loans to professional athletes is a legitimate cause for concern. Therefore, the NCUA had an alternative basis and justification for liquidation.
>
> - Finally, government agencies are so large that one hand does not know what the other hand is doing. NCUA had no way of knowing that the CDFI Fund was going to give KAPFCU the $100,000 grant.

---

73 See Appendix J: Federal District Court Hearing Transcript.

KAPFCU lost. The court ruled that post-deprivation hearings are constitutional, and that NCUA had presented an alternative rationale for liquidation. Despite all the "deficiencies" the NCUA claimed, KAPFCU had suffered only one loan loss, for less than $4,500, in its six-year existence. The NCUA had assessed KAPFCU over $6,700 for losses incurred by the liquidation of corporate credit unions.

The bench ruling enraged fraternity member Richard Maddox, a former Capitol Hill staffer turned lobbyist from Tupelo with a pronounced Southern drawl. As country as a pound of butter, when 'Mississippi' speaks, cornbread and buttermilk come out. After watching the ruling, he proclaimed, "He looked scared as a long-tail cat on a porch full of rocking chairs. Someone must have gotten to him, Vic."

Missed Opportunities

There were missed opportunities, other approaches our team could have taken.

- Our lawyer argued only that NCUA was mistaken, not malicious.
- We had no opportunity for rebuttal—for example, of the Region IV examiners, the data processing contract, or the adequacy of the allowance for loans and lease losses.
- Our lawyer did not argue that there was bias, or that NCUA had violated its own rules and regulations.
- He never argued racial discrimination.
- He refused assistance from Rainbow Push.
- We were never allowed the opportunity to stand in our own defense, nor to submit an affidavit.
- We never commented to the media.

Navigating The Race Card

The NCUA actions seemed hostile to KAPFCU as an African American-based institution—especially since credit unions, particularly Black ones, were started because African Americans were denied access to capital and commercial banking services because they were Black.

Following the disastrous hearing and ruling against KAPFCU, Victor and I drowned our sorrows with Old Fashioneds at the Old Ebbitt Grill, a local oyster bar and pub a few blocks away from the White House.

"We're stuck between a rock and a hard place, Vic," I said. "Ken did KAPFCU a favor by taking the case with minimal payment. But he refused to argue the case we wanted to present."

"Yeah, I talked to another firm in Chicago. They wanted $60,000 to argue our case," Victor said. "But you get what you pay for. Ken didn't want to play the race card like Jesse Jackson would."

"It's not just about the race card," I said. "We needed to play every damn card in the deck. We're fighting for KAPFCU's survival."

"That's just it, Mac," Victor said. "KAPFCU v. NCUA is just one case among many cases that Bynum and Jenkins currently has. And it's one case among many cases that Ken will have to litigate in the future."

"True."

Victor sighed. "So, it's not worth it for Ken to destroy the firm's reputation with the U.S. Attorney's Office and his relationship with a prominent African American Federal District Judge for one case?"

"You might get what you pay for—but you pay for everything you get," I said. "By only arguing mistake, federal regulations allow the NCUA to present an alternative theory to support liquidation. If they can do this, the court will deem the liquidation justified."

Vic said, "That's why they talked about the loans to NFL players and our rising delinquency rate."

> "Had KAPFCU argued racial discrimination, then federal law would provide an opportunity to argue that NCUA's alternative theory for liquidation was a mere pretext for racial discrimination. KAPFCU would have had the chance to present evidence of NCUA malfeasance," I shrugged. "We missed our chance in court. KAPFCU could have affirmed that NCUA previously verified our Allowance for Loan and Lease Losses account and could have exposed the lies in the ex parte liquidation hearing transcript. NCUA has intentionally misapplied the rules and regulations requiring ALLL in order to intentionally and maliciously liquidate KAPFCU."

NCUA's examiner, Cory Phariss, knew the KAPFCU board of directors received NCUA-sponsored training regarding implementing the ALLL requirements and had implemented an adequate ALLL methodology and policy. KAPFCU's loan delinquency was distorted because of one or two large loans to high net-worth individuals who were professional athletes. They paid the loans on a rolling quarterly basis. Region IV officials failed to adhere to the supervisory letter, which warned examiners to consider the effects that these types of distortions have on small, low-income, or community development credit unions. NFL athletes are paid quarterly, and the loan agreements should have been made correspondingly. Regrettably, the KAPFCU management team did not realize this option was available when these loans were executed.

Bynum and Jenkins took the case based on loyalty to the fraternity. However, the firm did not specialize in NCUA litigation or banking, finance, and credit union law. If they had, they probably would not have taken the case. Tragically, if KAPFCU had aggressive counsel who was knowledgeable of NCUA law, the outcome could have been different.

Kappa Alpha Psi FCU Liquidation, Federation Statement[74]

NCUA's liquidation of Kappa Alpha Psi Federal Credit Union is a fait accompli. But it is not the end of the story.

There will probably be another hearing in a month or two, unless the plaintiffs from KAPFCU decide it is no longer worth it. We hope they decide to have their day in court, and that the judge has the opportunity to offer his view on the procedure. For the Federation and others in the credit union movement, the logic of liquidation proceedings is puzzling. When an appeal can only be heard and decided after the liquidation is underway, it brings to mind Alice in Wonderland: "Let the jury consider their verdict," the King said, for about the twentieth time that day.

"No, no!" said the Queen. "Sentence first–verdict afterward."

As it is, the right to appeal a liquidation seems to us to be hollow. It would be more transparent to inform credit unions that NCUA's actions are irrevocable.

Several troubling questions remain after NCUA's actions. Why did NCUA not pursue a Purchase and Assumption, which would have allowed the 1,400 members of this credit union to continue to receive service? Was NCUA's restatement of the credit union's financials irrefutably correct; an issue that was also raised in the recent seizure of Arrowhead Credit Union in California? Was there truly "no prospect" of this tiny, young credit union obtaining or generating the few tens of thousands of dollars it needed to become "adequately capitalized" over the next four years?

NCUA can rarely be defeated in court unless it behaves in an "arbitrary and capricious" manner. That is an extremely high bar for any credit union plaintiff to meet: no credit union is flawless, and NCUA can always produce data and arguments to support its case. But that does not mean that the credit union movement will perceive NCUA's actions against credit unions as appropriate, unavoidable, and fair. Amid the continuing pain

---

74 August 18, 2010, by the National Federation of Community Development Credit Unions (New York, NY).

of the corporate credit union crisis, we believe the credit union movement's perception of the agency matters.

The CDFI Fund Announces Its Awards

A vapor-mist rose off busy city streets as precipitation fell from the overcast skies. It was a stormy day in New York City. Large raindrops tap danced on the subway windows in a staccato rhythm. It was daybreak on August 19 in the city that never sleeps. A slight man with a medium build swayed back and forth on the train. He had long raven hair with black horn-rimmed glasses—the type of guy that you could imagine in a tie-dyed tee shirt at Woodstock, although Brian Gately was a former NCUA examiner and was currently a senior consultant for small and emerging credit unions for the National Federation of Community Development Credit Unions.

Gately pushed his hair back, placed his glasses on his face, and sipped some dark roast coffee as he embarked on the subway to 37 Avenue B, the Lower East Side People's Federal Credit Union in New York City. Neighborhood activists organized the credit union in 1986 to fill the void left by the closing of the last bank branch in the neighborhood.

Since then, LES People's FCU has served over 9,000 members in neighborhoods such as Lower East Side, Central Harlem, East Harlem, North Shore of Staten Island, Jackson Heights, and other places, and reinvested over $150 million in housing, business, and consumer loans back into these communities.

He was excited because Donna Gambrell, the Director of the U.S. Department of Treasury CDFI Fund, would announce the CDFI funding awards at a restaurant that received a loan from the credit union. He rode on pins and needles because the Federation expected the CDFI Fund to distribute the largest amount of money in its history. Although nothing is guaranteed, since the CDFI Fund supported banks, revolving loan funds, and credit unions, the $247 million allocated in 2009 represented the very best chance that low-income, community development, and Federation credit union members would have for CDFI funding.

Donna Gambrell prepared to announce new technical assistance and financial assistance awards. Brian reviewed the powder-blue and gold CDFI program book as he waited for Donna Gambrell to begin the grant announcement. He greeted the ebony leader before she began her presentation. Something unexpected and unprecedented in the announcement surprised him.

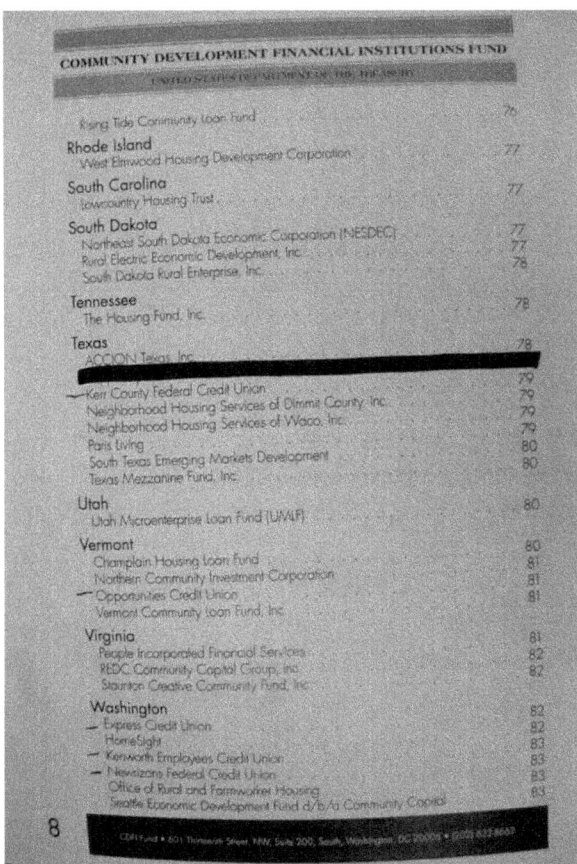

Community Development Financial Institutions Fund Award Program Book—Page 8

Redacted with Black Magic-Marker after printing—"Kappa Alpha Psi Federal Credit Union (KAPFCU) from Texas is included in this CDFI Grant Award Program."

After the announcement, Gately rushed back to his 33rd floor office at 116 John Street and sent an urgent email to Victor Russell and Michael McCray.

> *Mike and Vic,*
>
> *I attended the awards ceremony for U.S. Treasury CDFI grants today and let me say the timing for KAPFCU was not propitious. You would have gotten $100,000. It was in the final official program from CDFI.*
>
> *Brian*
>
> *Brian Gately, CUDE*
> *Senior Consultant, Small and Emerging Credit Unions*

After scanning the email, I immediately drafted a motion for reconsideration to document KAPFCU's objections to Judge Sullivan's ruling and dialed Ken Bynum.[75]

"Ken, get the transcript. We need to file an appeal ASAP. Judge Sullivan just doesn't get it."

Ken paused. "I didn't hear the judge say anything that was wrong."

"Judge Sullivan doesn't understand loan delinquency or balancing a CDCU loan portfolio at all," I said. "KAPFCU only had one bad loan."

"Yeah, but you've got rising delinquency rates, too."

I said, "We have $10,000 in loan loss reserves and an NCUA-approved allowance for loan and lease loss policy in place."

"It's over, Mac."

Flustered, I whispered direction to counsel.

"Ken, file the appeal."

"The charter is gone, the bank account is empty, and we had a fair judge," Ken scolded, "It's done!"

Ken refused to file a notice of appeal or to submit this motion for the record.

---

75 See Appendix K: Motion for Reconsideration.

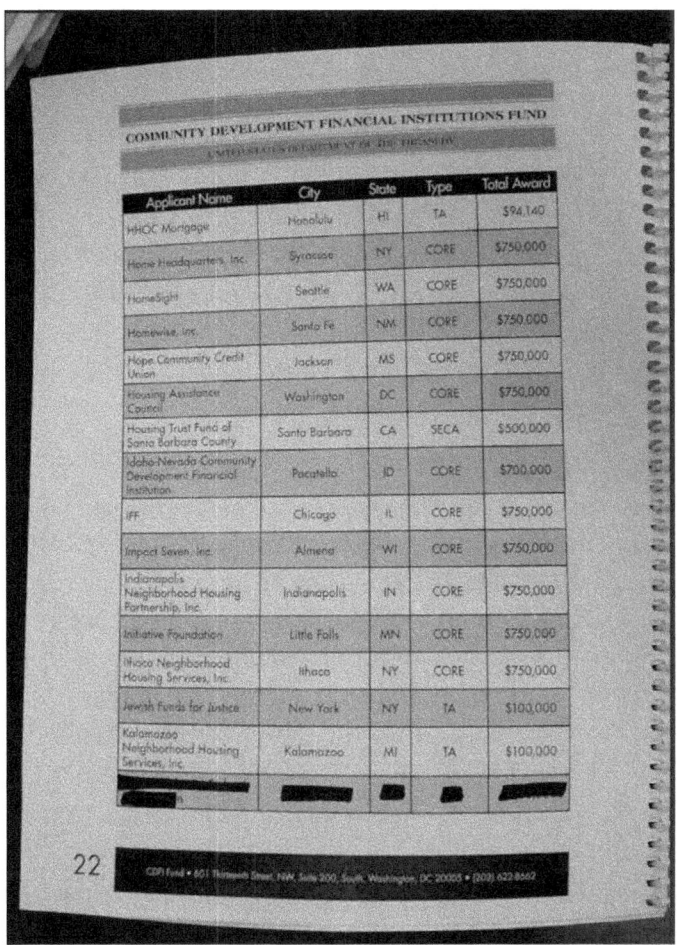

Community Development Financial Institutions Fund Award Program Book—Page 22

Redacted with Black Magic-Marker after printing – "Kappa Alpha Psi Federal Credit Union (KAPFCU) from Dallas, Texas was to be awarded a Technical/Assistance Grant for $100,000."

Brian Gately widened the loop and sent a follow-up urgent email to Helen Godfrey-Smith of the AACUC, Victor Russell, and Michael McCray.

> *Dear Helen, Dey, and Robert (separately), plus Mike and Vic:*
>
> *Cliff is off on his vacation, so I won't bother him, but this is horrible. What happened to Kappa Alpha Psi? NCUA had to have known they were in line to get an award (Robert, they were on the awardee list and were magic-markered off the hard copy at the last minute.)*
>
> *This may explain why NCUA was so eager to jump the gun and send out the liquidation checks even before the next hearing. I say, "they must have known," because by law, CDFI has to contact NCUA ahead of time before making a decision on an award. NCUA's reasoning in their court response that the credit union had no chance of becoming adequately capitalized is patently untrue. They would be over 16% [in net worth] if they had gotten their $100,000 award as was originally slated.*
>
> *Brian*
>
> *Brian Gately, CUDE*
> *Senior Consultant, Small and Emerging Credit Unions*

Gately debriefed the Federation's CEO, Cliff Rosenthal, on the KAPFCU debacle after he returned from vacation. To his credit, Cliff issued a public statement that described NCUA's aggressive regulatory actions against KAPFCU as *Alice In Wonderland*, much to the chagrin of NCUA Chairman, Debbie Matz.

Rosenthal Urges CUs to Challenge Overaggressive Examiners[76]

Cliff Rosenthal, National Federation of Community Development Credit Unions President/CEO, highlighted the liquidation of Kappa Alpha Psi FCU in a request for credit unions to take a stand against overaggressive examiners.

"The federation does not have access to the credit union's records, nor NCUA's examination documents, so it is difficult for us to evaluate the facts and merits of the case. It is important for credit unions who feel that they have been mistreated by their regulators to use all means available, ultimately including the courts, to assert their legal rights and argue their case publicly," Rosenthal said in a letter to his member credit unions.

We receive a steady stream of complaints from our member CDCUs about examiners acting overly aggressively or inappropriately. Almost no credit unions will take their cases public because they fear retaliation from their examiners—an obviously unacceptable situation. Kappa Alpha Psi has taken an important step in breaching the wall of silence," Rosenthal said.

---

76 Lindsey Siegriest, *Credit Union Times* (Updated on August 12, 2010).

PART THREE
Aftermath

CHAPTER 17

From New York to Washington: Leaving the Federation

Clifford N. Rosenthal

Rehearsal for Transition

There was a crucial lesson I needed to learn in my last years at the Federation.

In early 2008, I announced my plan for retiring from the Federation. In two years, 2010, I would turn 65 and mark 30 years at the Federation; the numbers sounded right for a departure. I had seen the challenges that organizations face when a long-time leader leaves, and so I welcomed an invitation to an intensive seminar sponsored by the Annie E. Casey Foundation specifically for founders and near-founders of organizations. It was an emotional and a clarifying experience. Leaving is hard. I learned about the stages leaders typically experience, through denial, bargaining, acceptance, and pivoting. I firmly decided that it would be a bad idea for me to linger offstage, as many departing CEOs do, in some sort of emeritus or "shadow" capacity; it works for some, but it would not work for me.

The board of directors began to address the succession process, soliciting requests for proposals from search firms. Meanwhile, I became increasingly anxious—in my daylight hours and in my sleep—about leaving. One morning in 2008, during the fall two-day board meeting at a San Francisco hotel, I awoke to a phone message from our board chair, Mrs. Rogers. "You know, we didn't ask you to leave. The situation in the country and for our members is tough. You don't *have* to leave." As she was quoted in *Credit Union Times,* "Because of this and other factors, the board unanimously decided to invite Cliff to extend his time as CEO of the federation."

Yes, retiring had been my decision and my plan. But I had not banished my terror at the blank scenario of retirement as a person who did not play golf, fish, or was otherwise really "retired." On my own, I would have been too proud to ask the board to reverse my decision. But Mrs. Rogers had thrown me a lifeline, and I gratefully accepted it. For two or three days, I felt that an enormous burden had been lifted from my shoulders. That was the good news. And then, the reality hit me—the economy was crashing, tottering on the brink after the Lehman Brothers and other collapses. I would have to help navigate the Federation through some of the toughest times we had ever experienced.

We lost some credit unions in the Great Recession. The disproportionate economic pain suffered by low-income communities and communities of color—the job losses, the home foreclosures—was transmitted to and shared by their credit unions. As described in Chapter 11, by 2010, we managed to achieve one of our greatest victories, accessing tens of millions of dollars for our members from the federal Community Development Capital Initiative—the summit of my decades-long campaigns to raise capital for our credit unions—but that was not nearly enough.

By 2011, the Great Recession was ebbing, although—as always—communities of color "recovered" more slowly and painfully than others. My initial departure date of 2010 had come and gone. The most pressing, immediate challenges had receded, and I turned my attention to what turned out to be my last major initiative. The International Year of the Cooperative was launched in October 2011, with ceremonies at the United Nations. I initiated a campaign to bring together New York City credit unions with cooperatives across the various sectors—housing, food, and worker co-ops. We convened 200 cooperators at the Ford Foundation, a block away from the United Nations. The City Council president unexpectedly joined us, along with other public officials. The steering committee for our event became the nucleus for a new organization, the Cooperative Economics Alliance of New York City (CEANYC).[77] The Federation was stable, with net worth sufficient to ensure its long-term survival barring cataclysmic management or economic failures. It was time for me to consider implementing my previous exit plan. Departing would also be an important test of what I had accomplished. Would the organization survive without me?

I began dropping hints to the board that my departure would come sooner than later. From my earlier training on "departure for founders," I had accepted the importance of "pivoting" to a new stage of my own life in order to remove the temptation to hover or encroach upon my successor. But my terror of a "purposeless" retirement terror had begun to return. Unexpectedly, the internet threw me a lifeline in the fall of 2011, when a post by the Americans for Financial Reform alerted me to an intriguing job opening. The new Consumer Financial Protection Bureau (CFPB), brainchild of (later Senator) Elizabeth Warren, was seeking someone to launch their Office of Financial Empowerment, which would be charged with addressing the issues of low-income consumers. "Perfect," I thought—except that it would be based in Washington, D.C. At the age of 67, how sensible would it be to embark on another career in another city? Nonetheless, the novelty of the idea cheered me up enough to apply, with the expectation that nothing would come of it.

Instead, as the Christmas holiday approached, I received a call from the CFPB inviting me to visit Washington for an interview. On

---

[77] The organization continued after my departure to Washington in 2012 (www.gocoopnyc.org), pursuing its mission of "closing the racial and gender wealth gap through cooperation." After I returned to New York City in 2014, I became a volunteer advisor.

January 3, 2012, I took an early train from New York to Washington, where on little sleep, I spent the day in a whirlwind succession of interviews with various staff, ending an exhausting day with the leadership team, Richard Cordray and Raj Date. My pitch for the job was simple: I had spent a long, successful career advocating for financial equity for impoverished communities. I did not need another job. It was the CFPB—and only the CFPB—that interested me.

I returned home on Amtrak thinking it likely that I would be offered the position. My wife, Elayne, and I contemplated the challenges of disrupting our lives in Brooklyn for a new chapter in another city. But ever since working in Washington in the 1970s, I had dreamed of returning "someday." This was the opportunity. If the job offer came, we decided that I would accept it.

I intensified my hints to the board that my departure was looming. Three weeks after my first interview, I returned to Washington for a final interview with my future boss. The offer was made, subject to background and security checks. To the considerable dismay of our board chair, Mrs. Lynda Milton, I informed the board that this was no dress rehearsal—I would be leaving, and in fairly short order, because the Bureau was pressing me to start immediately. I set the date for May, following a planned surgery. In March, our board met in Washington, where I introduced them to my soon-to-be boss. Mrs. Milton was not happy. My departure would complicate and add to her burden as board chair. But she was, as always, gracious and supportive. A staff member took a final picture of me with the board, which they signed and presented to me two months later amid my farewell events.

Final Months

As the word of my departure from the Federation spread within the credit union industry, I had various encounters with colleagues who half-jokingly commented on my defecting "to the dark side." Credit unions, no less than banks, hate regulations, and the new

Consumer Financial Protection Bureau would soon replace the National Credit Union Administration as their least-favorite Washington agency. On the other hand, our progressive allies in the credit union movement understood that my new position would enable me to continue to work toward financial equity for low-income consumers and communities of color. For better or worse, after 32 years, I was a fixture in the credit union industry. Acknowledging my decades of service (if not always as a "team player"), the New York State Credit Union Association graciously presented me with a token of their recognition.

The to-do list before departing included arranging for an interim successor. Several staff members, Latino and African American, were interested in applying. I advised the board against naming them; instead, I urged the board to accept my appointment of Pam Owens as interim CEO. Pam was an African American woman with more than a decade of service at the Federation. She was a consummate professional, popular among staff and our membership through her years of managing our hallmark residential seminar, the CDCU Institute™. I believed that after her years of outstanding service, the Federation owed her a chance to seek the permanent position. Knowing some of the challenges of the organization, she was not visibly enthusiastic about this opportunity—she knew the management problems I was dealing with. But the board knew and trusted her, as I did, and should she decide to pursue the CEO job, she would have a fair shot. Each of the other candidates clearly informed me that I should have chosen them. But I was unmoved.

The Federation's staff had arranged a local goodbye party for me in New York. Fittingly, I spent Friday, May 4, 2012, my last day working for the Federation, attending a White House conference on cooperatives. I flew back to New York, gathered a few personal things, and locked the door behind me for a final time. On Monday, I would start my new job in Washington.

To Washington

Accepting the position at the Consumer Financial Protection Bureau aligned well with my departure scenario. Federal regulations prevented me from engaging with my former employer for at least a year; I was physically separated from the Federation's New York headquarters and any temptation to meddle. Personally, I had a challenging new chapter in life—a new city, the first new job in decades, unfamiliar work in a large government bureaucracy, so different from the small nonprofits in which I had spent my career. I rented a room in Southeast Washington, returning to Brooklyn on weekends or having Elayne join me in the Capital.

The required separation from the Federation was so strict that I needed a waiver from the Bureau's general counsel even to attend the Federation's annual conference in Atlanta a month or so after I assumed my new job. The conference gave me the opportunity to say goodbye to my largest "extended family" from around the country, including credit union people I had worked with for decades. For my final appearance, I gave a too-long speech, detailing all that we, as a movement, had accomplished over the 32 years I had worked for the Federation.

Lingering Doubts

It did not take long for me to question my decision to join the CFPB. Two weeks into my new job, I was asked to write a blog (what was that?) introducing myself and my office's work. My draft came back with comments and criticisms from a host of lawyers and other bureau officials, cautioning me against sins including mentioning sensitive words like "unions"—as in credit unions. For thirty years, I had been the boss, crafting the Federation's public messages; now, I was a captive of a lawyer-ridden bureaucracy bent on eradicating any real or perceived deviation from the Bureau's "brand." Two weeks into my job, I happened to meet a fellow staff member on a walk in my neighborhood. I shared my fear that I had made a terrible mistake in becoming a "Fed." He reassured me that I would adjust, and I suspended my thoughts of reversing my choice. Still, my unconscious continued to take full measure of my departure from the organization that had been so central to me for half of my adult life. I had recurring, poignant dreams that I was attending a Federation event, but was treated as an outsider, not a member of the "family." Everyone refused to acknowledge me.

My new position prevented me from participating in the selection of a permanent successor for the Federation, even had I or the board wanted me to. Accordingly, I did not press for a candidate, and even rebuffed the aggressive push of a prominent New York acquaintance to recommend a former Congress member. By August, however, I was consulted in a final check about the board's proposed choice, Cathie Mahon. She had worked for the Federation in the late 1990s, managing our CDFI-related statewide and national advocacy. Later, she served as deputy commissioner of consumer affairs for New York City. She was superbly, uniquely qualified, with volunteer experience as a board member of the Lower East Side People's Federal Credit union, and I gave her my enthusiastic endorsement. Although the field was open for the board to find and choose a successor of color, they chose Cathie, a white woman.

It was emotional for me—the final step in my transition. I had complete confidence that Cathie would preserve and build upon the organization that had been my life's work. That she has done, and more.

My Career as a "Fed"

I survived my initial doubts and gradually adjusted to my life in a new federal bureaucracy, created by the Dodd-Frank legislation of 2010 that Elizabeth Warren had fought for. I was an assistant director at the bureau, managing a team of six charged with providing input and leadership on CFPB policies, regulations, and initiatives that impacted low-income consumers. My team was bright, energetic, and mostly a generation younger. They did their jobs so well that my supervisor complimented me on my management—praise that genuinely surprised me, given my own low opinion of my skills in that area.

The bureau had legions of lawyers, economists, and regulators. In general, they were impressively smart and experienced. Some came from consumer advocacy organizations, but few had worked primarily with low-income communities or on their particular issues and needs; for example, I was surprised to encounter economists who thought that savings were impossible and irrelevant for poor people. Neither did they have much awareness of CDFIs and their emerging role in the financial system. Consequently, I found a niche filling in some of the gaps in the bureau's expertise.

Our target group, as we defined it, was "the low-income and economically vulnerable population [that] includes as many as 100 million people, many of whom are unbanked, underbanked, or have thin or no credit files." Given that the agency had not defined a clear agenda to address the issues of low-income consumers, we had considerable scope to develop our own priorities. We embraced the success of financial coaching approaches and attempted to incorporate them into the programs of various federal departments, especially the U.S. Department of Labor and the U.S. Department of Health and Human Services. We learned that the people delivering social services were often only marginally more financially secure or knowledgeable than the clients they served, and we developed tools for those staff members. We elevated the financial needs of persons with disabilities, as well as people retiring from the military. We highlighted barriers to financial stability such as asset limitations for persons receiving government assistance—the "benefits cliff" over which people would fall if they made too much money, thus losing medical and other benefits.

I used my position to reach out to former colleagues and bring their work to the attention of the bureau. On November 28-29, 2012, six months into my tenure at the bureau, my team convened the CFPB's first conference on "Empowering Low-Income and Economically Vulnerable Consumers." We brought together more than 100 prominent advocates from consumer and antipoverty organizations; civil rights coalitions; credit unions and banks; funders and researchers; state and local programs; and other federal agencies, including the CDFI Fund and the National Credit Union Administration. We wrestled with the issues of data collection and pathways to scale. A year later, we published the conference proceedings[78] (cited below).

Leaving Washington. Again.

In 2014, as my two-year mark at the CFPB approached, I was finally comfortable in my job. We had launched several promising initiatives, and although we were never top-of-mind in the CFPB, we had established our place in the bureau's work. I felt that I had laid the foundation I was hired to create. My team knew their jobs and worked well.

Although I enjoyed my life in Washington, including especially the times my wife and I spent as tourists in the city, our respective weekend train trips back and forth between Brooklyn and Washington were taking a toll. I had joined the bureau with a vague notion that if I performed my job well, the bureau would eventually let me work in New York, where it had a small office, with occasional trips to Washington for important meetings. It seemed reasonable. I received excellent annual appraisals for my work. But when I proposed the arrangement, it was rejected—because I was a manager. It did not matter that the director of the agency himself flew home to Ohio every week. Nor did it matter that the bureau proudly proclaimed it was a "twenty-first century agency." Stay or go, that was my choice.

Reluctantly, I decided to go, to finally end our fragmented life, punctuated by the 700 hours we collectively had spent on Amtrak. I

---

[78] Consumer Financial Protection Bureau, *Empowering low income and economically vulnerable consumers. Report on a National Convening.* November 2013, Washington, D.C.

was briefly beset with the same pre-retirement terrors that had receded when I left the Federation and joined the Bureau. But one morning, as I rolled out of bed and looked out my window at the Library of Congress, the next phase of my life came into focus. I had a project—I would write the history of the community development financial institutions movement, which I had co-founded. It would close a circle for me, bringing me back to my roots as an aspiring historian.

My team graciously hosted a goodbye party, attended by dozens of my colleagues and Director Cordray. In March 2014, I returned to Brooklyn for good—the same house that I had moved to after my first departure from Washington in July 1980. Elayne and I celebrated with a trip to Hawaii, after which the next chapter of my life began. I secured several consulting assignments, one with a Washington policy organization advocating against payday lending, others to help start credit unions. I began researching my book, conducting more than 200 interviews with former colleagues and others who had helped shape the CDFI movement; visiting the Library of Congress, the Clinton Presidential Library, and the Ford Foundation archives; and doing extensive online research, which I found far easier than my graduate work in dusty libraries. In November 2018, I published *Democratizing Finance: Origins of the Community Development Financial Institutions Movement* (FriesenPress), bringing the story to events at Federal Reserve Banks, conferences in South Korea, university classrooms, and webinars.

CHAPTER 18

Change Came: Signs of Hope

> **It's been a long. A long time comin', but I know.
> A change gon' come. Oh, yes it will.**
> Sam Cooke, "A Change is Gonna Come," 1964

Change came!

In 1980, I joined the National Federation of Community Development Credit Unions and began my decades-long campaign for community-controlled capital. When I tell my story to younger generations, I'm sure some of them are incredulous; I joined the Federation before many of them had been born. Forty years is too long for change to come. But as Rev. Martin Luther King, Jr. urged us to remember, "the arc of the moral universe is long, but it bends toward justice." Often, it takes painful disruptions to wrench the moral arc from its too-gradual trajectory. In recent years, we have seen the arc bent by the Black Lives Matter movement, triggered by police killings and the COVID-19 pandemic.

Change has come in policies, actions, and especially, dollars. It has come among investors and philanthropists, federal agencies and regulators, corporations and nonprofits, credit union leaders and CDFI practitioners. Diversity, Equity, and Inclusion—DEI—seemingly have appeared on the agenda of every institution and organization. Multicultural business strategies and new staff positions have been created. "Hard conversations" have taken place as individuals scrutinized their own part in perpetuating inequity.

Without the killing of George Floyd and the massive Black Lives Matter protests, these changes may never have come. But I am hopeful that they will amount to more than a brief swing of a pendulum.

$12 Billion

The biggest headline arguably belonged to Congress. On December 27, 2020, Congress appropriated $12 billion for federally certified CDFIs and minority depository institutions (MDIs).[79] It was more investment than the field had ever seen. The Emergency Capital Investment Program (ECIP), administered by the Treasury Department, was allocated $9 billion to make equity-like investments in minority depositories, including CDFIs. The CDFI Fund received $1.25 billion to launch a Rapid Response Program (RRP), as well as an additional $1.75 billion to support lending in minority communities and by minority lending institutions.

The sum far exceeded the dreams of us CDFI founders. My 1988 concept paper, the first of its kind, called for a meager $25 million fund. After Bill Clinton won the 1992 election on a platform calling for the creation of a "national network of 100 community development banks and 1,000 microenterprise programs," a figure of $1 billion in appropriations was floated, soon reduced to $850 million. And when the legislation finally made its way through Congress, the new CDFI Fund emerged with only $50 million.

Was this $12 billion pot the "holy grail" I had pursued throughout my career? Certainly, the sheer volume of investment is a "game-changer." But the story is bigger than that. I welcomed not only the *scale* of investment, but the forms, targeting, and manner of distribution of this huge appropriation. I can't take credit for this progress; that belongs to my successors. I was gratified, and

---

79 Consolidated Appropriations Act of 2021 (Pub. L. 116-260).

felt vindicated, by seeing that issues I had raised for decades were being addressed.

Target: Minority Credit Unions and Banks

The Treasury Department's $9 billion Emergency Capital Investment Program was designated for Minority Depository Institutions (MDIs) and CDFIs, "supporting their efforts to provide financial products for small and minority-owned businesses and consumers in low-income and underserved communities . . . . especially communities of color and rural areas."[80] The help for insured depositories was long overdue: thirty years earlier, legislation had instructed regulators to "preserve and protect" minority financial institutions.[81] Through ECIP, Congress recognized that communities of color suffered disproportionately from the economic impact of the pandemic. It acknowledged that minority banks and credit unions were crucial in reaching those communities, and it recognized that Black financial institutions, in particular, were endangered species with compelling needs for capital.[82]

In a further advance toward equity, Congress set aside billions for smaller MDIs and CDFIs. It also incentivized "qualified lending" and "deep impact" lending to low-income borrowers for affordable housing, small businesses, and areas with persistent poverty. On December 14, 2021, Treasury Secretary Janet Yellin announced ECIP awards totaling $8.7 billion to 186 institutions, of which 54% were banks (101) and 46% (85) credit unions.[83] The program even reached one of the smallest institutions, a $1.4 million credit union serving a section of the Bronx, one of the poorest areas in the country.

---

80 *Emergency Capital Investment Program*. U.S. Department of the Treasury, March 4, 2021.
81 Section 308 of the Financial Institutions Reform, Recovery, and Enforcement Act (FIRREA).
82 Coronavirus response and Relief Supplemental Appropriations Act of 2021. I have used "minority" throughout this discussion because it tracks the legislative and policy language used.
83 The exact figures were not initially announced by Treasury, pending final contractual arrangements.

Unlike the CDFI Fund awards, ECIP investments were not grants. Banks received long term, low-cost equity in the form of preferred stock. Credit unions obtained equity-like subordinated debt. It was a product that the Federation had pioneered in 1996 for low-income credit unions. Although these investments were technically debt, they enabled institutions to leverage additional deposits and grow without endangering the capital ratios required by regulators.

The program was not perfect. There were exclusions and technical barriers that kept some deserving institutions out, including the *cooperativas* in Puerto Rico, as well as institutions that could not meet financial criteria. But overall, ECIP was major progress toward the congressional goal of preserving and protecting minority depositories, the providers of basic banking services and credit to underbanked, underinvested communities. For years, I had fought with limited success to address the erosion of Black credit unions. Now, the federal government had joined the effort.

ECIP helped redress what I had long argued was an inequity in the practice of the CDFI Fund. For more than 20 years, 80 cents of every CDFI Fund grant dollar went to nonregulated loan funds, while less than 20 cents went to credit unions and banks combined. If the Fund had prioritized depositories, could it have slowed the decline of Black banks and credit unions? That is uncertain. But I regarded the Fund's decades-long underinvestment in depositories as a missed opportunity, which I hope ECIP will help remedy.

Hope for Small Institutions: The Rapid Response Program (RRP)

From its beginning, the CDFI Fund's extensive, demanding application process effectively put it beyond the reach of the smallest CDFIs. To counteract this form of implicit bias, throughout the 1990s I had argued for a funding "window" through which small institutions could compete against their peers rather than against the largest, most sophisticated CDFIs. Finally, in 2000, the Fund established its Small and Emerging CDFI (SECA) program. With the Rapid Response Program, the Fund took a significant step toward equity by streamlining its application process and reducing the paperwork burden that had discouraged many small institutions.

The RRP reached CDFIs before other components of the $12 billion appropriation. The CDFI Fund opened the $1.25 billion program for applications on February 15, 2021. The RRP greatly streamlined the CDFI Fund's application process, removing the extensive paperwork that had discouraged small institutions. In a remarkably short time, on June 15, 2021, Vice President Harris joined Treasury Secretary Janet Yellen and key congressional supporters in announcing 863 awards to CDFIs. The simpler, formula-based approach ensured that successful CDFI applicants would obtain no less than $200,000. Consequently, the funding reached even some of the smallest CDFIs, including Black church credit unions with less than $2 million in assets. This streamlined funding approach may not become the norm, but it was an important step to enhance equity.

The RRP also redressed the imbalance between depositories and non-regulated CDFIs. Although the single largest share of awards and investments went to loan funds, for the first time, the combined share of banks and credit unions exceeded that of the loan funds.[84] Also advancing equity, credit unions and *cooperativas* in Puerto Rico, which had been devastated by Hurricane Maria in 2017, received $47.3 million, while Indigenous CDFIs received $54.6 million.

Equitable Recovery Program (ERP)

The remaining portion of the $12 billion went to create a pool of about $1.73 billion which the CDFI Fund used to create the Equitable Recovery Program. As described in congressional hearings, the pool was to include:

---

84 The winners including 463 CDFI loan funds ($571.3 million), 244 credit unions ($401.8 million), 149 banking entities ($267.1 million), and 7 venture capital funds ($9.4 million).

$1.2 billion for minority lending institutions. Minority lending institutions are a new category of CDFIs established in the December 2020 COVID-19 relief bill that predominantly serve minority communities and are either MDIs or meet other standards for accountability to minority populations, as determined by the CDFI Fund.[85]

Despite the congressional language, the Notice of Funds Availability (NOFA) adopted by the CDFI Fund made no mention of "minority lending institutions." Rather, the final language in the CDFI Fund application stated that

> The ERP will prioritize Applicants with a track record of: (1) making loans, grants, or investments in Low- or Moderate-Income Minority communities that are also ERP-Eligible Geographies; (2) making loans, grants, or investments to Minorities that have significant unmet capital or financial services needs; (3) making loans, grants, or investments in Persistent Poverty Counties, Native Areas, and/or U.S. Territories.

The definition of "eligible geographies" included those that "demonstrate severe impact" from COVID-19, taking into account severe mortality, high unemployment, median income at or below 120% of the Area Median Income, or are "Native Areas."

In the spring of 2022, an influential coalition of organizations with predominantly Black and Latinx membership argued that dropping "minority lending institutions" threatened to continue a discriminatory pattern. The coalition argued that Congress intended to assist those CDFIs "with leadership, governance *and* predominant lending activity that is determined to be of and for people and communities of color."[86] The coalition argued that:

---

85 Memorandum from Majority Staff to Committee on Financial Services, February 16, 2022, for Full Committee Hearing entitled, "An Unprecedented Investment for Historic Results: How Federal Support for MDIs and CDFIs Have Launched a New Era for Disadvantaged Communities."

86 Quoted from a letter to Jodie Harris, Director of the CDFI Fund, of February 4, 2022, signed by the African American Credit Union Coalition, Inclusiv, the African American Alliance of CDFI CEOs, and the National Association of Latino Credit Unions and Professionals.

Previous CDFI programs have been more targeted to high-resourced, white-led, and governed institutions over small Black-, Latino-, and Native American-led institutions. Most commonly, MDI credit unions have only been able to raise capital slowly through earnings and have not had access to outside bank or investor capital.

The program opened for applications on June 23, 2022, offering awards ranging from $500,000 to $15 million to certified CDFIs. On February 1, 2023, the CDFI Fund announced that "696 Community Development Financial Institutions (CDFIs) from across the country requested a total of $7.69 billion in awards, which is nearly 4.4 times the amount of available funding ($1.75 billion)."

Director Jodie Harris noted that "more than 50% of all certified CDFIs" applied for awards under the ERP. On April 10, 2023, Vice President Kamala Harris and Deputy Secretary of the Treasury Wally Adeyemo announced awards to 603 CDFIs headquartered in 44 states, the District of Columbia, Guam, and Puerto Rico received awards.

By CDFI sector, the awards were distributed as follows:

- 264 Loan funds ($615.5 million)
- 203 credit unions ($590.3 million)
- 129 banking entities ($513.7 million)
- 7 venture capital funds ($15.5 million)

The largest awards were approximately $6.2 million; the smallest, $500,000. The guidelines for the ERP stated that "eligible applicants may request no more than three times their annual average on-balance sheet Financial Products closed in their five most recent historic fiscal years or $15 million, whichever is less."

There were complaints about the exclusion of non-certified minority depositories, complaints about the certification process itself, and dismay that some likely candidates failed to get awards. Moreover, CDFIs led and governed by people of color tend to be smaller than white-led institutions; hence, the awards may not have proportionately reduced the disparity between Black-led and white-led institutions. But more than 85% of applicants received funding. For the most part, the organizations representing the various CDFI and minority bank sectors declared themselves satisfied with the results.

Investing in Equity: Corporate America Responds to BLM

Black Lives Matter movement and the massive public outpouring of shock and anger over George Floyd's killing transformed vague "concern" over racial inequity into action by corporate America and philanthropy organizations. Contributions and investments surged in to civil rights and economic justice organizations, including CDFIs.

For decades, banks had provided loans and grants to CDFIs, predominantly loan funds, for credit under the Community Reinvestment Act. But Black Lives Matter helped produce an unprecedented flow of bank capital into MDIs and CDFIs, and especially CDFIs of color. On February 16, 2022, the Committee on Financial Services of the U.S. House of Representatives held a hearing, "An Unprecedented Investment for Historic Results: How Federal Support for MDIs and CDFIs Have Launched a New Era for Disadvantaged Communities."[87] It detailed investments ranging from tens of millions to more than $1 billion. Sometimes the funding was intended to reach racial and ethnically diverse small businesses that had missed out on the

---

[87] Bank of America made a $50 million commitment to support MDIs and CDFIs; Citi committed $50 million, Goldman Sachs, $1.43 billion through PPP facilities with CDFIs and other partners, JPMorgan Chase, $100 million in equity to 16 MDIs, Morgan Stanley, $1.5 billion to MDIs and CDFIs, and Wells Fargo, $50 million in 13 African American MDIs. PNC, Trust, and U.S. Bank also made major commitments. Committee on Financial Services, "An unprecedented investment for historic results: How federal support for MDIS and CDFIs has launched a new era for disadvantaged communities: Virtual hearing before the Committee on Financial Services, U.S. House of Representatives, One Hundred Seventeenth congress, second session, February 16, 2022 § (n.d.)."

Paycheck Protection Program loans. Some large banks donated the fees that they earned in processing PPP loans. But by no means were all the large bank commitments actual grants or equity investments; much was in the form of loans, which fueled the skepticism of cynics.

What was qualitatively new was the outpouring of investment from other sources, including non-financial corporations and "impact investors." In 2020, Netflix announced that the company would allocate up to $100 million—2% of its cash holdings—"to financial institutions and organizations that directly support Black communities in the U.S.." Of the total, $25 million was to go to the Local Initiatives Support Corporation (LISC) for its Black Economic Development Initiative, while $10 million was designated for Hope Credit Union, the country's most prominent Black credit union. The investment was a piece of Hope's $100 million Transformational Deposit Initiative (TDI), launched in 2021. Netflix was followed by Nike, PayPal, Square, Chipotle, and Dick's Sporting Goods. By the end of the year, 274 corporations, banks, nonprofits, and high net-worth individuals had deposited $90 million into Hope via the TDI. Twitter committed $100 million to the Finance Justice Fund; a socially responsible investment fund started by the Opportunity Finance Network (OFN), which primarily makes loans of 2% to 3%.

Impact investors like the Olamina Fund provided capital to CDFIs led by people of color. The term "impact investor" seems inadequate to describe the multibillion-dollar donations that MacKenzie Scott made in 2020 from her Amazon-derived wealth to hundreds of nonprofit organizations. Dozens of CDFIs benefited, primarily loan funds, some of which were led by people of color, including the Latino Community Credit Union, the Oweesta Fund, the Community First Fund, and Hope CDFI. Strikingly, these were outright grants without strings, which increased the equity base of the recipients.

The Regulators: NCUA

The Great Recession changed the regulatory landscape for financial institutions, including how regulators were to deal with minority institutions. The National Credit Union Administration was not originally placed under Section 308 of the 1989 FIRREA legislation, which called for protecting and preserving minority banks. However, Section 367 of the Dodd-Frank Wall Street Reform and Consumer Protection Act of 2010 brought NCUA under those provisions and required the agency to report annually to Congress on its progress in protecting and preserving minority depositories. On January 21, 2011, the National Credit Union Administration established its Office of Minority and Women Inclusion (OMWI), and thereafter initiated its annual reports on Congress, which summarized "the composition and financial performance of the minority depository institutions (MDIs)" that NCUA supervised. The agency started a Minority Depository Institutions Preservation Program to "support and assist the growth of all credit unions, with a particular focus on low-income-designated credit unions and minority institutions," placing it under the agency's Office of Credit Union Resources and Expansion (CURE).[88]

What were credit union Minority Depository Institutions? As NCUA defined it, an MDI is "a credit union that has a majority of its current or potential membership composed of minorities (in this case Black American, Hispanic American, Asian American, or Native American) and a majority of minority members on its board of directors."[89] Credit unions obtain the MDI designation through self-certification. They provide a good-faith answer to two questions:

(1) Are more than 50% of your credit union's current and eligible potential members Black American, Native American, Hispanic American, or Asian American?

---

88 NCUA, *Preserving Minority Depository Institutions: 2019 Annual Report to Congress*. June 2020. As of December 31, 2019, the NCUA regulated 514 federally insured credit unions with the MDI designation.
89 Ibid.

(2) Is more than 50% of your credit union's current board of directors Black American, Native American, Hispanic American, or Asian American? (NCUA Interpretative Rule).

NCUA observed that "MDI credit unions are generally small, with 57% of all MDIs having less than $10 million in assets. These credit unions are typically located in a church, factory, or in small business locations." Certainly, NCUA's listing included many Black church credit unions, often with $1 million or less in assets. But the bulk of the collective assets of MDIs were concentrated in a handful of substantial institutions, each with hundreds of millions or even a billion in assets. Some of these had their roots in municipal or military credit unions, rather than being community-based.

"Safety and Soundness" vs. Equity

If advocates were hoping for a radical shift in regulatory policy, those hopes were soon dampened. In June 2015, NCUA issued an interpretive ruling and policy statement on the Minority Depository Institution Preservation Program. In response to public comments, NCUA declared "The Program will not interfere with supervisory enforcement actions duly undertaken by the other offices within the agency."[90] Monica Davy, the African American woman who became director of NCUA's Office of Minority and Women Inclusion in July 2015, explicitly addressed the tension between furthering equity and the agency's mission of preserving "safety and soundness" of the credit union system:

> There is a misconception that Dodd-Frank gives OMWI the authority to preserve minority depository institutions at all costs. That simply is not true. First and foremost, NCUA has to protect the safety and soundness of the credit union Share Insurance Fund.

---

90 Final Interpretive Ruling and Policy Statement 13-1. June 24, 2015.

For example, she went on to explain that the agency was not authorized to allow a merger of an MDI with another MDI if that wasn't the least-cost option for the agency. "Short of some regulatory change or different interpretation, our hands are tied in this regard."

The new order of things seemed much like the old order. During my decades at the Federation, ending in 2012, NCUA had made various attempts to aid low-income credit unions by designating Community Development Credit Union staff specialists. Many, if not most, were Black, and all of those I met and worked with were genuinely committed to helping and advocating for minority credit unions. But when the "regular" NCUA examiners decided to sanction or merge those credit unions, they simply overrode the CDCU specialists. The experience of Kappa Alpha Psi FCU sadly offered an example of this reality. In the new era, as well, as the agency explained, "NCUA has no plans to make MDI preservation a part of the examination and/or supervision processes."

Nonetheless, NCUA implemented various measures to "preserve and protect" MDIs. Each year, it provided thousands of dollars of technical assistance and monitoring grants—although not capital on a significant scale. There was, however, another source. On January 21, 2016, the National Credit Union Administration and the U.S. Treasury Department's Community Development Financial Institutions Fund signed an agreement to streamline the application process for low-income credit unions to become certified as community development financial institutions. NCUA declared its intention to double the number of CDFI certified credit unions, which then stood at 295. The streamlined process lasted until February 27, 2022. The number of certified CDFI credit unions indeed grew, although not as dramatically as NCUA hoped: by 2022, there were 461 federally insured CDFI credit unions. The growth was not primarily attributable to NCUA, but rather the increasing financial and other benefits available to CDFI certified institutions and the outreach efforts of Inclusiv, the primary association for CDFI credit unions. There was a major influx of certified credit unions and *cooperativas* in Puerto Rico following the disastrous Hurricane Sandy.

Little was achieved toward one purpose of the 1989 FIRREA legislation, namely fostering the creation of new institutions. In 2019, for example, NCUA chartered one new MDI credit union, Otoe-Missouria, in Red Rock, Oklahoma. That same year, NCUA noted a decline in the number of MDIs from 530 to 514. "Due primarily to mergers, the number of MDI credit unions declined between 2018 and 2019, mirroring the general long-term trend of consolidation in the financial services sector."

The long-term trend in the overall credit union industry was unfortunately clear—nearly 1,000 credit unions closed their doors over 2015-2020: a drop of 15%. In 2015, NCUA counted 626 MDIs out of 6,021 federally insured credit unions (10.4%). In the year ending 2020, the MDI count was 520, compared to 5,099 (10.2%) federally insured credit unions. In contrast, the number of low-income designated credit unions increased from 2,297 in 2015 (38.1%) to 2,642 (52.7%).[91] Why the disparity, growth in low-income designations, and the decline or stagnation among MDIs? Low-income designation brought tangible regulatory benefits, particularly the exclusive privilege of raising equity-like secondary capital loans, which enabled credit unions to leverage their balance sheets while adhering to regulatory capital standards.[92] The increase in the ranks of low-income designated credit unions did not necessarily suggest "mission conversion" of credit unions to the cause of serving communities of color. More indicative was the increase in the number of CDFI credit unions, because certification required a verifiable mission statement and data on services provided.

---

91 NCUA, *Preserving Minority Depository Institutions: 2019 Annual Report to Congress.* June 2020. As of December 31, 2019, the NCUA regulated 514 federally insured credit unions with the MDI designation.
92 Final Interpretive Ruling and Policy Statement 13-1. June 24, 2015.

Changing Institutional Culture

Although the trend toward consolidation within the credit union industry took its toll on small minority credit unions, the Dodd-Frank provisions brought significant change to NCUA—change that was intensified and deepened after the killing of George Floyd. NCUA, like the other financial regulators, was required to report to Congress annually about its progress in advancing equity in its workforce, its business practices, and among the institutions it supervised. The annual report includes detailed breakdowns of NCUA staffing by race and ethnicity, gender, and disability status. For example, among the findings in its report for 2021, it notes that "compared with the total workforce, the examiner series has lower representation across most minority groups;" about 26% of the examiner work force were classified as minority. Moreover, "the NCUA's Hispanic population continues to be an underrepresented group as compared to the [Civilian Labor Force]," as does the percentage of women.

The agency explicitly acknowledged the source of its concern for DEI. The report for 2020 cited "15 facilitated, open discussions on racial injustice and racism [that] were hosted by [the Office of Minority and Women Inclusion] in the aftermath of the killing of George Floyd and the nationwide Black Lives Matter demonstrations, and for nearly all special emphasis programs observances."

The agency established a "Culture, Diversity, and Inclusion Council" for employees, as well as employee resource groups respectively focusing on common race, ethnicity, gender, and disability status. In 2021, NCUA held a "Diversity, Equity, and Inclusion Summit" that attracted more than 800 participants from the credit union industry. As well, NCUA encouraged institutions to submit "voluntary credit union diversity self-assessments," although only 240 of about 5,000 did so in 2021.

Cultural change in an institution cannot proceed without support at the top. For several years, each NCUA board member has declared their support for diversity, equity, and inclusion. To me, perhaps the most remarkably frank statement came from former NCUA Board

Chairman J. Mark McWatters, a Trump appointee, on December 1, 2020 (quoted in American Banker). He described "white male privilege [as] the gift that kept on giving" throughout his life and career.

> There has never been a bad age or time as a white person or as a white male. It's truly impossible to distance yourself from the privilege even when you try.... The pandemic's final carnage will most assuredly fall disproportionately on persons of color, those of poverty, and those without privilege. COVID pandemic has caused communities to splinter along the lines of economic privilege.

As encouraging as these changes in regulatory tone and culture may be, it is important to recognize the legacy that must be overcome. On April 21, 2022, Kyle S. Hauptman, NCUA Vice Chairman who had formerly served on President Donald Trump's transition team, described the painful process undergone by a Black community group seeking to charter a credit union:[93]

> I recently found out that, at the same time as George Floyd's death in Minneapolis, a group was trying to start a new credit union in George Floyd's neighborhood in North Minneapolis, an area with many payday loan shops but few quality financial services options.[94] That group's organizer said last month that she felt 'humiliated' by how hard the NCUA made the de novo process. The group gave up on a federal charter and are now pursuing a state charter, but they still feel the NCUA wasted their time by

---

93 Prepared statement of NCUA Vice Chairman Kyle S. Hauptman Statement Following the Board Briefing, NCUA's Diversity, Equity, and Inclusion Program Update.
94 In 2017, responding to the killings of African Americans Jamar Clark (2015) and Philando Castile (2016) by the police in Minneapolis, the local Association for Black Economic Power and nonprofit community organizations decided to organize a credit union, the "Village Trust Financial Cooperative." It raised substantial pledges of support from the city government as well as private supporters. By mid-2022, the proposed Village Financial Credit Union was still well short of reality. Management controversies and a change of leadership were part of the problem. However, the effort continues and has won major support from the credit union movement, including a pledge of $250,000 from the CUNA Mutual Group in May 2022.

not clarifying the work needed for a federal charter versus just seeking NCUA insurance. . . .

Regardless of what we say about supporting small credit unions and minority depository institutions, neither of those categories include those trying to start a new credit union. . . . I urge all of us at the NCUA to remember what true financial inclusion means. We can't congratulate ourselves on our DEI efforts if we add any extra burdens on small credit unions and those seeking to start one. . . . The small credit unions, and those seeking a new charter, are people taking direct control of their financial well-being by forming their own credit union—a financial institution they own and control, dedicated to their specific needs. . . . Thus, if we are serious about financial inclusion, we must be sure these groups have a clear path to form their own credit union.

Recognizing the Difference

For decades, I argued that it was essential for the regulators to recognize the distinctive and socially significant conditions and roles of Black and other credit unions of color.[95] We counted it a success when NCUA's board issued supervisory guidance on CDCUs and other low-income credit unions—but too often, these went unheeded or were overridden by field examiners. Kappa Alpha Psi FCU explicitly argued that it was being compared unfairly to other credit unions that did not share its mission or membership characteristics.[96]

Not for the first time, but perhaps most unambiguously, NCUA's chairman acknowledged the differences and the need to preserve minority depository institutions. On February 27, 2023, NCUA Chairman Todd M. Harper addressed the thousands of credit unions representatives at the industry's largest gathering, CUNA's Governmental Affairs Conference:

---

95 See chapter 5.
96 See chapter 7.

> Our supervisory efforts here are aimed at creating a more equitable financial system that enables financial security for credit union members, especially those of modest means.
>
> And, thanks to the hard work of minority depository institutions, we all have made progress toward that goal. MDIs account for a sizable portion of the credit union system. In fact, one in ten federally insured credit unions is an MDI. Preserving MDIs is therefore fundamental to the NCUA's mission.
>
> That's why the NCUA implemented its support program for small credit unions and MDIs last year. The program assists these credit unions by identifying available resources, providing training and guidance, and supporting management in their efforts to address operational matters.
>
> But we are also assisting MDIs in other ways, such as adjusting our supervisory procedures to recognize MDIs' unique business models that often allow for higher expenses, charge-off rates, and delinquencies compared to federally insured credit unions overall. Using peer metrics to compare an MDI to a non-MDI in the same asset class is like comparing an apple to an orange. It makes little sense. [emphasis added]
>
> That is why the agency has recently developed new MDI-specific procedures to guide examiners. This customization will yield more useful peer metrics for MDIs to improve their policies, processes, and products to better serve their members' and communities' needs. And it will result in an apples-to-apples comparison. That's good for the entire credit union system.

It is too soon to say whether the policy and cultural changes in NCUA are irreversible. Still, looking back at my decades spent advocating with an agency that was overwhelming white and male (notwithstanding the various women board members), and too often was indifferent or hostile to the interests of credit unions and communities of color, I am hopeful that at long last, change has come for good.

The Bank Regulators

If anything, minority banks suffered greater chronic regulatory stress than credit unions. the number of Black-owned banks declined from 48 in 2001, to 18 in 2020.[97] The bank regulators elevated their support for minority depositories in a variety of ways. For example, in September 2021, the FDIC created the Mission-Driven Bank Fund, to help mission-driven banks, minority depository institutions (MDIs), CDFIs in supporting low- and moderate-income, minority, and rural communities. The agency emphasized that it would play only an advisory role rather than contributing capital for the fund, which had a maximum target of $1 billion. The FDIC released a statement of policy on June 15, 2021, that the National Bankers Association, which represents minority banks, applauded as "an essential step in the right direction. . . . The NBA looks forward to bank examiners increasing their understanding of the unique operating environments associated with our member institutions' economically distressed communities. . . . [Still] "much work remains to reverse the significant damage to minority communities and the steady decline of minority-owned banks. . . . We urge leaders of the prudential regulators to emphasize the current law's mandate of collaboration and encouragement in the regulatory treatment of our banks."[98]

It was a statement that I could have written about NCUA's treatment of minority credit unions.

---

97 It is important not to equate "Minority Depository Institutions" with Black-owned banks. The FDIC reported that as of March 31, 2021, there were 142 FDIC-insured MDIs. An analysis by the Brookings Institution indicated only 18 were "Black or African American"; numerically, the largest number (61) were Asian or Pacific Islander. Kristen Broady, Mac McComas, and Amine Ouazad, "An Analysis of Financial Institutions in Black-Majority Communities: Black Borrowers and Depositors Face Considerable Challenges in Accessing Banking Services," Brookings, March 9, 2022, https://www.brookings.edu/articles/an-analysis-of-financial-institutions-in-black-majority-communities-black-borrowers-and-depositors-face-considerable-challenges-in-accessing-banking-services/.

98 https://www.nationalbankers.org/news-6/national-bankers-association-applauds-house-passage-of-financial-services-racial-equity%2C-inclusion%2C-and-economic-justice-act, June 15, 2021.

The Awakening of the Credit Union Movement

For decades, change came gradually to the credit union industry. The faces of leadership long remained white and mostly male. Neither the Credit Union National Association nor the National Association of Federal Credit Unions has ever had a CEO of color.[99] Over the decades, there were few Black CEOs of statewide credit union associations, and the first Latinx CEO, Juan E. Fernández Ceballos, President and CEO of the Credit Union Association of New Mexico, was appointed only in 2021. Maurice Smith, a powerful African American voice for diversity, was elected to the CUNA board in 2010 and became president in 2018. He was responsible for introducing the proposal that "equity" be added to the seven founding principles of the cooperative movement.

Since Black Lives Matter, "DEI" has become the watchword of credit unions, their associations, and their suppliers. They have created diversity task forces, created new positions of diversity officer, and provided contributions to advance the work of equity. I have participated in dialogues and seminars about conscious and unconscious bias, personnel practices, lending, and the relationship of credit unions to their community. Some of the conversations became intensely personal, as African Americans tried to convey to their white peers the pain they suffered with each killing of an unarmed Black person, and the fear they felt as parents. There were "hard conversations," as they were often called, about the barriers to professional advancement.

Along with the DEI dialogues, staff training programs, and newly created positions, there have been notable examples of increased material support for credit unions serving communities of color. Through its foundation, CUNA Mutual Group, the industry's leading insurance company, has committed $1 million to build equity in credit unions led by and/or serving people of color through Inclusiv's Racial Equity and Resilience Investment Fund. In parallel with

---

[99] Lucy Ito, who is Asian American, served as CEO of a smaller industry group, the National Association of State Credit Union Supervisors, from 2014 through 2021.

the Minnesota Credit Union Foundation, it has pledged $250,000 in capital to support the launch of the Arise credit union (formerly Village Financial Cooperative) in North Minneapolis.

Never Easy

The drive for equity was strong and broad among credit unions. But it would be unrealistic to assume that racial tension was abolished or that change would be universally embraced.

On February 7, 2023, the *Credit Union Times* reported that "CUNA's Former Chief Advocacy Officer Claims He Was a 'Token Diversity Hire.'" Robert Lewis Jr. was terminated from one of CUNA's most senior positions less than one month after he was hired. Lewis's lawyers claimed that CUNA's CEO, Jim Nussle, told Lewis that he (Nussle) "'never had a Black direct report in his career before,' and then said, 'I do not know how to manage you.'"

As reported by the lawyers, "CUNA anticipated that Robert Lewis would be a token diversity hire. And when he attempted to actually do his job and exert authority over his majority white team, CUNA fired him after only 22 days."

CUNA denied the allegations, asserting that "Mr. Lewis's race was absolutely not a factor with regard to any employment decision and CUNA simply does not discriminate as to any protected characteristic."[100]

In a divided country, it would be too much to presume that everyone is aligned with the new focus on racial equity. At a major industry gathering in 2022, one participant asked the speakers on a diversity panel whether the credit union movement was becoming too "woke." I think there is little danger that the fundamentally centrist/conservative credit union movement is going to swing irrevocably to the extreme. On the other hand, like a large oceangoing vessel, the credit union industry may have been slow to turn in embracing racial equity, but it is hard to imagine a reversal of course.

---

100 Peter Strozniak, "Robert Lewis Suddenly Exits as CUNA's Chief Advocacy Officer," *Credit Union Times*, February 7, 2023, https://www.cutimes.com/2023/02/07/robert-lewis-suddenly-exits-as-cunas-chief-advocacy-officer/.

Leading Change:
The African-American Credit Union Coalition

With financial support from credit unions and even one bank, the African-American Credit Union Coalition has played a leading role in the industry's self-examination and change. Under the leadership of its President/CEO Renée Sattiewhite, the African-American Credit Union Coalition has greatly increased its programming, membership, and its financial support from the credit union industry. While describing itself as "a non-profit organization of African American professionals and volunteers in the credit union industry," it is an open and consciously inclusive organization that has readily partnered with many other credit union organizations, such as Inclusiv.[101] Throughout the pandemic, AACUC led widely attended weekly virtual webinars, "Commitment to Change: Credit Unions Unite Against Racism™." In frank, often emotional dialogues, African American professionals told of the barriers to professional advancement that they have experienced, while industry leaders reflected upon their personal commitment to diversity. Working to advance institutional change, AACUC sponsors the DEI Academy for Leadership Development.

In May 2021, AACUC was among 20 Black businesses featured in *The New York Times's* "virtual storefront," the paper's year-long recognition of the hundredth anniversary of the racist destruction of the Greenwood District of Tulsa, Oklahoma, once known as "Black Wall Street." In 2022, the National Credit Union Foundation presented AACUC with its rarely given Anchor Award "in recognition of its global efforts to unite financial industries in eradicating racism, particularly the organization's leadership in the wake of George Floyd's murder, the coronavirus pandemic, and political strife."

The Faces of Community Development Finance

For decades, community development loan funds dominated the CDFI field numerically and in terms of access to capital. The majority—and

---

101 Author's Note: In 2019, I was the first white inductee into the African American Credit Union Hall of Fame. Others have followed.

especially, the largest and most influential ones—were white-led.[102] Only in the last half-dozen years has change accelerated. The Great Recession, officially lasting over 2007-2009, widened the racial and wealth gap. The lack of diversity in CDFI leadership became increasingly obvious, and in the wake of the Black Lives Matter movement, increasingly urgent: why did so few CDFIs, especially loan funds, "look like" the capital-starved populations they were created to serve? CDFIs began to scrutinize their management structures, their personnel policies, their underwriting, and their investment procedures. The change has gathered momentum with each passing year, among both local and national CDFIs. The Nonprofit Finance Fund (NFF), a prominent first-generation CDFI loan fund, conducted a lengthy and far-reaching self-examination beginning in 2016.[103] In 2019, NFF produced its Plan 50%+, which included pledges that at least 50% of its investment would go to organizations led by people of color. Internally, at least 50% of its management positions would be held by people of color.

Representation: Raising Diverse Voices

Two decades after the formation of the national CDFI Coalition, new associations began to form to represent CDFIs led by and serving communities of color. They quickly attracted support from foundations and banks and expanded both as advocacy organizations and financial intermediaries.

First Nations Development Institute was active in the CDFI Coalition from the early 1990s, and later in the decade formed a CDFI, the Oweesta Fund. In 2009, the Native CDFI Network (nativecdfi.org) was formed, with the key policy priorities of: "adequate capital access by NCDFIs to serve Native Peoples" and "industry partnerships

---

102 In contrast, the leadership of community development credit unions and minority banks were predominantly people of color.
103 The fund was led at the time by South African-born Antony Bugg-Levine, who had served as a speech writer for Nelson Mandela.

and capacity to serve Native Peoples and Areas." The network launched its new capital intermediary in 2021. There are currently about 70 Native CDFIs, primarily loan funds.

The African American Alliance of CDFI CEOs (aaacdfi.org) was formed in 2018 as "the only organization leveraging African American CDFI CEOs' decades of expertise, relationships, and intellectual capital to change the odds and the outcomes for African Americans in underserved communities across America." The Alliance was motivated by the "inequitable access" to capital and capacity-building resources. It cited a study that from 2014 to 2017, the assets of white-led CDFIs grew by $21.8 billion, while the assets of minority-led CDFIs grew by only $682.5 million. With the mission of ensuring "that all Black communities have full and fair access to equitable financial tools," by 2022, it counted a membership of 56 Black-led CDFIs.[104] In August 2020, the U.S. Bank Community Development Corporation announced $1.15 million in grants to a dozen Black-led CDFI partners along with a grant to the Alliance. On September 27, 2022, the Alliance announced the launch of its Black Renaissance Fund, a $125 million fund to provide patient capital to Black-led CDFIs. Launched with an investment of $12.5 million from Bank of America, the Fund will provide below-market loans to its member institutions, strengthening their balance sheets and increasing their capacity.

The National Association of Latino Community Asset Builders (NALCAB) (nalcab.org) was formed shortly after 2000. It describes itself as "the hub of a national network of 140+ nonprofit organizations that serve diverse Latino communities in 40 states, Washington D.C., and Puerto Rico." Itself a certified CDFI, NALCAB also serves as an intermediary, channeling loans to Latino and Latino-serving CDFIs of various types among its membership. NALCAB notes that,

---

104 Donna Gambrell, former director of the CDFI Fund, is its board chairperson, and Lenwood V. Long Sr., a long-time community economic developer and advocate in North Carolina is its President and CEO.

"Approximately 70% or more of those served by the NALCAB Network are Latino, 20% are Black, and more than 40% are immigrants."

Launched in 2015 and incorporated in 2017, the mission of the National Disability Finance Coalition (disability-finance.org) is "to bridge the CDFI industry and the disability community, to ensure that CDFIs can respond effectively to address the needs of individuals with disabilities, and to offer technical assistance and support to CDFIs developing financing products and services."

Despite the regrettable demise, Victor Russell shared his dream to empower all African American credit unions and Divine Nine organizations through the example of KAPFCU's virtual business model and lessons learned from KAPFCU's sojourn to the promised land.

ALPHA KAPPA ALPHA SORORITY INC. ROLLS OUT DIGITAL CREDIT UNION FOR ITS MEMBERSHIP, AIMING TO HELP BUILD WEALTH[105]

Alpha Kappa Alpha, the nation's oldest Black sorority, is entering the financial services space to reportedly help build generational wealth.

The For Members Only Federal Credit Union in Chicago is being launched by the prominent organization. The institution has gained its federal charter and shares insurance coverage from the National Credit Union Administration (NCUA) and is expected to begin operations this year, based on this news release.

Founded in 1908 at Howard University in Washington, D.C., Alpha Kappa Alpha (AKA) is an international services organization with 355,000 members and 1,061 graduate and undergraduate chapters in the United States and in 11 countries per its website.

The credit union reportedly plans to offer safe, fair, and affordable financial products and services digitally. It will serve

---

105 Jeffrey McKinney, *Black Enterprise Magazine* (February 18, 2023).

members, future members, and their communities. It plans to provide members various savings and loan services its first year, including checking accounts, online banking, and debit cards.

"As the first Black-owned, woman-led, sorority-based, (and) 100% digital financial institution, we are poised to deliver innovative financial solutions that drive economic growth for our members, chapters, families and employees of Alpha Kappa Alpha Sorority," AKA International President Danette Anthony Reed shared in a letter written to members and reported by the *Atlanta Journal-Constitution.*

Unlike banks, credit unions often are non-profit institutions serving members. Being member and cooperatively-owned, they can sometimes offer higher rates on savings accounts and lower rates on loans because they have lower operating costs and don't pay profits to shareholders.

NCUA Chairman Todd Harper said among his comments, "This charter is also in keeping with AKA's current initiatives to assist members in building economic wealth, promote social justice, and uplift communities, all of which are fundamental to the statutory mission of credit unions."

Banking analyst William Michael Cunningham says the AKA Credit Union launch is a significant development that will have a positive impact on the Black community. He says he believes anyone can join a credit union if they are within the credit union's field of membership.

He says relative to the overall Black community, their common bond membership has higher income, is wealthier, has more stable employment, and are better educated. "This is a very attractive demographic around which to base a bank or financial institution."

Other Black Greek-letter organizations have previously or now operate credit unions. Reportedly, the Kappa Alpha Psi fraternity closed its credit union in 2010. And the Omega Psi Phi and Phi Beta Sigma fraternities purportedly launched credit unions in 1986.

The Challenges of Success

When the CDFI Fund opened its doors in 1996, there were about 300 institutions claiming to be CDFIs; today, there are some 1,300. Over the last decade, the number of credit unions and banks certified as CDFIs has multiplied. Especially among credit unions, some multi-billion-dollar institutions have newly dedicated themselves to the CDFI mission. Hundreds more could follow, reaching tens of millions of people. The public recognition and reputation of CDFIs have never been higher; arguably, their penetration among financially-excluded people and communities has never been greater.

Yet, despite the nearly 30-year history of the CDFI Fund, the need has not diminished; rather, it was exposed and magnified by Black Lives Matter and the COVID-19 pandemic. The emergence of issue-, race-, or ethnic-specific CDFI organizations could be read as a response to a failure of inclusion and equity of the first generation CDFIs. Rather, I would argue that it is a sign of the growth and success of the CDFI field: the sprouting of branches from the original tree.

Now, more than ever, I believe that CDFIs have become a permanent part of the country's financial ecosystem. Government, the private sector, and philanthropic organizations increasingly have found CDFIs the best channel for initiatives to reach underserved and hard-hit communities of color. The emerging organizations and leaders will enable CDFIs to reach more deeply among populations that remain underserved despite nearly 30 years since the launch of the CDFI Fund.

It has been gratifying for me to see that the critiques of financial inequity that I doggedly pursued for decades are finally being addressed. I count myself fortunate to have lived long enough to see the seeds I helped plant 40 years ago produce vibrant new life.

CHAPTER 19

Coda for KAPFCU

Michael R. McCray

Chip Filson: "The End of Kappa Alpha Psi FCU'S Journey To "The Promised Land" (Part II of II)"

In the previous article, I outlined the unprecedented action this young credit union took to oppose NCUA's efforts at forced liquidation.[106] The credit union's legal challenge stated in part

> "NCUA knowingly, intentionally attempted to summarily liquidate and revoke the charter of KAPFCU with total and reckless disregard for the truth."
>
> "Publication of the order of liquidation and revocation is defamatory, casts KAPFCU in a false light, and has caused erosion of public confidence. For these reasons, if the rushed liquidation continues, KAPFCU will suffer irreparable harm."
>
> Kappa Alpha Psi Federal Credit Union suffered irreparable harm. NCUA, an independent agency of the federal government, held all the resources and power and used it to destroy this new charter.

---

106 Chip Filson: The End of Kappa Alpha Psi FCU's Journey To "The Promised Land" (Part II of II)

Reviewing KAPFCU's Trajectory

On August 3, 2010, the NCUA served a surprise liquidation order on Kappa Alpha Psi Federal Credit Union. KAPFCU contended that the liquidation was based on the false impression in the press and media that KAPFCU's net worth ratio (NWR) had dropped to 1.95% and had no reasonable chance for recovery. The reality was KAPFCU was a new credit union, starting from scratch with a zero (0%) NWR. Instead, KAPFCU built its NWR up to 1.95% or "minimally capitalized" as of March 31, 2010, and even higher to 3.67% or "moderately capitalized" by June 30, 2010, after which NCUA elected to "liquidate" the credit union on August 3, 2010.

It is also troubling that NCUA chose the unusual and extreme measure of liquidation without consideration of conservatorship or a merger. KAPFCU had suffered only one loan loss, for less than $4,500, in its six-year operating history. NCUA rules and regulations give new credit unions ten years to become "adequately capitalized" and achieve a net worth ratio of 7%.

Under these conditions, the NCUA decision to liquidate KAPFCU on August 3, 2010, was ill-advised, improper, and legally actionable. NCUA rushed to liquidate KAPFCU not because they were failing, but because KAPFCU was becoming too successful, recovering too quickly. The steep decline in KAPFCU's NWR to 0.58% on December 31, 2009, resulted from the involuntary corporate stabilization assessment of $6,700 when KAPFCU had no exposure to real estate risk or mortgage-backed securities.

KAPFCU was required to contribute to recapitalizing larger corporate credit unions that suffered millions in losses from risky investments. The supervisory guidance regarding corporate stabilization stated that credit unions should not be prejudiced for losses because of corporate stabilization. Thus, KAPFCU's corporate-stabilized and cash-basis-adjusted NWR was 4.93% on June 30, 2010, which means KAPFCU operations complied with its previously-approved revised business plan (RBP).

KAPFCU PERFORMANCE

This chart illustrates KAPFCU's overall performance on a "modified cash basis" superimposed over the corporate stabilized net worth "hurdle" rates, thereby illustrating that KAPFCU had/would have exceeded NCUA's capital requirements before year-end.

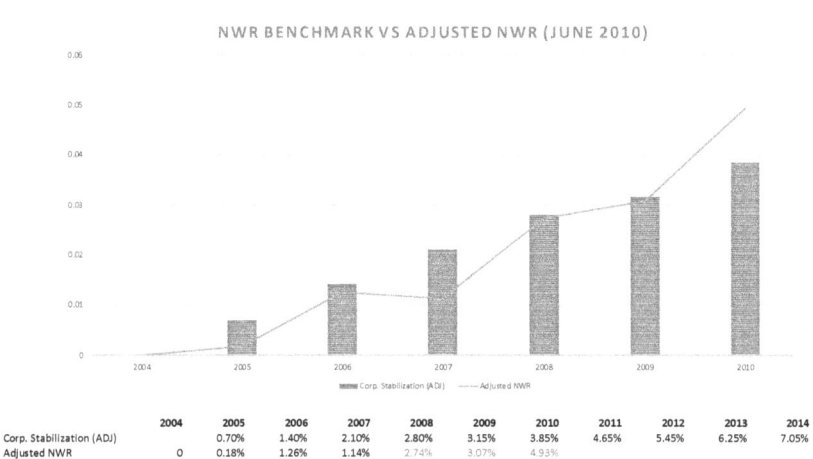

	2004	2005	2006	2007	2008	2009	2010	2011	2012	2013	2014
Corp. Stabilization (ADJ)		0.70%	1.40%	2.10%	2.80%	3.15%	3.85%	4.65%	5.45%	6.25%	7.05%
Adjusted NWR	0	0.18%	1.26%	1.14%	2.74%	3.07%	4.93%				

The NCUA offers technical assistance grants (TAG) and other benefits to designated low-income credit unions. They provide desperately-needed development and financial services to underserved and hard-to-serve populations. Therefore, there is a strong public policy need for these services. The NCUA evaluated KAPFCU as if it was a mature credit union with over $10 million in assets. The accounting rules and regulations are different, but NCUA examiners evaluated KAPFCU on the much higher standard.

KAPFCU reinstituted "modified cash" at year-end, and NCUA changed its policy in September 2009, so the examiners could no longer change credit union call reports without authorization, as was happening to KAPFCU. As a direct result, KAPFCU went from 0.58% on December 31, 2009, to 1.95% by March 31, 2010, and 3.67% on June 30, 2010. KAPFCU's financial performance had turned around, which NCUA opted to ignore and then moved forward with liquidating the credit union.

KAPFCU PROJECTED PERFORMANCE

This chart illustrates KAPFCU's overall performance on a "modified cash basis." It includes the CDFI technical/assistance grant superimposed over the corporate stabilized net worth "hurdle" rates thereby illustrating that KAPFCU had/would have exceeded NCUA's capital requirements before year-end.

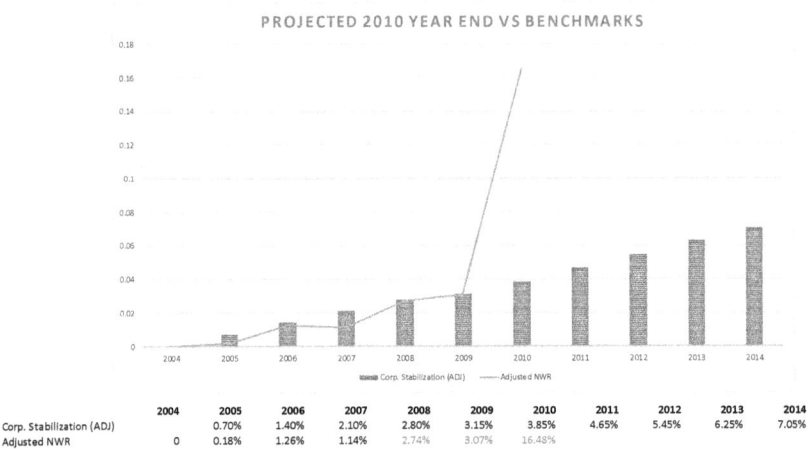

	2004	2005	2006	2007	2008	2009	2010	2011	2012	2013	2014
Corp. Stabilization (ADJ)		0.70%	1.40%	2.10%	2.80%	3.15%	3.85%	4.65%	5.45%	6.25%	7.05%
Adjusted NWR	0	0.18%	1.26%	1.14%	2.74%	3.07%	16.48%				

The Roots of Black Belief[107]

Recently, a friend shared reflections on Martin Luther King, Jr.'s last sermon ("I am a Man"), given on April 3, 1968, to support the Memphis garbage workers' strike.

We remember it as the "I have been to the mountaintop" speech, because King was assassinated the next day. Those last words were prophetic, but there were many other truths he spoke that are relevant to this day. I believe these are why Kappa Alpha Psi FCU stood up to the NCUA.

King said in part:

---

107 Ibid.

We've got to strengthen black institutions. (That's right, yeah.) I call upon you to take your money out of the banks downtown and deposit your money in Tri-State Bank. (Yeah.) [Applause] We want a "bank-in" movement in Memphis. (Yes.) Go by the savings and loan association. I'm not asking you something that we don't do ourselves in SCLC. Judge Hooks and others will tell you we have an account here in the savings and loan association from the Southern Christian Leadership Conference. We are telling you to follow what we're doing, put your money there. [Applause] You have six or seven black insurance companies here in the city of Memphis. Take out your insurance there. We want to have an "insurance-in." [Applause] Now these are some practical things that we can do. We begin building a greater economic base, and we are putting pressure where it really hurts. (There you go.) And I ask you to follow through here. [Applause]

Now the other thing we'll have to do is this: always anchor our external direct action with the power of economic withdrawal. Now we are poor people, individually we are poor when you compare us with white society in America. We are poor. Never stop and forget that collectively, that means all of us together, collectively we are richer than all the nations in the world, except for nine. Did you ever think about that? After you leave the United States, Soviet Russia, Great Britain, West Germany, France, and I could name the others, the American Negro collectively is richer than most nations of the world. We have an annual income of over thirty billion dollars a year, which is more than all the exports of the United States and more than the national budget of Canada. Did you know that? That's power right there if we know how to pool it.

Let us rise up tonight with a greater readiness. Let us stand with a greater determination. And let us move on in these powerful days, these days of challenge, to make America what it ought to be. We have an opportunity to make America a better nation. (Amen.)

A Lost Challenge—An Important Legal Precedent

Kappa Alpha Psi FCU's lost its unequal battle with a federal agency. The credit union's lawyers were not credit union attorneys. Nothing in their experience told them how unprecedented their challenge would be. But their effort to appeal NCUA's unilateral action may have lasting value, showing a legal path that could benefit credit unions and their members in the years to come.

Credit unions are member-owned, one-person, one-vote. The lawyers argued that NCUA's actions violated two individual constitutional rights: due process and equal protection. Could this Black-sponsored credit union have identified a legal standard that could benefit every credit union member which is subject to arbitrary NCUA dictates? Could NCUA have erred on both the facts of the case and the law? Or was this just a little regulatory nuisance that NCUA wanted to dispose of quickly?

When creditunions.com reported these events in August 2010, over 9,000 article views were recorded. Almost 100 comments were filed. Many similar experiences of regulatory arrogance were recounted in these posts. Kappa Alpha Psi FCU was not the only credit union to find its charter abruptly ended.

In September 2010, NCUA, without warning, liquidated five corporate credit unions with total assets of over $67 billion. The agency stated any appeal efforts would risk personal liability—the credit unions were marched straight to NCUA's chopping block. Other credit unions were subjected to this authoritarian power mode even though the economic crisis was almost a year into recovery. In June 2010, the $846 million Arrowhead CU was conserved to remove a management team that challenged examiners' exaggerated estimates of loan losses. Others were forced to merge, including the $600 million USA FCU into Navy FCU in September 2010.

The Continued Use of Summary Authority

But these were not just crisis incidents. NCUA continued to use this unchecked authority to end credit union charters without due process. On April 5, 2016, NCUA simultaneously liquidated six Philadelphia credit unions ending 308 total years of operations. These six were given no appeal rights. These credit unions had been through economic thick and thin for decades, and their total size—$4.8 million—could not pose a serious threat to the share insurance fund. They reported an average net worth of 17%. NCUA performed another instant liquidation on May 29, 2020, of IBEW Local Union 712 Federal Credit Union in Beaver, Pennsylvania. According to *CU Today*, "Chartered in 1964, IBEW Local Union 712 served 2,935 members and had assets of approximately $14.8 million according to the credit union's most recent Call Report. NCUA did not provide a reason for the liquidation."

This regulatory silence and lack of accountability continues to this day, for example, in all conservatorships in which NCUA takes total control of the credit union from the board and members. The reality, I have learned, is that being the federal government means you never have to say you're sorry. Federal examiners face zero accountability because the NCUA never has to face up to their errors when they can simply liquidate their own mistakes. Stuart Perlitsh, formerly a longtime CEO of a major California credit union, agreed:

> When it comes to the NCUA, I am never shocked. Just disappointed. This Kappa Alpha FCU is not the exception to the rule; it is the rule. The NCUA is arbitrary and capricious in dealing with 'problem credit unions.' The NCUA regulates them and examines them, and when things go bad, the NCUA is quick to dispose of the 'problem' to save themselves the embarrassment.
>
> Where was the NCUA at with the corporate credit unions, Kappa Alpha Psi FCU, Municipal CU, Telesis CU, CBS CU, etc.? No

one at the NCUA is held to account for mismanagement, gross incompetence in the exam cycle, or negligence. Nothing. Instead, they get promoted and move up a pay grade.

The Journey to the Promised Land[108]

Was Kappa Alpha Psi FCU's fate just another instance of a decades-long ongoing abuse of NCUA authority?

Does this credit union's unmatched courage taking a stand have any meaning today?

Why did these credit union novices fight when others did not dare?

I believe their actions were living out the charge that King gave that final day in Memphis:

> We just need to go around to these massive industries in our country (amen), and say, "God sent us by here (all right) to say to you that you're not treating His children right. (That's right.) And we've come by here to ask you to make the first item on your agenda fair treatment where God's children are concerned.

Will Kappa Alpha Psi's stand make a difference today? I think hearing this promise again should inspire everyone to realize that change is possible—even in those exercising unchallenged power.

Yes, I believe Kappa's example will be remembered.

Victor Russell reflects on KAPFCU's journey: "KAPFCU is a cautionary tale about NCUA abuse of power. We are a prime example of the challenges that African American credit unions, low-income credit unions, and community development credit unions face with NCUA examiners—individuals who do not appreciate the low-income

---

108 Ibid.

business model or community development-oriented business plans, and refuse to comply with mandatory NCUA rules, regulations and supervisory authority that relate to them."

KAPFCU's struggle was not forgotten. In August 2017, I introduced Victors Russell for his induction into the African American Credit Union Coalition's Hall of Fame. He joined another Kappa brother in the Hall of Fame, William "Bill" Bynum. Bill was inducted in March 2015, and received AACUC's Pete Crear Lifetime Achievement Award in 2017, a testimony to his impact in building the nation's foremost Black-led CDFI. A decade following its rushed liquidation, the KAPFCU example, influence, and message still resonate within the credit union industry. Like Cliff Rosenthal before him, NCUA Chairman Todd Harper gave remarks as an "ally" being inducted into the AACUC Hall of Fame during the CUNA Government Conference in Washington, D.C., in 2023.

NCUA Chairman Todd M. Harper Remarks at the African American Credit Union Coalition Hall of Fame Induction

I consider this honor to be among the very highest of my life, right up there with being nominated by the president and confirmed by the U.S. Senate to the NCUA Board. And this recognition means so much to me, especially knowing the caliber of the current and past honorees, several of whom I feel lucky to call friends.

After all, the list of Hall of Fame alumni reads like a who's who of leading voices for economic equity and justice within the credit union movement. Given all that AACUC does to advance financial security in historically under-resourced communities, to be counted among the trailblazers who comprise this class of inductees is inspiring.

I cried tears of joy when I first learned of my selection to the AACUC Hall of Fame because the recognition was totally unexpected. My emotions then took over because I felt affirmed for the things I hold as my core values—diversity, equity, and inclusion.

Even though I am a white male, I have experienced all of those things as a gay man. I know that many of you here have also exponentially experienced hatred and derision. But, acting from the heart and practicing the ‹power of one' can make an individual a change agent, and that's where I stand.

Thanks to the hard work of minority depository institutions, we all have made progress toward that goal. MDIs account for a sizable portion of the credit union system. One in ten federally insured credit unions is an MDI. Preserving MDIs is therefore fundamental to the NCUA's mission.

It's through our work that we will expand financial security and create opportunities for all Americans within the credit union system. It's why we at the NCUA have modified our rules to unlock the full potential of the Emergency Capital Investment Program for minority depository institutions. It's why we customized exams for minority depository institutions, allowing them to focus more on serving members than meeting peer metrics for credit unions operating under a different business model.

That's why the NCUA implemented its support program for small credit unions and MDIs last year. The program assists these credit unions by identifying available resources, providing training and guidance, and supporting management in their efforts to address operational matters.

We are also assisting MDIs in other ways, such as adjusting our supervisory procedures to recognize MDIs' unique business models that often allow for higher expenses, charge-off rates, and delinquencies compared to federally insured credit unions overall. Using peer metrics to compare an MDI to a non-MDI in the same asset class is like comparing an apple to an orange. It makes little sense.

That is why the agency has recently developed new MDI-specific procedures to guide examiners. This customization will yield more useful peer metrics for MDIs to improve their policies, processes, and products to better serve their members' and communities' needs. It will result in an apples-to-apples comparison. That's good for the entire credit union system.

It's why we are enhancing our fair lending supervision. And it's why we are working to root out racial bias in residential home appraisals and automated valuations. It's why we host an industry-wide diversity, equity, and inclusion summit. It's also why we created a grant initiative to assist credit unions in closing the racial wealth gap.

So, it's with a heart full of awe, joy, and gratitude that I humbly accept this deeply meaningful recognition. It's also why I will continue the fight to make our world a better place for all. We cannot rest until the credit and savings needs of all Americans are met, especially those of modest means.

KAPFCU provided access to capital and financial services to African Americans and low-income populations, traditionally hard-to-serve target markets. KAPFCU was a new credit union with less than $800,000 in assets. We were also a certified low-income and community development credit union. If NCUA had followed *its own* policy dictates, rules, and regulations, including its "Supervisory Letter to Credit Unions Related to Low-Income and Community Development Credit Unions," and its own rules regarding small credit unions with less than $10 million in assets, then KAPFCU would not have been subject to a letter of understanding and agreement and would never have been in any danger of liquidation. The forced change to full accrual accounting caused KAPFCU's record-keeping deficiencies and subsequent deterioration of KAPFCU's capital base, resulting in NCUA's punitive actions. But for the forced change to full GAAP accrual accounting, KAPFCU would never have been in the financial or management condition that subjected it to those actions at all.

PART FOUR

THE RECIEPTS:
KAPFCU v. NCUA

Michael R. McCray

APPENDIX

"The World's First Virtual National Low-Income Credit Union"
A Cautionary Tale of Premature Liquidation by NCUA

APPENDIX DOCUMENTS

A. NCUA Supervisory Letter to Examiners (LICUs/CDCUs)
B. KAPFCU Response to LUA and Request for Hearing
C. Dan Mouton, CPA. Email CPA Opinion (Cash Basis)
D. Balack & Williams, Legal Opinion (Product Defect)
E. NCUA Closed Door Board Transcript
F. KAPFCU Response to Ex Parte Hearing
G. NCUA TRO Press Release
H. KAPFCU Financial Performance (Quarterly Call Report)
I. NCUA "Sur Reply" to KAPFCU legal brief.
J. U.S. District Court Transcript & Final Court Order
K. KAPFCU Motion to Reconsider (Unfiled)
L. U.S. Treasury Department CDFI Debrief Report

Appendix A

NCUA SUPERVISORY LETTER TO EXAMINERS (LICUS/CDCUS)

APPENDIX A   285

NCUA LETTER TO CREDIT UNIONS

NATIONAL CREDIT UNION ADMINISTRATION
1775 Duke Street, Alexandria, VA 22314

DATE: January 2010   LETTER NO.: 10-CU-01

TO: Federally-Insured Credit Unions

SUBJ: Supervising Low Income Credit Unions and Community Development Credit Unions

ENCL: Supervisory Letter – Supervising Low Income Credit Unions and Community Development Credit Unions

Dear Board of Directors:

Enclosed is a Supervisory Letter entitled, *Supervising Low Income Credit Unions and Community Development Credit Unions*. We recently issued this guidance to all NCUA examiners. The primary focus of the guidance is to discuss the characteristics, benefits, and unique challenges of low income credit unions and community development credit unions. However, the contents of the Supervisory Letter are applicable to all credit unions in their continuing efforts to serve members of modest means.

One of the primary reasons for the creation of credit unions is to make credit available to people of modest means for productive purposes. This guidance was developed based on discussions with dedicated low income credit union management. You may find the enclosed guidance helpful as you strive to meet the needs of your membership.

Sincerely,

Debbie Matz
Chairman

Enclosure

Supervisory Letter

Supervising Low Income Credit Unions and Community Development Credit Unions

Introduction

The purpose of this document is to provide examiners guidance on issues they might face when supervising low income credit unions (LICUs) and self-designated community development credit unions (CDCUs). The guidance discusses the characteristics, benefits, and unique challenges of these types of credit unions and includes an appendix describing resources available to them. Examiners should remember, however, all federal credit unions have a continuing obligation to meet the financial service needs of people of modest means.[1] Therefore, most of this guidance will apply to most credit unions.

In 2005, NCUA issued a Letter to Credit Unions (LCU), entitled *Supervising Community Development Credit Unions*, LCU 05-CU-01 (February 2005). That letter included a white paper designed to facilitate examiners' understanding and ability to supervise the unique challenges faced by LICUs and CDCUs.

Low Income Credit Unions (LICUs)

In 1970, the Federal Credit Union Act was amended to authorize the NCUA Board to define "low income members" to permit credit unions predominantly serving them to take advantage of certain statutory benefits. The low-income designation criteria were amended in 2008 to use median family income or median earnings for individuals to determine if a credit union qualifies for a low-income designation and potential assistance through loans and grants from NCUA's Community Development Revolving Loan Fund (CDRLF). This amendment also helped better align the low-income designation criteria with the criteria for adding an underserved area to a federal credit union's field of membership. Adding an underserved area does not automatically qualify a credit union for the NCUA low-income designation.

All federally-insured credit unions may receive a low-income designation if they meet the qualifications.[2] Effective January 1, 2009, members qualify as low-income based on either median family income or median earnings for individuals, whichever is more beneficial to determining if the credit union qualifies for the designation.[3] Federally-

---
[1] State credit union laws reference provision of thrift and financial services to their members rather than serving people of modest means.
[2] 12 C.F.R. §§ 701.34, 741.204
[3] 12 C.F.R. § 701.34(a)(2).

insured credit unions serving a membership that consists of a majority of low income members qualify for the low-income designation.

With the low-income designation, credit unions gain access to additional sources of funding and resources, from both NCUA and outside parties.[4] Some additional sources of funding include:

- Nonmember deposits, 12 C.F.R. § 701.32;
- Secondary capital, 12 C.F.R. § 701.34;
- Loans and technical assistance grants under Community Development Revolving Loan Program, 12 C.F.R. Part 705; and,
- The United States Department of Treasury's Community Development Financial Institutions (CDFI) Fund.

LICUs are also eligible for an exception to the aggregate loan limit on member business loans.[5] Additionally, a credit union that qualifies for a RegFlex designation is exempted from the limits on nonmember deposits.[6]

Refer to the appendix *Resources for Low Income Credit Unions* for additional information.

Community Development Credit Unions (CDCUs)

NCUA does not designate or charter CDCUs. The term "CDCU" is not a term used in the Federal Credit Union Act or NCUA's regulations. Credit unions using the term CDCU generally define themselves as credit unions dedicated to serving and revitalizing low-income communities. NCUA understands CDCUs predominantly serve people of modest means and are committed to serving their members as well as the economic and development needs of the broader community. Self-designated CDCUs may be federally or state-chartered and can have a community, associational, occupational, or multiple common bond field of membership.

Characteristics of LICUs, CDCUs and the Members They Serve

LICUs and, generally, CDCUs typically serve a membership primarily composed of low income members. These credit unions face unique challenges serving members. The challenges are even more prevalent in small credit unions. Their members may face one or more of the following circumstances and characteristics:

- Unsteady employment (often temporary jobs with long hours);
- Part-time employment (often with multiple jobs or side businesses);
- Unstable residency (often rent or live in public or subsidized housing);
- No health insurance;
- Lack of affordable child care;
- Receive supplemental security income or social security disability benefits;
- English as a second language;
- Low share account balances;

---

[4] Federally insured state credit unions may have different sources pursuant to state law.
[5] 12 C.F.R. §§ 723.17 and 723.18.
[6] 12 C.F.R. §742.4(a)(2).

- Need for small dollar loans;
- Limited financial resources;
- Limited, negative, or no credit history; and,
- A need for labor-intensive services (e.g. money orders, financial education and/or counseling, check cashing).

Examiners should consider these member characteristics and take them into account when they evaluate LICU loan portfolios as well as the products and services these credit unions offer.

Characteristics of a Well-Managed LICU or CDCU

Characteristics of a well-managed LICU or CDCU will include most of the following:

- Maintains sound internal controls;
- Develops, follows, and adjusts comprehensive strategic, business and budget plans to meet the credit union's and members' needs;
- Retains skilled and dedicated staff because servicing members is a top priority;
- Maintains up to date, accurate records;
- Implements financial education and counseling, as applicable, for members as part of the lending process;
- Identifies and documents compensating factors supporting the loan decision, especially when income verification is difficult or credit history is limited, negative, or non-existent; and,
- Communicates regularly with membership.

In evaluating these credit unions, examiners should assure that the credit union's risk management efforts are commensurate with the size and complexity of the institution. Moreover, examiners should use appropriate or customized peer categories (e.g., other LICUs or CDCUs of similar asset size and complexity) to measure a credit union's risk management efforts.

Strategic Risk

Strategic risk is the current and prospective risk to earnings or capital arising from adverse business decisions made, improper implementation of decisions, or lack of responsiveness to industry changes. As in all credit unions, LICUs and CDCUs should carefully consider strategic risk when making decisions regarding the credit union's operations. In order to mitigate high strategic risk, the credit union should:

- Ensure risk exposure reflects strategic goals established by management;
- Develop, maintain, and adapt (as circumstances change) a business plan that directs the operation and is commensurate to the size and complexity of the credit union;
- Define acceptable levels of risk in different areas of operation that are compatible with business plan strategies;
- Develop quantitative measures to help assess progress with business plan goals;
- Adjust operations to address new circumstances, such as changing economic environment or changes to members' needs; and,
- Establish and maintain sound parameters for new member services.

APPENDIX A   287

LICUs and CDCUs should consider all ramifications of business decisions when starting a new program or service or adjusting a program or service already in place. When credit unions make these types of changes to operations, it is critical for credit union management to perform a thorough due diligence review. When beginning new programs, management should establish their limits, especially in regards to financial abilities and staffing needs. Once these limits are defined, management should work to stay within those boundaries to ensure risks remain within acceptable levels. New programs should have short-term, interim targets to allow credit unions to evaluate their processes and controls before reaching the limits established by the board. Examiners should evaluate management's plans to ensure the credit union has a guide to operating a financially sound institution that is meeting the realistic strategic and capital goals of the board of directors and will meet the needs of the membership.

Credit Risk

Credit risk is the risk of default on expected payments of loans or investments. LICUs and CDCUs may have a higher concentration of loans made to people with lower credit scores. This often increases the credit risk at the credit union. It is necessary for the credit union to manage the additional risk at a sound level for both the member and the credit union over the long term, while maintaining an acceptable level of strategic risk commensurate with the credit union's business plan. Strategies for managing this risk should be well documented in the policies, procedures, and strategic plan.

LICUs and CDCUs generally make credit available to their members by offering non-traditional lending products. These credit unions adapt their operations to fit the unique needs of their membership. Non-traditional products, procedures, and services that some credit unions use to better serve low income members include:

- Non-traditional loan underwriting, such as:
  - Explaining limited, negative, or no credit history;
  - Requiring payroll deduction for loan payments;
  - Documenting history of making timely rent and utility payments; and,
  - Using a qualified co-signor who sufficiently offsets credit risk;
- Loan restructuring; and,
- Financial literacy programs.

When offering non-traditional lending products, it is essential credit unions maintain strong collection programs to mitigate increased credit risk. A strong collection program should be in place before the credit union begins to make loans with a higher risk. A strong collection program should include:

- Firm and fair collection officer;
- Accurate, timely delinquency reports;
- Written collection policy that specifically outlines when the credit union will make contacts and by what means (e.g. telephone, postal mail, email, etc.);
- Quick reaction to first missed payment (contact should be made within one week);
- Quick reaction to missed promises to pay by delinquent members;

Supervisory Letter – Page 4

- Documenting, repeated contacts with delinquent members;
- Collateral liquidation procedures; and,
- Procedures for loan restructuring once a member begins making regularly scheduled payments.

Even though LICUs and CDCUs often offer higher risk loan products, maintaining credit risk within an acceptable level while meeting the needs of the members is still crucial to the operation of the credit union. Effective intervention by the credit union before the member falls further behind in his/her payment can serve to prevent the member from being placed in an increasingly worse financial position.

Financial Analysis

When reviewing the financial statements of a LICU, examiners must consider the effects the different types of funding available to LICUs may have on their balance sheets. Funding sources such as nonmember deposits, secondary capital, and loans from the CDRLF will affect the financial ratios of these usually small credit unions.[7] In addition to the effects of the additional funding, examiners must also consider the unique characteristics of members in LICUs and CDCUs.

Moreover, examiners should recognize that LICUs and CDCUs systematically show higher operating costs than other credit unions because of the nature of the field of membership they serve. Similarly, delinquency rates at LICUs and CDCUs, while often higher than other credit unions, do not automatically translate proportionally into charge-offs.

Examiners need to look beyond the financial ratios to analyze the credit union's financial condition accurately. The following table includes examples of items to consider when analyzing the financial condition of a LICU or CDCU.

---

[7] See appendix "Resources for Low-Income Designated Credit Unions" for additional information

Supervisory Letter – Page 5

288   COMMUNITY CAPITAL

Financial Ratio Trends	Items to Consider
↕ In Delinquent Loans / Total Loans	• Is the credit union's charge-off history increasing or remaining stable? • Analyze individual loan histories – does the borrower miss more than three payments in a year? • How often does the credit union communicate with delinquent borrowers? Is a strong collection policy being followed? • Could local economic reasons be a cause for the rise in delinquency? • Is the loan's principal balance reducing?
↕ In Return on Average Assets (ROAA)	• For LICUs, is there an increase in nonmember deposits, secondary capital, or loans from the CDRLF that increased average assets while earnings remained stable? • Is loan growth outpacing growth in income? • Is there an increase in expenses from new services offered?
↕ Operating Expenses / Gross Income	• Is there a program funded with grant money that causes the expenses to appear high, but is offset with income from the grant? • If expenses associated with a grant-funded program were backed out, would the ratio appear more reasonable? • Is the credit union eligible for grant funding that could offset the increase in operating expenses in the short-term? • Is the credit union's fee structure appropriate to offset the expenses of labor intensive services (e.g. share draft or check cashing)?

It is important that examiners view LICUs and CDCUs, rather than simply comparing them to other credit unions of similar asset size, which may benefit from such things as payroll deduction or higher-income members. Peer ratio data in AIRES and on the credit union's financial performance report (FPR) are not specific to LICUs. To understand the financial ratios of LICUs better, examiners can and should customize an FPR to include only LICUs of similar asset size on NCUA's internet site at [http://webapps.ncua.gov/ncuafpr/].

Some of the differences between LICUs and credit unions that are not low-income designated are illustrated in the following table. The table compares trends between two credit unions located in the same city with assets of approximately $40 million and explains obstacles the LICU must address.

Supervisory Letter – Page 6

	Low-Income Designated Credit Union Trend	Non Low-Income Designated Credit Union Trend	Items to Consider
	Grants 1,620 loans during quarter	Grants 327 loans during quarter	Even though the LICU granted four times as many loans as the non LICU, the average loan balance was greater on the 327 loans than the 1,620. This high volume of loans for the LICU is: • More labor intensive (i.e. time spent processing, time spent answering member questions); • More costly (i.e. requires more supplies to process); and, • More collection efforts due to number of members slow to pay (i.e. requires more collectors, delinquency notices, postage).
	Maintains 4,628 share draft accounts	Maintains 2,959 share draft accounts	Even though the LICU has more share draft accounts than the non LICU, the non LICU has approximately $2 million more in total share drafts. The low balance share draft accounts for the LICU are: • More labor intensive (i.e. volume of transactions translates to more staff needed and more financial education); and, • More costly (i.e. more supplies and equipment needed).

Examiners should recognize factors such as those discussed in this section when reviewing the financial condition of LICUs and CDCUs. The recognition of these factors will provide the examiner a better understanding of how and why the credit union operates as it does. This comprehensive understanding of the LICU and CDCU structure will allow examiners to appropriately assign CAMEL ratings based on risk to the National Credit Union Share Insurance Fund (NCUSIF) and not unduly lower the rating based solely on the LICU and CDCU business model.

Preserving LICUs and CDCUs

Examiners should work with LICUs and CDCUs to help them compete in their financial market. Within the constraints of regulations and safety and soundness, LICUs and CDCUs with the ability to succeed should be given the time and flexibility necessary to succeed. An examiner working with management and understanding the unique characteristics of these types of credit unions should afford them an opportunity to survive. In addition, the factors below should be considered in order to preserve LICUs and CDCUs.

Supervisory Letter – Page 7

Mentoring

Examiners should work with their supervisors to survey larger credit unions that may be interested in assisting LICUs and CDCUs. Many larger credit unions are often interested in assisting smaller credit unions with risk management or operational tasks. Larger credit unions can often provide office space, recordkeeping assistance, and collections assistance.

Supervising New Charters and Existing Charters

NCUA offers the assistance of Economic Development Specialists (EDSs), who are specialized examiners in NCUA's Office of Small Credit Union Initiatives, to newly chartered and existing credit unions. EDSs have expertise regarding small credit unions and can provide LICUs and CDCUs with needed guidance, such as "best practice" suggestions from other LICUs or CDCUs. These specialized examiners can also provide information and answer questions regarding the variety of potential funding sources available to LICUs and CDCUs.

In addition, NCUA offers the Small Credit Union Program (SCUP) to all credit unions with assets less than $10 million. This program is made up of SCUP examiners who are available to provide assistance to small credit unions on a regional level such as that provided by the EDS program on a national level.

Mergers

After considering all viable options, struggling LICUs and CDCUs sometimes merge into financially stronger credit unions. To ensure the merging credit union's members continue to receive services and efforts to serve people of modest means, NCUA and credit union officials should consider the possibility of merging with another LICU or CDCU. NCUA must merge any financially unsound credit union at the lowest cost to the National Credit Union Share Insurance Fund.[8] However, NCUA will take into consideration the best interests of the merging credit union's members when deliberating on potential merger partners.

Conclusions

There are some unique challenges to supervising and examining LICUs and CDCUs, but these credit unions face the same risks as other credit unions and must maintain safe and sound operations. As described in this supervisory letter, NCUA must provide appropriate oversight of higher risks that LICUs and CDCUs might pose to ensure all credit unions have the financial strength to continue serving people of modest means.

---

[8] See, 12 U.S.C. 1788.

Appendix
Resources for Low Income Credit Unions (LICUs)

Examiners should understand and make their LICUs aware of the available opportunities and resources. The information below outlines some opportunities and resources available for LICUs. For more detailed information, go to NCUA's Resource Connection located at http://www.ncua.gov/Resources/CreditUnionDevelopment/ResourceConnection/index.aspx.

Nonmember Deposits

LICUs may accept nonmember deposits from any source as stipulated in NCUA regulations.[9] Many different types of organizations, such as other financial institutions, will often consider making nonmember deposits in LICUs. With appropriate strategic, business, and budget planning and management, these funds can provide a fiscally sound source of funding for these credit unions.

Nonmember deposits may have interest rates at or below market rates allowing the opportunity for providing services on well thought out and financially sound programs. Some examples of programs credit unions have started with funds from nonmember deposits include: funding new loan programs, covering costs associated with establishing new member services, and adding employees to provide financial counseling for members. When considering whether to seek or accept nonmember deposits, credit unions should take into account the full ramifications the deposits will have on the financial safety and soundness of the credit union. Nonmember deposits may be a relatively expensive source of funds that can negatively affect earnings. Management should consider such questions as:

- How will the credit union use the funds made available with the nonmember deposit?
- What is the financial impact of the nonmember deposit to the credit union's net worth?
- Are there other or future benefits the credit union will receive because of the relationship with the organization providing the nonmember deposit?
- Does the credit union have a liquidity plan to repay the funds?
- Can a net positive return be achieved on the fund? Is the income generated on the additional funds greater than the dividend cost paid to have the funds on deposit?

In computing the cost-benefit of nonmember deposits, examiners should be cognizant of several factors:

- Servicing a single large deposit may be considerably less costly than serving a large number of deposits with very small share balances.

---

[9] 12 C.F.R. § 701.32

- Nonmember deposits are often a "relationship" business. Returning nonmember deposits before maturity may jeopardize the relationship of the credit union to a foundation, government, social investor, or other philanthropic source; and,
- Nonmember deposits may lower net worth in the short-term, but additional income earned from the deposits could strengthen long-term net worth.

NCUA regulations limit the amount of public unit and nonmember deposits to the greater of 20 percent of the credit union's total shares or $1.5 million.[10] Deposits in excess of this limitation are subject to regional director approval.[11] However, this limitation does not apply to accounts maintained in Treasury Tax and Loan Depositaries or Depositaries and Financial Agents of the Government,[12] matching funds required by NCUA's Community Development Revolving Loan Program for credit unions with outstanding loans,[13] and credit unions qualifying for RegFlex.[14]

Secondary Capital

LICUs should take into account the same financial considerations for secondary capital as discussed with nonmember deposits. LICUs may accept secondary capital in accordance with the requirements in NCUA regulations, 12 C.F.R. § 701.34(b). Before accepting secondary capital, however, the credit union must develop, adopt, and submit a secondary capital plan to the appropriate regional director. The secondary capital plan ensures the credit union has considered the impact the funds will have on its financial performance. The credit union plan should show specific uses for the funds along with including appropriate plans to replace or continue without the funds as the funds mature.[15]

Secondary capital typically serves to increase net worth and allow the credit union to increase lending. Secondary capital accounts have the longest term at most credit unions, and should have a beneficial ALM effect. For example, one possible use of secondary capital could be to implement a new lending program. The credit union should match the loan maturities to the term of the secondary capital account or have another source of funds planned to replace the funds as they mature.

NCUA regulations stipulate specific accounting treatment for secondary capital accounts, and credit unions need to consider the impact to their net worth as they are depreciating or "writing down" the capital account and adjusting financial operations as needed.

Community Development Revolving Loan Program

Since 1986, NCUA has administered the Community Development Revolving Loan Fund (CDRLF), funded by Congress. NCUA's Community Development Revolving Loan Program is described in part 705 of NCUA regulations.[16] The purpose of this program is to:

---

[10] 12 C.F.R. §701.32(b), 741.204
[11] 12 C.F.R. § 701.32(b)(2).
[12] 12 C.F.R. § 701.37.
[13] 12 C.F.R. § 705.7(b).
[14] 12 C.F.R. §742.4(a)(2).
[15] 12 C.F.R. §701.34(b)(1).
[16] 12 C.F.R. Part 705.

- Provide basic financial and related services to residents in low-income communities; and,
- Stimulate economic activities in low-income communities, which will result in increased income, ownership, and employment opportunities for low-income residents, and other community growth efforts.

Only LICUs are eligible to participate in the Community Development Revolving Loan Program. These credit unions can receive up to $300,000 in aggregate loans from the CDRLF. Within one year of receiving the loan, the recipient must match the loan amount with share deposits. Examiners are encouraged to discuss the availability of these funds with their LICUs. Credit unions can also access applications and monthly reports regarding the funds available through this program at http://www.ncua.gov/Resources/CreditUnionDevelopment/Finance.aspx

Technical Assistance

In years past, Congress has earmarked $1 million to be used specifically for technical assistance grants as part of NCUA's Community Development Revolving Loan Program. These cash grants are intended to help LICU officials, management, and staff acquire specialized skills, equipment, or other forms of assistance to improve member services and enhance their credit union's financial strength. In addition to congressional appropriations, interest earned on the CDRLF loans is used to fund technical assistance grants. The average technical assistance grant is under $5,000. Applications for technical assistance grants are located at http://www.ncua.gov/Resources/CreditUnionDevelopment/Finance.aspx

Community Development Financial Institutions Fund

The Riegle Community Development and Regulatory Improvement Act of 1994 established the Community Development Financial Institutions (CDFI) Fund, which is operated by the United States Department of Treasury. The fund expanded the capacity of financial institutions to provide credit, capital, and financial services to underserved populations and communities in the United States. Many LICUs and other credit unions with a demonstrated concentration of members located in investment areas (i.e. underserved areas) as defined by the CDFI can become CDFI certified through the CDFI Fund and be eligible to apply for larger dollar grants and capital funds. Details about certification and funding programs are available at http://www.cdfifund.gov

Appendix B

KAPFCU RESPONSE TO LUA AND REQUEST FOR HEARING

APPENDIX B   293

Board of Directors
Victor F. Russell
Chairman/President

William Whitehead
Chief Financial Officer

Karey Burnett
Secretary

Kenny Henderson
Supervisory Committee

Steven Ellis
Media & Public Relations

Tim Witte
Technology

Joe Williams
Credit Committee

CU Counsel & Legal Affairs
Micheal McCray, Esq.
Administrator

Associate Board Members
Dwight H. Hamilton
Joseph C. Newton
Michael Jasper

Co: Dwight Thomas
Derrick Harris
Larry Gilmore
Kevin Wilson
Darryl Carter
Stephone Coward

Kappa Alpha Psi Federal Credit Union
New Accounts Administrator

"Financial benefits for Kappa's, their families, and associations"

[KAPFCU Logo]
P.O. Box 703047,
Dallas, TX 75370
(972) 394-3324 Direct Line
Email: VRusse@kapfcu.org

April 12, 2010

Debbie Matz, Chair
National Credit Union Administration
1775 Duke Street
Alexandria, VA 22314-3428

RE: RESPONSE TO LUA AUDIT LETTER AND FORMAL REQUEST FOR HEARING

Chair Matz,

Please find this correspondence as our response to two letters from Regional Director Keith Morton dated February 2, 2010 and April 9, 2010 about the current status and planned implementation of our LUA, and a request for assistance regarding CDCI funding. We also write this because we are concerned that our examination reports cast us in a false light and may impair our ability to receive NCUA funding or participate in the Treasury's CDCI program.

KAPFCU was the first credit union that NCUA authorized to operate on a virtual basis and we are the only certified Community Development Financial Institution (CDFI), Community Development Credit Union (CDCU) and a Low Income Credit Union (LICU), that operates through a national service delivery area. Accordingly, thank you for the Supervisory Letter you issued on January 15, 2010 acknowledging our strong public policy supporting for LICUs. Historically, our examiners have treated KAPFCU as an "ugly duckling" when we should have been embraced and celebrated our innovative business model.

Unfortunately our examiner (CAROLYN PENALUNA) never appreciated our community development business model or our low-income oriented mission.

In the April 9, 2010 letter, Regional Director Keith Morton identifies three areas of concern based on our most recent LUA contact:

1. **Net Worth** – Regional Director Keith Morton expresses concern that after examination adjustments that KAPFCU will be near insolvent with an anemic Net Worth of 0.59%. Unfortunately, our Net Worth is currently understated due to unnecessary "full accruals" forced on KAPFCU by our examiner. When KAPFCU is reviewed on a "Modified Cash" basis, which we are allowed to utilize, pursuant to 12 U.S.C. § 1782(6)(C)(iii), our Net Worth increases to 3%. Additionally, we have submitted a Revised Net Worth Restoration Plan on March 31, 2010 in which we project to achieve a Net Worth Ratio of 7% by December 31, 2016. However, with NCUA approval, we plan to apply for the Treasury Department's CDCI Secondary Capital Program that will provide KAPFCU with an additional $26,000 or 3.5% boast to our NWR. Moreover, we have identified an additional $100,000 secondary capital match for the requested CDCI funds. If we are approved to pursue these funding opportunities our NWR will exceed 17% by year end.

2. **Lending Practices** – Regional Director Keith Morton expresses concern that KAPFCU has potential problems due to poor quality loans. We admit we have some issues with slow pays – but this is not unusual or unexpected for Low Income Credit Unions. Despite lending to credit challenged borrowers, KAPFCU has experienced only one loan default in our five year lending history (which we believe was actually a fraudulent loan and we are seeking prosecution). More importantly, our "credit challenged" borrowers have routinely made advance payments and voluntary capital contributions in excess of their required loan payouts – in one case as much as $7,000 in additional contribution (which our examiner refused to give us full credit for). KAPFCU has been impacted more by improper examiner adjustments rather than poor credit quality or bad lending policies. We have experienced less than $5,000 in losses due to our lending practices; in contrast, we have experienced nearly $35,000 in losses due to improper examination adjustments and unnecessary forced accruals.

3. **Record Keeping** – Regional Director Keith Morton expresses concern over what our examiner considers "poor" record keeping. The record keeping deficiencies reflected in the examination contacts are the direct result of inadequate full-time staff that are necessary to implement GAAP full accrual accounting. However, due to our size, KAPFCU is not required to utilize full accrual accounting – and was not. Unfortunately our examiner did not take this exception into consideration when she evaluated our management/record keeping and found it lacking. However, our management/record keeping is more than adequate for our size and community development business model. **We were improperly evaluated and examined in comparison to large credit unions with full-time staff and not our low-income peer group.**

We believe that these ratings are unwarranted and inaccurate because our examiner (1) failed to consider or apply the NCUA regulations applicable to small credit unions, (2) never considered or complied with the policy mandates outlined in the January 15, 2010 Supervisory Letter, and (3) ignored the strong public policy considerations regarding community development and low-income credit unions. **The problem is KAPFCU has never been examined or compared with our LICU peer group of credit unions with $1 Million in assets or less.**

Ultimately, our examiner has consistently acted in the interest that best protects the NCUIF deposit; not the best interest of KAPFCU. She consistently presents the worst case scenario – not the best case scenario, or even the most likely case scenario - e.g., a third-party audit of a member loan account proved that our examiner failed/refused to recognize $1,300 of a $7,000 gift of contributed capital to KAPFCU. Another third-party audit of our accrued interest/dividend account proved that our examiner over accrued our expenses by $3,800 dollars. The effect of this was to understate our income by $5,000 – for an institution our size, and considering the volatile environment, i.e., corporate stabilization, this could be the difference between profitability and insolvency.

Perhaps, the biggest issue is the fact that our examiner forced us to use "full accrual" accounting when we are allowed to use Modified Cash. When we started, we timed our transaction and recorded our books using a method short of full accrual accounting, but we are allowed to do so for institutions our size. That all changed after Carolyn Penaluna started examining us. When she would literally go into the system and change our call report figures. SHE – not our board – put KAPFCU on full accrual accounting. That decision caused the precipitous decline in our NWR. It seems clear that other credit unions probably had similar problems with their examiners, which is probably why he NCUA changed the rules so that the examiners can't change our call reports directly anymore.

As you know, NCUA regulations require large credit unions to use GAAP. However, the NCUA regulations allow small credit unions (under $10 million in assets) to operate on a Modified Cash Basis. After we filed our financial statements, and over our objections, our examiner simply went into the system and changed our call reports to reflect full accruals. This went on for three years, and we thank the NCUA for making recent policy changes that prevent NCUA examiners from changing credit union call reports. We estimate that this one change will improve our NWR by nearly 3%. However, our examiner's insistence on requiring "full accrual" also impacts the CAMEL management ratings. We designed our business model to operate around the human resources we have available. We operate with an active volunteer board of directors – but we don't have a full-time employee.

This works for KAPFCU because there is actually less record keeping required to operate on a Modified Cash Basis – which we were. Unfortunately, our examiner raised the record keeping bar by placing us on "full accrual" and then wrote our management up for failing to maintain the record keeping necessary to implement a "full accrual" system. We don't think that this is fair. We believe that our CAMEL management rating would be drastically improved if we had actually been compared to our peer group of low-income credit unions under $1 Million in assets – rather than large credit unions with the human resources and capital base to apply full GAAP accounting (i.e., Credit Unions over $10 million).

APPENDIX B   295

If we had been properly examined (under modified cash basis) and compared to our actual low-income peer groups; KAPFCU would have a significantly higher NWR and probably would not be subject to the existing LUA. Consequently, we object to criticism regarding our LUA because KAPFCU was forced to agree to operate under a LUA that conflicts with our low-income mission and the January 15, 2010 Supervisory Letter from Debbie Matz.

In the previous February 2, 2010 letter, Regional Director Keith Morton stated that our prior response failed to completely, adequately and/or satisfactorily addresses the following three questions:

1. Why We Have Not Complied With The LUA – We respectfully disagree with this assertion. Although we have not completely complied, we have been diligently working through the process of complying with the LUA. This process has taken longer than we originally anticipated, due to the complexity in establishing, and transitioning to a third-party back office; and the fact that we have simultaneously been operating a national platform – with an all volunteer board and no full-time staff.

<u>LUA COMPLIANCE TIMELINE</u>

- May, 2009 – Executive Board Planning Meeting (Washington, DC)
- May, 2009 – Five State Regional Conference (Jackson, MS)
- **June, 2009 – Executed Letter of Understanding and Agreement**
- June, 2009 – Engaged Texas Credit Union League for Bank Reconciliations
- August, 2009 – Bi-annual International Conclave (Washington, DC)
- September, 2009 – CRW Leadership Conference (Hattiesburg, MS)
- November, 2009 – **Submit Revised Net Worth Restoration Plan**
- November, 2009 – Submit Comprehensive CDFI / TA Application
- November, 2009 – NCUA Annual Review for 2008
- November, 2009 – NCUA Quarterly Review for 2009
- December, 2009 – Established Texas Credit Union League Connectivity and Total/1 System Access
- December, 2009 – Initiated Texas Credit Union League G/L Journal Entry Process Training
- December, 2009 – Initiated Texas Credit Union League Weekly Batch Reports and Deposit Reconciliations
- December, 2009 – Hosted 5th Annual Shareholder's Meeting
- December, 2009 – Held 1st Election of New Board Members
- December, 2009 – Begin Texas Credit Union League Opening New Member Accounts; 130 New Member Applications
- December, 2009 – Texas Credit Union League Conducts Annual Audit
- January, 2010 – Texas Credit Union League Conducts ACH Audit
- January, 2010 – Formally Engage Texas Credit Union League Back Office
- **February, 2010 – Letter of Understanding and Agreement Review**

For the record, KAPFCU provides development and financial services on a national foot-print, through our relationship with Kappa Alpha Psi Fraternity Inc. Consequently, we participate with the executive planning and leadership of the fraternity; and therefore must plan and attend national, international and regional meetings and conferences. Consequently, our expenses are higher than other association credit unions because we are a LICU – and they are not. Additionally, our expenses are moderately higher than other LICUs because they are local/state based; while KAPFCU services a national delivery area.

2. How We Intend to Comply With The LUA in The Future -- Over the last eight months, as demonstrated, we have made and continue to make significant progress towards fully implementing the LUA as agreed; especially, when you take into consideration the other major business planning and ongoing activities we have also had to execute during the corresponding time period.

Consequently, we continued to implement our back office transition to the Texas Credit Union League and anticipate that this third-party relationship became fully functional and complete as of March 31, 2010. Once in place, the back office greatly enhanced our record keeping capabilities; and hopefully eliminates most, if not all, of the persistent reconciliation difficulties we have been experiencing. This third party arrangement has laid the foundation to improve our overall day-to-day operations.

3. Why The NCUA Board Should Not Publish The LUA -- As we understand Letters of Understanding and Agreement (LUAs) are supervisory tools used by the NCUA. An LUA is essentially a contract between NCUA and a credit union and/or its officials, in which the credit union or officials agree to take, or not take, certain specified actions. Normally, LUAs are negotiated when credit unions have not adequately responded to less severe measures, such as Documents of Resolution (DOR). NCUA also requires LUAs for newly chartered credit unions and to grant permanent special assistance.

The Federal Credit Union Act requires that the NCUA Board publish and make available to the public "any written agreement or other written statement for which a violation may be enforced by the Board unless the Board, in its discretion, determines that publication would be contrary to public interest." Violations of the terms of a published LUA constitute grounds for administrative actions. The NCUA Board may therefore take administrative actions against credit unions or officials that fail to comply with the terms of published LUAs.

On January 15, 2010 the National Credit Union Administration (NCUA) issued *Letter to Credit Unions 10-CU-01 -- Supervising Low Income Credit Unions and Community Development Credit Unions*. The Letter, which was provided to NCUA examination staff and shared with the boards of directors of all federally insured credit unions, provides guidance on the characteristics, benefits, and unique challenges of low-income credit unions and community development credit unions.

"NCUA is very aware of the distinct qualities inherent in credit unions that primarily serve consumers in low and moderate-income areas. The challenges these credit unions face are real but by no means insurmountable, and I am confident that this new guidance will enhance both the quality of NCUA supervision, and the credit union's ability to serve those consumers who need affordable financial services the most," commented NCUA Chairman Debbie Matz. "This is a reasoned, flexible and sensible regulatory approach, and it can have a real and positive impact in distressed communities."

An appendix listing resources available to credit unions with low-income designations (LICU), and those credit unions that are self-designated community development credit unions, (CDCU) was included with the Supervisory Letter. It also highlights additional sources of funding available, including Community Development Revolving Loan Fund access, Treasury Department-Administered Community Development Financial Institution grants, as well as non-member deposit and secondary capital funds. Thus, the NCUA offers Technical Assistance Grants (TAG) and other benefits to designated Low-Income Credit Unions because they provide desperately needed development and financial services to traditional underserved and hard-to-serve populations. There is a strong public policy need for these services. KAPFCU is a prime example of the challenges that LICUs and/or CDCUs face with NCUA examiners that do not fully appreciate low-income business models or community development oriented business plans.

APPENDIX B

KAPFCU engaged its second examiner during 2007. We were initially hopefully, because this new examiner is one of, if not the, top examiners in Region IV. We thought her expertise would be a great learning opportunity for KAPFCU. Unfortunately, despite her extensive experience with large credit unions – our examiner did not have a history with, or appreciation for low-income credit unions (LICU), community development credit unions (CDCU) or community development financial institutions (CDFI). Consequently, our examinations for 2007, 2008 and 2009 and the resultant LUA do not incorporate these important considerations or the January 15, 2010 supervisory letter.

Our examiner never demonstrated or provided any tangible proof that she ever considered KAPFCU's status as a LICU and CDCU, nor evaluated KAPFCU in relationship with other LICU peers – as opposed to large or mature credit unions– as required by the Supervisory Letter. Therefore, it would seem unwise and even unfair for the NCUA to publish a LUA for KAPFCU which is a LICU, CDCU and CDFI institution, within weeks following a January NCUA Supervisory Letter concerning LICU/CDCU without first ensuring that our examiner actually adhered to the policy mandates contained in the supervisory letter before actually publishing the contemplated LUA.

Over the last few years, KAPFCU has engaged in a constant and consistent debate with our examiner about our "business model" and the significance, meaning and impact of our LICU and CDFI certifications, as well as the fact that we operate a national platform on a virtual basis. Ironically, the January 15, 2010 supervisory letter encapsulates our previous arguments and concerns. Unfortunately, our examiner simply refused to take into account our pleas about these issues or the NCUA policy. For example:

(1) Our examiner forced us to report on a full accrual basis in violation of applicable federal law. As a credit union with less than $10,000,000 in total assets KAPFCU is allowed to report on a "cash basis" or "modified cash" basis. See 12 U.S.C. § 1782(6)(C)(iii) – which states that small credit unions are exempted from the mandatory GAAP treatment that our examiner imposed on KAPFCU under the "de minimus exception" to the standard accounting principals.

However, our examiner refused to honor these regulations and has forced us to use "full accrual" accounting and actually changed our call reports. Worse, she repeatedly forces us to create "special reserve accounts" which are unnecessary, unwarranted and understate our Net Worth by nearly **$30,000**. Due mainly to these forced accruals, our Net Worth Ratio dropped to 0.5% or **Minimally Capitalized**. However, without these "special reserves" our Net Worth Ratio should be 3.5% – that is **Moderately Capitalized**. This material difference is based solely on our examiner's individual discretion, and is in contradiction to KAPFCU directives and federal law applicable to credit unions of our size and composition.

(2) Our examiner repeatedly wrote us up for failure to supply complete bank statements. However, the missing pages are the blank "sample reconciliation" worksheets that banks include with bank statements. Our examiner never asked us to include these worksheets before – but includes their absence in the list of LUA required records.

(3) As a part of the LUA audit, our examiner repeatedly criticizes us for failure or delays in establishing a "lock box" system. However, there is no requirement for a "lock box" actually contained in the signed LUA. Writing us up for so-called deficiencies outside the LUA – as a measure of our LUA compliance– is another example of our examiner attempting to micro-manage the operations of the credit union, rather than simply examine them.

(4) Our examiner also refuses to accept legitimate miscellaneous income. Due to the internationally respected brand and valuable goodwill of "Kappa Alpha Psi" – we sell "Kappa Alpha Psi, FCU" logo dress shirts, polo shirts, pens and pencils as gifts and small dollar fundraisers. Seeking these types of grants and small donor donations are common revenue sources for low-income and community development based organizations. However, our examiner refuses to accept these receipts as operating revenue and forces us to record it as non-operating income.

(5) Our examiner has written us up for failing to produce a "phantom check." The examiner demands that we produce check number "14400" as a reconciling issue. We are a small institution with a very limited number of transactions. Consequently, we do not have, and have not written any checks with five (5) digit numbers. We produced check number "1440" but our examiner is still not satisfied. This is clearly some sort of error, but our examiner wrote this up – just the same.

(6) As a part of the LUA audit, our examiner noted that KAPFCU failed to get an "opinion audit." 12 U.S.C. § 1782(6)(D) only requires credit unions with assets exceeding $500,000,000 to have "opinion audits." We resisted this request and argued back and forth with our examiner that is was unnecessary and too expensive. We received a $25,000 price quote from the CPA firm she recommended. More importantly, there is no requirement for an "opinion audit" actually contained in the LUA. Writing us up for so-called deficiencies outside the LUA – as a measure of LUA compliance– is unfair and another example of our examiner attempting to micro-manage the operations of the credit union.

(7) Finally, as the only Black Financial Institution in the Dallas Metropolitan area, our Board is planning to participate in a high-dollar fundraiser and charitable gala to raise money for the credit union, local Historically Black Colleges and Universities, and the Congressional Black Caucus. When our examiner found out about this event, she became obstinate and immediately attempted to micro-manage this process as well.

We can only guess that her resistance is due to her limited experience working with and examining minority, LICU or CDCUs. Nearly everything she has forced KAPFCU to do is more consistent with the requirements for large credit unions. Unfortunately, they are totally inconsistent with the requirements for small, LICU and CDCU institutions. As a result, we feel our prior examinations and the resultant LUA have been out of compliance with NCUA rules, regulations and the recent supervisory letter. More importantly, we feel this type of excessive scrutiny places KAPFCU in a "false light" because it appears that our outstanding LUA deficiencies are larger and more extensive than they truly are.

Additionally, this pattern of "overzealousness" is clear evidence of bias or extreme indifference to our institution and our mission as a LICU and CDCU. Whether that bias is against low-income credit unions, (LICU) community development credit unions (CDCU), or African-American credit unions (AACUC) is debatable. The point is, there is more than a "reasonable basis" to believe that our examiner has engaged in a pattern of bias against KAPFCU and our low-income business model.

Moreover, our examiner has never included any indication that she was aware that KAPFCU is a LICU, CDCU and CDFI; or that any consideration has ever been given to our low-income and community development mission and business model. Unfortunately, a NCUA examiner, in her sole discretion, has the individual power to undermine the will of Congress.

We speak specifically about the ability of an individual examiner to cut off access to NCUA and other federal funding based upon subjective components in the CAMEL rating system. Simply stated, congress provides grant funding for LICU and CDCU – but an individual examiner has the ability to "veto" this funding by issuing misleading exam reports or a poor CAMEL rating. For example, KAPFCU's financial condition would have been vastly improved if it received a $15,000 NCUA/TAG we applied for. We were told that we had a highly competitive grant application, but could not be approved because we possessed an unacceptable CAMEL 4 rating – rather than CAMEL 3. We have subsequently learned, that almost no funders will award significant grants to credit unions with a CAMEL 4 rating.

This would not be so disturbing and problematic, if the CAMEL ratings were objectively determined. Unfortunately, there are subjective components contained in the CAMEL determination. Thus, an individual examiner has the subjective power to cut off federal funding to LICU and CDFI in contradiction to Congressional intent and clear public policy.

In closing, we concede that the NCUA Board has the discretion to publish a LUA. However, we contend that the NCUA Board should not exercise that discretion in a discriminatory, arbitrary or capricious manner, or in a manner that could

APPENDIX B 299

reasonably appear to be discriminatory, arbitrary or capricious. As a matter of public policy, we do not believe that the LUA should be published until and unless our examiner can demonstrate and prove that she complied with the requirements of January 15, 2010 Supervisory Letter and all other applicable rules and regulations applicable to credit unions of our size and composition.

We are preparing to apply for the Treasury Department's CDCI Secondary Capital Program, but we were notified that we may not receive funding due to our overall CAMEL 4 ratings and/or misleading information included in our examination reports – particularly our CAMEL 5 management rating. Consequently, we believe the NCUA Board should be very careful that KAPFCU receives all appropriate due process before any such a drastic and potentially deleterious action is taken. Therefore, we argue that it is against public policy to publish this LUA under the present circumstances and we respectfully ask for an opportunity to formally address the entire NCUA Board before any such publication occurs.

Respectfully,

Victor Russell, Chairman/President

Enclosure: NCUA Supervisory Letter – January 15, 2010.
Keith Morton LUA Letter – February 2, 2009
Keith Morton LUA Letter – April 9, 2009

cc: C. Keith Morton, Region IV Director
Cory Phariss, Supervisory Examiner

Appendix C

DAN MOULTON, CPA. EMAIL CPA OPINION (CASH BASIS)

From: "Dan Moulton" <dmoulton@ocmcpa.com>
Date: February 15, 2010 10:25:15 PM CST
To: "Victor F Russell" <vicrussell@mmi-realtyadvisors.com>
Cc: "Stephone Coward" <scoward@kapfcu.org>, "Karey Barnett" <mccray.michael@gmail.com>, "Michael McCray" <kbarnett@kapfcu.org>, "Tim White" <twhite1dr1@yahoo.com>, "Steve Ellis-KAPFCU" <steveell@us.ibm.com>, "Bill H. Whitehead-Kappa" <bill.whitehead@fedexkinkos.com>, "Michael Jasper" <jasperm@aol.com>, "Kenneth E. Henderson-KAPFCU" <ken.henderson@att.net>, "Joe Williams-KAPFCU" <Joe.Williams21@att.net>
Subject: RE: Recap Saturday and Thank You !!!

Hi Vic

I couldn't grab the full document in PDF, but this link will get you to the NCUA Accounting Manual in parts. Within this manual, you will find the definitions I have reproduced below.

http://www.ncua.gov/GenInfo/GuidesManuals/accounting_manuals/Manual/TableOfContents.aspx

Hope this helps some! -Dan

MODIFIED CASH BASIS

Generally under a cash basis of accounting, income is recorded and accounted for when actually collected and expenses are accounted for when actually paid. Under the modified cash basis prescribed herein, the accounting is based on the actual receipts and disbursements of the credit union except that provisions should be made to reflect:

- Liabilities which are not promptly paid when due,
- Dividends and interest refunds applicable to the accounting period but not yet paid,
- Deferred income or expenses applicable to future periods,
- Estimated losses to be sustained on loans outstanding,
- Estimated unrealized losses associated with mutual fund investments, and
- Depreciation on fixed assets.

The foregoing exceptions to maintenance of accounting records on a strictly cash basis are designed to recognize in the accounts certain significant financial transactions not involving the concurrent receipt or disbursement of cash and to reflect their effect in financial reports prepared from the accounts. In unusual circumstances, there may be other significant non-cash financial transactions that should be recorded. Therefore, the above list is not all-inclusive.

Credit unions for which adoption of the accrual basis of accounting is not required or practicable should use the modified cash basis of accounting.

ACCRUAL BASIS

The accrual basis of accounting refers to that method under which liabilities and expenses are recorded when incurred, whether or not paid, and income is recorded when earned, whether or not received. It is intended that credit union accounting be maintained on the accrual basis by all credit unions for which they deem such basis practicable.

Generally accepted accounting principles require the accrual basis of accounting.

Daniel C. Moulton, CPA, Partner
Orth, Chakler, Murnane & Company, CPAs
(214) 878-6758 - cell phone

From: dmoulton@ocmcpa.com - email
Sent: Victor F Russell [mailto:vicrussell@mmr-realtyadvisors.com]
Monday, February 15, 2010 12:59 PM
To: Dan Moulton
Cc: Stephone Coward; Michael McCray; Karey Barnett; Tim White; Steve Ellis-KAPFCU; Bill H. Whitehead-Kappa; Michael Jasper; Kenneth E. Henderson-KAPFCU; Joe Williams-KAPFCU
Subject: Recap Saturday and Thank You !!!

Hey Dan,

Dan, thank you for taking a few hours out of your schedule and meeting with us on short notice to assist in shedding some light on our concerns with how to adjust and provide a little more "dry powder" to compete in this CU space with the Examiners.

Once you shoot the manual for operating CU's under $10M, we'll dig right in and see if it has any application to this platform. Seek you opinion or thoughts accordingly.

The recommendation to expand our current Audit from the League to cover 12/31/2009, essentially annualize 2008 and 2009 is a good to eliminate the deficit reflected 10/31/2009 report. Once Cheryl get back to us on Chad's approval then we'll proceed.

Additionally, of the $12.8k 2008, 4th Quarter adjustment, how much resulted in 2007, if any....... Cheryl and I have all of the Loan Histories pulled through June 30, 2009. I would presume its a small number of the total $12.8k. On a percentage bases, if it looks like 20% plus of the $12.8k falls into 2007, then we'll get the League to adjust back into 2007 too.

Lastly, Saturday we returned to the office and reviewed the "NSF" check file for the "Savage" loan to confirm in detail that the $3.4k was in fact a check that "never" cleared on the second re-deposit. To this point it should not have been credit per the "Loan History" analysis and the pay should have reflective of $43k and some change. This alone takes the $3k theory to zero. I attached the "Loan History" analysis which is just an FYI to look at one more time.

Thx,

Vic

Appendix D

BALACK & WILLIAMS, LEGAL OPINION
(TOTAL/1 PRODUCT DEFECT)

BLALACK & WILLIAMS

A PROFESSIONAL CORPORATION
ATTORNEYS AND COUNSELORS
5599 LBJ FREEWAY, SUITE 600
DALLAS, TEXAS 75240
214-850-1914
214/934-1112 (FAX)

MIKE BLALACK
CHARLES L. WILLIAMS
SHANNON R. ENGSTROM
RANDY ROBERTS*
MARC F. KAZEMBA

THOMAS H. DUKE
TOM W. SHARP
ROBERT A. WOODCOCK
CHRIS BLALACK
JARED TARBE

*BOARD CERTIFIED CIVIL TRIAL LAW
TEXAS BOARD OF LEGAL SPECIALIZATION

May 12, 2010

SENT BY E-MAIL TO vfrussell@mmr-realtyadvisors.com
AND BY FIRST CLASS MAIL

Mr. Victor F. Russell
President
Kappa Alpha Psi Federal Credit Union
P.O. Box 703047
Dallas, TX 75370

Re: TOTAL/1 Services Corporation
    Data Processing Service Agreement

Dear Mr. Russell:

Kappa Alpha Psi entered into a Data Processing Service Agreement with TOTAL/1 Services Corporation on May 21, 2005. The contract is for the credit union's core data processing services, and it remains in effect today.

Recently, you have advised us of an error in the TOTAL/1 data processing system. You have related that the system is incapable of correctly applying principal and interest to the loan balance when a borrower makes payments in advance. In particular, if a borrower pays ahead on a loan, we understand that the system allocates all of the advance payment to interest and no amounts to principal. The credit union discovered this error in December 2008. Although TOTAL/1 has since offered a workaround, the error initially caused the credit union a loss of approximately $13,000. You have asked us to review the TOTAL/1 Data Processing Service Agreement and provide an opinion of whether TOTAL/1 has breached its contract with Kappa Alpha Psi Federal Credit Union.

We have not had an opportunity to examine the TOTAL/1 data processing system directly, so we have assumed for purposes of this opinion that there is in fact a programming error. Section 1.a. of the Agreement provides for the following performance standards:

> "Services will be provided in a professional manner as considered standard in the data processing industry and commensurate with the type of services being provided."

Section 1.b. further provides that:

> "Services provided will comply with all terms and conditions as stated in this agreement and its attached Schedules."

Section 6 provides for online access to the TOTAL/1 Credit Union Computer Systems via VPN

00177653.WPD

Mr. Victor F. Russell
May 12, 2010
Page 2

Schedule "A" to the agreement provides for several core data processing services, including a full member central information system, integrated general ledger, and monthly statistical and delinquency reports.

It is a fundamental premise that any acceptable financial institution data processing system will comply with generally accepted accounting principles and apply any type of loan payment correctly. Accordingly, the failure of the TOTAL/1 system to perform in this regard, which caused the credit union a loss, is a breach of the performance standards set forth in the agreement for which the credit union may pursue its contract remedies.

Very truly yours,

BLALACK & WILLIAMS, P.C.

Mark E. Kazemba

From: Victor F. Russell <vicrussell@mmr-realtyadvisors.com>
Subject: Calling Me
Date: March 15, 2006 9:00:25 AM CST
To: Marc R Lafitte <rlafitte@total1services.com>, Dan Winburn <dwinburn@total1services.com>, Nel Lafitte <nlafitte@total1services.com>, Harry Buzek <hbuzek@total1services.com>
Cc: Steve Ellis <steveell@us.ibm.com>, "Julius L. Thompson, Esq." <julius@jlitlawfirm.com>, Don W. Davis <ddavis01@elp.rr.com>, "TA Brooks, Jr" <tbrooks@onebox.com>, Bill H. Whitehead <bill.whitehead@fedexkinkos.com>, Larry L. Williams <LWilliam@w-w-i-s.com>, Tony Rausch <RASCH@NCUAGOV>, Lance Van Tuyle <lylevn@ncuagov>, Kenneth E. Henderson <ken.henderson@tigta.treas.gov>, Efrain Duran <efrain@gemchecking.com>, Mike McMath <MMcMath@w-w-i-s.com>, Anna Robinson <ARobinso@w-w-i-s.com>

Marc,

Is there something that I haven't done" to piss you off ??? In retrospect, it can't be something that I have said, because, I haven't spoken to you since February 8,2006. There are some small things that I need to get to you to discuss. Technical issue that, my understanding can only be handled by you !!!!! I have been text messaging you, calling the office, calling your cell----------no response---------- short of getting on an airplane to come to Houston to your the office, to raise hell about not returning my, MY phone calls !!!!!! I have Tony Rausch, Lance and the NCUA in my ass about small, insufficient shit. Call me man !!!!! Godamit .... what is it with you !!!!!!!!

Larry, cancel the damn WWI service today !!!!!! I am not getting a call from the people that hook me into your system and this is bullshit ?????????

Marc, I thought we were cooler than this. We bought into your idea and can't find you as the CEO / President / Chairman or the point person for Total /1. If I have to take out full page ads in the CU Magazine and attend conferences to discount your company, I will do that. If I have to start litigating this issue, than lets get it on !!!!!!! I will tie you up in order "till hell" freezes over. This is bullshit, Marc !!!!!!! I am pissed !!!!!!!!!!!!!!!!!!!!!!!!!!!!!!!!!!!!

Vic

Victor F. Russell-Managing Principal
MMR Realty Advisors
3701 Maywood Ct, Ste 101
Carrollton, Texas 75007
(972) 394-3324-Direct
(972) 492-6753-fax
URL: www.MMR-Realty-advisors.com
Email: VicRussell@MMR-Realty-advisors.com

TEXAS BUSINESS & COMMERCE CODE - CHAPTER 2. SALES

§ 2.725. STATUTE OF LIMITATIONS IN CONTRACTS FOR SALE.

(a) An action for breach of any contract for sale must be commenced within four years after the cause of action has accrued. By the original agreement the parties may reduce the period of limitation to not less than one year but may not extend it.

(b) A cause of action accrues when the breach occurs, regardless of the aggrieved party's lack of knowledge of the breach. A breach of warranty occurs when tender of delivery is made, except that where a warranty explicitly extends to future performance of the goods and discovery of the breach must await the time of such performance the cause of action accrues when the breach is or should have been discovered.

(c) Where an action commenced within the time limited by Subsection (a) is so terminated as to leave available a remedy by another action for the same breach such other action may be commenced after the expiration of the time limited and within six months after the termination of the first action unless the termination resulted from voluntary discontinuance or from dismissal for failure or neglect to prosecute.

(d) This section does not alter the law on tolling of the statute of limitations nor does it apply to causes of action which have accrued before this title becomes effective.

Appendix E

NCUA CLOSED DOOR BOARD TRANSCRIPT

APPENDIX E   309

NATIONAL CREDIT UNION ADMINISTRATION (NCUA)

CLOSED BOARD MEETING

Tuesday, August 3, 2010

Alexandria, Virginia

MS. MATZ: I now call this meeting to order. I certify that the Board did not receive a request to reconsider its decision to close discussion of these items.

The first item will be the liquidation of Kappa Alpha Psi Federal Credit Union pursuant to Section 207(a)(3)(t) of the Federal Credit Union Act. Staff presenting via video: Keith Morton, Region IV Director, and Richard Lynn, Senior Analyst, Region IV. Good morning, gentlemen.

MR. MORTON: Good morning, Chairman Matz and Board Members Hyland and Fryzel. We are requesting NCUA Board approval to liquidate Kappa Alpha Psi Federal Credit Union under Prompt Corrective Action due to its continued low level of net worth without reasonable prospects of becoming adequately capitalized.

Kappa Alpha Psi Federal Credit Union is an $800,000 single common bond credit union located in Dallas, Texas. As of March 31, 2010, the credit union was minimally capitalized with a net worth ratio of 1.95%. According to the recently uploaded June 30 call report, this ratio has increased to 3.6% due to the reversal of its data processing expense. Kappa has a history of inaccurate recordkeeping and we believe the true net worth ratio continues to be below 2%.

We have denied eight revised business plans since 2008 and we believe this credit union does not have any reasonable prospect to become adequately capitalized as required by regulation. The credit union has consistently failed to recognize the seriousness of its situation and has not been willing to implement suggestions, recommendations or requirements set forth by NCUA to improve its operations. Insurance analyst Richard Lynn will provide further details.

MR. LYNN: Kappa Alpha Psi Federal Credit Union was chartered in 2004 to serve the members of the national professional fraternity of the same name. While total assets have grown somewhat during its existence, the credit union has had great difficulty maintaining the records, granting quality loans, collecting delinquent loans and achieving positive net earnings and a growing net worth position. NCUA field staff cites continued poor recordkeeping, weak collections and loans being granted out of compliance with the credit union's lending policies. As of March 31, 2010, delinquent loans and net charge offs exceeded 22% and 4% respectively. The officials are not receptive to NCUA's suggestions, recommendations or requirements to improve the operational and financial condition of the credit union.

Since being chartered in 2004, the credit union has only met 2 of 20 net worth goals that were part of their revised business plans. Net worth has consistently been less than 2% since June 2008, when it reached its historical high net worth ratio of 3.12%. The credit union continually submits new revised business plans that are not acceptable because they do not adequately address the problems and place excessive reliance on grants rather than operationally generated income to increase the net worth position.

The most recent plan projects the credit union will not achieve a 6% net worth ratio within 10 years of being chartered. Thus, it is in violation of the regulation.

The credit union is currently out of compliance with most of the items in the outstanding published LUA. Further, the preliminary warning letter sent earlier in 2010 has not had any real positive effect. The region recommends involuntary liquidation under Prompt Corrective Action because no viable alternative exists. The credit union serves a unique nationwide field of membership and operates using a virtual platform. We do not believe a small credit union would be able to afford implementation of the additional internal controls that a merger with this credit union would require. Further, a larger credit union with more resources would likely be unable to retain the current membership due to the fraternal structure and nature of the organization.

APPENDIX E   311

We do not believe this credit union is an attractive merger partner to another credit union of any size and the officials are not interested in a merger. The estimated loss for this liquidation is $133,922. By acting now, NCUA can prevent further losses to the NCUSIF. We are available to answer any questions you may have.

MS. MATZ: Thank you very much. I know you have worked hard on this small credit union given the number of business plans that you have reviewed.

Can you characterize for us and describe the relationship with management and their responsiveness to your requests?

MR. MORTON: Sure. It has been a real challenge working with management. Chairman Russell is actually the de facto CEO. He handles most day-to-day aspects of the operation and it has become increasingly difficult to work with them, to a point that they will not do anything except comply with rules or regulations that are explicit or legal requirements per the Federal Credit Union Act. They essentially have taken a posture that they do not agree with addressing safety and soundness concerns.

MS. MATZ: Thank you. I support this liquidation and have no other questions.

Board Member Hyland.

MS. HYLAND: Thank you, Chairman Matz. Thank you both for your work on this. I know it has been a long process in terms of a new credit union trying to help them be successful and unfortunately we are at a situation where you are recommending liquidation. There was some dispute over whether or not the credit union was operating on a cash basis or whether it could operate on a cash basis. Do you want to go into a little bit of that and the disagreement potentially between the region and the credit union on that issue?

MR. MORTON: Yes, I would be glad to. Approximately two years ago, our examiners were on site at the credit union and recommended that they go to a full accrual basis of accounting. A big reason for that had to do with the data processing expense. They had a large outstanding liability related to the data processor and failure to record that essentially materially, in our opinion, overstated their net worth position. The credit union was in agreement at that time to go to the full accrual basis of accounting and did go to the full accrual basis of accounting. Subsequent to that point, as they saw their net worth continuing to deteriorate, their difficulty achieving the revised business plans, etc., the credit union we believe took a posture that they wanted to go to the cash basis of accounting just in essence to reverse these other liabilities that had not been paid that were on their books.

MS. HYLAND: Okay. That is great. And the second question is are you confident that our inadvertent failure to respond to the credit union's submitted revised business plan, which technically meant we approved it, will not legally impair our case to liquidate the credit union? I know you have had some dialogue with general counsel on that issue.

MR. MORTON: That is a great question. It is a very fair question. As you noted, and as I advised the Board about a week ago, we tacitly approved the revised business plan in error. It was administrative oversight on our part, which I advised the Board I take full responsibility for. We were due to respond to the revised business plan on July 21 and we did not do so.

We looked at the record carefully and, in my opinion, and Bob I certainly will ask you weigh in on this question as well, I think it is important that we both answer it, but looking at the facts, the regulation says, do they have a reasonable prospect of becoming adequately capitalized, and that is to a point of getting to 6% net worth. The highest net worth ratio they have ever been able to achieve was 3%, and that was in 2008 and they have continuously declined since then. So they have had less than 2% net worth since 2008. So they are not going in the right direction.

Secondly, they have only met 2 of 20 net worth goals that they have established based on their own assumptions and projections, etc. They have only met 2 of 20 historically since they have been chartered. So that gives us certain reason to believe that they are going to have difficulty moving forward.

Third, their net worth restoration plan that was tacitly approved did not project that they would achieve an adequate capitalized level within ten years of being chartered, which is the requirement of the regulation. So it resulted in a net worth ratio a little over 4%, not the 6% that is required by the rule.

And then I would say fourth, given the safety and soundness concerns that are present at the credit union, given the fact that delinquency was 22% in March. It increased I want to say—

MR. LYNN: Twenty-four.

MR. MORTON: To 24%, in June with $400,000 outstanding in loans, the potential for loss in the loan portfolio is great. While the credit union suggests that the members are good for those loans, the loan documentation is poor. Their collections are weak. Their recordkeeping has been weak. So we believe there are a lot of other reasons to believe there are potential losses that have not been recognized that will be recognized going forward.

So, with all those factors together coupled with the current management, Chairman Matz asked about the Chairman, Victor Russell, we noticed several different irregularities with

APPENDIX E 313

him and his management of the credit union. One, he had booked a loan to his wife in the amount of $7,000 and it took two months for him to record it on the books. And then when questioned about that, he indicated that he did not back date the loan to November of 2008 and we have documentation that says otherwise. So the integrity and honesty of him as the Chairman and CEO is questionable and that gives us additional pause.

He also spent over $1,000 that we found on a debit card at the credit union at an NBA All-Star game where he was apparently treating folks at the game to $1,000 of the credit union money when they only have $15,000 in net worth. There are different concerns we have at the credit union with management, too, that question whether or not we really can rely on the management to do what is right and what is appropriate. I mean they really cannot afford to spend this money.

So in totality, I believe that we do have a case that shows that there is no reasonable prospect of becoming adequately capitalized even though we did tacitly approve the RBP.

MS. HYLAND: Do you have anything to add, Bob?

MR. FENNER: Well, I would just say, I think we all recognize that the failure to disapprove the revised business plan within our regulatory timeframe complicates things, but the law is on our side and the overwhelming weight of the facts are on our side if we are challenged. I mean there are no guarantees in litigation but I am comfortable that we should prevail if we are challenged.

MS. HYLAND: I appreciate both of you just running through the two levels of evidence. One, in terms of our failure to respond to the revised business plan but also the preponderance of the evidence, which is fairly compelling in terms of a variety of issues related to this credit union. I am supportive of the package but I appreciate you putting all of that on the record. I have no further questions. Thank you, Chairman.

MS. MATZ: Mr. Fryzel, any questions?

MR. FRYZEL: I have no questions, Chairman.

MS. MATZ: Is there a motion?

MS. HYLAND: Yes. I move that the NCUA Board place Kappa Alpha Psi Federal Credit Union into liquidation pursuant to Section 207(a)(3)(A) of the Federal Credit Union Act.

MS. MATZ: Is there a second?

MR. FRYZEL: Second.

MS. MATZ: All in favor say "Aye."

MS. HYLAND: "Aye."

MR. FRYZEL: "Aye."

MS. MATZ: "Aye." The ayes have it. The motion passes. Thank you both very much.

MR. MORTON: Thank you.

MR. LYNN: Thank you.

Appendix F

KAPFCU RESPONSE TO NCUA EX PARTE HEARING

NCUA Closed Board Meeting
August 3, 2010

KEITH MORTON – request to liquidate KAPFCU due to continued low level of net worth without reasonable prospects of becoming adequately capitalized. KAPFCU has a history of inaccurate recordkeeping and we believe the true net worth continues to be below 2%.

NCUA should not have rushed to liquidate KAPFCU based merely on Region IV subjective belief. At worse they should have waited for the next quarterly supervisory examination and determined whether KAPFCU's FPR/Call report was in fact or wrong. The rush to liquidation based on subjective belief was unnecessary and unfair.

We have denied eight revised business plans since 2008.

True, however this demonstrates more malice/callousness on NCUA. Every time NCUA rejected KAPFCU proposed RBP they would list 5 or 6 reasons. KAPFCU would address each of the reasons provided and submit another RBP. Which NCUA would reject and give another 5 or 6 reasons. This went on eight times, which proves that KAPFCU was diligently trying to comply – but NCUA was being mean-spirited, stubborn and obstinate.

As of March 31, 2010 – delinquent loans and net charge offs exceeded 22% and 4% respectively. The officials are not receptive to NCUA suggestions, recommendations, and requirements to improve operations and financial conditions.

While true, this criticism fails to consider the January 15, 2010 Supervisory Letter concerning Low Income and Community Development Credit Unions. As a Small, Low Income and Community Development – KAPFCU small loan size allows its delinquency ratios to be skewed by one or two large loans. This level of delinquency is not desirable but not unusual for credit unions of our size and character.

KAPFCU has met 2 of 20 net worth goals they have established on their own assumptions and projections in its approved revised business plans (July 2008).

Not True / Misleading, KAPFCU met its net worth goals before CP discovered a software defect with its data processing company that resulted in an immediate $12,800 loss in the second quarter of the approved business plan. From that point on, the baseline assumptions of the plan were unachievable without a significant adjustment/concession from the data processor – which KAPFCU finally did in June 30,

2010, which caught us up to both the approved July 2008 RBP, and the tacitly approved RPB.

KAPFCU had a 3.12% high in June 2008 and is not going in the right direction.

Wrong, this is the effect of being forced to change from modified cash to full GAAP accrual. When KAPFCU results are analyzed on the proper accounting basis for institutions of their size and character – KAPFCU trends are all significant, positive and heading for adequate capitalization.

RBP are not acceptable because they place excessive reliance on grants rather than operationally generated income to increase net worth.

Wrong, this criticism fails to consider the January 15, 2010 Supervisory Letter concerning Low Income and Community Development Credit Unions. In fact Region IV has completely ignored this regulatory/supervisory authority completely. It recognizes that Low Income and Community Development Credit Unions often rely on substantial grant funding to operate and provide financial services to traditionally hard-to-serve populations.

KAPFCU is out of compliance with Published LUA.

KAPFCU believes that it is in compliance or substantial with the Published LUA and would like some form of mediation or objective review of its compliance.

The Preliminary Warning Letter has had no real positive effect.

Wrong, as a result of the PWL, KAPFCU engaged in a full court press to restore its net worth, including implementing detailed Regulatory Action Plan, filling a new Revised Strategic Business Plan and Net Worth Restoration Plan (which was tacitly approved by NCUA), sought qualified full time management staff, etc.

Region IV recommends involuntary liquidation under Prompt Corrective Action because no viable alternative exists. We do not believe KAPFCU is attractive for any size and officials are not interested in a merger.

Wrong KAPFCU authorized a potential merger with HOPE Community Credit Union – in a formal BOD resolution which was submitted/available to the NCUA.

KEITH MORTON - our examiners recommended full GAAP accrual (to record data processing expense). The credit union was in agreement with going to full GAAP accrual accounting. We believe the credit union wanted to go back to cash basis just to reverse the data processing entries.

Absolute Bull Shit. The examiner (CAROLYN PENALUNA) did not recommend anything to KAPFCU – she simply went into the system and changed our FPR/Call reports to reflect full GAAP accrual accounting over KAPFCU express objections. The NCUA did not change Call Report access policy until September 2009. KAPFCU never agreed to utilize full GAAP accrual accounting – but was forced and cajoled into believing that we had to.

The reason KAPFCU desired to use modified cash was to improve its CAMEL rating. The "record keeping" problems are the direct result of the increased bookkeeping requirements necessitated by full GAAP accrual. KAPFCU can properly maintain modified cash basis records – it could not do so under full GAAP accrual without dedicated full time staff. The increased boost in capitalization was merely a secondary concern and benefit. KAPFCU discovered that no other small, low income or community development credit union under $10 Million was utilizing full GAAP accrual accounting.

KEITH MORTON – it is a real challenge working with management, VICTOR RUSSELL is the defacto CEO. They will only follow rules and regulations. They are not interested in safety and soundness concerns. Apparently, he advanced a loan to his wife (ALMA RUSSELL) without processing the loan. He denies it happened despite evidence to the contrary. His integrity and honesty are now in question.

VICTOR RUSSELL contends that he booked the loan before advancing the money. He now acknowledges, that he may have become distracted and did not complete transaction in the system – when he thought he had. The loan was repaid in full with interest within 60 days.

"He also spent over $1,000 that we found on a debit card at the credit union at an NBA All-Star game where he was apparently treating folks at the game to $1,000 of the credit union money when they only have $15,000 in net worth... I mean they really can not afford to spend this money."

Bold-faced lie. KAPFCU underwrote the travel expenses for 2 or 3 board and/or associate board members to attend the Southwest Provincial (Regional Meeting) for Kappa Alpha Psi Fraternity. KAPFCU attends all national, regional and executive meetings of the Fraternity. This particular meeting happened to coincide with NBA All-Star weekend in Dallas. VICTOR RUSSELL did not spend over $1,000 at an NBA All-Star game. VICTOR RUSSELL did not treat anyone to an NBA All-Star game. VICTOR RUSSELL, paid for drinks and hors-d'oeuvres at a lobby bar while meeting with CU officials and major depositors, including professional athletes/agents, that occurred during NBA ALL-Star weekend (but was totally unrelated to the ALL-Star game). The KAPFCU supervisory committee reviewed these charges and required VICTOR RUSSELL to repay $94 which was returned to the institution.

I believe that we do have a case that shows that there is no reasonable prospect of becoming adequately capitalized even though we did tacitly approve the RBP. Approved business plan on July 21, 2010 – tacitly approved in error.

Appendix G
NCUA TRO PRESS RELEASE

Kappa Credit Union Blocks NCUA Liquidation

WASHINGTON, DC (August 6, 2010) – Federal District Court for the District of Columbia issued a Temporary Restraining Order today against the National Credit Union Administration blocking the surprise liquidation and revocation of Kappa Alpha Psi Federal Credit Union.

Last week, Region IV of the National Credit Union Administration (NCUA) served a surprise liquidation order on Kappa Alpha Psi Federal Credit Union (KAPFCU), the first *"virtual"* credit union authorized by the NCUA and the only Low Income designated credit union (LICU) that operates on a national footprint. KAPFCU is also a Certified Community Development Financial Institution (CDFI).

Unfortunately, the NCUA issued an Order of Liquidation and Revocation on August 3, 2010. The basis of this decision was that KAPCU was *"minimally capitalized"* with a Net Worth Ratio of 1.95% on March 31, 2010 with no reasonable prospect to recover.

As of March 31, 2010 KAPFCU had a NWR of 1.95% or "minimally capitalized" which was still the highest NWR that KAPFCU had achieved historically. However, KAPFCU's second quarter results were 3.67% or *"moderately capitalized"* for June 30, 2010 – after which, NUCA elected to *"Liquidate"* the credit union on August 3, 2010.

The August 3, 2010 liquidation was based on the false impression in the press and media was that KAPFCU's NWR had **dropped down** to 1.95% and had no reasonable chance for recovery. The reality is that KAPFCU is a new credit union, starting from scratch 0%, which had built its NWR **up to** 1.95% as of March 31, 2010 and **even higher** to 3.67% by June 30, 2010. This chart is a visual depiction of KAPFCU Net Worth Growth since its inception in November 2004 through June 30, 2010 – right before its involuntary liquidation on August 3, 2010.

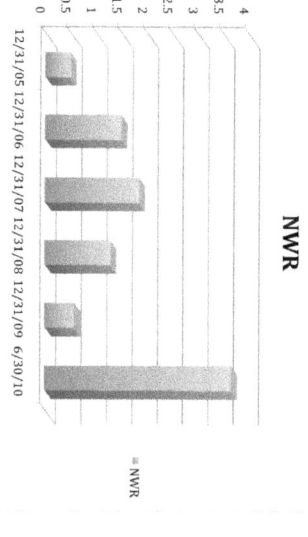

Thus, KAPFCU insists that any adverse NCUA action in August – that was based on March 31, 2010 data as opposed to the June 30, 2010 financial statements is arguably *"intentional, malicious and discriminatory"* treatment. It is also troubling that NCUA chose the unusual and extreme measure of liquidation, without consideration of a merger, when KAPFCU had suffered only one loan loss (for less than $4,500) in its six year operating history.

NCUA Rules and Regulations give new credit unions ten (10) years to become "adequately capitalized" and achieve a Net Worth Ratio of 7%. Net Worth is a measure of financial health and stability. KAPFCU is in its sixth year of operation and has a current NWR of 4% (7/31/2010). It was 3.67% according to its 2nd Quarter call report (6/30/2010). Therefore, KAPFCU was within the applicable NCUA Rules and Regulations for an institution of its size and character.

Consequently, the NCUA decision to liquidate KAPFCU on August 3, 2010 under these conditions was ill-advised, improper and legally actionable. NCUA rushed to liquidate KAPCU – not because they were failing, but because KAPFCU was becoming too successful. This was a NCUA abortion.

The Net Worth History of KAPFCU is as follows –

NWR	12/31/05	12/31/06	12/31/07	12/31/08	12/31/09**	6/30
	0.49	1.49	1.84	1.28	0.58	3.6

** *The shaded areas show where KAPFCU was improperly placed on "full accrual" instead of "modified cash."*

NCUA chastised KAPFCU for failing to comply with its approved Revised Business Plan (July 2008). However, they fail to acknowledge that this RBP was approved prior to the Corporate Stabilization assessments. KAPFCU has sustained $18,000 loss due to NCUA Corporate Stabilization assessments. These are involuntary costs assessed on all credit unions to recapitalize large corporate credit unions following real estate related losses. KAPFCU had no exposure to the real estate or mortgage-backed securities. This was money taken from KAPFCU to fund other large corporate credit unions – these assessments were completely unrelated to KAPFCU operations.

The precipitous decline in KAPFCU's NWR to **0.58%** on 12/31/2009 was a result of the involuntary Corporate Stabilization Assessment of $18,000 – KAPFCU had no exposure to real estate risk or mortgage-backed securities, nevertheless we were required to contribute to the recapitalization of larger corporate credit unions that suffered millions in losses from risky investments.

Additionally, the supervisory guidance regarding Corporate Stabilization states that credit unions should not be punished/prejudiced for losses due to Corporate Stabilization. Thus, KAPFCU Corporate Stabilization Adjusted NWR is actually **4.29%** (3/31/2009) and **5.97%** (6/30/2010), which means KAPFCU operations are actually in compliance with the previously approved RBP.

On January 15, 2010 the National Credit Union Administration, NCUA Chairman Debbie Matz issued *Letter to Credit Unions 10-CU-01 "Supervising Low*

¹ Pursuant to 12 U.S.C. §1782(6)(C)(iii) KAPFCU is reporting on a "**Modified Cash**" basis. KAPFCU was previously examined on "full accrual" accounting. As a credit union with less than $10,000,000 in total assets KAPFCU is allowed to report on a "cash" basis or "modified cash" basis. See 12 U.S.C. §1782(6)(C)(iii) – which states that small credit unions are exempted from the mandatory GAAP treatment that the NCUA examiner imposed upon KAPFCU under the "de minimus exception" to the standard accounting principals.

Income Credit Unions and Community Development Credit Unions." The Letter, which was provided to NCUA examination staff and shared with the boards of directors of all federally insured credit unions, provides guidance on the characteristics, benefits, and unique challenges of low-income credit unions and community development credit unions.

The NCUA offers Technical Assistance Grants (TAG) and other benefits to designated Low-Income Credit Unions because they provide desperately needed development and financial services to traditional underserved and hard-to-serve populations. There is a strong public policy need for these services.

Unfortunately, NCUA examiner (CAROLYN PENALUNA) evaluated KAPFCU as if it was a mature institution with over $10,000,000 in assets. KAPFCU is a new credit union with less that $850,000 in assets, and a certified low income and community development credit union. The accounting rules and regulations are different – but KAPFCU was improperly evaluated on a much higher standard.

The Real Problem: overzealous examiners, forcing full accrual accounting, in total disregard to important policy implication for Low Income or Community Development Credit Unions – is a recipe for disaster. An examiner can lose their jobs if they fail to "flag" a credit union that subsequently fails. Unfortunately, the NCUA imposes no penalty for destroying a credit union. This creates an incentive for examiners to become excessively overly critical and over scrutinize small credit unions in order to cover their own professional careers. However, there is NO penalty for destroying a perfectly good, albeit small credit union.

KAPFCU is a prime example of the challenges that LICUs and/or CDCUs face with NCUA examiners that do not fully appreciate low-income business models, community development oriented business plans or comply with NCUA Rules, Regulations and Supervisory Authority.

KAPFCU's chief complaint is that it has not been afforded the full flexibility allowed under NCUA rules, regulations and supervisory letters for institutions of like size and character. KAPFCU's remedies appear to be in federal court. The hearing for permanent injunction is set for Tuesday at 2:30 PM (est) August 10, 2010 in Washington, DC.

APPENDIX G

Appendix H

KAPFCU QUARTERLY CALL REPORT (FINANCIAL PERFORMANCE)

APPENDIX H 323

Cycle Date: June-2010
Run Date: 07/19/2010
Interval: Quarterly

Page	Click on links below to jump to FPR contents
1	Summary Financial Information
2	Ratio Analysis
**	
4	Assets
5	Liabilities, Shares & Equity
6	Income Statement
7	Delinquent Loan Information
8	Loan Losses, Bankruptcy Information, & Loan Modifications

KAPPA ALPHA PSI
Federal Credit Union
PO Box 703047
Dallas TX 75370

Count of CU : 1
Asset Range : 0 - 2,000,000
Peer Group Number : 1
Count of CU in Peer Group : 0

Charter-Region-SE-District:
24732 - 4 - K - 5

*Note to Users: The peer groups and resulting peer average ratios are based upon all federally insured credit unions within the asset range. Peer average ratios are not available for aggregate reports.
The ratios on aggregate FPRs are consolidated ratios for the group of credit unions included in the report and do not represent a peer average for that group.

** Page 3 - Supplemental Ratios - is not included

Summary Financial Information
For Charter : 24732
Count of CU : 1
CU Name: KAPPA ALPHA PSI
Asset Range : 0 - 2,000,000
Peer Group: 1
Criteria : N/A
Count of CU in Peer Group : 0

	Jun-2009	Sep-2009	% Chg	Dec-2009	% Chg	Mar-2010	% Chg	Jun-2010	% Chg
ASSETS:	Amount	Amount		Amount		Amount		Amount	
Cash & Equivalents	245,076	302,960	23.6	326,242	7.7	367,830	12.7	315,386	-14.3
TOTAL INVESTMENTS	113,602	113,601	0.0	4,671	-95.9	2,104	-55.0	2,104	0.0
Loans Held for Sale	0	0	N/A	0	N/A	0	N/A	0	N/A
Real Estate Loans	0	0	N/A	0	N/A	0	N/A	0	N/A
Unsecured Loans	64,154	69,518	8.4	56,525	-18.7	50,216	-11.2	98,704	96.6
Other Loans	431,374	376,980	-12.6	363,344	-3.6	358,578	-1.3	365,853	2.0
TOTAL LOANS	495,528	446,498	-9.9	419,869	-6.0	408,794	-2.6	464,557	13.6
(Allowance for Loan & Lease Losses)	(4,986)	(9,239)	101.5	(9,329)	1.0	(7,058)	-24.3	(8,417)	19.3
Land And Building	0	0	N/A	0	N/A	0	N/A	0	N/A
Other Fixed Assets	361	271	-24.9	181	-33.2	0	-100.0	0	N/A
NCUSIF Deposit	7,934	7,934	0.0	7,934	0.0	7,934	0.0	7,233	-8.8
All Other Assets	12,193	8,623	-29.3	11,197	29.9	250	-97.8	250	0.0
TOTAL ASSETS	870,008	870,548	0.1	760,765	-12.6	779,854	2.5	781,113	0.2
LIABILITIES & CAPITAL:									
Dividends Payable	5,179	9,893	91.0	6,000	-39.4	3,969	-33.9	4,168	5.0
Notes & Interest Payable	0	0	N/A	0	N/A	0	N/A	0	N/A
Accounts Payable & Other Liabilities	28,577	25,227	-11.7	27,010	7.1	22,461	-16.8	1,274	-94.3
Uninsured Secondary Capital	0	0	N/A	0	N/A	0	N/A	0	N/A
TOTAL LIABILITIES	33,756	35,120	4.0	33,010	-6.0	26,430	-19.9	5,442	-79.4
Share Drafts	0	0	N/A	0	N/A	0	N/A	0	N/A
Regular shares	623,533	624,916	0.2	623,297	-0.3	638,156	2.4	646,929	1.4
All Other Shares & Deposits	199,000	199,000	0.0	100,000	-49.7	100,000	0.0	100,000	0.0
TOTAL SHARES & DEPOSITS	822,533	823,916	0.2	723,297	-12.2	738,156	2.1	746,929	1.2
Regular Reserve	8,480	9,350	10.3	9,350	0.0	9,351	0.0	10,131	8.3
Other Reserves	0	0	N/A	0	N/A	0	N/A	0	N/A
Undivided Earnings	5,239	2,162	-58.7	-4,892	-326.3	5,917	221.0	18,611	214.5
TOTAL EQUITY	13,719	11,512	-16.1	4,458	-61.3	15,268	242.5	28,742	88.2
TOTAL LIABILITIES, SHARES, & EQUITY	870,008	870,548	0.1	760,765	-12.6	779,854	2.5	781,113	0.2
INCOME & EXPENSE									
Loan Income*	20,483	41,814	36.3	52,110	-6.5	6,640	-49.0	16,239	22.3
Investment Income*	2,824	4,013	-6.3	3,406	-36.3	755	-11.3	1,079	-28.5
Other Income*	7,773	9,073	-22.2	13,473	11.4	-1,525	-145.3	-500	83.6
Salaries & Benefits*	0	0	N/A	0	N/A	0	N/A	0	N/A
Total Other Operating Expenses*	17,960	36,833	36.0	53,421	9.4	11,409	-14.6	14,211	-37.7
Non-operating Income & (Expense)*	5,475	1,875	-77.2	-919	-136.8	11,093	4,928.3	30,641	38.1
NCUSIF Stabilization Income*	N/A	5,475		5,475	-25.0	0	-100.0	0	N/A
Provision for Loan/Lease Losses*	1,813	6,466	137.8	6,557	-23.9	1,288	-21.4	2,648	2.6
Cost of Funds*	7,071	11,785	11.1	13,221	-15.9	711	-78.5	0	-100.0
NET INCOME (LOSS) BEFORE NCUSIF STABILIZATION EXPENSE*	9,681	7,366	49.3	346	-96.5	3,555	4,009.8	30,600	330.4
NCUSIF Stabilization Expense*	6,665	6,665	-33.3	6,665	-25.0	0	-100.0	0	N/A
Net Income (Loss)*	3,016	701	-84.5	-6,319	-776.1	3,555	325.0	30,600	330.4
TOTAL CUs	1	1	0.0	1	0.0	1	0.0	1	0.0

* Income/Expense items are year-to-date while the related %change ratios are annualized.
# Means the number is too large to display in the cell

1. Summary Financial

324 COMMUNITY CAPITAL

APPENDIX H   325

	Liabilities, Shares & Equity									
Return to cover	For Charter : 24732									
07/19/2010	Count of CU : 1									
CU Name: KAPPA ALPHA PSI	Asset Range : 0 - 2,000,000									
Peer Group: 1	Criteria : N/A									
	Count of CU in Peer Group : 0									
	Jun-2009	Sep-2009	% Chg	Dec-2009	% Chg	Mar-2010	% Chg	Jun-2010	% Chg	
LIABILITIES, SHARES AND EQUITY										
LIABILITIES:										
Uninsured Secondary Capital	0	0	N/A	0	N/A	0	N/A	0	N/A	
Other Borrowings	N/A	N/A		N/A		N/A		N/A		
Other Notes, Promissory Notes, Interest Payable, & Draws										
Against Lines of Credit	0	0	N/A	0	N/A	0	N/A	0	N/A	
Borrowing Repurchase Transactions	0	0	N/A	0	N/A	0	N/A	0	N/A	
Subordinated Debt	0	0	N/A	0	N/A	0	N/A	0	N/A	
Accrued Dividends and Interest Payable	5,179	9,893	91.0	6,000	-39.4	3,969	-33.9	4,168	5.0	
Accounts Payable & Other Liabilities	28,577	25,227	-11.7	27,010	7.1	22,461	-16.8	1,274	-94.3	
TOTAL LIABILITIES	33,756	35,120	4.0	33,010	-6.0	26,430	-19.9	5,442	-79.4	
SHARES AND DEPOSITS										
Share Drafts	0	0	N/A	0	N/A	0	N/A	0	N/A	
Regular Shares	623,533	624,916	0.2	623,297	-0.3	638,156	2.4	646,929	1.4	
Money Market Shares	0	0	N/A	0	N/A	0	N/A	0	N/A	
Share Certificates	0	0	N/A	0	N/A	0	N/A	0	N/A	
IRA/KEOGH Accounts	0	0	N/A	0	N/A	0	N/A	0	N/A	
All Other Shares[1]	0	0	N/A	0	N/A	0	N/A	0	N/A	
Non-Member Deposits	199,000	199,000	0.0	100,000	-49.7	100,000	0.0	100,000	0.0	
TOTAL SHARES AND DEPOSITS	822,533	823,916	0.2	723,297	-12.2	738,156	2.1	746,929	1.2	
EQUITY:										
Undivided Earnings	5,239	2,162	-58.7	-4,892	-326.3	5,917	221.0	18,611	214.5	
Regular Reserves	8,480	9,350	10.3	9,350	0.0	9,351	0.0	10,131	8.3	
Appropriation For Non-Conforming Investments (SCU Only)	0	0	N/A	0	N/A	0	N/A	0	N/A	
Other Reserves	0	0	N/A	0	N/A	0	N/A	0	N/A	
Equity Acquired in Merger	0	0	N/A	0	N/A	0	N/A	0	N/A	
Miscellaneous Equity	0	0	N/A	0	N/A	0	N/A	0	N/A	
Accumulated Unrealized G/L on AFS Securities	0	0	N/A	0	N/A	0	N/A	0	N/A	
Accumulated Unrealized Losses for OTTI (due to other factors) on HTM Debt Securities	N/A			0		0		0		
Accumulated Unrealized G/L on Cash Flow Hedges	0	0	N/A	0	N/A	0	N/A	0	N/A	
Other Comprehensive Income	0	0	N/A	0	N/A	0	N/A	0	N/A	
Net Income	0	0	N/A	0	N/A	0	N/A	0	N/A	
EQUITY TOTAL	13,719	11,512	-16.1	4,458	-61.3	15,268	242.5	28,742	88.2	
TOTAL SHARES & EQUITY	836,252	835,428	-0.1	727,755	-12.9	753,424	3.5	775,671	3.0	
TOTAL LIABILITIES, SHARES, & EQUITY	870,008	870,548	0.1	760,765	-12.6	779,854	2.5	781,113	0.2	
NCUA INSURED SAVINGS[2]										
Uninsured Shares	0	0	N/A	0	N/A	0	N/A	0	N/A	
Uninsured Non-Member Deposits	0	0	N/A	0	N/A	0	N/A	0	N/A	
Total Uninsured Shares & Deposits	0	0	N/A	0	N/A	0	N/A	0	N/A	
Insured Shares & Deposits	822,533	823,916	0.2	723,297	-12.2	738,156	2.1	746,929	1.2	
TOTAL NET WORTH	13,719	11,512	-16.1	4,458	-61.3	15,268	242.5	28,742	88.2	

Means the number is too large to display in the cell
[1] PRIOR TO JUNE 2006, INCLUDED MONEY MKT, SHARE CERTS, IRA/KEOGHs, AND NONMEMBER SHARES FOR SHORT FORM FILERS
[2] PRIOR TO 10/03/08 SHARES INSURED UP TO $100,000; 10/03/08 to 05/20/09 SHARES INSURED UP TO $100,000, and $250,000 FOR IRAS; 5/20/09 AND FORWARD SHARES INSURED UP TO $250,000

5. Liab/Sh/Equity

	Income Statement									
Return to cover	For Charter : 24732									
07/19/2010	Count of CU : 1									
CU Name: KAPPA ALPHA PSI	Asset Range : 0 - 2,000,000									
Peer Group: 1	Criteria : N/A									
	Count of CU in Peer Group : 0									
	Jun-2009	Sep-2009	% Chg	Dec-2009	% Chg	Mar-2010	% Chg	Jun-2010	% Chg	
* **INCOME AND EXPENSE**										
INTEREST INCOME:										
Interest on Loans	20,453	41,814	36.3	52,110	-6.5	6,640	-49.0	16,239	22.3	
Less Interest Refund	(0)	(0)	N/A	(0)	N/A	(0)	N/A	(0)	N/A	
Income from Investments	2,824	4,013	-5.3	3,406	-36.3	755	-11.3	1,079	-28.5	
Income from Trading	0	0	N/A	0	N/A	0	N/A	0	N/A	
TOTAL INTEREST INCOME	23,277	45,827	31.3	55,516	-9.1	7,395	-46.7	17,318	17.1	
INTEREST EXPENSE:										
Dividends	7,071	11,785	11.1	13,221	-15.9	711	-78.5	0	-100.0	
Interest on Deposits	0	0	N/A	0	N/A	0	N/A	0	N/A	
Interest on Borrowed Money	0	0	N/A	0	N/A	0	N/A	0	N/A	
TOTAL INTEREST EXPENSE	7,071	11,785	11.1	13,221	-15.9	711	-78.5	0	-100.0	
PROVISION FOR LOAN & LEASE LOSSES	1,813	6,466	137.8	6,557	-23.9	1,288	-21.4	2,648	2.8	
NET INTEREST INCOME AFTER PLL	14,393	27,576	27.7	35,738	-2.8	5,396	-39.6	14,670	35.9	
NON-INTEREST INCOME:										
Fee Income	7,773	9,073	-22.2	13,473	11.4	-1,525	-145.3	-500	83.6	
Other Operating Income	0	0	N/A	0	N/A	0	N/A	0	N/A	
Gain (Loss) on Investments	0	0	N/A	-3,029	N/A	0	100.0	0	N/A	
Gain (Loss) on Disposition of Assets	0	0	N/A	0	N/A	0	N/A	0	N/A	
Gain from Bargain Purchase (Merger)	0	0	N/A	0	N/A	0	N/A	0	N/A	
Other Non-Oper Income/(Expense)	5,475	1,875	-77.2	2,110	-15.6	11,093	2,002.9	30,641	38.1	
NCUSIF Stabilization Income	N/A	5,475		5,475	-25.0	0	-100.0	0	N/A	
TOTAL NON-INTEREST INCOME	13,248	16,423	-17.4	18,029	-17.7	9,568	112.3	30,141	57.5	
NON-INTEREST EXPENSE										
Total Employee Compensation & Benefits	0	0	N/A	0	N/A	0	N/A	0	N/A	
Travel, Conference Expense	606	1,636	80.0	2,015	-7.6	1,645	226.6	3,625	10.2	
Office Occupancy	0	0	N/A	0	N/A	0	N/A	0	N/A	
Office Operation Expense	8,576	19,952	55.1	27,049	1.7	8,110	19.9	0	-100.0	
Educational and Promotion	1,032	2,849	84.0	3,796	-0.9	687	-27.0	1,047	-23.8	
Loan Servicing Expense	0	0	N/A	0	N/A	0	N/A	0	N/A	
Professional, Outside Service	6,866	10,190	-1.1	14,895	9.6	409	-89.0	5,484	570.4	
Member Insurance	0	0	N/A	0	N/A	0	N/A	0	N/A	
Operating Fees	0	0	N/A	0	N/A	0	N/A	0	N/A	
Misc Operating Expense	880	2,006	52.0	5,696	113.0	558	-80.8	4,055	263.4	
TOTAL NON-INTEREST EXPENSE	17,960	36,633	36.0	53,421	9.4	11,409	-14.6	14,211	-37.7	
NET INCOME (LOSS) BEFORE NCUSIF STABILIZATION EXPENSE	9,681	7,366	-49.3	346	-96.5	3,555	4,009.8	30,600	330.4	
NCUSIF Stabilization Expense	6,665	6,665	-33.3	6,665	-25.0	0	-100.0	0	N/A	
NET INCOME (Loss)	3,016	701	-84.5	-6,319	-776.1	3,555	325.0	30,600	330.4	
RESERVE TRANSFERS:										
Transfer to Regular Reserve	1,738	2,609	0.1	2,609	-25.0	0	-100.0	781	N/A	

* All Income/Expense amounts are year-to-date while the related % change ratios are annualized.
# Means the number is too large to display in the cell

6. Inc/Exp

326   COMMUNITY CAPITAL

Appendix I

NCUA "SUR REPLY" TO KAPFCU COMPLAINT

APPENDIX I

UNITED STATES DISTRICT COURT
FOR THE DISTRICT OF COLUMBIA

KAPPA ALPHA PSI FEDERAL
CREDIT UNION,

    Plaintiff,

v.   Civil Action No. 10-01321 EGS

NATIONAL CREDIT UNION
ADMINISTRATION,

    Defendant.

SUR-REPLY TO PLAINTIFF'S OPPOSITION TO DEFENDANT'S RENEWED RESPONSE TO THE SHOW CAUSE ORDER

The opposition filed by plaintiff, Kappa Alpha Psi Federal Credit Union ("KAPCU"), is long on rhetoric but short on verifiable facts that support its arguments. Page after page contains statement after statement unsupported by citations to the record. Where plaintiff's opposition does cite to the record, the arguments it makes are wrong. Given that the Court's review of this case is under the Administrative Procedure Act's deferential "arbitrary, capricious, an abuse of discretion, or otherwise not in accordance with law" standard — a standard of review that is conceded by plaintiff — there is no merit to the opposition. The show-cause order should be discharged.[1]

---

[1] On September 3, 2010, this Court issued an order advising the parties that it was unhappy with their filing of same-day motions for extension of time and with the filing of motions for extension of time after the due date, noting that plaintiff had already done the latter in this case. The Court advised the parties that in the future such motions would be summarily denied. Plaintiff was ordered to file its opposition to defendant's Renewed Response To The Show Cause order by September 27. It did not do so. Instead, it filed the opposition on September 28, unaccompanied by a motion to permit it to do so. Under Smith v. District of Columbia, 430 F.3d 450, 456-57 and n. 5 (D.C. Cir. 2005), this Court has the authority to strike the late-filed opposition and discharge the order to show cause, based solely on plaintiff's disregard of the Court's order and plaintiff's failure to file a motion for leave to file the opposition late. Defendant submits that the Court do so in this case.

SUMMARY OF ARGUMENT

The heart of plaintiff's opposition is its contention that the National Credit Union Administration ("NCUA") "knowingly and intentionally used improper dated 3/31/10 net worth numbers [1.95%] rather than the more accurate 6/30/10 net worth number[] [which plaintiff contends was 3.67%] to argue for the rushed liquidation of KAPCU in the ex parte board meeting." Opposition at 8. As shown below, plaintiff's argument for a 3.67% net worth ratio on 6/30/10 is based on an unacceptable accounting sleight of hand. Other arguments made by plaintiff are equally deficient. Plaintiff was not "forced" to use GAAP accrual accounting, and plaintiff's recordkeeping deficiencies were not the result of accrual accounting. The deficiencies reflected a much more fundamental problem with the management and operation of the credit union. Plaintiff's suggestion that it, as a new credit union, was entitled to ten years in which to reach an acceptable net worth level is without foundation in the governing regulations. Plaintiff also erroneously argues that its actual loan delinquency ratio should have been ignored because the ratio was "skewed" as a result of a "handful" of loans made to "professional athletes and/or entertainers." (It is unclear why a low income credit union such as plaintiff is making a significant portion of its loans to "high income and high net-worth individuals." See Opposition at 14.) Plaintiff attacks NCUA's concern over its management. That concern is fully supported by the administrative record, as were the decisions to disapprove plaintiff's secondary capital plans. Finally, the provisional Technical Assistance Grant award to plaintiff occurred after the liquidation order was issued and can not be used to attack that decision. Additionally, for reasons explained below, the Technical Assistance Grant would not have addressed plaintiff's financial problems.

ARGUMENT

A. NCUA's Judgment That Plaintiff's 6/30/10 Net Worth Ratio Was Below 2% Is Fully Supported By The Record. Plaintiff argues that its net worth ratio significantly increased after it converted from full accrual accounting to modified cash accounting: from 0.58% on 12/31/09 to 1.95% on 3/31/10 to 3.67% on 6/30/10.

Plaintiff then asserts:

> Region IV Officials knowingly and intentionally used improper dated 3/31/10 net worth numbers to argue for the rushed liquidation of KAPFCU in the *ex parte* board meeting.

Opposition at 12.

It is correct that the package of materials provided to the NCUA Board on June 30, 2010, (see Administrative Record ("AR") at 000006) contained the 3/31/10 net worth ratio. The 6/30/10 net worth ratio was, however, also discussed at the August 3, 2010, NCUA Board meeting where the Board voted to liquidate KAPFCU. The Region IV Director made the following statement:

> Kappa Alpha Psi Federal Credit Union is an $800,000 single common bond credit union located in Dallas, Texas. As of March 31, 2010, the credit union was minimally capitalized with a net worth ratio of 1.95%. According to the recently uploaded June 30 call report, this ratio has increased to 3.6% due to the reversal of its data processing expense. Kappa has a history of inaccurate recordkeeping and we believe the true net worth ratio continues to be below 2%.

AR 000076.

Plaintiff further asserts:

> Region IV Officials improperly usurped the prerogatives of the KAPFCU board of directors in an attempt to bankrupt KAPFCU by forcing them to book/record an unenforceable debt, KAPFCU had a contract dispute with a data processing vendor, KAPFCU elicited a Legal Opinion and a CPA Opinion about the proper accounting treatment of the disputed matter. See, Exhibits G and H.
>
> Additionally, after the four year Texas Statute of Limitations expired, KAPFCU passed a formal Board resolution deeming the debt, [sic] uncollectible and released the special reserved [sic] into retained earnings. See, Exhibit J.
>
> Nevertheless, Region IV Officials exceeded their authority and usurped the prerogatives of the KAPFCU board of directors by improperly contacting the third party vendor in a tortuous and malicious attempt to reaffirm an unenforceable debt and bankrupt the credit union. See, Exhibit J."

Opposition at 12.

Virtually every one of the statements quoted above is wrong. It is useful to start first with the exhibit (the exhibits are attached to plaintiff's Opposition) that plaintiff claims supports its position that the four-year Texas statute of limitations has run on its data-processing contract.

This is Exhibit G, a vituperative email dated March 15, 2006, from Victor R. Russell, the Chairman of the KAPFCU Board of Directors, to Marc R. Laffite, an official at TOTAL/I Services Corporation, the contractor. The email, which was addressed to a number of people, contains this statement: "Larry, cancel the damn [sic] WWI service today!!!!! I am not getting a call from the people that hook me into your system and this is [expletive deleted].??????!!." This suggests that a contract with a provider may have been cancelled in 2006, but there is more to the story.[2]

---

[2] Undersigned counsel (Fred E. Haynes) has been advised by an NCUA examiner who supervised KAPFCU that at the time of the email the credit union had contracts with TOTAL/I Services and an entity referred to as WWI. KAPFCU still has contracts with these entities. This is not, however, in the administrative record.

Plaintiff asserts that it obtained a legal opinion supporting its action of releasing the special reserve for the unpaid data processing services. This is Exhibit H, a May 12, 2010, letter from a Dallas, Texas, law firm. The letter starts:

> Kappa Alpha Psi entered into a Data Processing Service Agreement with TOTAL/1 Services Corporation on May 21, 2005. The contract is for the credit union's core data processing services, and it remains in effect today.

The letter goes on to state that KAPFCU may have a contract cause of action against TOTAL/1 based on the representation by KAPFCU to the law firm as to a problem with TOTAL/1's data processing system, a problem as to which the letter states TOTAL/1 has offered a "workaround." Nowhere in this letter is there any statement that the alleged error in the software justifies the release of the special reserve being retained on plaintiff's books to pay for the core data processing services that the credit union has already received.

Plaintiff also asserts that it elicited a CPA opinion about the proper accounting treatment of the disputed matter. This is, apparently, a reference to Exhibit K, which is an email from an individual who may be a CPA. The email nowhere suggests that plaintiff would be justified in releasing the special reserve. It merely provides to Mr. Russell the relevant portion of the NCUA's accounting manual that describes the modified cash basis of accounting. The part of the manual provided to Mr. Russell directly contradicts plaintiff's argument that it did not need to account for its unpaid bills from TOTAL/1:

> Generally under a cash basis of accounting, income is recorded and accounted for when actually collected and expenses are accounted for when actually paid. Under the modified cash basis prescribed herein, the accounting is based on the actual receipts and disbursements of the credit union <u>except that provisions should be made to reflect</u>:
>
> - Liabilities which are not promptly paid when due,
> - Dividends and interest refunds applicable to the accounting period but not yet paid,
> - Deferred income or expenses applicable to future periods,
> - Estimated losses to be sustained on loans outstanding,
> - Estimated unrealized losses associated with mutual fund investments, and
> - Depreciation on fixed assets.

Exhibit K to the Opposition (emphasis added).

Plaintiff's interpretation of this language, as set forth in the Opposition at 10, is at odds with its plain meaning. Plaintiff asserts that the modified cash basis of accounting enables it to have "more control" over the operational performance of the credit union by enabling it "to better match revenues to expenses." Opposition at 10. Plaintiff then makes the following statement, which is directly contrary to the modified cash basis of accounting and contrary to fundamental principles of accounting:

> From an operational management perspective, it is helpful to hold off on certain larger expense [sic], and pay them during periods when we have increased income. This is perfectly legal, legitimate and allowable under Modified Cash basis accounting. And contrary to Region IV Officials contentions, there is nothing nefarious or improper about doing so.

Opposition at 10. This appears to be an attempt to justify not reflecting the unpaid bills on KAPFCU's accounting statements, a course of action that is forbidden under the modified cash accounting method described in the NCUA's accounting manual, which requires that the accounting statement reflect liabilities that are not promptly paid when due.

Plaintiff also argues that it was improper for one of the NCUA examiners to contact the data processing company, TOTAL/I Services Corporation, to confirm the amount owed to it by plaintiff. This contention is meritless on its face, and no authority for it is cited. In fact, NCUA examiners have broad power to conduct such investigations as are required to evaluate the financial condition of a credit union. See 12 U.S.C. § 1784(a); 12 C.F.R. § 741.1. Plaintiff attaches an email from TOTAL/I Services as Exhibit J, but this email does not help plaintiff.

The TOTAL/I Services official states, in pertinent part, the following:

> We have, sadly, felt we could not participate in any way in the brou-ha-ha between the Credit Union and NCUA. I learned a hard lesson when I spoke unwittingly to NCUA's Corey (last name?) about amounts due to TOTAL/I. I told him I did not know a number, but agreed to a number he mentioned as a possible amount – he then used that information to help NCUA's case. I should never be so agreeable !!!.

The email in no way negates NCUA's decision that plaintiff had improperly deleted from the calculation of its net worth ratio the debt that it owed to its data processing company. See AR 000080.

B. **NCUA Did Not Force Plaintiff To Use GAAP Accrual Accounting And Plaintiff's Record Keeping Deficiencies Were Not The Result Simply Of Accrual Accounting.** The administrative record establishes that plaintiff was not "forced" to use the accrual accounting method. As explained in the Region IV Director's letter to the Chairman of plaintiff's Board, dated July 12, 2010:

> You have repeatedly asserted your previous examiner forced you to report on a "full accrual" accounting basis when you were permitted to utilize the "modified cash" basis of accounting. In reviewing agreements reached with Kappa Alpha Psi Federal Credit Union (KAPFCU) officials in examination and supervision reports for the three years the previous examiner examined KAPFCU, there is no evidence of any formal request for the credit union to change its accounting basis. In fact, KAPFCU board members have consistently voted to adopt NCUA recommendations at the close of each examination or supervision contact. Further, at the time the previous examiner began examining KAPFCU, the credit union was already utilizing full accrual accounting, albeit imprecisely.

Exhibit H to defendant's Renewed Response To The Show Cause Order, docket entry 10, hereafter referred to as Renewed Response.

And as explained in defendant's Renewed Response, the recordkeeping problems experienced by plaintiff were of a very fundamental nature. See Renewed Response at 11 to 16. They were not attributable to any esoteric aspect of GAAP accrual accounting. Instead, they reflect the fact, as admitted by plaintiff, that the credit union does not have any full-time staff:

> KAPFCU has – NO – full-time staff. It operates through an all volunteer board. Consequently, KAPFCU has developed a streamlined and simple operational model, one that can be implemented with the limited/non-existent staff?

Opposition at 9. As noted in defendant's Renewed Response, and not disputed by plaintiff's opposition, one of the problems with the credit union's operation is that the Chairman of the Board "continues to post accounting entries and make disbursements," despite repeatedly being told not to do so. This is a basic failure of internal controls. See Renewed Response at 17-18.

Plaintiff also argues, without any support in the record, that full accrual accounting required it to maintain 35 to 40 sub-ledger accounts for every month whereas modified cash accounting only requires that plaintiff maintain 4 to 5 sub-ledger accounts per month. By contrast, NCUA believes that the difference in the maintenance of sub-ledger accounts is much smaller, although this fact is not in the record, since it was not relevant to the NCUA's decision.

C. A New Credit Union Is Not Guaranteed A Ten-Year Period In Which To Reach An Acceptable Net Worth Ratio. Plaintiff argues that it should have been allowed the full ten-year period to achieve an adequate capitalization level. Opposition at 4-5. As explained in NCUA's Renewed Response at 9-10, NCUA has the authority to liquidate a new credit union before the expiration of the ten-year period, even where the credit union is moderately capitalized, which plaintiff contends was its status as of June 30, 2010. This follows from the language of the statute and the regulations. The statute and regulations define a "new" credit union as one that is less than ten years old, 12 U.S.C. § 1790d(b)(2) and 12 C.F.R. § 702.301(b), and the regulations provide NCUA with authority to liquidate a "new" credit union, 12 C.F.R. § 702.304(c), which by definition is one that is less than ten years old. The finding that NCUA is required to make when a new credit union is liquidated before the ten-year period is that it "has no reasonable prospect of becoming adequately capitalized." This finding was made by the NCUA Board on August 3, 2010, as reflected in the order of liquidation. AR 000002.

D. Plaintiff's Actual "Loan Delinquency Ratio" Should Not Have Been Ignored. Plaintiff asserts that its loan delinquency ratio was "skewed by a handful of large loans from [sic] high income and high net-worth individuals." Opposition at 14. Plaintiff contends that NCUA's Supervisory Letter 10-CU-01 (January 2010) "explicitly recognizes the distortion that a few loans have on a small credit union's loan portfolio." Opposition at 15. The Supervisory Letter is attached to the opposition as Exhibit A. There is absolutely nothing in the Supervisory Letter that, explicitly or otherwise, authorizes a low income credit union to exclude from its loan delinquency ratio large loans made to high-income and high net-worth individuals.

E. NCUA's Concern About The Credit Union's Management Is Supported By The Administrative Record. The Opposition at 17 to 20 argues that NCUA's negative assessment of plaintiff's management is not supported by the facts and was a personal vendetta and a "malicious effort." Opposition at 19, to remove Victor Russell as the Chairman of the credit union's Board of Directors. As explained in the Renewed Response, at 10 to 19, there had been a lengthy effort by NCUA to get plaintiff's management to correct the many deficiencies in the operation of the credit union. For example, NCUA spent a total of 891 hours working with plaintiff — 229.5 hours of examination time; 418.7 hours of supervisory contact; and 253 hours of work by Economic Development Specialists. See Renewed Response at 10. The concerns about the management of the credit union are fully supported by the administrative record, and they were also repeatedly explained to KAPFCU. See Exhibits A to H attached to the Renewed Response.

Additional concerns about the Chairman's actions were made in the Risk Management Review Comments that were presented to the NCUA's Board as part of the record in support of the recommendation that the Board liquidate KAPFCU. AR at 000026-27:

[T]he CEO [Mr. Russell] recently disbursed funds on a loan to his spouse without booking the loan. No entry was posted on the credit union's books at the time the funds were dispersed. Two months later, he booked the loan and the loan payoff (including interest), backdating the entries to the date funds were transferred. The entry was made twenty-three days after the loan payoff. This is similar to a teller taking money from the credit union and paying it back later, with interest.

Despite repeated demands by NCUA staff, the credit union's board chairman [Mr. Russell] continues to post accounting entries and make disbursements. This failure to follow even basic internal controls raises the possibility of inappropriate transactions occurring. Given the condition of the credit union's records, discovering errors in a timely manner is unlikely.

F. **NCUA Did Not Arbitrarily Deny Plaintiff's Secondary Capital Plan And, In Any Event, That Decision Is Not Properly Before The Court In This Case.** Plaintiff argues that its net worth problems would have been resolved had NCUA authorized it to pursue a secondary capital plan. NCUA's staff denied the proposed plans. It bears emphasis that permitting plaintiff to pursue a secondary capital plan would not have guaranteed that someone would have been willing to provide such capital to the credit union, in light of its problems and questionable viability. See AR 000033.

The reasons that the NCUA staff rejected plaintiff's secondary capital proposals are spelled out in the regional summary that was submitted to the NCUA Board as part of the recommendation to liquidate the credit union:

> Secondary capital proposals by the credit union have been denied due to its poor financial condition and prospects for increased risks to the NCUSIF. KAPCU's stated purpose for the secondary capital requested in recent proposals is to stabilize and increase net worth, as well as support additional non-member deposits. Credit union management specifically stated in their April 19 and April 22, 2010 secondary capital requests that they would not earn investment or loan income on the secondary capital since they plan to put the funds into a non-interest bearing cash account.
>
> In recent secondary capital proposals, the credit union has assumed the interest rate charged on secondary capital would be 1.5 percent. This is unrealistic due to KAPCU's precarious financial condition. The interest rate charged for secondary capital for this credit union would likely be significantly more than 1.5%. Therefore, the credit union would likely not be able to service the secondary (subordinated debt) during the first few years of the plan. Also, its projected net income would not be enough to replace the reduction in net worth as secondary capital rolls into Subordinated CDCU Debt. Thus, if the credit union grew significantly under the

artificial capital level, its net worth ratio would be less favorable than it is now when the secondary capital was due to be repaid.

> An infusion of cash from secondary capital funds, which would allow them to achieve rapid growth by removing net worth constraints, could result in the creation of more substandard loans to support share dividends and interest expense. Since the credit union has not corrected its safety and soundness issues, adding additional funds solely for the purpose of temporarily increasing the net worth ratio to allow for more aggressive growth would be ill-advised. For that reason, the credit union has repeatedly been counseled to resolve outstanding safety and soundness issues and secondary capital proposals have been deferred until such time as the noted concerns are properly addressed and corrected.

AR 000028. See also AR 000045.

Even if one were to assume that the decision to deny plaintiff's secondary capital proposals is properly before this Court, the rationale for the decision cannot be characterized as arbitrary or capricious. It was a well-reasoned decision based on NCUA's expertise in supervising federally-chartered credit unions.

G. **Plaintiff's Application For A Technical Assistance Grant Was Not Relevant To The NCUA's Liquidation Decision And Likely Would Not Have Affected Plaintiff's Financial Condition.** The merits of NCUA's decision to liquidate KAPCU must be judged by the record that was before the Board when it made the decision. The fact that, post-liquidation, plaintiff was advised that it had been awarded a Technical Assistance Grant does not change the Board's analysis. Plaintiff, however, sees NCUA's liquidation decision in suspicious terms:

> Region IV Officials rushed to liquidate KAPCU because they knew about the pending CDFI/TA award. The NCUA has been in contact with the U.S. Department of Treasury CDFI Fund regarding KAPCU funding application since April 2010. Thus, NCUA "rushed to liquidate" the credit union because [they] knew

that KAPFCU was going to receive a $100,000 T/A award from the CDFI Fund.

Opposition at 19.

There is not a scintilla of evidence that supports this factually unsupported suspicion, and plaintiff cites none. NCUA denies that it had prior knowledge of the decision by the Department of Treasury to possibly award a Technical Assistance Grant to KAPFCU under the Community Development Financial Institutions ("CDFI") Program. Although KAPFCU was a CDFI-certified institution eligible for grants, the CDFI Program is independently run by the U.S. Department of the Treasury ("Treasury"). See "Who We Are," Community Development Financial Institutions Fund, United States Department of the Treasury, available at http://www.cdfifund.gov/who_we_are/. Applications are made directly to the Treasury Department through the CDFI Program. See "Overview of What We Do, " Community Development Financial Institutions Fund, United States Department of the Treasury, available at http://www.cdfifund.gov/what_we_do/overview.asp.

Although Treasury typically consults with a CDFI institution's primary regulator during its consideration process, NCUA represents that it was not notified that Treasury was awarding a Technical Assistance grant to plaintiff prior to the Board meeting of August 3, 2010. Thus, the Board did not consider such a possibility in making its determination to issue the liquidation order. Notwithstanding this fact, Technical Assistance Grants are explicitly made only for use to "build their capacity by acquiring prescribed types of products or services including technology (usually efficiency enhancing technology such as computers and loan management software), staff training, consulting services to acquire needed skills or services (such as a market analysis

or lending policies and procedures), or staff time to conduct discrete, capacity-building activities (such as website development)." See "Technical Assistance Awards," Community Development Financial Institutions Fund, United States Department of the Treasury, available at http:// www.cdfifund.gov/what_we_do/programs_id.asp?programID=7. Therefore, even had KAPFCU received a Technical Assistance Grant, it would not have directly altered the relevant calculus of whether KAPFCU was adequately capitalized.

CONCLUSION

For the reasons set forth above and in the Renewed Response and above, the order to show cause should be discharged.

Respectfully submitted,

RONALD C. MACHEN JR., D.C. Bar #447889
United States Attorney
for the District of Columbia

RUDOLPH CONTRERAS, D.C. Bar #434122
Chief, Civil Division

BY: /s/ Fred E. Haynes
FRED E. HAYNES, D.C. Bar #165654
Assistant United States Attorney
555 Fourth Street, N.W., Room E-4110
Washington, D.C. 20530
202.514.7201
fred.haynes@usdoj.gov

OF COUNSEL:

JON J. CANERDAY
DAMON P. FRANK
Trial Attorney
Office of the General Counsel
National Credit Union Administration

Appendix J

U.S. DISTRICT COURT TRANSCRIPT & FINAL COURT ORDER

APPENDIX J   337

```
                    UNITED STATES DISTRICT COURT
                    FOR THE DISTRICT OF COLUMBIA
                    ----------------X
KAPPA ALPHA PSI FEDERAL     :
CREDIT UNION,               :
            Plaintiff,      :  Washington, D.C.
                            :  Docket No. CA 10-1321
         v.                 :  November 9, 2010
                            :  10:50 a.m.
NATIONAL CREDIT UNION       :
ADMINISTRATION,             :
            Defendant.      :
                    ----------------X

               SHOW CAUSE HEARING
     BEFORE THE HONORABLE COLLEEN KOLLAR-KOTELLY
           UNITED STATES DISTRICT JUDGE

APPEARANCES:
For the Plaintiff:     BYNUM & JENKINS, PLLC
                       By: Mr. Kenneth D. Bynum
                       901 N. Pitt Street
                       Suite 320
                       Alexandria, VA 22314
                       703.549.7211
                       kbynum@bynumandjenkinslaw.com

                       COOPER & CRICKMAN, PLLC
                       By: Mr. Kenneth C. Crickman
                       1625 Massachusetts Avenue, N.W.
                       Suite 425
                       Washington, D.C. 20036
                       202.265.4520
                       kcrickman@cocrlaw.com

For the Defendant:     U.S. ATTORNEY'S OFFICE
                       By: Mr. Fred E. Haynes
                       555 4th Street, NW
                       Room E-4110
                       Washington, D.C. 20530
                       202.514.7201
                       fred.haynes@usdoj.net

Court Reporter:        Catalina Kerr, RPR, CRR
                       U.S. District Courthouse
                       Room 6509
                       Washington, D.C. 20001
                       202.354.3258
                       catykerr@msn.com

Proceedings recorded by mechanical stenography, transcript
produced by computer.
```

                    P-R-O-C-E-E-D-I-N-G-S
                    (10:50 A.M.; OPEN COURT.)

THE DEPUTY CLERK: Civil Action 10-1321, Kappa Alpha Psi Federal Credit Union versus National Credit Union Administration. Counsel identify yourselves for the record.

MR. BYNUM: May it please the Court, Ken Bynum of Bynum & Jenkins on behalf of Kappa Alpha Psi Federal Credit Union, along with Ken Crickman from Cooper & Crickman. Good morning.

THE COURT: Good morning, Counsel.

MR. HAYNES: Your Honor, Fred Haynes for the Government. With me at counsel table is Damon Frank, a trial attorney with the Credit Union Administration. We have the regional director, Keith Morton, M-o-r-t-o-n. He's Region IV which supervises this credit union, and we have the supervisory examiner, Cory Phariss, who supervised it.

THE COURT: All right. Good morning to everyone.

MR. HAYNES: Thanks for indulging the Court. I had to continue the matter without any significant advance notice for compelling reasons at the time. Sorry if I inconvenienced anyone, but everyone wants their cases decided yesterday and sometimes criminal matters take priority.

THE COURT: Well, every time criminal matters, especially matters involving people who are incarcerated, take priority over civil matters. So that principally was the reason for

1 the continuances.
2   The Court did note the errata that was filed by the
3 Government yesterday and also the Administrative Record
4 filing. It appears to the Court that the Administrative
5 Record NCUA had originally filed on the public docket did not
6 contain the meeting minutes of the August 3rd, 2010 board
7 meeting where the board voted to place Plaintiff into
8 liquidation.
9   While at first glance it seems like a serious
10 omission, it is in fact merely a filing error. Both the Court
11 and Plaintiff were provided with the full administrative
12 record, including the meeting notes by on or before August 13,
13 2010. And in that regard, see Docket No. 6. Accordingly, in
14 the Court's view, no party was prejudiced by the late filed,
15 corrected administrative record yesterday.
16   Do you disagree, Counsel?
17   MR. BYNUM: No, Your Honor.
18   THE COURT: All right. I absolutely have no
19 questions. I'm prepared to rule and will do so. Plaintiff
20 Kappa Alpha Psi Federal Credit Union brought this action
21 against the National Credit Union Administration, NCUA,
22 pursuant to 12 U.S. Code Section 1787(a)(1)(B). Plaintiff
23 claims that NCUA improperly ordered liquidation and revocation
24 of its charter as a Federal Credit Union.
25   On August the 11th of this year, the Court issued

1 an order granting Plaintiff's motion to show cause and ordered
2 NCUA to show cause why it should not be prohibited from
3 continuing its liquidation of the credit union.
4   Upon consideration of the renewed response to the
5 order to show cause, the reply and the sureply thereto, the
6 applicable law and the entire record in this case and for the
7 following reasons that I will articulate, the Court finds that
8 NCUA has successfully demonstrated that its order of
9 involuntary liquidation and revocation of the Credit Union's
10 charter was in accordance with applicable law, and
11 accordingly, the Court will discharge the show cause order and
12 dismiss this action.
13   The NCUA is an independent agency in the executive
14 branch of the federal government that charters supervisors and
15 insures federal credit unions under the Federal Credit Union
16 Act, and I'll refer to that as the "Act." The NCUA is
17 administered by -- and the Act is decided at 12 U.S. Code
18 Section 1751, et seq.
19   The NCUA is administered by a board that consists of
20 three members appointed by the President pursuant to 12 U.S.
21 Code Section 1752(a), in parens, and (b). And this case
22 involves the Board's exercise of its powers regarding
23 liquidation of a, quote, new, end quote, credit union that it
24 supervised. A new credit union is defined as one that has
25 been in existence less than ten years and that has less than

1 $10 million in total assets, and that's pursuant to 12 CFR
2 Section 702.301(b).
3   The Act requires the Board to design a system that
4 gives a new credit union a, quote, reasonable time to
5 accumulate net worth and to become adequately capitalized
6 under 12 U.S. Code Section 1790d(b)(2)(B).
7   The Act also requires the Board to, quote, establish
8 regulations that prescribe a system of prompt corrective
9 actions that shall apply to new credit unions, end quote, and
10 that's also pursuant to Section 1790d(b)(2)(A), and quote, to
11 impose adequate restrictions and requirements on new credit
12 unions that do not make sufficient progress toward becoming
13 adequately capitalized. Same section, 1790d(b)(2)(B)(iv).
14   The net worth category classifications for new
15 credit unions are the following: Well capitalized, in other
16 words, the credit union has a net worth ratio of capital equal
17 to 7 percent of total assets or higher; adequately
18 capitalized, net worth of 6 percent; moderately capitalized, a
19 net worth of 3.5 to 5.99 percent; marginally capitalized, a
20 net worth of 2 percent to 3.49 percent; minimally capitalized,
21 a net worth of 0 percent to 1.99 percent; and uncapitalized,
22 net worth -- net worth of less than 0 percent, and that's all
23 set forth in 12 CFR Section 702.302.
24   The Act and its regulations establish prompt
25 corrective action the Board can take for, quote, moderately

1 capitalized, end quote, quote, marginally -- marginally
2 capitalized, end quote -- quote/unquote, or, quote, minimally
3 capitalized, end quote, new credit unions. Specifically, the
4 Board is empowered to place a new credit union into
5 liquidation without prior notice or opportunity to be heard
6 pursuant to 12 CFR Section 702.304(c), and that section is
7 important. I'll read it in relevant part, and I'm quoting.
8   Notwithstanding any other actions required or
9 permitted to be taken under this section, the NCUA Board may
10 place a new credit union, which is, quote, moderately
11 capitalized, end quote; marginally capitalized, quote/unquote;
12 or quote, minimally capitalized, end quote, into liquidation
13 pursuant to 12 U.S. Code Section 1787(a)(3)(A)(1) provided
14 that the credit union has no reasonable prospect of becoming,
15 quote, adequately capitalized, end quote.
16   In turn, Title 12, U.S. Code 1787(a)(3)(A)(ii), reads
17 in relevant part: Under Subsection 3, liquidation to
18 facilitate prompt corrective action. The Board may close any
19 credit union for liquidation and appoint itself . . . as
20 liquidating agent of that credit union if (A) the Board
21 determines that the credit union is significantly
22 undercapitalized . . . and has no reasonable prospect of
23 becoming adequately capitalized.
24   The Kappa Alpha Psi Federal Credit Union was
25 chartered by NCUA in November -- strike that -- in

1 November 2004 to serve the membership and associations of the
2 Kappa Alpha Psi national fraternity. It provides financial
3 services to African-Americans and low-income populations. Its
4 headquarters are located in a suburb of Dallas but it operates
5 as a virtual credit union, which means its members conduct
6 business over the internet or by mail.
7   Between March 2005 and March 2008, the Credit
8 Union's level of capitalization fluctuated between marginally
9 and minimally capitalized, and that's set forth in the
10 administrative record at 61. Following an examination of the
11 Credit Union in early 2008, the NCUA determined that the
12 Credit Union was experiencing financial and operational
13 problems.
14   Specifically, Defendant noted problems with lending
15 practices: Loan documentation was inadequate, loan limits
16 were not based on credit risk and income levels and debt
17 ratios were not calculated to determine whether members had
18 the capacity to pay. And that's set forth in Defendant's
19 Memorandum Exhibit A.
20   There were also recordkeeping problems. There were
21 outstanding items on bank record -- bank reconciliations that
22 were over a year old, reconciliations generally were not
23 performed timely, and recordkeeping lacked sufficient detail
24 to identify specific information about transactions.
25   And finally, Plaintiff was not in compliance with

1 its own Revised Business Plan. Now, with respect to the
2 Revised Business Plan, the Court's understanding is that all
3 new credit unions must file business plans outlining their
4 strategy to reach adequate net worth ratios. When a credit
5 union's net worth does not increase consistent with this
6 strategy, it must file a Revised Business Plan addressing
7 problems and explaining how it will correct them, among other
8 requirements. That's also set forth in the Code of Federal
9 Regulations at 702.206.
10   Now, as a result, the parties entered into a letter
11 of understanding and agreement in March 2008, and that's also
12 set forth in Defendant's Memorandum Exhibit A, "A" as in
13 apple. The letter of Understanding outlining actions that the
14 Plaintiff agreed to take in order to address these problems,
15 specifically Plaintiff agreed to the following: (1), to
16 develop a recordkeeping process allowing for the timely
17 reconciliation, identification and clearing of outstanding
18 items.
19   (2), research and clear all outstanding items on
20 particular bank statements.
21   (3), to prepare reconciliations on specifically
22 identified bank statements.
23   (4), to obtain training on how to properly evaluate
24 and to underwrite a loan.
25   (5), to cease granting unsecured loans in excess of

1 $2500 until completion of items (3) and (4).
2   And finally, to submit a Revised Business Plan and
3 wait for approval before accepting new nonmember deposits or
4 implementing new products or services not approved in the
5 Current Business Plan.
6   On August 22nd, 2008, the parties entered into a
7 Modified Letter of Understanding and Agreement, and that's
8 Exhibit B of Defendant's Memorandum. The NCUA identified the
9 same problems as it had in the first Letter of Understanding.
10 The Plaintiff again agreed to five of the six actions it had
11 agreed to in the first Letter of Understanding.
12   NCUA conducted another examination of the Credit
13 Union in September 2008. Following that examination, on
14 January 16, 2009, NCUA Regional Director C. Keith Morton sent
15 a letter to Plaintiff. Morton advised Plaintiff that it was,
16 quote, operating in an unsafe and unsound manner for which
17 substantial immediate corrective action must be taken.
18 Specifically, and I'm quoting, I have grave concerns about the
19 recordkeeping and loan underwriting in your credit union.
20 Further, the board of directors has not complied with the
21 August 22nd, 2008 Modified Letter of Understanding and
22 Agreement. This is all set forth in Defendant's Exhibit C.
23   The letter continues, and I quote, The underwriting
24 deficiencies noted, given the dollar amount and types of loans
25 are alarming. Poor recordkeeping, including untimely posting

1 of payments, has overstated income and rendered asset quality
2 ratios unreliable. The dollar amount of delinquency is
3 considerably more than current Net Worth, which has declined
4 to 1.33 percent, and the account -- and the Account for
5 Loan -- declined to 1.33 percent in the Account for Loan
6 Losses Balance. Recognizing one loss of any significant
7 amount from the loan portfolio could render the credit union
8 insolvent.
9   The January 2009 letter set forth a list of
10 mandatory actions for the Credit Union to take, many of which
11 echoed the actions agreed to in the previous Letters of
12 Understanding. And finally, the letter advises that if the
13 Credit Union's board of directors does not address these
14 issues, NCUA will, and I quote, consider administrative action
15 against the credit union, end quote.
16   Despite these letters, the same conditions
17 persisted. As a result, the parties entered into a third
18 Modified Letter of Understanding and Agreement in July 2009.
19 The credit union agreed to make significant changes in its
20 recordkeeping and loan policies, and in exchange, the regional
21 director agreed to refrain from recommending formal
22 administrative action against the Credit Union as long as it,
23 and I quote, made a sustained, effective and good faith effort
24 to comply with all terms of this agreement. That's set forth
25 at Exhibit D in Defendant's Memorandum. The letter

1 specifically stated that the administrative action against the
2 Credit Union could include an order to liquidate.
3   Unfortunately, the problems continued. A NCUA
4 examination on or about September 30th, 2009 revealed that
5 the Credit Union was nearly insolvent and that it had not
6 complied with several conditions of the most recent Modified
7 Letter of Understanding. Once again, on December 31, 2009,
8 Regional Director Morton sent the Credit Union a letter
9 memorializing the Credit Union's continuing problems with
10 recordkeeping, lending practices and net worth. That's
11 Defendant's Exhibit E.
12   Morton advised the Plaintiff that he was considering
13 publishing the most recent Letter of Understanding and
14 Agreement unless Plaintiff addressed its continuing problems.
15   Normally, letters of understanding are private, but
16 when a credit union demonstrates repeated or serious
17 noncompliance with the letter's terms, NCUA has the authority
18 to publish the letter. Morton told the Credit Union to
19 respond to his letter by January 15, 2010. He explained that
20 shortly thereafter NCUA staff would contact the Credit Union
21 to review its status, and shortly after that Morton would
22 decide whether to publish the Letter of Understanding.
23   In response, the Credit Union requested an extension
24 of time to submit its Revised Business Plan. By letter dated
25 February the 2nd, 2010 Morton agreed — Strike that. Morton

1 granted Plaintiff's request for an extension to submit the
2 Revised Business Plan only. That's Exhibit F of Defendant's
3 memorandum.
4   Plaintiff did not request an extension to otherwise
5 comply with the conditions set forth in the Letter of
6 Understanding or the Regional Director's letter and Morton did
7 not grant such extensions. Morton also noted that, as set
8 forth in his December 31, 2009 letter, NCUA examiners had
9 contacted the Credit Union to attempt to review its affairs,
10 but the Credit Union had failed to provide the examiners with
11 complete access to its books and records.
12   By letter dated April 9, 2010, Morton issued a
13 Preliminary Warning Letter to the Credit Union due to its
14 continued extremely poor financial and organizational
15 situation. Morton noted that after NCUA personnel made
16 corrections to the general ledger, the Credit Union remained
17 nearly insolvent. Serious recordkeeping deficiencies
18 persisted, including inaccurate ledgers and account balances,
19 outdated and untimely reconciliations and inadequate
20 documentation.
21   Moreover, while the Credit Union had hired a third
22 party to perform recordkeeping duties, it had not actually
23 transferred responsibility to the third party.
24   Finally, the Credit Union continued to grant loans
25 based on insufficient documentation and did not make or

1 document collection efforts for delinquent loans. And that's
2 Defendant's Exhibit G.
3   In his letter, Morton also advised Plaintiff that
4 NCUA would publish the July 2009 Modified Letter of
5 Understanding and Agreement and if the Credit Union did not
6 demonstrate compliance with the terms -- with its terms, it
7 would be subject to further administrative action, including
8 liquidation.
9   Finally, Morton advised Plaintiff that a NCUA
10 examiner would make an onsite visit to the Credit Union within
11 the next 30 days to assess Plaintiff's compliance and to
12 provide assistance.
13   NCUA's offers of assistance to Plaintiff were not
14 new. Since the Credit Union's inception, NCUA made extensive
15 efforts to help it succeed. From late 2004 to March 2010,
16 NCUA staff spent over 900 hours working with Plaintiff. This
17 is all set forth in the Administrative Record at pages 39 to
18 45.
19   It examined the Credit Union on several occasions
20 and worked repeatedly with Credit Union officials to review
21 its records, make recommendations and develop plans to assist
22 in resolving its problems. Moreover, from June 2007 through
23 September 2009, NCUA's economic development specialists spent
24 over 250 hours working with the Credit Union. Economic
25 development specialists have expertise regarding small credit

---

1 unions, low income credit unions and community development
2 credit unions.
3   Despite NCUA's assistance, Plaintiff's situation did
4 not improve. As of June, 2010, it remained out of compliance
5 with 10 of the 12 terms it agreed to in the June 30, 2009
6 Letter of Understanding and Agreement. This is set forth in
7 Defendant's Exhibit H, the July 9, 2010 letter from Morton to
8 Plaintiff.
9   Based on the Credit Union's longstanding history of
10 lending and recordkeeping deficiencies, its failure to resolve
11 these issues and its continued low net worth, Regional
12 Director Morton issued a 12-page Regional Summary recommending
13 that the Board exercise its authority to liquidate the Credit
14 Union. This is all set forth in the Administrative Record,
15 pages 25 to 36.
16   This recommendation was premised upon the following
17 major issues: Minimal capitalization, otherwise known as low
18 net worth; extensive recordkeeping errors; continued granting
19 of loans without appropriate underwriting or documentation;
20 high delinquency rates; failure to collect on delinquent loans
21 or to document collection efforts; and unresponsiveness to
22 requests for corrective action.
23   The Regional Director concluded that based on all of
24 these factors, Plaintiff had no reasonable prospect to
25 becoming adequately capitalized and therefore that the Board

1 was authorized to liquidate. In a regional summary, NCUA also
2 considered five alternatives to liquidation, including other
3 corrective action, merger, special assistance and
4 conservatorship but ultimately concluded that none of these
5 options were advisable for a variety of reasons. Again,
6 that's all set forth in the Administrative Record.
7   The Regional Summary was reviewed by NCUA's Director
8 of Examination and Insurance and General Counsel. Both
9 offices concurred with the recommendation to liquidate set
10 forth in the Administrative Record at pages 12 to 18.
11   Finally, on August the 3rd, 2010, the Board met to consider
12 whether Plaintiff should be liquidated. The Board discussed
13 Plaintiff's self-reported net worth ratio of 3.67 percent
14 June 30, 2010, and considered whether this improving ratio
15 altered its analysis.
16   The Board concluded that the self-reported ratio was
17 not reliable because the Credit Union's recordkeeping had
18 historically been inaccurate and NCUA personnel had repeatedly
19 found, after examination, that Plaintiff's net worth was
20 significantly lower than it had self-reported.
21   The board unanimously -- unanimously concluded that
22 given Plaintiff's high delinquency rate over 22 percent in
23 March 2010, weak recordkeeping, failure to meet 18 out of 20
24 net worth goals in its Revised Business Plan and lack of
25 compliance with the outstanding published letter of

---

1 Understanding, the Credit Union did not have a reasonable
2 prospect of becoming adequately capitalized within ten years
3 and that involuntary liquidation was appropriate. And this is
4 all set forth in the Administrative Record, pages 75 to 84.
5   The Board issued an Order of Liquidation and
6 Revocation of Charter on August the 3rd, 2010 as set forth in
7 the Administrative Record, pages 1 to 3.
8   Now, with respect to this action -- this -- this
9 action initially came before the Court on August the 6th, 2010
10 as a motion for a temporary restraining order against NCUA
11 during a status hearing in open court on August the 18th,
12 2010. However, Plaintiff informed the Court that it no longer
13 sought an injunction pending the Court's decision on the
14 merits of the order to show cause which the Court had already
15 issued on August the 11th, 2010. The Court was also
16 informed during this status hearing that the parties had
17 agreed to extend the briefing schedule and hearing on the
18 order to show cause.
19   The Defendant then filed a renewed response to the
20 order to show cause, and after several requests for extensions
21 of time by both parties, briefing was completed. The motion
22 is ripe for determination by the Court. In its order of
23 August 11, 2010 and its minute order of August 18, 2010, the
24 Court directed the parties to brief the proper standard of
25 review, the Board's Order of Liquidation and Revocation of

APPENDIX J   345

1 Charter, the scope of materials this court should consider in
2 its review and whether the Plaintiff is entitled to an
3 evidentiary hearing. These questions will be explored as
4 follows.
5   Turning first to the standard review of the Board's
6 Order of Liquidation, Defendant has argued, and Plaintiff
7 concedes, that the deferential arbitrary and capricious
8 standard of review set forth in the Administrative Procedure
9 Act governs this case, that is, whether the agency's action
10 was arbitrary, capricious, an abuse of discretion or otherwise
11 not in accordance with the law, and support for that is set
12 forth in the following cases, Recording Industry Association
13 of America, Inc. versus Library of Congress, 608 F.3d 861;
14 also in the Matter of the Bricks -- In the Matter of the
15 Bricks Community Federal Credit Union Charter versus National
16 Credit Union Administration, 50 F. Supp. 2d 509, and that's --
17 Plaintiff has indeed referenced that, that case, at
18 Plaintiff's Memorandum at page 4.
19   Under this standard of review, an agency must,
20 quote, examine the relevant data and articulate a satisfactory
21 explanation for its action pursuant to authority of
22 longstanding, the Motor Vehicle Manufacturers Association of
23 United States, Inc. versus State Farm Mutual Automobile
24 Insurance Company, 463 U.S. 29, 43.
25   Therefore, the NCUA's finding that the Plaintiff

17

1 Credit Union was less than adequately capitalized and, quote,
2 had no reasonable prospect of becoming adequately capitalized,
3 end quote, was not arbitrary and capricious, then this court
4 must uphold the liquidation under 12 CFR 702.304(c).
5   Second, the Court must determine the scope of
6 material it should consider in its review, and as part of that
7 question, whether Plaintiff is entitled to an evidentiary
8 hearing. Defendant argues, and Plaintiff does not contest,
9 that APA review is based on the administrative record, not a
10 de novo review of the facts in the district court. And again,
11 that's -- that's pursuant to authority of longstanding, the
12 APA, the Administrative Procedure Act, also Community for
13 Creative Non-Violence versus Lujan case, 908 F.2d 992.
14   There is a limited opportunity for the parties to
15 supplement the administrative record. First, Plaintiff may
16 supplement where the Government has presented an incomplete
17 record. Second, the agency must provide what's referred to
18 as, quote, explanatory, end quote, declarations so long as
19 they merely explain the agency's decision and do not provide
20 any new rationalization for it, and again pursuant to
21 authority of longstanding, Bunker Hill Company versus
22 Environmental Protection Agency, 572 F.2d 1286.
23   Here, in this case, the Defendant has provided the
24 administrative record as well as two explanatory declarations,
25 and Plaintiff has supplemented the record with additional

18

19

1 documents, all of which the Court has considered.
2   Neither party argues that an evidentiary hearing is
3 appropriate or necessary. Accordingly, the Court conducts its
4 review based on the party's submissions and in accordance with
5 the Administrative Procedure Act.
6   Now, Plaintiff has challenged the Board's decision
7 as arbitrary and capricious. Moreover, the Court has asked
8 the parties to address the issue of whether NCUA provided
9 Plaintiff with sufficient preliquidation notice and an
10 opportunity to be heard, and I'll address those issues in
11 turn.
12   NCUA argues that based on Plaintiff's record of
13 serious systemic problems and based on its failure to correct
14 the vast majority of those problems, it properly liquidated
15 the Credit Union.
16   The Credit Union, in turn, attacks NCUA's
17 substantive decision to liquidate it on several grounds,
18 arguing that the Board abused its discretion in making the
19 determination that Plaintiff had, quote, no reasonable
20 prospect of becoming adequately capitalized and therefore
21 could be liquidated. And I'll address those arguments.
22   First, it claims -- Plaintiff claims that NCUA, and
23 I use the word "forced," forced it to use a full accrual
24 method, a-c-c-r-u-a-l, full accrual method of accounting in
25 2007 to 2009, which resulted in both recordkeeping problems

20

1 and lower net worth.
2   When the Credit Union returned to, a quote, modified
3 cash accounting, end quote, in 2010, it claims its net worth
4 ratio increased by 600 percent in a matter of months.
5 Specifically, Plaintiff claims its net worth ratio increased
6 from 0.58 percent on December 31, 2009 to 1.95 percent in
7 March 2010, to 3.67 percent on June two-thousand- -- in
8 June 2010, demonstrating a clear trend toward adequate
9 capitalization. The Court is not persuaded.
10   First, there's nothing in the record, or Plaintiff's
11 supplemental submissions, to suggest that the Credit Union
12 was, quote, forced, to use Plaintiff's words, to utilize a
13 full accrual method of accounting at any point.
14   Second, NCUA disputes the accuracy of the Credit
15 Union's self-reported net worth ratios of 1.9 percent and
16 3.67 percent in 2010. Defendant provided evidence that
17 neither figure is supported by the facts and that after
18 correcting for recordkeeping errors, Plaintiff's true net
19 worth ratio is much lower. The Credit Union has not provided
20 any evidence to rebut these conclusions.
21   Third, the record reveals that when the Credit Union
22 was operating on a, quote, modified cash, end quote, method of
23 accounting in 2005 and 2006, its net worth ratio was
24 consistently minimally capitalized, only rising above
25 2 percent once during that period, and that's set forth in the

1 administrative record at page 61.
2   Accordingly, the Court has no basis to conclude the
3 Credit Union's performance was significantly impacted by the
4 use of one accounting method over another. And finally, as a
5 matter of common sense, the Court cannot accept Plaintiff's
6 argument that the substantial well-documented evidence
7 supporting NCUA's findings that the Credit Union suffered
8 serious long-term systemic problems can be explained away by a
9 change in accounting methods.
10   Accordingly, even assuming, for argument's sake, the
11 Defendant compelled Plaintiff to use the full accrual method
12 of accounting from 2007 to 2008, this does not show the
13 agency's decision to liquidate was arbitrary and capricious.
14   In a related argument, Plaintiff claims that the
15 Board arbitrarily considered its March 2010 net worth ratio of
16 1.95 percent as opposed to its June 2010 net worth ratio,
17 which was a substantially higher 3.67 percent. This argument
18 also fails. As discussed in the background section of my
19 previous — of this ruling, NCUA presented significant
20 evidence that Plaintiff's self-reported net worth figures were
21 inaccurate on a number of different occasions, and after
22 corrections were made by NCUA examiners, its net worth ratios
23 were lower than its self-reported numbers.
24   For example, Plaintiff's self-reported 1.95 percent
25 net worth ratio in March 2010 was disputed by NCUA whose own

1 figures showed the Credit Union's net worth as 1.30 percent,
2 that's AR 25. With respect to the Credit Union's June 30th
3 2010 net worth, the numbers reported by Plaintiff and found by
4 NCUA were even more divergent. Plaintiff reported that its
5 net worth ratio in June 30th -- on June 30th, 2010 was
6 3.67 percent; however, the agency never corrected that number.
7 To the contrary, once NCUA examiners corrected reporting
8 errors, the agency determined that the Plaintiff's net worth
9 was actually only 1.09 percent. That's set forth in the
10 Administrative Record at page 9.
11   While Plaintiff provides conclusory assertions that
12 its numbers are correct, it has not provided any evidence
13 refuting NCUA's accounting, much less shown that Defendant's
14 reliance on such accounting was arbitrary and capricious.
15   Third, the Credit Union claims that the NCUA
16 arbitrarily failed to consider, quote, an adjusted delinquency
17 ratio, end quote, on its delinquent loans. Plaintiff does not
18 clearly explain how the adjusted delinquency ratio works. It
19 suggests that it involves ignoring delinquencies on a few
20 large loans the Credit Union made to, quote, high income and
21 high net worth individuals, such as profession athletes or
22 entertainers, end quote, because the effect of these
23 delinquencies is disproportionately high given the small size
24 of the Credit Union's loan portfolio. This is set forth in
25 Plaintiff's Memorandum at page 14.

Plaintiff does not cite to any authority in support of its claims that the agency should exclude these loans when considering its delinquency rates. The authority it does cite to, a supervisory letter from the NCUA, merely cautions NCUA to compare low income and community development credit unions such as Plaintiff with other low income community development credit unions as opposed to their wealthier peers.

Contrary to Plaintiff's claim, this letter does not instruct the agency to exclude large delinquencies when evaluating low income or community development credit unions. Moreover, as the Defendant points out, even if it was agency position to be more lenient with loan delinquencies in low income populations, the loans at issue here were not made to low income individuals. And that's -- can be hardly overlooked.

Accordingly, the Court concludes that the decision not to exclude large loans to high net worth individuals in calculating the Plaintiff's delinquency ratio, which the Court notes was a troubling 24.3 percent as of March 31, 2010 was not arbitrary and capricious.

Fourth, the credit Union claims that NCUA arbitrarily denied its request for a secondary capital plan. Specifically, in April 2010, Plaintiff requested the NCUA approve $100,000 in secondary capital which would permit the Credit Union to borrow $100,000. In June 2010, Defendant refused to approve the request. Plaintiff claims that NCUA arbitrarily denied its access to -- denied it access to capital which would have improved its net worth ratio which in return could have permitted it to avoid liquidation. The Court is not persuaded.

As a threshold matter, the agency decision before this court for review is NCUA's decision to liquidate the Credit Union in August 2010, not its decision to deny Plaintiff's request for a secondary capital plan in June 2010.

Even assuming, for argument's sake, that the secondary capital decision was properly before the Court, Plaintiff has not shown it was arbitrary and capricious. In the administrative record, NCUA sets forth several reasons for its denial. First, Plaintiff's request for the loan was based on an assumption it would only be charged 1 percent to 1-1/2 percent interest on the loan. Plaintiff provided no documentation in support of that assumption, which NCUA concluded was, quote, unrealistic due to Plaintiff's precarious financial position, and that can be found at AR 28.

Second, based on the Plaintiff's historical and present condition, NCUA determined the likelihood that Plaintiff would be able to service the debt, or ultimately repay it, was small. Finally, NCUA concluded that although a 100,000-dollar loan of secondary capital would allow Plaintiff to achieve rapid growth, such growth is undesirable given the

APPENDIX J   349

1 Plaintiff's fundamental safety and soundness issues. As set
2 forth throughout the administrative record, as set forth,
3 Plaintiff has not provided evidence to rebut these
4 conclusions, much less to demonstrate that they were arbitrary
5 and capricious. -- Strike that.
6   Plaintiff -- Delete the words "as set forth
7 throughout." Delete those words.
8   Plaintiff has not provided evidence to rebut those
9 conclusions, much less demonstrate that they were arbitrary
10 and capricious.
11   Finally, the Credit Union argues that the board's
12 decision to liquidate was arbitrary and capricious because it
13 was a result of a, to use Plaintiff's word, personal vendetta,
14 end quote, against the Credit Union's management, and
15 that's -- that can be found in Plaintiff's memorandum at page
16 17. The Court does not agree.
17   The Court has no doubt that the relationship between
18 NCUA and the Plaintiff was far from ideal. However, the
19 Plaintiff has submitted no evidence and the Court has found
20 none to support a conclusion that this acrimony resulted in an
21 arbitrary and capricious decision by the board to liquidate
22 Plaintiff. To the contrary, record reflects that the agency
23 undertook a series of well-documented, careful reviews of the
24 facts at several levels within the agency before making the
25 decision to liquidate.

1 For all of those reasons, the Court concludes that
2 the board's decision to liquidate Plaintiff pursuant to U.S.
3 Code 1787(a)(3)(A)(i) was not arbitrary, capricious or
4 otherwise an abuse of discretion.
5   Now, in its orders of August the 11th and August the
6 18th, 2010, the Court directed the parties to address the
7 following, quote, NCUA's authority and/or discretion to act
8 pursuant to 12 U.S. Code Section 1787(a)(3), including whether
9 Plaintiffs are entitled to preliquidation notice hearings
10 and/or appeals, end quote.
11   NCUA made three arguments in response. First, it
12 explained that federal regulations specifically give it
13 authority to liquidate a new federal credit union without
14 preliquidation notice or opportunity to be heard when the
15 credit union is not adequately capitalized and, quote, has no
16 reasonable prospect to become -- of becoming adequately
17 capitalized. And I referred to this before. It's 12 CFR
18 Section 702.304.
19   Second, the Defendant pointed out that Plaintiff had
20 abundant preliquidation notice as follows: No fewer than
21 seven occasions over the course of several years NCUA put its
22 concerns in writing and notified the Credit Union that failure
23 to correct its problems could result in corrective action by
24 the agency, including liquidation.
25   Finally, NCUA explained the policy reason for its

1 decision to liquidate without even more notice. As a
2 federally chartered credit union, Plaintiffs is covered by the
3 National Credit Union Share Insurance Fund which insures the
4 accounts of credit union members up to $250,000 per account.
5 At the time of liquidation, NCUA estimated that the -- the
6 National Credit Union Share Insurance Fund would lose
7 approximately $134,000 due to the Credit Union's poor
8 financial status, and this can be -- this is discussed at
9 pages 10, 14 and 16 of the Administrative Record.
10   Based on its findings that Plaintiff's net worth was
11 not likely to increase, NCUA determined that, quote, the
12 problems facing the Credit Union are serious and need
13 immediate aggressive action to protect the interests of the
14 members and the National Credit Union Share Insurance Fund.
15   Plaintiff did not respond to those points in its
16 brief. Indeed, Plaintiff does not address the due process
17 argument at all apart from a conclusory assertion that it was
18 not given a, quote, fair opportunity to be heard, end quote,
19 prior to liquidation. That's at page 2 of Plaintiff's memo --
20 memorandum.
21   It's -- you know, it's proper for the Court to treat
22 that argument as conceded. And in that regard, the Court
23 relies on Sewell, S-e-w-e-double l, versus Chao at 532 F.
24 Supp. 2d 126.
25   For all those reasons, the court discharges this

1 order to show cause and dismisses this action. I'll issue an
2 appropriate written order dismissing this case.
3   Anything further?
4   MR. HAYNES: No, Your Honor.
5   MR. BYNUM: Just one thing, Your Honor.
6   THE COURT: Sure.
7   MR. BYNUM: Thank you for the time that the Court
8 took to deal with this matter, but other than noting our
9 objection for the record, we have nothing else, Your Honor.
10   THE COURT: All right.
11   MR. HAYNES: Your Honor, I misspoke actually.
12 There's an issue that we're not sure if you're the right court
13 to deal with it or whether we've got to go down in Texas. The
14 Credit Union --
15   THE COURT: Texas.
16   MR. HAYNES: Okay.
17   (LAUGHTER.)
18   THE COURT: No, no, just playing.
19   MR. HAYNES: There's an issue about whether we've
20 got all of the records, but this is something maybe we can
21 talk with counsel and work out.
22   THE COURT: I'm sorry, whether you have all the
23 records?
24   MR. HAYNES: Yeah. There's some missing records.
25 There's a list of them that we can give to Mr. Bynum.

APPENDIX J

29

```
 1         THE COURT:  What's the impact of that on what the
 2  Court just did?
 3         MR. HAYNES:  Nothing, Your Honor.  It's just --
 4         THE COURT:  All right.
 5         MR. HAYNES:  Somewhere we've got to get a judge to
 6  say, "Give them all of this material."
 7         THE COURT:  All right.  If indeed this is the proper
 8  court, I'll be happy to accommodate the parties.  If not, I
 9  hate to send you to Texas to get that relief, I mean, but if
10  it's not appropriate for this court to take action, I won't do
11  it, but just let me know.  I mean, speak with Plaintiff.
12         MR. HAYNES:  Will do, Your Honor.
13         THE COURT:  Well, I'm not going to guess about
14  whether I have the authority or not.  I'm not quite sure I
15  understand.
16         MR. HAYNES:  Well, I don't know who has the
17  authority either, but I think you would have to do it as a
18  miscellaneous.
19         THE COURT:  Your question is whether or not the
20  Credit -- whether or not the Government has all of the proper
21  records?
22         MR. HAYNES:  Yes, Your Honor.
23         THE COURT:  The proper records in what regard?
24         MR. HAYNES:  Well, there are a list -- it goes on
25  pretty lengthy, including things like the tax records for all
```

30

```
 1  years, contracts and correspondence from vendors, credit -- I
 2  mean, it goes on and on, original bank statements from Wells
 3  Fargo, Capital One and Southwest --
 4         THE COURT:  Are these records that a credit union
 5  has to submit on an annual basis pursuant to some sort of
 6  audit process or something?
 7         MR. HAYNES:  I think they're supposed to keep them,
 8  Your Honor, but maybe Mr. Bynum -- they should have --
 9  Apparently, Your Honor, I'm told by Mr. Frank that these
10  records should have been turned over lock, stock and barrel
11  when we liquidated, but there is an issue as to --
12         THE COURT:  All right.  These records arise -- All
13  right.  These records, there was an obligation on the part of
14  the institution to turn the records over as part of a
15  liquidation order.  The liquidation order, did it order the
16  institution to do that?
17         MR. HAYNES:  I'm sure it did, Your Honor.  I don't
18  actually recall, but I'm sure.
19         THE COURT:  I don't whether I have the authority to
20  do that.  I'm sitting really as a -- I'm reviewing the record
21  in this case.  This is an APA case.  It may be related.  I
22  don't know.  I'll leave it to counsel to work it out.
23         MR. HAYNES:  I don't know.
24         THE COURT:  It may be part and parcel of my scope of
25  review, and again, if I have the authority, let me know,
```

1 Counsel. I just don't know off the top of my head whether I
2 have the authority or not, but arguably, I probably do, but
3 see if you can work it out; otherwise, you may have to file
4 some petition in another court. All right. Thank you. The
5 parties are excused. Thank you.
6   MR. HAYNES: Thank you, Your Honor.
7   THE DEPUTY CLERK: This honorable court now stands
8 in recess.
9   (PROCEEDINGS END AT 11:43 A.M.)
10   *-*-*-*

CERTIFICATE OF REPORTER

13   I, Catalina Kerr, certify that the foregoing is a
14 correct transcript from the record of proceedings in the
15 above-entitled matter.

_____
Catalina Kerr   Date

Appendix K
KAPFCU MOTION FOR RECONSIDERATION

APPENDIX K

UNITED STATES DISTRICT COURT
FOR THE DISTRICT OF COLUMBIA

KAPPA ALPHA PSI FEDERAL
CREDIT UNION

    Plaintiff

-vs-   Civil Action No. 10-01321 EGS

NATIONAL CREDIT UNION
ADMINISTRATION

    Defendant

MOTION FOR RECONSIDERATION

COMES NOW BEFORE THE COURT, Kappa Alpha Federal Credit Union ("KAPPCU") by counsel to file this Motion For Reconsideration because we contend it is reversible error as a matter of law to sustain the liquidation order while KAPPCU was operating under and in compliance with NCUA approved Revised Business and Net Worth Restoration Plans.

Ultimately, the liquidation was based on the NCUA determination that *"KAPPCU was Minimally Capitalized with no reasonable chance to reach Adequate Capitalization within 10 years."* However, in the August 3, 2010 closed board meeting, NCUA board members acknowledged that KAPPCU was operating under a NCUA approved Revised Business Plan and Net Worth Restoration Plan. *See NCUA Closed Hearing Transcript.*

ARGUMENT 1. IT IS IMPROPER AND ERRONEOUS TO LIQUIDATE KAPPCU WHILE IT IS IN COMPLIANCE WITH AND OPERATING UNDER NCUA APPROVED REVISED BUSINESS PLANS AND NET WORTH RESTORATION PLANS.

KAPPCU submitted a Revised Business Plan and Net Worth Restoration Plan pursuant to §702.206 on May 28, 2010. NCUA acknowledged receipt but failed to respond within the statutory time period, consequently the Net Worth Restoration Plan was approved on July 12, 2010.

§702.206 (f) *Review of NWRP*— (1) *Notice of decision.* Within 45 calendar days after receiving an NWRP under this part, the NCUA Board shall notify the credit union in writing whether the NWRP has been approved, and shall provide reasons for its decision in the event of disapproval.
(2) *Delayed decision.* If no decision is made within the time prescribed in paragraph (f)(1) of this section, the NWRP is deemed approved.

By definition, an approved NWRP is likely to succeed in restoring the credit union's net worth and outlines the steps the credit union will take to increase its net worth ratio so that it becomes "adequately capitalized" by the end of the term of the NWRP. Therefore, it is legally inconsistent —*if not legally impossible*— for NCUA to argue that KAPPCU had No reasonable prospect to achieve adequate capitalization when NCUA acknowledged that KAPPCU was operating under NCUA approved Revised Business and Net Worth Restoration Plans (NWRP).

§702.206 (d) *Criteria for approval of NWRP*. The NCUA Board shall not accept a NWRP plan unless it — (1) Complies with paragraph (c) of this section; (2) Is based on realistic assumptions, and **is likely to succeed in restoring the credit union's net worth**; and

§702.206 (e) *Contents of NWRP*. An NWRP must —
(1) Specify — (i) A quarterly timetable of steps the credit union will take to increase its net worth ratio so that it **becomes "adequately capitalized" by the end of the term of the NWRP**, and to remain so for four (4) consecutive calendar quarters.

Assuming for the sake of argument that the NCUA did in fact approve the KAPFCU Net Worth Restoration Plan in error; the tacitly approved NWRP was still in full effect until notification by the NCUA of the error. At which point KAPFCU should have been allowed to submit a new or revised NWRP within 30 calendar days of receiving such notice, unless the NCUA Board notified the credit union in writing that the NWRP was to be filed within a different time frame.

§702.206 (a)(3) *Filing of additional plan*. Notwithstanding paragraph (a)(1) of this section, **a credit union that has already submitted and is operating under a NWRP approved under this section is not required to submit an additional NWRP due to a change in net worth category** (including by reclassification under §702.102(b)), unless **the NCUA Board notifies the credit union that it must submit a new NWRP**. A credit union that is notified to submit a new or revised NWRP shall file the NWRP in writing with the appropriate Regional Director within 30 calendar days of receiving such notice, unless the NCUA Board notifies the credit union in writing that the NWRP is to be filed within a different period.

Net Worth Restoration Plans are subject to quarterly review. Consequently, since KAPFCU's Net Worth Restoration was tacitly approved on July 12, 2010 KAPFCU should have been afforded at least until the September 31, 2010 examination contact to prove its compliance with the approved NWRP.

ARGUMENT 2. KAPFCU WOULD HAVE EXCEEDED THE NET WORTH RESTORATION PLAN GOALS AND ACHIEVED "ADEQUATE CAPITALIZATION" BEFORE THE END OF THE QUARTER.

But For the NCUA's premature and improper liquidation on August 3, 2010 KAPFCU would have received $100,000 Technical Assistance award from the U.S. Department of Treasury CDFI Fund on August 17, 2010. As a result, KAPFCU would have immediately increased its NWR to 14.6% under the Modified Cash Basis of Accounting.[1] *See CPA Opinion Letter*.

Even if we were to concede the outstanding balance of the disputed data processing contract; KAPFCU would have remained *"adequately capitalized"* because the T/A adjusted Net Worth Ratio would still exceed 11.4% Thus, contrary to NCUA assertions, KAPFCU would have achieved *"adequate capitalization"* by the end of the quarter and would not have been subject to liquidation or further prompt corrective action.

CONCLUSION

In closing we contend that it is reversible error for the court to sustain NCUA's assertion that KAPFCU had No

---

[1] The NCUA incorrectly argues that the $100,000 T/A Award would not positively impact KAPFCU's overall NWR because of the offsetting Grant Liability. This assertion would be correct under Full GAAP Accrual Accounting, however, it is incorrect under the Modified Cash Basis.

reasonable prospect of reaching adequate capitalization when KAPFCU was operating under and in compliance with a NCUA approved Net Worth Restoration Plan and would have achieved *"adequate capitalization"* by the end of the month. To hold otherwise would raise significant due process and equal protection concerns.

Appendix L

U.S. TREASURY DEPARTMENT CDFI DEBRIEF REPORT

APPENDIX L   359

CDFI Program Application Debriefing

Organization Name: Kappa Alpha Psi Federal Credit Union
Control Number: 101TA008799

The Application Review Process

After an Application is submitted, the CDFI Fund determines whether it meets basic eligibility requirements. If the Application is found to be eligible, it receives a two-part substantive review in accordance with the criteria and procedures described in the Notice of Funding Availability (NOFA) and the Combined Application.

The CDFI Fund usually rejects or declines an Application at one of three phases. First, at the Application deadline phase, the CDFI Fund will reject an Application if it is received late. Second, at the completeness and eligibility review phase, the CDFI Fund will reject an Application received on time - if it is found to be incomplete or ineligible. The CDFI Fund will notify an Applicant declined for one or both of these reasons via email usually within two months of the Application deadline. Third, at the Application review stage, the CDFI Fund may decline an Applicant that satisfies the eligibility and completeness requirements for score resulting from a poorly presented Comprehensive Business Plan). The CDFI Fund will notify an Applicant declined for substantive reasons after awards are announced.

The FY 2010 CDFI Program application review process required three reviewers to independently review and evaluate each Financial Assistance application. The reviewers were private/non-profit sector professionals with strong credentials in community development finance and federal agency staff working in other community development finance programs. Reviewers were required to evaluate and score each application independently from the other reviewers who were scoring the same application.

The following five sections in the application were scored:

1. Market Analysis;
2. Business Strategy;
3. Community Development Performance and Effective Use;
4. Management; and
5. Financial Health and Viability.

Within each of these sections, reviewers evaluated the responses to specific questions, and provided an overall section score with the following range: Weak (0-5 points); Limited (6-10 points); Average (11-15 points); Good (16-20 points); and Excellent (21-25 points). An Applicant must receive a minimum score in each section to be considered for an award.

The CDFI Fund made award selections based on the rank order of Applicants by their scores and the amount of funds available. TA-only Applicants, Category I/ SECA and Category II/Core Applicants were ranked separately. In addition, the CDFI Fund considered the institutional and geographic diversity of Applicants when making its funding decisions.

Scoring Range of Your Application

The *Combined Application for Financial Assistance and/or Technical Assistance* provides the most extensive information on how to prepare a submission for CDFI Program assistance. The technical guidance in the application included specific questions that reviewers were instructed to score. All questions raised in the application should have been addressed in the Comprehensive Business Plan.

Please refer to the application for more information. It is available on the CDFI Fund website at: <http://www.cdfifund.gov/what_we_do/programs_id.asp?programID=7>

Additionally, please bear in mind that since the number of qualified Applications exceeded the available CDFI Program funding, many Applicants scoring in the "good" and even "excellent" range did not receive an award due, in large, to the CDFI Fund's limited funding.

A. Market Analysis:

The overall section score range for Kappa Alpha Psi Federal Credit Union in Market Analysis was: Good.

B. Business Strategy:

The overall section score range for Kappa Alpha Psi Federal Credit Union in Business Strategy was: Good.

C. Community Development Performance and Effective Use of Funds:

The overall section score range for Kappa Alpha Psi Federal Credit Union in Community Development Performance and Effective Use was: Average.

D. Management:

The overall section score range for Kappa Alpha Psi Federal Credit Union in Management was: Good.

E. Financial Health and Viability:

The overall section score range for Kappa Alpha Psi Federal Credit Union in Financial Health and Viability was: Limited.

Thank you for your application!

Index

Note: Page numbers in *italics* refer to illustration, and those followed by "n" refer to notes.

#

9/11, 130, 133, 147–48

– A –

AACUC. *See* African American Credit Union Coalition
accounting, cash-basis, 103n40, 178, 182, 186
   See also modified cash-basis accounting
accrual accounting, 87–88, 103n40, 177, 179–81, 186, 202, 279
ACORN, 166
adequate capitalization, 200–201. *See also* Kappa Alpha Psi Federal Credit Union (KAPFCU)
Adeyemo, Wally, 249
African American Alliance, 265
African American Credit Union Coalition (AACUC), 143–44, 167, 263
   Anchor Award to, 263
   Hall of Fame, 163–66, 207–9, 277–79
   virtual webinars, 263
African Americans. *See* Black community (credit unions/financial institutions)
ageism, 145–46
AIM. *See* American Indian Movement
AKA. *See* Alpha Kappa Alpha (AKA)
Alayon, Adolfo ("Al"), 31, 32–34
Allison, Herbert, 158
Alphabet City, 109
Alpha Kappa Alpha (AKA), 266–67
American Indian Movement (AIM), 18–19
American Indians for Development, 18
Americans for Financial Reform, 235
Analysis of the Role of Credit Unions in Capital Formation and Investment in Low- and Moderate-Income Communities, An, 99
Angelou, Maya, 142–43
Annie E. Casey Foundation, 233
anti-poverty programs, 24
anti-Semitism, 6
anti-war movement, 11
ASI FCU, 149n53
Atlanta Journal-Constitution, 60, 267
Atwell, Clyde, 53

– B –

Bank of America, 265
bank regulators, 260
Banks, Carl, 175
Banks, Dennis, 18
Barnett, Karey, 189
Barry, Marion, 25
"Bill" (farmworker coalition's executive director), 26, 27
Black Caribbean immigrants, 53
Black community (credit unions/financial institutions), 53–54
   CDFI Fund and, 68–71
   churches, 112–16
   leaders/leadership, 143–44
   See also communities of color; low-income credit unions; National Federation of Community Development Credit Unions (Federation)
Black Economic Development Initiative, 251
Black Lives Matter, 4, 47, 116, 136, 243, 244, 250–51, 261, 264, 268
Black Panthers, 12, 13–14
Black Renaissance Fund, 265
Blouch, Ron, 193
Blue Hills Food Co-op, 16
Bricks Community Federal Credit Union, 126
Brown, Wilmette, 8n2
Brown v. Board of Education of Topeka, 347 U.S. 483 (1954), 198n62
Bugg-Levine, Antony, 264n103
Bureau of Federal Credit Unions, 37–38, 81.
   See also National Credit Union Administration (NCUA)
Burkhart, Elizabeth Flores, 98
Burnett, Kenny, 183

Burnett, Kevin, 189–90
Bush, George H. W. (Bush Administration), 94, 100
   presidential campaign of 1988, 98
Bush, George W. (Bush administration), 77n28
Bynum, Ken, 198, 203–4, 210, 212, 220, 221, 225
Bynum, William "Bill," 79, 166, 277

– C –

CABS. *See* Community Action for Bedford-Stuyvesant
CAMEL score/rating, 86, 180–81
   of KAPFCU, 88, 177, 178, 181, 200
Camus, Albert
   Stranger, The, 9
Capitalization Committee, 126, 138, 143
CARE Program (Credit Abuse Resistance Education), 121n48
Carter, Jimmy (Carter Administration), 24, 25, 40, 41
casework, 91
cash-basis accounting, 103n40, 178, 182, 186. *See also* accounting; modified cash-basis accounting
Castile, Philando, 257n94
Castillo, Leonel, 23
Catholic women's orders, 44
CDC. *See* Community Development Corporations
CDCI. *See* Community Development Capital Initiative
CDCU. *See* community development credit unions
CDFI. *See* Community Development Financial Institutions
CDFI Coalition, 49, 51, 66, 69, 71, 72, 74, 79, 264
Ceballos, Juan E. Fernández, 59n22, 261
Center for Farm and Food Policy, 17
Central Brooklyn FCU, 75
Central Intelligence Agency (CIA), 13
CFBP. *See* Consumer Financial Protection Bureau
Chasen, Simon, 8n2
Chavez, Cesar, 24, 25
Chisholm, Shirley, 32
Church Connections, 114
civil rights, 11, 65, 66
Clark, Jamar, 257n94

Clark, Jim, 30, 33–34, 42
Clark, Mark, 13
Clinton, Bill (Clinton Administration), 3, 50–51, 60, 65, 68, 72, 73, 77, 78, 101, 166, 215, 244
Clinton Place Junior High School, 6–7
collective bargaining, 5
collective self-help, 3
"Color of Money, The" *(Atlanta Journal-Constitution),* 60
Columbia University in New York City, 8–9, 12, 109
   student strike of 1968, 14
communities of color, 111, 136, 140, 141, 142, 151
   automation in banking and, 48, 82, 93
   CDCUs and, 26, 56, 103
   CDFI Fund, 74–75, 78, 248, 264, 268
   DEI (*See* DEI (Diversity, Equity, and Inclusion))
   discrimination against, 93
   Great Recession and, 234
   large credit unions and, 61
   loan funds and, 71
   MDIs and (*See* Minority Depository Institutions (MDI))
   redlining and, 60
   resource-poor credit unions and, 63
   victimization of, 154, 155
   See also Black community (credit unions/financial institutions)
Community Action Agencies (CAAs), 37, 67, 112
Community Action for Bedford-Stuyvesant (CABS), 31, 32
community-controlled capital, 243
Community Development Capital Initiative (CDCI), 153–54, 155, 156–59, 234
Community Development Central, 56, 99
Community Development Corporations (CDC), 67
community development credit unions (CDCU), 3, 26, 56
   being different from other credit unions, 83–85
   investments in, 57
   loan delinquency, 83
   as nonprofit cooperatives, 52
   See also credit union(s); Kappa Alpha Psi Federal Credit Union (KAPFCU); National Federation of Commu-

INDEX 363

nity Development Credit
    Unions (Federation)
Community Development Financial
    Institutions (CDFI) Fund, 3, 43,
    65–80, 144–45, 268
  application process, 74
  Black financial institutions and, 68–71
  certified institutions, 254–55, 268
  community development and, 66–68
  disability community and, 120, 266
  establishment, 49, 74
  Evelyne's confrontation with, 76–78
  financial ecosystem and, 268
  first round of awards, 75–76, 144
  growth and success of, 268
  impact investor, 251
  institutions claiming, 268
  as law, 72–73, 75
  leadership, 65, 71, 77
  legislative process, 71–72
  New York State, 49–50
  origins of, 65–66
  policy change, 78–79
  SECA program, 79, 80, 247
Community Development Partners, 150–51
Community Development Revolving Loan
    Program, 33
Community Housing Development Organizations (CHDO), 67
Community Reinvestment Act (CRA), 57,
    60–61, 73, 115
Community Services Administration (CSA),
    24, 54–55
compassionate conservatism, 98–99
Congress of Racial Equality (CORE), 66
Consumer Financial Protection Bureau
    (CFPB), 235–42
Cooper, Robert, 212
Cooperative Economics Alliance of New
    York City (CEANYC), 235
co-op organizer, 15–16
Cordray, Richard, 236, 242
CORE. *See* Congress of Racial Equality
corporate credit unions, 169, 185–87
corporate stabilization, 88, 170, 186–87, 270
COVID-19 pandemic, 4, 69, 243, 248, 268
CRA. *See* Community Reinvestment Act
Crear, Pete, 58–59
credit union(s)
  accounting and financial reporting, 82
  bank-like services, 56, 106
  Black community and churches, 53–54,
    112–16

  capital crisis, 39–40
  concept, 26
  conditions affecting, 104–5
  corporate credit unions, 169, 185–87
  CRA regulations and, 60–61
  disability outreach, 118–20
  examiners and, 85–90
  history, 26
  Latinx, 116–18
  leaders/leadership, 143–44
  as limited income, 82
  loan delinquency, 83, 92, 104, 221
  loss of, 89–90, 92–93
  mainstream, 83
  MDIs (*See* Minority Depository Institutions)
  mergers, 90–91
  mission conversion, 255
  natural-person, 212–13
  organizers, 52–53
  overaggressive examiners and, 229
  prompt corrective action, 102–4, 168
  as pure cooperatives, 81
  safety and soundness assessment, 82
  vulnerabilities, 92
  as working-class movement, 53
  youth and, 120–21
  See also Kappa Alpha Psi Federal Credit
    Union (KAPFCU); National Federation of Community Development Credit
    Unions (Federation)
Credit Union Membership Access Act, 101
Credit Union National Association
    (CUNA), 55–64, 124, 214, 261
  battle fatigue, 54
  cardinal rule of political representation,
    60
  cooperative agreement with, 57–58
  crisis (business lines failure), 62
  Diekmann on, 55
  as dues-paying statewide associations, 55
  financial support, 58, 62
  Governmental Affairs Conference,
    62–64, 258–59
  location/headquarters, 55, 58
  Mutual Group, 261
  structure, 55
  taxation and, 57, 60
  termination of Lewis, 262
  War on Poverty and, 54, 56
Credit Union Times, 234, 262
Culture, Diversity, and Inclusion Council

(NCUA), 256
CUNA. *See* Credit Union National Association
Cunningham, William Michael, 267

– D –

data processing contract, 178, 182, 195
Date, Raj, 236
Davis, Milton, 65, 66
Davy, Monica, 253–54
DeFilippi, Pablo, 118
DEI (Diversity, Equity, and Inclusion), 243–44
    NCUA staffing and, 256–58
    as watchword of credit unions, 261
Del Rio, Deyanira, 116
Democratizing Finance (Rosenthal), 52n18, 242
deposit insurance
    qualifying for, 81–82
    solvency of, 86
Diekmann, Frank J., 55
disability outreach, 118–20
"Diversity, Equity, and Inclusion Summit" (NCUA), 256
Divine Nine organizations, 266
Dodd-Frank Wall Street Reform and Consumer Protection Act, 239, 252, 253, 256
Donovan, Annie, 80
Doughton, Morgan, 98–99
due process, 168, 212–17
    banks *vs.* natural-person credit unions, 212–13
    KAPFCU *vs.* NCUA, 214–17
    procedural, 213
    substantive, 213

– E –

Eakes, Martin, 78
eligible geographies, 248
Ellis, Steve, 185
embezzlement, 94, 95n37, 96, 132, 141
Emergency Capital Investment Program (ECIP), 244, 245–46
"Empowering Low-Income and Economically Vulnerable Consumers" (CFPB conference), 241
Empowerment Zones and Enterprise Communities Program, 166
Engel, Barbara, 14
Episcopal Community Federal Credit Union, 112
Episcopal Relief and Development, 112
Equitable Recovery Program (ERP), 247–50
    guidelines for, 249
Esteban, Ignacio, 116
Evelyne (Federation's board chairman), 59, 60, 61, 62n24, 76, 78, 124–33
examiners (NCUA), 85–90, 172–82
    supervisory letters and guidance to, 104–6
    See also Kappa Alpha Psi Federal Credit Union (KAPFCU); liquidation of KAPFCU (NCUA's arbitrary and capricious action/decision)
explicit bias, 93. *See also* implicit bias

– F –

faith-based credit unions, 113–16
Faith Community United Credit Union, Cleveland, 115
Faithful Stewardship, 114
farmworker coalition, 23–26
Fauntroy, Walter, 166
FDIC. *See* Federal Deposit Insurance Corporation (FDIC)
Federal Bureau of Investigations (FBI), 13
    COINTELPRO operation, 13–14
Federal Credit Union Act, 81, 170, 209
Federal Deposit Insurance Corporation (FDIC), 81, 260, 260n97
Federal Housing Administration, 93
feminism, 15
Filson, Charles "Chip," 91–92, 206, 269
Financial Institutions Reform, Recovery, and Enforcement Act (FIRREA), 68, 255
    Section 308, 68, 252
First Nations Development Institute, 264
Flake, Floyd, 113, 115
Fletcher, James, 65–66
Floyd, George, 244, 250, 263
Foley, Lee, 42
food co-op, 15–21, 23, 24, 30, 110
Food Stamps, 24
Ford, Gerald, 94
Ford Foundation, 44, 45, 100, 113, 151, 235
Foxwoods Casino and Resort, 21

Frank, Damon, 203
Franklin Community Federal Credit Union scandal of 1988, 94–95, 97
full accrual accounting. *See* accrual accounting
full faith and credit, 89n35

– G –

Gambrell, Donna, 182, 182n57, 223–24, 265n104
Gately, Brian, 182–83, 223, 224–28
Geithner, Timothy, 156
G.I. Bill, 5
Gilliam, James, 137
Godfrey-Smith, Helen, 207–9
    Gately's email to, 226–27
Golden Hill Paugussetts, 19, 20
Government Accounting Office (GAO), 38
Governmental Affairs Conference (GAC), 62–64, 258–59. *See also* Credit Union National Association (CUNA)
Grameen Bank in Bangladesh, 65
Great Recession, 153, 154, 155–56, 234, 251–52, 264
Great Russian Encyclopedia, 15
Grzywinski, Ron, 65

– H –

Hammerman, Charlie, 120
Hampton, Fred, 13
Harper, Todd M., 43n15, 258–59, 267, 277–79
Harrington, Michael, 37
Harris, Jodie, 249
Harris, Kamala, 249
Hartnett, Johnette, 119
Hauptman, Kyle S., 257–58
Haynes, Fred, 203, 204, 209–10
Haynes, Rita, 53–54, 115–16
Hayward, Richard "Skip," 21
Henderson, Kenny, 184, 189
Hoover, J. Edgar, 10, 12
    on Black Panthers, 14
Hope Community Federal Credit Union, 166, 209–10
Hope Credit Union, 251
Hope Enterprise Corporation, 166
Houghton, Mary, 65

Hurricane Katrina, 148–49, 158
Hurricane Maria, 118n47, 247

– I –

implicit bias, 93. *See also* explicit bias
Inclusiv, 121–22. *See also* National Federation of Community Development Credit Unions (Federation)
Indigenous people, 18–20, 22
Individual Tax Information Numbers (ITIN), 118
International Year of the Cooperative, 234
Ito, Lucy, 261n99

– J –

Jackson, Jesse, 130–31, 214–15
Jackson, Robert, 100–101, 101n38
Jepsen, Roger, 95
John D. and Catherine T. MacArthur Foundation, 45, 149
Johnson, Earnest, 62n24
Johnson, Eddie Bernice, 165, 197–98
Johnson, Lyndon, 11, 37
Julius Thompson PLLC, 171, 184

– K –

KAPFCU. *See* Kappa Alpha Psi Federal Credit Union (KAPFCU)
KAPFCU v. NCUA (court case and hearing), 203–6, 211–12
    due process rights, 214–16
    final judgement, 217–18
    missed opportunities for KAPFCU, 219
Kappa Alpha Psi Federal Credit Union (KAPFCU), 258, 269–79
    achievements, 191
    administrative costs, 84–85
    auto financing, 85
    call report, 205, 207
    CAMEL score/rating of, 88, 177, 178, 181, 200
    CARE Program, 121n48
    CDFI denying grant to, 153
    CDFI Fund certification and award, 167, 182, 223–27

compliance and operational improvement, 199
corporate stabilization assessment, 88, 170, 185, 186–87, 270
data processing contract, 178, 182, 195
deterioration of capital base, 88
emergency funds, 167
extra reserves (arrears), 174–75
federal deposit insurance fund, 169
foundation of, 69, 163–65
Hope Community FCU and, 209–10
legal challenge, 269
liquidation of, by NCUA (*See* liquidation of KAPFCU (NCUA's arbitrary and capricious action/decision))
loans, 84–85, 169, 221, 270
as moderately capitalized, 194–96
modified cash-basis accounting, 178, 178n55, 179–81, 186, *186*, 201, 202, 271–72
net worth ratio (NWR), 168–69, 170, 201, 202, 207, 270
office expenses, 183–84
performance on a "modified cash basis," *271*
portfolio risk, 85
purpose of, 70–71
record-keeping deficiencies, 87–88, 177, 279
Revised Business Plan (RBP) compliance, 169, 186
secondary capital plan (equity-like debt), 175–76
second-chance credit, 167
telephonic board meeting for, 189–90
as virtual credit union, 69, 83, 266
youth outreach, 121n48
zero-default rate, 190
See also Russell, Victor
Kappa Alpha Psi (fraternity), 69, 121n48
central tenets of, 185
Ken (Federation's board chairman), 58, 124–25
Kennedy, John F., 10
Kennedy, Robert F., 12
Kennedy, Ted, 25
King, Lawrence, 94–96, 97, 141
embezzlement charges, 94, 95n37, 96
sexual abuse of children, 95
King, Martin Luther, Jr., 10, 243, 272–73
assassination, 12
"Beyond Vietnam" speech, 11
Operation Breadbasket, 214n71

King, Rodney, 112
Kutchey, John, 188

– L –

Lamb-Richmond, Trudie, 18n8
Latino Community Credit Union (Cooperativa Latino), 117
Latinx credit unions, 116–18, 142. *See also* credit union(s); low-income credit unions
Lawyers Alliance of New York, 157
Lawyers' Committee for Civil Rights Under Law, 96
Letter of Understanding and Agreement (LUA), 88
KAPFCU's compliance with, 178, 183, 195, 199
Lewis, Robert, Jr., 262
Libby, Margaret, 121
Lingenfelter, Paul, 45
liquidation of KAPFCU (NCUA's arbitrary and capricious action/decision), 170, 222–23, 269–79
assessment/examination prior to, 172–82
basis/reasons for, 168–69, 207
being improper, 194–96
board (NCUA) voting for, 192–94
court case challenging (*See* KAPFCU v. NCUA (court case and hearing))
GAAP record-keeping discrepancies, 177, 178
as malicious and intentional effort, 196–200
merger with Hope Community FCU to avoid, 209–10
race card (discrimination) perspective, 220–21
in rush to judgment, 200–202
secondary capital plan and, 175–76
loan delinquency, 83, 92, 104, 221
Long, Lenwood V. Sr., 265n104
Louis, Errol, 36, 36n12, 100
Lower East Side People's Federal Credit Union, 110–11
low-income communities, 26, 48, 75. *See also* communities of color; credit union(s)
low-income credit unions, 83–84
"20% rule" and, 96–97

capital crisis, 39–40
CDCU Revolving Loan Fund and, 42
CDFI Fund (*See* Community Development Financial Institutions (CDFI) Fund)
corporate credit unions *vs.*, 187
discrimination against, 96
GAO study, 38
loan delinquency, 83
NCUA and (*See* National Credit Union Administration)
secondary capital, 156–57
See also Kappa Alpha Psi Federal Credit Union (KAPFCU)
Lynn, Richard, 184–85

– M –

Maddox, Richard, 219
Mahon, Cathie, 121, 239
Malcolm X, 10, 10n3
Mandela, Nelson, 264n103
Manuel (Navajo man), 19–20
Manufacturers Hanover Trust, 109–10
March on Washington for Jobs and Freedom, 9–10
Martinez, Kathy, 119
Mashantucket Pequot Museum and Research Center, 21
Matz, Debbie, 188, 192, 197, 198, 210, 228
Maxwell, Dora, 110, 110n44
McKechnie, John, 216
McWatters, J. Mark, 257
MDI. *See* Minority Depository Institutions
Means, Russell, 18
mergers and liquidations of credit unions, 90–91, 100, 149–50. *See also* liquidation of KAPFCU (NCUA's arbitrary and capricious action/decision)
Milton, Lynda, 115–16, 236
Minnesota Credit Union Foundation, 262
Minority Depository Institution Preservation Program (NCUA), 253
Minority Depository Institutions (MDI), 67, 244, 245, 248, 250, 250n87, 252–55, 259, 260, 260n57, 278–79
Mission-Driven Bank Fund, 260
modified cash-basis accounting, 87n34, 178, 178n55, 179–81, 186, *186,* 201, 202, 271–72
Morris, Michael, 119
Morrisey, Dan, 188
Morton, Keith, 193
Mosley, Walter, 174
Muhammad, Elijah, 124
Myers-Briggs personality inventory, 135–36
MyPath, 121

– N –

Nader, Ralph, 130
NAFO, 26, 27
NALCAB. *See* National Association of Latino Community Asset Builders (NALCAB)
National Association of Community Development Loan Funds, 50
National Association of Latino Community Asset Builders (NALCAB), 265–66
National Bankers Association (NBA), 68–69, 260
National Credit Union Administration (NCUA), 35, 251–53
   "20% rule," 95–97
   CDRLF grants, 43n15
   corporate stabilization, 88, 169, 186–87, 228, 270
   "CRA-lite" regulation, 61
   Culture, Diversity, and Inclusion Council, 256
   DEI and cultural change, 256–58
   "Diversity, Equity, and Inclusion Summit," 256
   Dodd-Frank provisions and, 256
   Evelyne's response to, 126–27
   Filson on, 91–92
   KAPFCU and (*See* Kappa Alpha Psi Federal Credit Union (KAPFCU))
   LUA (*See* Letter of Understanding and Agreement (LUA))
   MDIs and (*See* Minority Depository Institutions)
   Office of Minority and Women Inclusion (OMWI), 252
   peer statistics (as a tool), 82–83
   policy and cultural changes, 258–59
   rating system, 82
   Rules and Regulation, 87n34
   secondary capital regulations and, 157

small credit unions and, 187–88
supervisory letters and guidance, 104–6, 169, 258
National Credit Union Foundation, 62
National Credit Union Share Insurance Fund (NCUSIF), 81, 88–89, 211
National Disability Finance Coalition (disability-finance.org), 266
National Disability Institute (NDI), 119–20
National Economic Development and Law Center, 111
National Federation of Community Development Credit Unions (Federation), 3, 29–33
  as an intermediary, 144–45
  Black community and churches, 53–54, 112–16
  Capitalization Committee, 126, 138, 143
  Capitalization Program, 36, 44, 46, 47, 126, 144
  as 501(c)(3) charity, 126
  Community Development Partners, 150–51
  conflicts (board/staff relations, Evelyne's conflict of interest), 125–32
  CUNA and (*See* Credit Union National Association (CUNA))
  description, 107
  disability outreach, 118–20
  election for board chairman, 124–25
  external crises, 4
  funding, 33, 34
  governance crisis, 3–4
  Latinx population and, 116–18
  membership, 122, 149–51
  national conferences, 31
  organizing new credit unions, 108–12
  real estate project, 123–24
  rebranding (name change) of, 121–22 (*See also* Inclusiv)
  staff, 31–32
  strategies, 107–22
  succession process, 233
  survival plan, 33–34
  Twenty-Fifth Anniversary Conference, 130–31
  youth and, 120–21
Nation of Islam, 10, 124, 130
Native CDFI Network, 264–65
natural-person credit unions, 212–13
Navajos, 19–20
NCUA. *See* National Credit Union Administration (NCUA)
NCUSIF. *See* National Credit Union Share Insurance Fund
Neighborhood Banking Corporation, 50
Netflix, 251
net worth ratio (NWR), 168–69, 170, 201, 202, 207, 270. *See also* Kappa Alpha Psi Federal Credit Union (KAPFCU)
Newark, New Jersey, 5
New England Federation of Cooperatives, 17
New Left, 13
New Markets Tax Credit (NMTC), 72, 80, 152
Newton, Huey, 13
New York State Corporation for Community Banking, 49
New York State Credit Union Association, 237
New York Times, The, 263
Nixon, Richard, 6
No FEAR. *See* Notification and Federal Employee Anti-discrimination and Retaliation Act of 2002
No FEAR Institute, 166
Nonprofit Finance Fund (NFF), 264
North Carolina Minority Support Center, 126–27
Notice of Funds Availability (NOFA), 248
Notification and Federal Employee Anti-discrimination and Retaliation Act of 2002 (No FEAR), 166–67
Nussle, Jim, 262

– O –

Obama, Barack (Obama Administration), 15, 152–53. *See also* Community Development Capital Initiative (CDCI)
OCS. *See* Office of Community Services
OEO. *See* Office of Economic Opportunity
Office of Community Services (OCS), 42
Office of Economic Opportunity (OEO), 24, 38, 39, 41–42, 66
Office of Financial Empowerment, 4, 235
Office of Management and Budget (OMB), 41

Olamina Fund, 251
Omega Psi Phi, 267
Operation Breadbasket, 214n71
Operation Grassroots, 57
Operation Moneywise, 35, 38
Opportunity Finance Network (OFN), 251
Other America, The (Harrington), 37
Oweesta Fund, 264
Owens, Pam, 119, 237

– P –

Panther 21, 14
Paragon Association, 53
Pastor, Luis, 117
"Paul," 63–64
Paycheck Protection Program (PPP) loans, 251
PCA. *See* Prompt Corrective Action (PCA)
Penaluna, Carolyn, 176–77, 178, 193, 208–9
Perlitsh, Stuart, 275–76
Pete Crear Lifetime Achievement Award, 166
Phariss, Cory, 193–94, 203, 204, 221
Phi Beta Sigma, 267
Phillip (board member of the Federation), 131
Pierce, Samuel, 94
Plan 50%+ (NFF), 264
Plot Against America, The (Roth), 6
"Political Influence and TARP Investments in Credit Unions", 159
Ponzi scheme, 95
Powell, Armistice, 31–32
powwows, 19
procedural due process, 213
program-related investments (PRIs), 44
Prompt Corrective Action (PCA), 102, 104, 168, 175, 177, 183

– R –

racism/racial discrimination, 9, 12, 60, 76, 87–88, 91–93, 97, 127, 142, 220–21, 256, 262
  ageism and, 145–46
Rainbow PUSH Coalition, 214n71
Rapid Response Program (RRP), 244, 246–47
Ratigan, Terry, 159

Rausch, Tony, 171–74, 176, 209
Reagan, Ronald (Reagan Administration), 97–98
  CDCU Revolving Loan Program, 33, 41–43
  funding for antipoverty efforts, 34
  inauguration, 33
Reed, Danette Anthony, 267
Republicans, 97–98
revolutionary populism, 15
Richardson Plano Guide Right Foundation (RPGRF), 163–64
Riegle Community Development and Regulatory Improvement Act, 182
Rogers, Eunice J., 115–16
Rosenberg, Julius and Ethel, 6
Roth, Philip, 7
  Plot Against America, The, 6
RPGRF. *See* Richardson Plano Guide Right Foundation
Russell, Victor, 153, 167, 177, 183, 212, 224, 266
  AACUC's Hall of Fame induction, 163, 166, 207, 208, 277
  on founding of RPGRF and KAPFCU, 163–65
  Gately's email to, 226–27
  Godfrey-Smith and, 207–9
  on KAPFCU's journey, 276–77
  KAPFCU *vs.* NCUA (court case hearing and judgment), 203, 204–5, 214–17, 219, 220
  Lynn (NCUA's Region IV director) on, 184–85
  NCUA liquidating KAPFCU, 193–95, 197–98, 200
  personal vendetta against, 193
  Rausch *vs.*, 172–74
  telephonic board meeting, 189–90
Russia, 13–15

– S –

Sattiewhite, Renée, 263
savior syndrome, 140–41
Scott, MacKenzie, 251
secondary capital, 156–57
  regulations and restrictions, 157
Second Mount Sinai Baptist Church, Cleveland, 115
Servicemen's Readjustment Act of 1944. *See* G.I. Bill
Shorebank, 65–66, 66n26

Shulman, Alix Kates, 15n5
Small and Emerging CDFI (SECA), 79, 80, 247
Smith, Maurice, 59n23, 261
socially responsible investment (SRI) movement, 44
South Central People's FCU, 112
Stevenson, Adlai, 6
Stockman, David, 41, 98
Students for a Democratic Society (SDS), 13
subprime mortgages, 154, 155. *See also* Great Recession
substantive due process, 213
Sullivan, Emmet, 203–6, 209–10, 211, 212, 215–18, 225–26
"Supervising Community Development Credit Unions" (NCUA), 104–5
"Supervising Low Income Credit Unions and Community Development Credit Unions" (NCUA), 105
Sutton, Willie, 142

– T –

TARP. *See* Troubled Asset Relief Program
technical assistance grants (TAG), 271
Texas Credit Union League, 183
Texas League of Credit Unions, 164–65
Thompson, Julius, 170–71, 174
Transformational Deposit Initiative (TDI), 251
Treasury Department. *See* U.S. Department of Treasury
Trinity Church, 113
Troubled Asset Relief Program (TARP), 155–59
Trump, Donald, 257

– U –

unionization, 5, 27, 28
United Food and Commercial Workers, 27
University of Hartford, 17
U.S. Bank Community Development Corporation, 265
U.S. Central Credit Union, 154–55
U.S. Department of Agriculture (USDA), 67, 166, 182
U.S. Department of Commerce, 67
U.S. Department of Health and Human Services (HHS), 67

U.S. Department of Housing and Urban Development (HUD), 67
U.S. Department of Treasury, 49, 67, 155, 156, 157–58, 159, 182, 245. *See also* Community Development Financial Institutions (CDFI) Fund
U.S. Small Business Administration (SBA), 67

– V –

Vamper, Annie, 3, 35–36, 134–35
Velasquez, Baldemar, 24–25
Vieth, Harvey, 42
Village Trust Financial Cooperative, 257n94
Village Voice, 94–95

– W –

War on Poverty, 24, 31, 35, 37–38, 39, 54
Warren, Elizabeth, 235, 239
Watts Riots, 174
Western Pequots, 19, 21
Whitehead, Bill, 177, 189
White House, report for, 98–99
white savior syndrome. *See* savior syndrome
Wilkerson, Isabel, 146
Wounded Knee, 18
Wright, Richard, 146

– Y –

Yellen, Janet, 245, 247

Acknowledgments

Cliff Rosenthal

My thanks to those colleagues and friends who offered encouragement, comments, and helpful criticism as I wrote this memoir. Among these were Mrs. Rita L. Haynes, State Senator Robert Jackson, Pete Crear, Deborah Washington, Pamela Owens, Cathie Mahon, Onika Lewis, Susanne James, Sondra Townsend-Browne, Terry Ratigan, Jeff Wells, Randy Chambers, Cheyenna Weber, Renée Sattiewhite, and Maurice Smith. Steven Dubb read an early version and provided valuable suggestions. Thanks to Meryl Ann Butler for her insightful and extensive editing assistance and guidance. Mark Winston Griffith graciously provided the foreword that is informed both by his journalistic skill and his hard-won knowledge of the life of a regulated financial institution.

Special thanks to Michael McCray and Victor Russell, both for their contributions to this book and for their work in starting and fighting for the Kappa Alpha Psi credit union. Their story is an important one not only for the credit union movement, but for all those who would seek against the odds to build community power. I am especially indebted to Michael for his patient, persistent, and enlightening collaboration throughout the long journey of creating this book.

My greatest thanks, as always, go to my wife, Elayne Grant Archer—teacher, editor, writer—for her support not only in my writing of this memoir, but for sharing with me the sometimes tumultuous journey that demanded decades of unrewarded sacrifice from her.

While they did not contribute to the writing of this book, many institutions and individuals made possible the career that defined my memoir. It is no exaggeration to say that the Revson Foundation, through its fellowship, enabled me to preserve and rebuild the Federation when otherwise it might have perished. In the last decades of my career, I was privileged to receive awards and recognition from many organizations: the National Credit Union Foundation (Herb Wegner Award), the Opportunity Finance Network (Ned Gramlich Award), the Insight Center for Community Economic Development, the Urban Homesteading Assistance Board, the Lawyers Alliance of New York City, and the Network of Latino Credit Unions and Professionals. In 2009, the ASI Federal Credit Union named its community center in the Upper Ninth Ward of New Orleans after me in recognition of the support I organized after Hurricane Katrina. The African-American Credit Union Coalition gave me one of the greatest gifts of my career by inducting me into its Hall of Fame in 2019, the first non-African American so chosen. I was introduced by Sheilah Montgomery, AACUC cofounder and the Federation's former board member, and accompanied by my colleague, Pamela Owens. Appearing in the pages of this memoir are many other AACUC Hall of Fame inductees, including Victor Russell, cofounder of Kappa Alpha Psi FCU; my long-time colleague Bill Bynum, rightly honored as the foremost Black-led CDFI in the country; the Federation's former board chair, Mrs. Rita L Haynes; and posthumously, my Federation partner of the 1980s, the late Annie Wilma Vamper. In 2024, I have been chosen for induction into the national Cooperative Hall of Fame.

Finally, my thanks to the people of the community development credit union movement and the organization now known as Inclusiv that represents them. Serving them for 32 years was the greatest professional privilege of my life.

Michael McCray

First and foremost, I want to thank my lovely wife, Chandra McLeroy McCray, and my doting parents, Dr. Jacquelyn McCray and Parnell McCray. This book would not be possible without the love and support of my family along with Victor Russell and Alma Russell, who have become my extended family.

I also want to thank the Honorable Eddie Bernice Johnson for always supporting KAPFCU in our quest for achievement in every field of human endeavor including financial services and for providing remarkable constituent services to the only African American-owned federally chartered financial institution in the great state of Texas.

Next, I offer additional thanks to Kappa Alpha Psi leadership (National and Regional) former Grand Polemarchs (National Presidents) Sam Hamilton, Dwayne Murray, Esq., and Tommy Battle and the Mighty Southwest Polemarch Ron Julian–One Kappa–for believing in and supporting this Kappa dream for economic empowerment for African American men, our families, and our community.

More importantly, special thanks to KAPFCU founders, organizers, and board members, the men in the arena–gone but not forgotten–the people who gave the time, put in the work, risked their reputation, fought the battles, suffered the loss, felt the pain, and displayed fidelity in the face of adversity. The individuals who made history: Victor Russell, Julius Thompson, Steve Ellis, Kenneth Henderson, Bill Whitehead, Derrick Harris, Karey Burnett, Kevin Burnett, Tim White, Joe Williams, and T.A. Brooks.

Final thanks to AACUC Leaders Helen Godfrey Smith, Bill Bynum, Lynda Milton; Federation Leaders Cliff Rosenthal and Brian Gately; and former NCUA executives Carl Banks and Chip Filson as our most ardent supporters within the credit union industry. And particularly to Cliff Rosenthal for helping me refine my voice and providing this opportunity for the real story of KAPFCU to be preserved, revered, and not lost to obscurity.

About the Authors

Clifford N. Rosenthal

After receiving his master's degree in Russian history at Columbia University, Clifford Rosenthal worked as a freelance translator while organizing food cooperatives in New York City and Connecticut. He brought his skills to successive nonprofit jobs for a statewide Indigenous organization and a national farmworker advocacy organization. He joined the National Federation of Community Development Credit Unions in 1980, becoming its executive director in 1983.

Under his leadership, the federation became the credit union industry's leading voice on issues affecting low-income and minority communities. To bring resources to the federation's member credit unions, he launched its Capitalization Program, raising more than $100 million from faith-based and social investors, foundations, banks, and government. He cofounded and co-led the coalition that successfully advocated for the Community Development Financial Institutions Fund. He personally assisted the organizing of nearly a dozen credit unions around the country and wrote *Organizing Credit Unions: A Manual.* After leaving the federation (now known as Inclusiv) in 2012, he headed the Office of Financial Empowerment of the Consumer Financial Protection Bureau. In 2018 he published the groundbreaking volume, *Democratizing Finance: Origins of the Community Development Financial Institutions Movement.*

He served on the Consumer Advisory Council of the Federal

Reserve Board and the advisory board of the New York City Office of Financial Empowerment. Rosenthal was honored with the highest awards of the National Credit Union Foundation, the Opportunity Finance Network, the Insight Center for Community Economic Development, and the Lawyers Alliance of New York City. Recognizing his aid after Hurricane Katrina, in 2009 the ASI Federal Credit Union in New Orleans named its community center after him. In 2019, he was inducted into the African-American Credit Union Coalition's Hall of Fame.

Michael McCray

Michael McCray was an advisor and official of the Kappa Alpha Psi Federal Credit Union. A public policy expert on community and economic development finance and grassroots organizing, Michael participated in KAPFCU's rare, almost unprecedented battle to save the credit union, bringing its case to the second highest court in the land.

Michael was "to the manner born," raised with a strong family tradition in education and community organizing and development. His mother, Jacquelyn McCray, held a PhD in housing from Florida State University, and sat on the board of directors, along with Hillary Clinton, of Southern Bancorp, which became a model for the CDFI Initiative. She also developed the USDA Center of Excellence in Regulatory Science at the University of Arkansas at Pine Bluff.

Michael is an alumnus of Georgetown Law, Howard University, American University, and Florida A&M University. His diverse educational and professional background includes Fortune 500 experience in marketing at Johnson & Johnson, Personal Products Company; accounting at Honeywell Information Systems; and investment banking at SunTrust Bank. He began his career in community development finance when he worked for the Federal Empowerment Zone and Enterprise Communities (EZ/EC) Program, a White House Economic Development Initiative of the Clinton Administration. Michael pioneered new technology for community development nationally and oversaw the grant recipients from Arkansas, Tennessee, and Mississippi, including Hope Enterprise Community, one of the nation's leading CDFIs. He followed his passion for community empowerment by working for various community and faith-based development organizations, including T.D. Jakes Ministries (i.e., Metroplex Economic Development Corporation). Michael also taught community development finance for the Graduate Community Development Program at Prairie View A&M University.

He received statewide recognition from the OMNI Center for Peace, Justice, and Ecology, which in 2008 honored him as an Arkansas Peace and Justice Hero. In 2011 he published the breakthrough volume, *Race, Power, and Politics: Memoirs of an ACORN Whistleblower.* Most recently, McCray is a 2021 recipient of the Cliff Robertson Sentinel Award for his advocacy with the ACORN 8 from the Association of Certified Fraud Examiners (ACFE).

For decades, New Orleans played host to one of the most feared and revered political organizations in America, the Association of Community Organizations for Reform Now, better known as ACORN. Yet, most people hadn't heard of ACORN before the historic election of President Barack Obama. And many more don't know what community organizers actually do, why they do it, or how they get things done.

While not everyone has always approved of ACORN's confrontational tactics, many know some of the impressive results achieved for poor people over the years, such as living wage laws to fight poverty, building partnerships with unions to assist workers, or creating housing programs to get Americans one step closer to the American dream. These are real, tangible victories that improve people's lives.

But equally real was the tarnish to the group—the multi-million-dollar embezzlement of funding that should have gone to support members and campaigns for social and economic justice. And the stain of accusations of voter fraud, voter registration fraud, unpaid taxes, employee mistreatment, and undercover videos of ACORN assistance to pimps and prostitutes have all led to a devaluation of the original legacy of ACORN to help the underserved and disenfranchised through direct community action. Yet, regardless of how ACORN started, it evolved into something else.

Eight courageous low-income board members fought back against the 400,000-member association and internal corruption following the embezzlement. Dubbed the ACORN 8, Michael McCray led the fight first as a national spokesman and then as a breakthrough author. His gripping memoir gives an insider's account of ACORN at a crossroads and the rise and fall of the Rathke family empire. Tom Devine, leader of the Washington-based Government Accountability Project (GAP), called this story "one of the most important corporate whistleblower stories in twenty-five years." It is the story of systematic waste, fraud, and abuse at a powerful nonprofit organization.

www.ingramcontent.com/pod-product-compliance
Lightning Source LLC
Chambersburg PA
CBHW050849160426
43194CB00011B/2085